Lawyers as Leaders

LAWYERS AS LEADERS

DEBORAH L. RHODE

OXFORD
UNIVERSITY PRESS

OXFORD
UNIVERSITY PRESS

Oxford University Press is a department of the University of Oxford.
It furthers the University's objective of excellence in research, scholarship,
and education by publishing worldwide.

Oxford   New York
Auckland   Cape Town   Dar es Salaam   Hong Kong   Karachi
Kuala Lumpur   Madrid   Melbourne   Mexico City   Nairobi
New Delhi   Shanghai   Taipei   Toronto

With offices in
Argentina   Austria   Brazil   Chile   Czech Republic   France   Greece
Guatemala   Hungary   Italy   Japan   Poland   Portugal   Singapore
South Korea   Switzerland   Thailand   Turkey   Ukraine   Vietnam

Oxford is a registered trademark of Oxford University Press
in the UK and certain other countries.

Published in the United States of America by
Oxford University Press
198 Madison Avenue, New York, NY 10016

© Oxford University Press 2013

Library of Congress Cataloging-in-Publication Data
Deborah L. Rhode
Lawyers as leaders / Deborah L. Rhode
p. cm.
Includes bibliographical references and index.
ISBN 978-0-19-989622-6 (hardback : alk. paper)   1. Lawyers—United States—Psychology.
2. Leadership—United States.   3. Leadership—United States—Psychological aspects.
4. Leadership—Moral and ethical aspects—United States.   5. Practice of law—United States—
Psychological aspects.   I. Title.
KF298.R48 2013
340.068'4—dc23
2013011935

1 3 5 7 9 8 6 4 2
Printed in the United States of America
on acid-free paper

For Ralph

Contents

Acknowledgments

THIS BOOK OWES many debts. Amanda Packel, Executive Director of Stanford's Center on the Legal Profession, provided insightful comments on an earlier draft, and served as my coauthor on a text of leadership teaching materials on which this book draws, *Leadership, Law, Policy, and Management* (2011). David McBride of Oxford University Press offered wisdom in the shaping and editing of the project. Donald Polden, Dean of Santa Clara Law School, provided helpful comments and convened inspiring leadership roundtables at which chapters of this book were presented. The staff of the Stanford Law library provided invaluable research assistance; I am particularly indebted to Paul Lomio, Sonia Moss, Rich Porter, Rachael Samberg, Sergio Stone, George Vizvary, Erika Wayne, and George Wilson. Laurel Schroeder, my extraordinarily gifted assistant at the Stanford Law School, made this and all my other academic efforts possible. Barbara Kellerman, the James MacGregor Burns lecturer in public leadership at Harvard University's Kennedy School of Government, helped lure me into the field of leadership, and enriched my understanding of its dynamics. Finally, in this endeavor, as in all others, my deepest debt is to my husband, Ralph Cavanagh. His support, wisdom, and example of leadership in law mean more than I can ever express.

Lawyers as Leaders

I

Lawyers as Leaders

IT IS IRONIC that the occupation most responsible for producing America's leaders has focused so little attention on that role. The legal profession has supplied a majority of American presidents, and in recent decades, almost half the members of Congress.[1] Many of our nation's most revered and most reviled public figures have been attorneys: Abraham Lincoln and Thurgood Marshall; Joseph McCarthy and Richard Nixon. Although they account for just 0.4 percent of the population, lawyers are well-represented at all levels of leadership, as governors, state legislators, judges, prosecutors, general counsel, law firm managing partners, and heads of corporate, government, and non-profit organizations.[2] Even when they do not occupy top positions in their workplaces, lawyers lead teams, committees, task forces, and charitable initiatives. Yet rarely have these lawyers received training for leadership responsibilities. Although leadership development is now a forty-five billion dollar industry, and an Amazon search reveals close to 88,000 leadership books in print, the topic is largely missing in legal education.[3]

This book is a step toward filling the gap. Its aim is to shed new light on why we trust lawyers with so much power and why we are so often disappointed in their performance. My central claim is that the legal profession attracts a large number of individuals with the ambition and analytic capabilities to be leaders, but frequently fails to develop other qualities that are essential to effectiveness. The focus of legal education and the reward structure of legal practice undervalues interpersonal capabilities and ethical commitments that are necessary for successful leadership. Drawing on a broad array of interdisciplinary research, as well as biographical and autobiographical profiles, the book explores leadership competencies that are too often missing in practice.

Discussion proceeds in three parts. The first section of the book offers an overview of leadership traits, styles, and development. This introductory chapter focuses on the role of lawyers, and explores why they so frequently occupy positions of power even though the public has little faith in their qualifications for those positions. Chapter 2 looks at the nature of leadership more generally and identifies its defining characteristics and predominant styles. Chapter 3 surveys leadership development. It explores how lawyers learn to lead and the forces shaping their paths to leadership. Chapter 4 addresses core leadership capabilities: influence, decision making, innovation, conflict management, and communication.

A second section of the book addresses ethics in leadership. Chapter 5 focuses on the role of ethics, the influences on ethical conduct, the tensions between means and ends, and the strategies for fostering ethics in organizations. Chapter 6 explores scandals: the role of hypocrisy, the corrosion of judgments involving money and sex, and the dynamics of crisis management and corrective action.

A third section of the book views leadership in context. Chapter 7 addresses diversity: the nation's historical patterns of exclusion, the persistence of bias, the limits of law, the case for inclusiveness, and the most effective diversity-related strategies for leaders and those who aspire to leadership roles. Chapter 8 centers on leaders in law firms: their challenges, their successes, and their failures. Chapter 9 focuses on lawyers in social movements: the conditions of social change, and the leadership strategies that have been most and least effective in producing it. A final chapter looks at the legacy of leaders. Drawing together themes from the preceding chapters as well as empirical research on successful leadership, the book concludes with thoughts on what lawyers can do to advance their individual commitments and the public interest.

The Paradox of Trust

To put this exploration of leadership in context, it makes sense to begin with a paradox. According to a PEW public opinion poll, honesty is the most important leadership trait.[4] This is not a characteristic commonly associated with lawyers. The most recent Gallup poll finds that less than a fifth of Americans rated lawyers high or very high in honesty and ethical standards.[5] In another poll in which people were asked to volunteer what profession they trusted least, lawyers ranked highest (26 percent), with over twice as many votes as the next highest, members of Congress and sellers of used cars (11 percent).[6] Only 11 percent of Americans have "a great deal of confidence in people in charge of running law firms," while almost a third have "hardly any."[7]

Yet Americans place lawyers in leadership roles in much higher percentages than other countries. Only one nation (Colombia) has a higher proportion of lawyers in the national legislature.[8]

Part of the reason for this seeming mismatch in public attitudes and actions may stem from ambivalence in the public's views. Although they distrust lawyers as a group, Americans like their own lawyers. In one survey, over half of those questioned were very satisfied with the quality of legal services provided and another fifth were somewhat satisfied; only 12 percent were very or somewhat dissatisfied.[9] When the public is asked about lawyers' positive qualities, the characteristic most commonly chosen is that their "first priority is to their clients."[10] But that is also what the public dislikes in other people's lawyers. The most negative quality attributed to lawyers, by some three-quarters of Americans, is that attorneys are "more interested in winning than in seeing that justice is served."[11] In short, people want an advocate who will serve their own interests, but not the professional norms that result when everyone else wants the same.

These ambivalent attitudes do not, however, fully account for why lawyers in the United States are so much more likely to occupy leadership roles than lawyers in other societies. Researchers have attributed the distinctive influence of American lawyers to several factors. First, the centrality of law in American culture has contributed to the centrality of the legal profession.[12] The country's longstanding tendency to frame questions of social policy and morality in legal terms has elevated lawyers to positions of authority. As de Tocqueville famously noted, "[i]n America, there are no nobles or literary men, and the people are apt to mistrust the wealthy; lawyers consequently form the highest political class and the most cultivated circle of society."[13] Because lawyers functioned, in de Tocqueville's phrase, as the "American aristocracy," upwardly mobile individuals who aspired to public influence often chose law as their career. Lawyers' ability to practice part-time reinforced that decision because many state legislatures were also part-time.[14] As law became associated with positions of influence, those who were interested in leadership increasingly saw it as the occupation of choice. Woodrow Wilson captured prevailing wisdom when he noted: "The profession I chose was politics; the profession I entered was the law. I entered one because I thought it would lead to the other.[15] The similarity in functions required in law and politics has pushed in similar directions. According to some researchers, these are convergent professions: skills in investigation, drafting, procedure, and oral advocacy all work to advantage lawyers who seek public office.[16]

Whatever the causes for the centrality of lawyers in leadership positions, there is reason to question whether they are well-qualified for their role. Almost two-thirds of Americans believe that the nation faces a leadership crisis, and only 15 percent have confidence in the national government, which is heavily staffed by lawyers.[17] Part of the problem may stem from the mismatch between the traits associated with leaders and those associated with lawyers.

Although, as chapter 2 notes, what constitutes effective leadership depends on context, certain qualities are rated as important across a vast array of leadership situations. The most well-documented characteristics cluster in five categories:

- values (such as integrity, honesty, trust, and an ethic of service);
- personal skills (such as self awareness, self-control, and self-direction);
- interpersonal skills (such as social awareness, empathy, persuasion, and conflict management);
- vision (such as a forward-looking and inspirational); and
- technical competence (such as knowledge, preparation, and judgment).[18]

A survey of leaders of professional service firms (including law firms) similarly found that the most important leadership qualities involved personal values and interpersonal skills, such as integrity; empathy; communication; and abilities to listen, inspire, and influence.[19] Particularly in times of stress, a key capacity is the ability of leaders to inspire others with a vision that is both emotionally compelling and attainable.[20] This research is consistent with other surveys of law firms and professional service firms, which stress interpersonal qualities such as the ability to chart a direction, gain commitment to that direction, and set a personal example.[21] A leader, in Napoleon's phrase, "is a dealer in hope."[22]

Not all of these leadership qualities are characteristic of lawyers. Several decades of research have found that attorneys' distinctive personality traits can pose a challenge for them as leaders, particularly when they are leading other lawyers. For example, attorneys tend to be above average in skepticism, competitiveness, "urgency," autonomy, and achievement orientation.[23] Skepticism, the tendency to be argumentative, cynical, and judgmental, can get in the way of what George Walker Bush famously dismissed as the "vision thing."[24] "Urgency," defined as the need to "get things done" can lead to impatience, intolerance, and a failure to listen.[25] Competitiveness and desires for autonomy and achievement can make lawyers self-absorbed, controlling, combative, and difficult to manage.[26] Lawyers also rank lower than the general population in sociability, interpersonal sensitivity, and resilience.[27] They are less likely to be comfortable in initiating social interactions and participating in activities requiring emotional rather than analytic intelligence. Lawyers' relative lack of resilience or "ego strength" makes for difficulties in accepting criticism, and in responding without defensiveness to performance evaluations.[28] Lawyers lacking in "soft skills" tend to devalue their importance rather than address their absence.[29]

Of course, general tendencies do not accurately predict individual behavior, and lawyers who reach a leadership position may have profiles more suited to that role. The point is not to paint an overly bleak or simplistic portrait of the "lawyer personality." Rather, it is to identify some ways in which lawyers are not ideally suited for leadership, and to suggest that formal preparation is often essential for lawyers to perform effectively in that role.

The Paradox of Power

Another paradox arises from the disconnect between the qualities that enable lawyers to achieve leadership positions and the qualities that are necessary for lawyers to succeed once they get there. What makes leaders willing to accept the pressure, hours, scrutiny, and risks that come with their role? For many individuals, it is not only commitment to a cause, an organization, or a constituency. It is also an attraction to money, power, status, and admiration. But successful leadership requires subordinating these self-interests to a greater good. The result is what is variously labeled the "leadership paradox" or the "paradox of power."[30] Individuals reach top positions because of their high needs for personal achievement. Yet to perform effectively in these positions, they need to focus on creating the conditions for achievement by others. As the philosopher Laotse famously put it, "A leader is best when people barely know he exists. When his work is done, his aim fulfilled, they will say: 'we did it ourselves.'"[31]

If left unchecked, the ambition, self-confidence, and self-centeredness that often propel lawyers to leadership roles may sabotage their performance in those roles. Research on personality and organizational effectiveness finds that narcissistic individuals are frequently selected for leadership positions because they project the confidence and charisma that makes a positive impression. Yet over time those characteristics can translate into a sense of entitlement, overconfidence, and an inability to learn from mistakes.[32] Strong ego needs can also prevent leaders from letting go of their positions when an organization would benefit from change.[33] These personal weaknesses are compounded by the environments in which leaders function, which often fail to supply honest criticism. Subordinates may be understandably unwilling to deliver uncomfortable messages. And the perks that accompany leadership may inflate an individual's sense of self-importance and self-confidence. Being surrounded by those with less ability or less opportunity to display their ability encourages what psychologists label the "uniqueness bias:" people's belief that they are special and superior. Such environments reinforce narcissism and entitlement; leaders may feel free to disregard rules of ethics, or norms of courtesy and respect that apply to others.[34] As Abraham Lincoln reportedly put it, "nearly all men can stand adversity, but if you want to test a man's character, give him power."

The most effective leaders are those who can see past their own ambitions, and retain a capacity for critical reflection on their own performance. In Peter Drucker's phrase, successful leaders "think and say we."[35] Enduring legacies are left by those who advance collective purposes and transcend personal needs in pursuit of common values.

2

The Nature of Leadership

WHAT EXACTLY IS leadership? Does it involve traits that are generalizable across different situations? What qualities and styles are most and least effective? What challenges do contemporary leaders confront? The discussion that follows explores these questions and casts doubt on conventional wisdom about the nature of leadership.

Characteristics of Leadership

What defines a leader? That issue has generated a cottage industry of commentary, and by some researchers' accounts, over 1,500 definitions and forty distinctive theories.[1] The term "leader" dates to the thirteenth century, but "leadership" appeared only in the nineteenth.[2] Although popular usage sometime equates leadership with power or position, most contemporary experts view it rather as a relationship. John Gardner, founder of Common Cause, noted that heads of organizations often mistakenly assume that their status "has given them a body of followers. And of course it has not. They have been given subordinates. Whether the subordinates become followers depends on whether the executives act like leaders."[3] Leaders must be able to inspire, not just compel or direct their followers. To borrow a metaphor from Harvard Professor Joseph Nye, holding a title is like "having a fishing license. It does not guarantee that you will catch any fish."[4] Moreover, some leaders exercise influence without the formal status that would convey their role. Paul Hoffman's *Lions in the Streets*, a celebrated profile of elite New York law firms in the 1970s, noted that their heads were often not those known as leaders in the outside world. An attorney he interviewed put it this way: "The man who really runs the firm is the guy who tells the secretaries whether or not they have to work on Washington's Birthday."[5]

What qualities are necessary for leadership? The traditional assumption has been that leadership requires exceptional personal traits, particularly intelligence. Max Weber added the concept of charisma, a term that Catholic theologians applied to gifts manifesting God's grace.[6] Weber used the term in a secular sense to convey the magnetism and persuasiveness that made individuals able to attract a wide following, especially in times of crisis or rapid change. Building on Weber's insight, traditional theorists have defined charisma in terms of qualities such as emotional expressiveness, empathy, self-confidence, and control.[7] By their definition, leaders are charismatic figures whose inspirational appeals tap into followers' values and identity.[8]

Recent research, however, has challenged these "trait theories" of leadership, and has stressed the importance of context.[9] The skills needed to run a thousand-person law firm with multiple branches in multiple countries are not the same as those needed to launch a small public interest organization or to win a state governor's race. Over the last half century, some one thousand studies on leadership characteristics have produced no clear profile of the ideal leader.[10] Even the much celebrated quality of charisma is not necessarily related to performance. Charisma does not explain popular support or organizational success.[11] Indeed, some studies find that the leaders of the most continuously profitable businesses have tended to be self-effacing and lacking in the qualities commonly considered charismatic.[12] Biographies of many highly successful lawyers reveal similar traits. Burke Marshall, the head of the Justice Department's Civil Rights Division in the Kennedy Administration, was "modest," "mild mannered," and "self-deprecating"; Warren Christopher, secretary of state under Clinton, was equally reserved and reluctant to self-promote; Archibald Cox, solicitor general in the Kennedy Administration, was shy and lacking in a "natural, easy social sense"; Erwin Griswold, solicitor general under the Johnson Administration and dean of the Harvard Law School, was "shy, stiff, formal and sometimes gruff"; and John Doar, head of the civil rights division under Johnson and counsel to the Watergate Committee that recommended Nixon's impeachment, was "dry, methodical," and able to read the *Happy Hooker* aloud in a way that would "put you to sleep."[13] Paul Cravath, architect of the modern system of law firm training, viewed " "sound and steady" as the key to effectiveness.[14]

Even when a lawyer is widely viewed as charismatic, what exactly is meant by the term is not always clear or uncontested. Barack Obama is the most recent prominent example. Some commentators credit him with remarkable personal magnetism and an ability to connect with different constituencies;

he can reportedly adjust his style to church basements, huge stadiums, back-yard barbecues, and elite policy forums.[15] Yet other commentators fault him for being "aloof," "detached," "professorial," "technocratic," "tone deaf," and susceptible to "policy speak disaster."[16] "Cannot emote" is a common assessment.[17] This description of "no drama Obama" is hard to reconcile with the candidate who gave us some of the most memorable rhetorical moments in recent political history with his 2008 campaign messages on hope, change, and racial reconciliation.[18] At his best, he seemed "able to call us back to our highest selves, to the place where America exits as a glittering ideal, and where we, its honored inhabitants, seem capable of achieving it...."[19] These varying views underscore the larger point that historian James McGregor Burns made about "charisma" as a leadership trait. As he put it, the term is "so ambiguously and inconsistently used...[that] it is impossible to restore the word to analytic duty."[20] Often it seems to function as a conclusory label that fails to specify what accounts for the appeal described.

Although what constitutes an ideal leader depends on context, and charisma is not an essential attribute, certain other qualities do appear effective in the vast array of leadership situations. As chapter 1 noted, the most well-documented characteristics involve vision, ethics, interpersonal skills, technical competence, and personal capabilities such as self-awareness and self-control. Consistent predictors of leadership failures are to some extent the flip side of those traits: incompetence, rigidity, arrogance, callousness, dishonesty, indecision, and intemperance.[21] Inability to establish a clear mission, learn from mistakes, model integrity, and respond to the needs of others are among the fatal flaws that can derail an otherwise promising career.[22] Ambition is one of the most common traits that can propel it.[23]

Yet the relative importance of those qualities varies across contexts, and successful leadership requires a match between what the circumstances demand and what the individual has to offer.[24] So, for example, Ralph Nader was extraordinarily effective during the activism of the 1960s and 1970s in galvanizing a progressive consumer movement. But he was far less successful decades later in running a presidential campaign on similar issues. The self-righteous iconoclasm that stood him well in one historical era worked against him as a third-party candidate in a different political climate.[25] Warren Burger is another leader whose skill set was reportedly not a good match for his role as Chief Justice. To his colleagues he seemed "pompous," "petty," "overbearing," and sometimes incompetent—incapable of recording votes accurately and unwilling to stop speaking long after he had run out of things to say.[26]

John Gardner notes that history makes leaders and leaders make history; no single pattern of styles and traits is apparent. What produces leadership are "great opportunities greatly met."[27] The most effective leaders are those who have a good sense of their capabilities, and are able to place themselves in positions where their strengths are critical and where they can minimize or compensate for their weaknesses. According to the Center for Creative Leadership, self-awareness is the primary characteristic that distinguishes successful leaders and, as chapter 3 indicates, such self-knowledge provides the foundation for professional development.[28]

Challenges of Leadership

Part of leaders' self-awareness is an appreciation of how well they are addressing the situational challenges that stand in the way of effective leadership. Although the contexts in which lawyers lead vary considerably, most share some common features. Increases in competition, complexity, scale, pace, and diversity have all complicated the lives of leaders, and heightened difficulties in their role.

Competition

Over the last several decades, competition has intensified within and across many organizations that lawyers lead. Their success in those positions often depends on the ability to achieve short-term results, sometimes at the expense of long-term goals.[29] In law firms, internal rivalries have bred acrimony, defections, and sometimes dissolution.[30] According to one consultant, the result is a low-trust environment, in which more and more partners are behaving as "bands of warlords, each with his or her followers...acting in temporary alliance—until a better opportunity comes along."[31] In the public and nonprofit sectors, competition for support and resources also has intensified, particularly during the recent economic downturn, and budgetary difficulties have become an often debilitating fact of daily life.[32] These pressures pose difficulties on an interpersonal as well as a financial level. All too often "competition brings out the best in products and the worst in people."[33]

danger of competition

Scale and Complexity

Other challenges arise from the growth in scale and complexity of legal organizations, as well as the problems that they confront. Over the last half century, the size of the fifty largest law firms has increased more than ten times and the staff of the most prominent public-interest legal organizations has more than doubled.[34] In the corporate sector, the number of in-house counsel has also doubled since 1970; general counsel's offices have expanded to keep pace with the growth of their organizations.[35] Legal employers are operating in many more locations, and they have more alliances, subsidiaries, and outsourcing arrangements that also require oversight.

This increase in scale, together with other social, economic, and technological changes, has significantly complicated the landscape of leadership. Governments, markets, organizations, and professions are interacting in more complex ways, and leaders' actions play out on a larger stage.[36] Technological advances have increased both the pace of decision making and the accessibility of decision makers. Leaders often face a barrage of information along with pressure to make complex judgments instantly.[37] As one former deputy attorney general noted, "if you don't like an issue before you, wait fifteen minutes…Somebody will give you a new one."[38] Leaders remain tethered to their workplaces through electronic communication, and the personal costs can be substantial: stress, burnout, substance abuse, and related mental health difficulties.[39]

Additional challenges arise from increased diversity within the legal profession and its clients. As chapter 7 notes, this trend has had many organizational payoffs, but it has also complicated the lives of leaders. Among their responsibilities is ensuring that institutions deal productively with differences across race, ethnicity, class, gender, age, culture, and sexual orientation in an increasingly interconnected world.

The Role of Leaders

"Mt. Rushmore syndrome"

The nature of the leadership role brings further complications. Although the extent and complexity of demands on contemporary leaders frequently argues for shared authority, many stakeholders still want a single heroic figure at the helm. As Joseph Nye describes it, this "Mt. Rushmore syndrome" rests on a fundamental "leader attribution error"—a tendency to ascribe undue credit or blame for performance to the person at the top.[40] The dynamic is common in all sectors of the legal profession. Stakeholders often expect quick fixes to complex problems and intractable market dynamics, and fail to value or to institutionalize shared leadership.[41]

So too, although lawyers might want, or benefit from, the results of strong leadership, they may not like to be led, and may not welcome the changes and sacrifices that it demands. As chapter 1 noted, attorneys value independence and are well-prepared to challenge authority when they disagree. By training and temperament, lawyers are experts at locating loopholes and are attached to precedent; leaders' efforts at innovation are often met with skepticism and counterexamples.[42] In public sector bureaucracies, rigid legal constraints, job protection for civil servants, insulation from market pressures, and potential political landmines can also foster resistance to change.[43] Many policy settings tend toward what experts describe as "organized anarchy." No one is really in charge: power is dispersed among shifting coalitions and interest groups, which require considerable leadership skills to align in pursuit of societal goals.[44]

authentic *humility* A final challenge for leaders lies in maintaining a sense of humility in circumstances that push in the opposite direction. Recent research finds that authentically humble leaders are more effective; they are more likely to view themselves objectively, more open to new ideas and critical feedback, and more willing to admit mistakes.[45] Yet as chapter 1 noted, the power and perks of leadership often reinforce arrogance and overconfidence.[46] Soliciting criticism and remaining self-reflective about one's own weaknesses are critical leadership skills.

Styles of Leadership

The mystery of what leaders can and ought to do in order to spark the best performance from their people is age-old. In recent years, that mystery has spawned an entire cottage industry: literally thousands of "leadership experts" have made careers of testing and coaching.

DANIEL GOLEMAN[47]

Harvard psychology professor Daniel Goleman is unusual among those experts in that his conclusions about effective leadership have a broad empirical base. Drawing on a sample of almost four thousand leaders worldwide, Goleman has identified six styles, each reflecting distinctive forms of "emotional intelligence."[48] Effective leaders "do not rely on only one leadership style; they use most of them in a given week—seamlessly and in different measure—depending on the [situation]."[49] Goleman summarizes the styles as follows:

Daniel Goleman's leadership styles

Coercive leaders demand immediate compliance.
Authoritative leaders mobilize people toward a vision.

Affiliative leaders create emotional bonds and harmony.
Democratic leaders build consensus through participation.
Pacesetting leaders expect excellence and self-direction.
Coaching leaders develop people for the future.[50]

All of these styles are readily recognizable among lawyer leaders, and other commentators have added variations that are relevant for professional development.[51]

The Coercive or Intimidating Style

Coercion, the style most often associated with positions of power, is typically the least effective. Goleman suggests a number of reasons why. A leader's "extreme top-down decision making" kills new ideas. People feel so "disrespected that they…won't even bring…ideas up" or so "resentful that they adopt the attitude, 'I'm not going to help this bastard.' "[52] Because the leader has not conveyed a sense of shared mission, people can become "alienated from their own jobs, wondering, 'How does any of this matter?' "[53] Research on lawyers similarly suggests that while this approach may accomplish short-term results, it often does so at the expense of longer-term problems of morale.[54]

That is not to suggest that coercive styles are always ineffective. They are often useful in conditions of crisis or emergency, or with " 'problem' employees with whom all else has failed."[55] Stanford business school professor Roderick Kramer also suggests that a certain form of coercion, practiced by "great intimidators," can yield impressive bottom-line results.[56] These leaders, while not above using a few "ceremonial hangings" are not your "typical bullies."[57] Their motivation does not involve "ego or gratuitous humiliation"; rather, they are impatient with impediments, including human ones, and willing to use anger to achieve their ends.[58] One of Kramer's examples is Clarence Thomas, whose capacity for intimidation was on display during Senate confirmation hearings on his appointment to the Supreme Court. In response to questions about whether he had sexually harassed Anita Hill, Thomas accused Senate committee members of engaging in a "high tech lynching for uppity blacks…."[59] The result was to silence critics and help secure his nomination.

Moreover, according to Kramer,

A calculated "loss of temper" does more than help intimidators prevail in the heat of the moment, though. It also serves as a chilling deterrent for potential challengers. While in some instances they are clearly putting on an act, intimidators aren't always in full control of their emotions when they go off on tirades. But even then a loss of control can be useful.[60]

The biographies of famous lawyers are laced with examples of coercion and intimidation. Wisconsin Senator Joseph McCarthy was one of the profession's most infamous bullies. His abusive tactics ruined countless careers of suspected communist sympathizers until his cruelty in televised congressional hearings appalled the nation and eroded his political support.[61] Less extreme examples involve leaders whose desire for control sapped the morale and imitative of those around them. A profile of Paul Cravath, founder of Cravath, Swaine & Moore, noted that "most of the young men who worked in his offices disliked him heartily" largely because of his insistence that "everything be done his way."[62] Washington insider Edward Bennett Williams, founder of Williams, Connolly & Califano, could be similarly autocratic. He demanded "total control" over the firm's decision making, was notoriously "unforgiving of errors" by others, and could fly into a "rage on demand."[63] Jeff Kindler, the lawyer who became CEO of Pfizer, reportedly lost his position because of a combative, abusive micromanagement style.[64] Ralph Nader, another micromanager, structured the public interest organizations that he founded so that "everything passed through [him]."[65] Nader even opposed unionization in those organizations, a position hard to square with his progressive ideals. As one staffer put it, Nader just felt that the workplace was "his baby and he want[ed] to run things his way."[66] That way even included a ban on soft drinks in his flagship organization, the Center for the Study of Responsive Law.[67] On discovering a contraband Coca-Cola can in the trash, Nader personally telephoned the staffer responsible. "This is a breach of trust," he explained to an incredulous reporter. "Soda is bad all the way around. It has no nutrition. It causes cavities. It is taste manipulation. Companies that make it should not be supported."[68] Steven Kumble, the founder of Finley Kumble, similarly obsessed about lawyers and clients who carried coffee cups without lids, threatening the firm's $300,000 carpet. "I think I'm just going to have to take the coffee away from them," he announced.[69]

Coercive and intimidating styles are less common in women leaders. Not only are they socialized differently, they also are punished for such "unfeminine" conduct.[70] What seems merely assertive in a man can seem abrasive in a woman.[71] "Attila the Hen" and "the Dragon Lady" have difficulty gaining respect, support, and cooperation from coworkers.[72] Indeed, some leadership coaches have developed a market niche in rehabilitating "bully broads"— women who come across as insufficiently feminine.[73] Still, the history of the legal profession offers examples of unrepentant female leaders who were at least partly successful despite their intimidating styles. Congresswoman Bella Abzug, a leader on many women's rights issues, was known as "rude," "cantankerous," "abusive" to her staff, and "not kind to stupid people."[74] That insensitivity to the needs of others exacted a heavy toll. She experienced constant turnover among employees, and was fired as chair of an influential Presidential Advisory Committee on Women, because of her inability to "cooperate" with the administration, including President Carter himself.[75]

Kramer claims that the "great intimidators" are not "typical bullies" because their motive is not humiliation. But it is by no means clear how much motive matters to those who are on the receiving end of abusive conduct. Most research suggests that likeability is correlated with effective leadership and that continued bullying impairs the performance both of leaders and their subordinates.[76] About half the targets of such abuse leave their job as a result.[77] Those who stay are unlikely to volunteer constructive criticism. Few wish to risk antagonizing leaders with the attitude of Hollywood's Darryl Zanuck, known for suggesting that subordinates "don't say yes until I stop talking."

Another form of intimidating behavior involves the use of knowledge in ways that preempt competing views. "Informational intimidators," as Kramer terms them, "always have an abundance of facts, and intentionally or unintentionally invoke them in ways that suppress opposition."[48] This, of course, can sometimes be a highly useful skill for lawyers, particularly in litigation. But in leadership contexts, where the goal is to understand and inspire others, this behavior can be counterproductive. It is especially damaging if done with insufficient concern for truth. In the short run, as Kramer notes, "[o]ften, it doesn't even matter all that much whether the 'facts' are right… Even the misleading or inaccurate factoid—when uttered with complete confidence and injected into a discussion with perfect timing and precision—can carry the day."[79] But in the long run, that tactic can be costly, particularly if the errors are made in public and someone has sufficient incentive and ability to expose them. Given the importance that people attach to honesty among leaders, informational intimidators can suffer serious credibility costs if they are flexible with facts.

A final type of coercive tactics arises from what is sometimes labeled a "drive to overachievement."[80] Leaders with this tendency focus too much on their own performance and need to show up not only competitors but also subordinates. Such leaders don't truly listen to others; instead, they soak up "all the oxygen in the room" by pushing their own ideas and even answering their own questions.[81] This approach may yield some short-term advantages if the leader is gifted, but the ultimate result is likely to be disengagement and dependency among followers.

The Authoritative Style

Goleman's research suggests that the authoritative style is generally the most effective.[82] This approach combines clarity about ends with flexibility about means.   *Clarity about ends*
                         Flexibility about Means

> The authoritative leader is a visionary; he motivates people by making clear to them how their work fits into a larger vision for the organiza- tion. People who work for such leaders understand that what they do matters and why.... An authoritative leader states the end but generally gives people plenty of leeway to devise their own means. Authoritative leaders give people the freedom to innovate, experiment, and take cal- culated risks.[83]

Yet as Goleman also notes, the authoritative style is not effective in every situ- ation. It fails, for example, "when a leader is working with a team of experts or peers who are more experienced than he is; they may see the leader as pompous or out-of-touch. Another limitation ... [is that] if a manager trying to be authoritative becomes overbearing, he can undermine the egalitarian spirit of an effective team."[84] These circumstances are particularly common in law firms; many partners are reluctant to cede too much power to a single individual.[85]

So too, an authoritative manner in women bumps up against the gender stereotypes noted earlier. An overview of more than a hundred studies con- firms that women are rated lower as leaders when they adopt authoritative, seemingly masculine styles, particularly when the evaluators are men, or when the role is one typically occupied by men.[86] This leaves female leaders in a double bind. They risk seeming too feminine or not feminine enough. Those with a soft-spoken approach may appear unable or unwilling to make the tough calls that leadership positions require. Those who lean in the opposite direction are often viewed as strident, arrogant, or overly aggressive.[87] During her presidential campaign, Hillary Clinton sought to strike an elusive bal- ance, described as "something between a country-club, golf playing, hedge fund executive, with a whiff of bingo games Sunday churchgoing, supermar- ket aisles, and coffee clatches."[88] As chapter 7 indicates, these persistent, often unconscious gender biases help explain women lawyers' continued underrepresentation in leadership roles. One recommended response, is to be "relentlessly pleasant" without backing down.[89] Researchers propose frequently smiling, expressing appreciation and concern, invoking common interests, focusing on others' goals as well as their own, and taking a problem-solving rather than a critical stance.[90]

The Affiliative Style

The "affiliative" style of leadership puts people first. Its adherents focus on maintaining satisfaction and harmony among followers. They tend to be "natural relationship builders" who supply frequent positive feedback, value personal relationships, and celebrate group accomplishment.[91] The result is a high level of trust, loyalty, communication, and innovation.

Many successful politicians and heads of law firms and in-house counsel offices have been known for such relational skills. Robert Kennedy was a prominent example. Shortly after his appointment as attorney general, he astonished Justice Department lawyers by walking into their offices announcing, "I'm Bob Kennedy" and then asking where they had gone to law school and what they were working on.[92] He got minor officials their first invitation to the White House, sent thank-you notes to staff whom he saw working on holidays, and called or wrote lawyers with congratulations when they had accomplished some difficult task.[93] As Victor Navasky summed it up, this leadership style "brought out the best in others and enlarged their sense of possibility."[94] Hillary Clinton has earned similar praise in her position as secretary of state. She has been famously "big on feedback;" an Internet "Secretary's Sounding Board is bringing the suggestion box into the modern age."[95] Clinton also gains respect for following through on the ideas that she hears. After receiving complaints that full benefits for domestic partners were not yet available, she cut through bureaucratic obstacles with a simple directive: "Fix it."[96]

Similar examples are common in the private sector. Michael Kelly's *Lives of Lawyers Revisited* profiles a general counsel who made it a priority to sponsor social events and to meet individually with staff and find out what they would like changed.[97] Larry Sonsini, one of the founders of the Silicon Valley legal establishment, including the law firm that bears his name, is legendary for "bridge build[ing]" and having "a firm grasp of what is important to others."[98] Louis Brandeis, who distinguished himself in many leadership positions on and off the bench, recognized the value ✳

of knowing the affairs of others, including clients, "better than they do" and using that knowledge to forge personal relationships. As he advised a young lawyer, "the ability to impress [others] grows from...confidence [that] can never come from books; it is gained by human intercourse."[99] Used exclusively, however, affiliative approaches have limitations. In some leadership contexts, too much praise and desire for harmony "can allow poor performance to go uncorrected" and internal conflicts to go unresolved.[100] Whatever its short term advantages in minimizing stress and unpleasantness, conflict avoidance should be avoided.[101] As chapter 4 indicates, unaddressed problems can fester, impair performance, and lead to more costly confrontations later on.

The Democratic Style

One way to handle conflicts, as well as other leadership challenges, is through democratic processes. By giving stakeholders a say in decisions that affect them, leaders can generate new ideas, encourage buy-in, and build morale, trust, respect, and commitment.[102] Many heads of public interest legal organizations employ this approach and rely heavily on legal staff to shape organizational priorities.[103]

However, as experts including Goleman note, the democratic style has drawbacks that make it ill-suited for many leadership contexts.[104] Most lawyers have had experience with the problems, such as "endless meetings where ideas are mulled over, consensus remains elusive, and the only visible result is scheduling more meetings."[105] Participatory processes can also defer decisions in ways that leave individuals "confused and leaderless."[106] Many accomplished leaders have paid a price for this approach. Observers of Hillary Clinton's presidential campaign chronicled the downsides of her democratic style and refusal to resolve internal staff conflicts.[107] A year into her campaign, her advisors were still "squabbling over [the] message," and, rather than establish clear lines of authority, Clinton allowed them to share power.[108] The result was that "nobody knew who was in charge. Nobody wanted to be in charge."[109]

The broader lesson from such examples is that democratic processes work best when leaders are themselves uncertain about the best direction to take and need ideas and commitment from stakeholders. Alternatively, even when leaders have a strong vision of what needs to change, democratic styles can generate constructive strategies for making that change happen, and buy-in from those most affected.[110] But there are also times when leaders simply have to decide; the problem with democracy can be the same as with socialism, which in a classic phrase, "takes too many evenings."[111]

The Pacesetting Style

A fifth leadership style emerging from large-scale research involves pacesetting. A leader employing this approach

> sets high performance standards and exemplifies them himself. He is obsessive about doing things better and faster, and he asks the same of everyone around him. He quickly pinpoints poor performers and demands more from them. If they don't rise to the occasion, he replaces them with people who can.[112]

This is a readily recognizable strategy among prominent lawyers. A textbook example comes from William Kuntsler's autobiography, *My Life as a Radical Lawyer*.[113] He describes his first meeting with a law student intern who had just started working for the firm. Kuntsler handed him a motion to file immediately and added, with little more by way of instruction, "If you screw this up, don't come back."[114] In explaining his strategy, Kuntsler noted,

> Clearly I had no time to babysit law students if they couldn't do the work... My goal for anyone who works with me is, simply, to get the job done.... I expect a lot from people... and I don't want to hear... [their] complaints or problems. I often yell when someone makes a mistake, which, I admit, is not pleasant, but that's how I function.[115]

If subordinates couldn't handle the pressure, Kuntsler had a simple solution: "I let them quit."[116]

Ralph Nader combined control and pacesetting. He created an entire consumer movement by recruiting students and recent law graduates and giving them substantial responsibility. "I'm not interested in the Lone Ranger effect," he famously insisted.[117] "The function of leaders is to produce more leaders."[118] To that end, he looked for Nader Raiders who would be "highly self-directed as well as highly motivated." "Advice-giving [was] a luxury he [didn't] have much time for."[119] "Don't ask me questions" he told his staff. "Just go get at them."[120]

This style has some of the same downsides as the coercive approach. According to Goleman,

> Many employees feel overwhelmed by the pacesetter's demands for excellence, and their morale drops. Guidelines for working may be clear in the leader's head, but she does not state them clearly; she expects people to know what to do and even thinks, "If I have to tell you, you're the wrong person for the job." Work becomes not a matter of doing one's best along a clear course so much as second-guessing what the leader wants. At the same time, people often feel that the pacesetter doesn't trust them to work in their own way or to take initiative.[121]

Of course, as Goleman notes, "the pacesetting style isn't always a disaster. The approach works well when all employees are self-motivated, highly competent, and need little direction or coordination."[122] Given a talented team, "pacesetting does exactly that: [it] gets work done on time or even ahead of schedule."[123] Ralph Nader was revered by some staff for being "the best teacher in the world…partly because he doesn't teach you."[124] He gave junior lawyers major policy, press, and political organizing responsibilities and enabled them to rise to the occasion. Their efforts laid foundations for major consumer, environmental, and occupational safety regulations, and many of those lawyers went on to lead other public interest initiatives.[125] Yet not all "Nader's Raiders" were up for the pressure and the "hundred hour work week" that Nader thought was "perfect"; "flameout" was a significant problem.[126] The lesson is that pacesetting, like other styles, requires discretion. Leaders need to exercise judgment about when those on the receiving end are up to the task.

The Coaching Style

A final style involves coaching. Leaders taking this approach

> help employees identify their unique strengths and weaknesses and tie them to their personal and career aspirations. They make agreements with their employees about their role and responsibilities in enacting development plans, and they give plentiful instruction and feedback. Coaching leaders excel at delegating; they give employees challenging assignments, even if that means the tasks won't be accomplished quickly. In other words, these leaders are willing to put up with short-term failure if it furthers long-term learning.[127]

Leaders who have made coaching a priority have been responsible for some of the profession's greatest achievements. Charles Houston, the Dean of Howard Law School and head of the NAACP legal office in the 1930s and 1940s, nurtured the careers of many civil rights leaders, including Thurgood Marshall, who did the same for others.[128] Former Secretary of State Warren Christopher was revered for supporting junior lawyers; one of his mentees recounted thirty years of assistance, ranging from recruitment to Stanford Law School, to critical support and advice concerning his appointment as Associate Attorney General and judge on the 9th Circuit Court of Appeals.[129] In legal education, founding mothers such as Barbara Babcock and Herma Hill Kay not only served in leadership roles themselves, but also launched the careers of innumerable women's rights advocates and prominent public servants.[130]

Yet despite its frequent effectiveness, the coaching style is the least common leadership approach that Goleman's research identified. The reason, according to interviewed leaders, is that they "don't have the time in this high-pressure economy for the slow and tedious work of teaching people and helping them grow."[131] Other explanations involve interpersonal obstacles to candid feedback, such as leaders' desires to be liked or to avoid conflict, and concerns about damaging relationships and reducing chances of retention.[132] Particularly in large organizations with high turnover rates, leaders often see little reason to invest in subordinates who are likely to leave.[133] As a consequence, many legal workplaces lack adequate mentoring and leadership development.[134] The problem is compounded by some leaders' lack of skills and comfort in coaching those who are different along lines of race, ethnicity, or gender.[135] Although increasing numbers of legal workplaces have responded by creating formal mentoring programs, these initiatives often lack effective oversight and reward structures.[136] Mentors take a "call me if you need me approach" that leaves subordinates uncomfortable in asking for assistance. Also lacking are well-designed leadership development strategies. Only a quarter of surveyed firms have leadership succession plans.[137]

Of course, like other leadership styles, extensive coaching is not appropriate in all circumstances. The employee needs to be capable and motivated, and the effort should be proportional to the circumstances. I can still recall my first exposure to intensive mentoring when I was about the age of Kuntsler's intern, and it was not a happy experience. After my second year in law school, I spent the summer at a prominent Washington law firm. One of my assignments involved a client who raised chickens. He was suing the Department of Agriculture because it had condemned some diseased chickens and provided what he felt was inadequate compensation. I invested a week reading condemnation cases in search of possible precedents and lines of appeal. The junior partner who reviewed my research memo treated it like a draft for a Supreme Court decision or a tenure article in a leading law review. Every paragraph was redlined with stylistic and substantive revisions, along with long digressions based on the partner's own rhetorical peeves and preferences. I was astonished. We were, after all, not writing for the ages here. This was just a memo. About dead chickens. I tried to imagine an explanation. Did the partner not have enough other work and needed to run up hours at the client's expense? Did he not have enough other opportunities to exercise power and control? Or was he so taken with his craft that every work product had to reach a state of polished perfection regardless of the stakes or the client's preferences? Whatever the explanation, if this is how the firm let associates "sink or swim," I wanted out of the water.

In the contemporary law firm, however, such micro-mentoring is rare. Not-so-benign neglect is far more common, and it exacts a substantial price.[138] Retention of talented junior lawyers is a major problem in many legal workplaces, and high attrition rates of women and minorities are of particular concern. A major contributing factor to premature departures is lack of guidance and professional development opportunities.[139] In one American Bar Association study, two thirds of women of color and over half of white women and men of color would have liked better mentoring.[140] Failure to develop subordinates has been identified as one of the "fatal flaws" of unsuccessful leaders.[141] In today's increasingly competitive climate, organizations need those who occupy positions of power to support and model effective mentoring. Indeed, Goleman puts the point directly: "[a]lthough the coaching style may not scream 'bottom-line results,' it delivers them."[142]

A Repertoire of Styles and a Redeeming Sense of Humor

As this overview makes clear, no single leadership style is effective in all contexts, although some are more likely to be effective than others. Leaders need multiple approaches and an understanding of when each is most appropriate. The best leaders are "exquisitely sensitive to the impact they are having on others," and able to adjust their styles accordingly.[143]

These leaders also tend to have a sense of humor. The research available suggests that outstanding leaders outperform their counterparts in the use of humor and that this ability correlates with leadership effectiveness.[144]

Humor serves multiple functions in the workplace; it can deflect and diffuse tension, relieve stress, and foster collegiality.[145] A capacity for irony and self-deprecating wit is not only appealing in itself, but also signals emotional intelligence. One leader who embodied these qualities was Thurgood Marshall. He was legendary among colleagues, clerks, and even opponents for his spontaneous humor and telling anecdotes. He used that strategy to build relationships, attract donors, relieve tensions, and ridicule injustice; his stories managed not only to "evoke a laugh [but also to]...make a point."[146] He was equally able to "chew the fat" with a white sheriff during a racial protest and to spar with royalty during a trip abroad.[147] While working in London on a constitution for the newly created state of Kenya, Marshall had an opportunity to meet with Prince Philip. When the Prince inquired if Marshall would "care to hear my opinion of lawyers," Marshall responded in kind: "Only if you care to hear my opinion of Princes."[148]

Another pointed example occurred during Marshall's 1950 efforts in Japan, where the NAACP sought to challenge the racial discrimination pervasive under General MacArthur's command.[149] The task was complicated by MacArthur's refusal to acknowledge the problem, despite ample evidence of racially disparate treatment in job assignments, promotions, and court martials. When Marshall pointed out the absence of blacks on the entire headquarters' staff and the General's personal guard, MacArthur insisted that no blacks were qualified for such positions. Marshall then pointed out that the base's military band also had no blacks, and added "Now General, just between you and me, goddammit, don't you tell me that there is no Negro that can play a horn."[150]

There are, to be sure, downsides to this strategy, when humor is used to deflect attention from serious and personally inconvenient issues. But for leaders like Marshall, who was never afraid to face tough questions, the wit was part of his greatness. My own favorite Marshall anecdote is a story he told during my clerkship about his initial appointment to the bench. He was one of the first African-Americans to sit on a federal appellate court, and shortly after his term began, he and his colleagues were scheduled for a group photograph to mark his new membership. Marshall arrived a bit late, just after the photographer had blown a fuse and everyone was milling around in semi-darkness. As he entered the chambers, the Chief Judge's secretary, who had not yet met him, announced with evident relief, "thank God, the electrician's arrived." To which Marshall reportedly responded, "Ma'am, you'd have to be crazy to think they'd let me in that union."[151]

Today, of course, they would, and part of the reason is Marshall's own leadership.

It seems somewhat ironic to close a chapter on lawyers and leadership with a plea for irony. The legal profession is not known for self-deprecating humor. But neither is it known for its attention to leadership. Both need to change. For better or worse, law is the occupation from which vast numbers of American leaders emerge. They need to become more informed and adept in developing the characteristics and styles that make for effective leadership.

3

Developing Leadership

WHY HAS THE occupation that produces the nation's greatest proportion of leaders done so little to prepare them for that role? Only 20 percent of large firms have formal leadership development programs, and even schools whose stated mission includes producing leaders almost never have even a single course on the subject.[1] One reason for the omission may be that the field has only recently emerged, and its reputation has been tarnished by pop publications. "Leadership lite" includes classics such as *Leadership Secrets from Attila the Hun* and *Leadership Lessons from the Toys You Loved as a Child*. A second obstacle to leadership preparation is the assumption that great leaders are born not made. Yet contemporary research suggests the contrary. It indicates that most leadership skills are acquired, not genetically based, and decades of experience with leadership development indicate that its major capabilities can be learned.[2] In effect, the "best leaders are the best learners."[3] Individuals who demonstrate leadership potential early in their careers tend to be particularly gifted learners; they are able to absorb ideas and criticisms and translate them into practical strategies.[4]

Although formal curricula are a modern development, informal learning has been common. Many lawyer leaders have sought guidance from history, psychology, and other relevant fields. As a youth, Huey Long read every book on leaders he could lay hands on.[5] President Barack Obama looked to historical accounts of Franklin Roosevelt's first one hundred days as president.[6] Yet informal education often falls short. This chapter suggests why, and suggests more effective learning strategies and pathways to leadership for aspiring lawyers.

Preparation for Leadership
The Learning Process

How people learn to be learners varies considerably. What improves learning ability depends on the individual and the particular qualities at issue. Reading, discussion, observation, coaching, and group interaction can all be valuable techniques, and lawyers need to seek out the formal and informal learning structures that are best for them.[7] As a general matter, experience is the most common and effective teacher, but it can also be the most expensive. In their book *Judgment*, Noel Tichy and Warren Bennis tell the story of a young lawyer who wants to know what accounts for the leader's success.

"People respect my judgment," the leader responds.
"Why do they have respect?"
"Well, I guess I have made the right decisions."
"On what basis did you make the right decisions?"
"Experience."
"What's experience based on?"
"Wrong decisions."[8]

grow after Failure

Virtually all managing partners say they learned their job while doing it, but some of them drove into a ditch in the process.[9] The costs of on-the-job learning are well-illustrated by a story about Tom Watkins, the founder of IBM. An up-and-coming employee involved the company in a risky venture that proved financially disastrous. When Watson called the man into his office, he offered his resignation. Watson reportedly responded, "You can't be serious. We just spent $10 million educating you."[10]

Not all aspiring leaders are as fortunate, and the goal of leadership preparation is to help them avoid errors that can sabotage careers. Learning is a *lifelong process*. Its foundations should be laid early in legal education and reinforced continuously in legal workplaces. Part of the learning process should involve self-assessment of strengths as well as weaknesses, and the kinds of positions that will best match individuals' talents and commitments. A flaw in many leadership development programs is their attempt to improve performance by focusing solely on deficiencies.[11] Feedback becomes a predominately negative experience, which discourages individuals from seeking it, and erodes self-confidence. Although constructive criticism is necessary for leadership, it is not sufficient. Individuals often develop best by capitalizing on their strengths, pursuing their most fundamental goals and values, and receiving positive recognition for their successes.[12] To that end, lawyers need to be self-aware and proactive in enhancing the capabilities necessary to realize their own aspirations. As Peter Drucker put it, those who manage others need to become experts in managing themselves.[13] Developing that capacity bumps up against several obstacles.

Obstacles to Learning

The first obstacle is the failure to acknowledge the need for continuous learning and to invite the criticism on which it depends. Leadership experts James Kouzes and Barry Posner put the problem bluntly: "[M]ost leaders don't want honest feedback, don't ask for honest feedback, and don't get much of it unless it's forced on them."[14] In Kouzes and Posner's survey of some seventy thousand high-ranking individuals, the least frequent of some thirty leadership behaviors was a request by a leader "for feedback on how his/her actions affect others' performance."[15] Similar observations might be made about lawyers who lead. Indeed, as chapter 1 noted, attorneys tend to be worse than average in responding to criticism. This tendency toward self-protection is particularly problematic because most legal workplaces do not institutionalize feedback from subordinates. Only 40 percent of law firms offer associates the opportunity to evaluate their supervisor, and of those who engage in the process, only 5 percent report a change for the better.[16]

Yet without feedback, leaders may fail to identify problems in their own performance. Harvard economist John Kenneth Galbraith once noted that "[f]aced with the alternatives between changing one's mind and proving it unnecessary, just about everybody gets busy on the proof."[17] Defensiveness and denial are particularly apparent when leaders' own self-evaluations are at issue because various cognitive biases help shield individuals from uncomfortable insights. One common problem is the "self-serving" or "self-enhancing" bias: people's tendency to see themselves in a favorable fashion and to attribute their successes to factors such as competence and character, while attributing their failures to external circumstances.[18] A related problem stems from confirmation and assimilation biases. People tend to seek out evidence that confirms a favorable vision of themselves, and to avoid evidence that contradicts it. They also assimilate information in ways that favor their preexisting beliefs and self-images.[19] In one random sample of adult men, 70 percent rated themselves in the top quarter of the population in leadership capabilities; 98 percent rated themselves above average.[20]

Other obstacles to learning arise from the specific circumstances of leadership positions. Lawyers who achieve such positions often have high needs for approval. For these individuals, as one consultant notes, "the intention to *look* good displaces the intention to *be* good;" the result is to undervalue concerns that do not translate into immediate recognition.[21] So too, the intense demands of many leadership positions provides a ready rationalization for not making the effort necessary to change behavior; "I don't have time" is a common response to opportunities for leadership programs or coaching.[22] Avoiding such opportunities permits lawyers to stay within their comfort zones but at the cost of developing new strengths and insights.[23]

Failures in mentoring pose another obstacle to professional development. Overcommitted supervisors are often reluctant to invest the time in coaching others, or to take risks in giving inexperienced employees the responsibilities that would best expand their competence.[24] As Morgan McCall puts it, ~~Mentors~~ "developing leadership requires leadership," and it is not always forthcoming.[25]

A final barrier to learning is the assumption that leadership education is a "touchy-feely process," unworthy of attention from intellectually sophisticated individuals. Lawyers are particularly prone to this view.[26] As noted earlier, by training and temperament, they tend toward skepticism and emphasis on analytic rather than interpersonal skills.[27] Yet precisely because of these tendencies, lawyers need to develop their "emotional intelligence."[28] For many, "the soft stuff is the hard stuff."[29]

Learning Strategies

A more constructive approach to leadership development would include formal programs during and after law school, together with related workplace support structures. Lawyers need the lifelong commitment described by Darwin Smith, the attorney who served Kimberly Clark as CEO for over two decades. In reflecting on his contribution to the company's success, Smith said simply, "I never stopped trying to be qualified for the job."[30]

There are, of course, limits to what can effectively be taught in academic settings, particularly to students with limited work experience. But as researchers note, skills relevant to leadership not only *can* be taught, they *are* being taught, although not always intentionally, in classrooms as well as workplaces.[31] The process would be more effective if it were more mindful, and more informed by research on leadership. At a minimum, formal leadership programs can increase individuals' understanding of how to exercise influence and what cognitive biases, interpersonal responses, and organizational dynamics can sabotage effectiveness. Through exposure to leadership research, case studies, historical examples, role simulations, and guided analysis, individuals can discover models and prepare for dilemmas that they will face in practice.[32]

Even seemingly fixed traits are not entirely beyond influence. Law schools cannot directly teach integrity, but they can teach about it in ways likely to be useful to future leaders. Significant changes occur during early adulthood in peoples' basic strategies of moral reasoning and well-designed curricula have been found to assist the developmental process.[33] Case histories, problem solving, and simulations all can enhance skills in ethical analysis and build awareness of the situational pressures that skew judgment.[34] Moreover, the best ways to promote ethical conduct are often through regulatory standards and organizational reward structures, and educational programs can equip future leaders to pursue those strategies. Law schools and continuing legal education could also do much more to teach crucial leadership skills such as problem solving, teamwork, influence, organizational dynamics, and conflict management.[35]

Leaders and aspiring leaders also need safe spaces to explore mistakes and the rationalizations that often underlie them. Lawyers who are reluctant to take time out for intensive programs can benefit from coaching, mentoring, and on-the-job assignments designed to develop leadership skills.[36] Whatever the setting, the objective should be to ensure opportunities for guided reflection. That preparation can enable aspiring leaders to take risks with the understanding that "failure is as vital as it is inevitable."[37] The key is to "crash and learn…[not] crash and burn."[38]

To become effective learners both during and after law school, individuals need to think strategically about their goals, capabilities, and needs.[39] They also need to act on their aspirations and to seek experiences, positions, and assignments that develop leadership skills.[40] Students should look not just for relevant courses, but also for pro bono and other extracurricular opportunities. Junior lawyers should find both paid and unpaid opportunities to lead and to learn from their mistakes. Mid-career professionals may need to switch jobs or specialties, or take on substantial pro bono projects, in order to broaden skills and networks.[41] High levels of responsibility and pressure, coupled with mentoring, often provide the best learning experiences.[42]

Organizational Learning

Leaders need to focus not only on their own learning process, but also on creating what Peter Senge termed "learning organizations." By his definition, these are institutions in which individuals are "continually learning how to learn together to expand their capacity to create the results they truly desire."[43] Other experts describe a learning organization as one "skilled in creating, acquiring and transferring knowledge, and at modifying its behavior to reflect new knowledge and insights."[44] Leaders can foster such learning environments by becoming "multipliers" of collective intelligence; they can optimize talent by extending opportunities, and by sharing credit, control, and ownership of organizational objectives. By focusing on organizational capacities, leaders can ensure that their own goals are tied to broader collective purposes.[45]

To build such capacities, Harvard Business School professor Chris Argyris suggests distinguishing between single-loop and double-loop learning; the first involves finding a solution to a problem, the second involves understanding one's own contribution to that problem. In Argyris' view,

> most people define learning too narrowly as mere "problem solving,"
> so they focus on identifying and correcting errors in the external environment. Solving problems is important. But if learning is to persist, managers and employees must also look inward. They need to reflect critically on their own behavior, identify the ways they often inadvertently contribute to the organization's problems, and then change how they act.[46]

As an example of such unintended contributions, Argyris cites a leader who urged department heads to serve the interests of the organization as a whole, but established budget policies that put the heads in direct competition with each other. In an effort to be diplomatic, the leader assumed a consensus that did not exist, leaving subordinates feeling confused and wary. Only by focusing on his own rather than his subordinates' conduct could the leader effectively advance organizational objectives.[47] Such examples underscore the need for individual leaders to pursue organizational learning, and to remain conscious of "how the very way they go about defining and solving problems can be a source of problems in its own right."[48]

Paths to Leadership

Another productive leadership strategy is learning from the careers of others. What affects the paths to power? As the following discussion suggests, what distinguishes successful leaders in law is a strong sense of their goals, resilience in the face of setbacks, and a capacity to learn from advice and from experiences that chance has thrown their way.[49]

Self-Awareness

The first step on the path to leadership is self-knowledge. Lawyers must be reflective about what they want and what experiences and abilities will be necessary to achieve it.[50] What are their deepest aspirations, what capabilities are they missing, and what is standing in their way?[51] In thinking through objectives, lawyers must be honest about their tolerance for risk, failure, conflict, competition, pressure, and extended hours. At every stage of their careers, they also need occasions to step back and reflect on their talents and passions. If the position they hold is not a good fit, or at least a useful training ground, aspiring leaders should actively look for an alternative.[52]

That is, in essence, the advice that young lawyers get from Margaret Marshall, the first woman Chief Judge of the Massachusetts Supreme Judicial Court, who also served as president of the Boston Bar Association and General Counsel for Harvard. "Ask yourself what do you enjoy doing every single day of your life.... Ignore the 'should dos' of your life. Have an honest dialogue with yourself about the role money will play in your life."[53]

Other leaders also emphasize the importance of such self-scrutiny. Marian Wright Edelman, the head of the Children's Defense Fund, quotes an entry from her journal as a civil rights organizer in the 1960s:

> The time has come for you, Marian, to have a frank talk with yourself. Where are you headed? You are in the midst of a history-making epoch...and here you stand helpless. Get a hold of yourself and then forget yourself. What do you really want more than anything in life?[54]

She figured it out in short order, and a career in civil rights and children's rights followed. Constance Baker Motley, the first black woman appointed to the federal courts, the first black borough president of New York City, and the first female attorney at the NAACP, came to a similar realization. On finding that "race, racism, and [their connection to] American law simply were not part of the course of study" at Columbia Law School in the 1940s, she began volunteering at the NAACP Legal Education and Defense Fund, which led to a permanent job after graduation.[55]

Ralph Nader is another famously self-directed leader, who has wanted none of the perks and personal life that others value. In a *Chicago Tribune* interview, Nader described some of the country's most prominent CEOs as "a little pathetic," driven by desires for "money, success, and power."[56] His own motivation, as he described it, was "trying to improve society. That's the highest work of human beings on earth."[57] That work has reportedly occupied him for twelve to fourteen hours a day, seven days a week. "Rebel without a life," was one observer's description.[58] After Nader detailed his "no frills" schedule, which rarely included time for friends, family, books, or recreation of any sort, the *Tribune* reporter asked him if he was happy. Nader responded, "What's happy? Happiness is applying your ideals."[59] But, the reporter also wanted to know, "what do you do when you want to be good to yourself? Reward yourself?"[60] To which Nader responded, "I achieve goals. I set sub-goals that are achievable. I want to get alar out of apples."[61]

Some leaders come to self-knowledge relatively early. Ralph Nader grew up in a family of Lebanese immigrants, where social justice was a focus of dinner table conversation. By his own account, at "four years of age…I used to say, 'that was the wrong thing, what the mayor did.'"[62] Hillary Clinton focused on leadership and civic issues early on, organizing a babysitting service for immigrant families and earning community service awards from the Daughters of the American Revolution while in high school.[63] Her door-to-door campaign effort to become student government president at Wellesley was an early version of the "listening tour" that gained traction in her New York race for the Senate.[64] Other leaders stumbled into legal careers from backgrounds far removed. Sandra Day O'Connor spent her formative years on a Montana cattle ranch. By age eight, she could brand a cow and drive a truck; by college, she was focusing less on cattle and more on justice.[65]

Many leaders bounced around in their initial years in practice, but with an eye to broader goals. While Thurgood Marshall tried to make a living as a solo practitioner, he handled NAACP civil rights cases on a part time or pro bono basis, which enabled him to land a full-time position with the organization.[66] Then he knew when to stay and when to leave. Although his accomplishments as an NACCP litigator created opportunities to run for Congress or seek a state court appointment, he had no appetite for soliciting campaign contributions or for currying favor with certain political insiders, whose endorsements would be critical.[67] It was not until later in life that he sought an alternative. Then, a desire for greater economic security for his family and a discomfort with the militant turn in civil rights activism made a federal appellate court appointment attractive.[68]

Family Commitments and Cultural Biases

Family commitments affect the career path of many leaders and how they cope with detours and constraints holds broader lessons. Former Assistant Attorney General and Solicitor General Drew Days describes being en route to "fame and fortune" in a Chicago law firm practice when he fell in love with a woman about to enter the Peace Corps.[69] He ended up accompanying her to the Honduras and organizing agricultural cooperatives for impoverished farmers. When his term ended, he presented his experience as useful for work with the NAACP Legal Defense Fund. That was the position he had wanted after graduating from law school, but then he had lacked the practical experience that the organization required.

In more typical circumstances, the gender patterns have been reversed. Women lawyers often have followed their husbands, bumped up against bias, and charted unconventional paths to the top. In the nineteenth century, Clara Foltz, the first woman admitted to the California bar, became a lawyer after eloping with a soldier who later abandoned her and their five children.[70] Unable to support the family through conventional feminine occupations like dressmaking and taking in boarders, she began studying law.[71] Her talents in both courtroom advocacy and self-promotion made her a leading figure in major reform movements of her times, including women's rights and criminal justice.[72]

A century later, both Hillary Rodham Clinton and Sandra Day O'Connor broke through gender barriers by similarly unconventional routes. Clinton left a promising public sector career in Washington D.C. to "follow my heart instead of my head" and relocate to Arkansas, where her future husband was building his political future. When a friend asked repeatedly if "I knew what I was doing, I gave her the same answer every time. 'No, but I'm going anyway.' "[73] After a stint as one of the nation's first female law professors, she joined a prominent Arkansas firm, and by the 1980s, was winning awards both as the state's "Young Mother of the Year," and one of its best business litigation attorneys.[74] O'Connor, after graduating at the top of her Stanford Law School class, found no law firm willing to hire her except as a secretary, and her marriage to a classmate limited her geographic options.[75] But she talked her way into creating a position in a county district attorney's office and then started a two-person firm in a shopping center. After giving birth to two sons and losing her babysitter, she decided to take time out. As she put it, "I stayed home myself for about five years and took care of [my family]."[76] In fact, a biographer observed, she "didn't really stay home."[77] She became more active in Republican politics and civic activities, which paved the way for positions with the state attorney general and election to the state legislature. That political involvement laid the groundwork for her appointment to the Supreme Court.[78] In later commenting on the impact of gender norms and family commitments on her career, O'Connor noted, "[I]t never occurred to my husband or me that he should assume a major childrearing role. Of course, as my husband was also fond of pointing out, things did turn out all right for me in the end."[79]

Bias has, of course, been a persistent and pervasive feature of the leadership landscape. Ruth Bader Ginsburg was denied clerkships and law firm positions due to the combination of being a woman, a Jew, and a mother. That experience helped paved the way for her later work as director of the ACLU Women's Rights Project. There she sued some of the New York firms that had refused to hire her or other women, or had relegated them to second-class status.

Other leaders also brought landmark litigation to challenge the bias they had encountered in their own careers. Thurgood Marshall had the satisfaction of winning a discrimination lawsuit against Maryland Law School, which had denied him admission.[80] Clara Foltz relished her victory over Hastings Law School, which had found the prospect of her presence too distracting for male students.[81] She also succeeded in removing the ban on female lawyers in Oregon. In passing through the state on a lecture tour, she learned of a local woman's rejection from the bar. She immediately "seated herself at her desk, drew up [a bill,] and announced, 'There, I think that will cover our case.'"[82] It did after she lobbied the bill through the state legislature.[83]

But for most leaders most of the time, the common response was to look for ways around the obstacles, rather than to confront them directly.[84] Bella Abzug famously refused to learn to type so that she would not be given clerical tasks.[85] Thurgood Marshall put up with many indignities of racism in the course of his civil rights work. When suing the University of Oklahoma's all-white law school, Marshall faced the challenge of feeding his legal team. No restaurant in Norman would serve blacks, and the noon recess was not long enough to drive anywhere else. After discovering the problem on the first of day of trial, Marshall emptied his pocket change into a courthouse vending machine and bought peanuts for the group. He then told the plaintiff, "I'm going to put you in charge of baloney sandwiches" until a local restaurant could be persuaded to open a segregated section.[86]

The Role of Chance

When asked about his secret of success, Nelson Rockefeller reportedly responded, "Get up early. Work late. Strike oil."[87] So too, many lawyers owe their leadership to the role of non-merit-based concerns in ostensibly merit-based processes. Some potential leaders received positions for which they had no experience, largely because of political considerations or personal connections. Burke Marshall went from being an antitrust litigator at a large Washington D.C. law firm to Aassistant Attorney General for Civil Rights because Attorney General Robert Kennedy wanted "a first class lawyer" who would "do the job in a technically proficient way" and who had no record on race-related cases that would offend southern whites.[88] When New York District Attorney Robert Morgenthau invited Arthur Liman, a leader of the Wall Street bar, to run a special unit prosecuting securities fraud, Liman raised concerns that he "knew almost nothing about stocks, let alone stock fraud. He had never studied securities law at Yale nor even so much as read the federal securities statutes."[89] Morgenthau did not care. "Arthur," he pointed out, "neither have the crooks."[90]

Warren Christopher received his first international position as a negotiator for textile trade agreements not because he had any background in diplomacy or textiles, but because he had "no public record" of "free trade" sympathies that might evoke opposition.[91] Later, despite a distinguished record as Assistant Secretary of State, he was passed over for Secretary of State, primarily on political grounds. As Christopher noted without resentment in his memoirs, Bill Clinton needed to "bolster his stature on Capitol Hill in a presidential election season," and Christopher was not the right candidate for that task.[92] But the result turned out to be fortuitous. Christopher received the central role in high-stakes negotiations over return of American hostages held by Iran. In commenting on the opportunity, Christopher later wrote,

> Washington is a place of political, not merit-driven decision making.... The lesson I drew from this chapter of my life is simple and a little ironic; the chance of a lifetime is not necessarily the next rung up the ladder. It may be the one on which you already stand.[93]

Many other leaders have received key positions because of equally fortuitous events. Harvard Professor Archibald Cox was appointed Solicitor General when his colleague Paul Freund opted to stick with scholarship and recommended Cox instead.[94] Sandra Day O'Connor lacked the typical pedigree for a Supreme Court Justice and later acknowledged that her "experience on Arizona's courts, as nice as it had been, had [not] prepared me for the appointment."[95] The American Bar Association agreed and rated her only "qualified," not "very qualified," for the position.[96] Ronald Reagan, however, had made a campaign promise to appoint a woman and found O'Connor's legislative and ranching experiences to have appealing parallels with his own background.[97] It also helped that other possible choices turned out to have "oversized skeletons" in their closets.[98] So too, Janet Reno became Bill Clinton's Attorney General only after other candidates had to withdraw for failing to pay social security taxes for their domestic help.[99] When asked about the issue, Reno quipped that she benefitted from having a dirty house, something not typically seen as a virtue in women.

In public life, as Richard Nixon once observed, "the road to victory is sometimes paved with defeat."[100] As an example, he cited his own loss in the California governor's race in 1962. Had he won, he would undoubtedly have been drafted for the Republican presidential ticket in 1964, and would have lost to Lyndon Johnson. Had he not run for governor, he would have launched an unsuccessful campaign for the presidential nomination. Running and losing the California race kept him on the sidelines in 1964, and positioned him to win in 1968. Such experiences taught Nixon the importance of taking risks and remaining resilient when things don't work out as planned.

Many leaders in the private sector also stumbled into their positions. Some "just got lucky. There was a void in…[their law] firm and it needed to be filled."[101] Others stepped in during a crisis, "played a significant role," and ended up as managing partner.[102] Lawyers interested in acquiring a "new skill set" and facing new challenges have taken advantage of responsibilities that came their way.[103] Dorian Daley, General Counsel of Oracle, "never really had a plan. It was more a matter of trying new things and learning as much as I possibly could as often as I could."[104] Being willing to take risks when chance threw an opportunity in their direction has been equally important for other general counsel.[105] By contrast, other leaders like Eliot Richardson remained trapped in positions that fell short of their expectations because a "draft movement" on their behalf never materialized, and they did not take steps to create one.[106]

As these examples make clear, leaders need to acknowledge the role of chance but should also refuse to be bound by it. Leaders cannot script every career move. But simply waiting for fate to take its course is not a path to success. Aspiring leaders need to behave as if hard work and outstanding performance will pay off, and to be proactive when they do not. The Justice

Department official who investigated O'Connor's background noted that "she was always looking for the next opportunity to assume a leadership role."[107] Despite considerable gender bias, she managed to find one. From similar stories, aviator Elinor Smith drew the right conclusion: "It has come to my attention that people of accomplishment... rarely [stayed] back and let things happen to them. They went out and happened to things."[108]

Mentoring and Advice

One other crucial leadership skill is finding honest and informed advice, but also knowing when to disregard it. Experts note that the "more elevated [a person's] position, the more important it is to solicit [candid criticism]" because subordinates are unlikely to volunteer it. [109] The feedback can come in varying forms: objective measures of behavior, observations by others, bottom-up evaluations, and mentoring.[110] Leaders need to know who and what to ask, but also to know themselves well enough to weigh competing advice and to steer their own course.

Many lawyers from unprivileged backgrounds were discouraged from choosing law as a career. Constance Baker Motley recalled that "no one thought that [becoming a lawyer] was a good idea." Her mother thought she should be a hairdresser, and her first employer after graduating from college, a female government aid worker, told her that going to law school would be a "complete waste of time" because "women don't get anywhere in the law."[111] By contrast, others succeeded through the support of family and mentors. As Stanford Professor Barbara Allen Babcock noted in her review of early women lawyers, "male allies" were essential to female leaders; many were "encouraged and aided at every turn" by husbands, brothers, and advisors.[112]

Finding trusted and supportive mentors at early career stages is particularly important because aspiring leaders may lack the life experience to know which opportunities are most likely to pay long-term dividends. Elliot Richardson, who ultimately held a series of high-level national positions, credited the advice that he received from Archibald Cox at a critical turning point. After a Supreme Court clerkship, Richardson received a job offer in the State Department under Dean Acheson. Although attracted by the prospect, Richardson had political ambitions and worried that "if I stayed in Washington, I might end up...a government hack."[113] He sought advice from Cox, his former labor law professor at Harvard. Recalling wisdom he had received from presidential advisor Harold Ickes, Cox responded, "When

I was in Washington, I always thought it important to come *from* somewhere."[114] Richardson took the advice, became a U.S. attorney and Lieutenant Governor from Massachusetts, and then returned to the capitol as Attorney General.

Other leaders, however, were warned off local politics, often with equally good reason. When Edward Bennett Williams toyed with the idea of running for senator, friends who knew him well did their best to discourage the idea. Williams did not like to compromise, cede control, or engage in cocktail party chitchat.[115] His law partner Brendon Sullivan suggested that before Williams threw his hat in a senatorial race, he should go to the local Safeway and "spend thirty minutes shaking hands."[116] Then he should ask himself: "You want to do that for two years?"[117]

Williams, for his part, provided some astute advice to others about the downside of non-elective political office. When Arthur Liman received an offer to head the Iran-Contra investigation, Williams counseled against taking it. According to Liman, Williams described Washington as a

> Puritan Salem; they burned a new witch each month. He warned me that I'd become one. It would be impossible, he said, to convince every faction in Washington that the investigation was fair.... Unless we brought down the President, the media would criticize me as blind and incompetent...no matter what we turned up by way of evidence.[118]

Other Washington insiders, including Cyrus Vance, took a different view and urged Liman to accept. In the end, Liman knew himself well enough to know how to respond. This was, in his view, a "challenge of historic proportions."[119] And Liman loved a challenge.

So did Barack Obama, and advice during the run-up to the 2008 presidential election helped convince him to enter the race. He had begun his Senate career publicly insisting that "there's no way that I'm running—I have two small children and I'm not that presumptuous."[120] Privately, he appeared to be keeping his options open and consulting political advisors and mentors.[121] When Senate majority leader Harry Reid advised Obama to declare his candidacy and other senators concurred, Obama was inclined to agree.[122] He had a window of opportunity that might not open again for a decade. As his strategist David Axelrod put it, "usually the politician chooses the moment, [but] sometimes the moment chooses the politician."[123] By all accounts, however, the decisive advice for Obama came from his wife. Michelle had "veto power," and as she later put it, she had to be confident that "our family would stay grounded and stable through the process."[124]

AS THESE EXAMPLES suggest, there are multiple paths to leadership and lawyers have only partial control over the possibilities that come their way. Those who are most successful are proactive in developing and taking advantage of the opportunities that circumstances make possible. That requires self-awareness, mentoring, and a recognition that leadership education can be helpful in identifying "what you didn't even know you didn't know."[125] In the final analysis, however, one of the key skills of leadership is knowing not only when to listen but also when to stop listening, and to follow an inner compass. Attorney General Janet Reno kept on her a wall a quotation from Abraham Lincoln:

> I do the very best I know how—the very best I can; and I mean to keep doing so until the end. If the end brings me out all right, what is said against me won't amount to anything. If the end brings me out wrong, ten angels swearing I was right would make no difference.[126]

4

Leadership Capabilities

ALTHOUGH LEADERSHIP NEEDS vary by context, certain competencies are central to most positions. The discussion that follows focuses on five: decision making, influence, innovation, conflict management, and communication. Leaders need not excel in all of these areas, but failure to master basic skills in any of them can undermine performance.

Decision Making
The Decision-Making Process

One essential leadership skill is the ability to make sound decisions and to develop decision-making processes that will enable subordinates to do the same. Decision making generally has two core objectives: quality and acceptability. Both are subject to external constraints, such as time and cost, and trade-offs are often necessary. For example, broad participation often enhances the soundness and legitimacy of decisions, but it generally requires more effort and expense. In many contexts, the optimal decision is out of reach due to the complexity of issues, the limitations of information, and the costs of obtaining it. Difficulties can also arise from too much rather than too little information. The brain can only process so many facts at any one time and an overload may misdirect our focus. As Herbert Simon has noted, "a wealth of information creates a poverty of attention."[1] In effect, leaders, like other decision makers, operate in a universe of what Simon has termed "bounded rationality."

In this environment, one important task of leaders is to create systems for decision making that are most cost-effective and least subject to distortion. That requires some basic understanding of the ways that individuals make judgments and the cognitive biases that get in the way. There is, in effect, an "immense gulf between the way we think and the way we think we think."[2] For most decisions, the process is intuitive rather than deliberative.[3] Typically, when individuals receive information from their surroundings, they attempt to fit it into existing knowledge structures, or "schemas." These impose meaning on perceptions and organize them into predictable patterns. Schematic processes are inevitable but often inaccurate.[4] The need to impose order leads people to see patterns that do not exist; sometimes it encourages stereotypes, including those based on race, gender, and class.

To avoid such errors, decision makers may monitor their intuitive judgments through a deliberative process that can override initial responses. In its ideal form, this process begins by framing the issues to be resolved and identifying and prioritizing the relevant values, interests, and objectives. Effective decision makers then select the most plausible response and later assess and learn from the outcomes. In structuring the deliberative process, leaders need to take into account concerns such as:

- How important is the quality of the decision and how much information does a reasonably good decision require?
- Who has the relevant information and do these individuals have personal interests that could skew their judgment?
- How important is commitment to the outcome among followers, and how much is that commitment likely to depend on whether they had a meaningful role in the process?
- What constraints of time and cost are involved?[5]

In creating appropriate processes, leaders also need to be conscious of the cognitive biases that can impair results. A threshold difficulty is "bounded awareness"—the failure to see, seek, use, or share information that is relevant to a decision.[6] Intense focus on a particular objective is especially likely to lead to tunnel vision. A graphic example of the problem comes from an experiment in which participants watch a short film of two teams passing basketballs. One team wears white shirts, the other black. Viewers are asked to count the passes made by one of the teams, a task demanding full concentration. In the middle of the film, a woman wearing a gorilla suit appears for nine seconds, thumps her chest and moves off screen. Of the thousands who have viewed the film, half never notice her, and many are adamant that she didn't appear.[7] That and related experiments underscore psychologist Daniel Kahneman's observation that "we can be blind to the obvious and....also blind to our blindness."[8] Given the demands on their time and the information overload in their environments, leaders are particularly vulnerable to "focusing failures."

Another common problem is self-serving or confirmation bias. People are likely to perceive information in ways that favor their own interests and confirm their own abilities. For example, individuals tend to inflate their contributions to joint efforts.[9] In explaining outcomes, people also are subject to the fundamental attribution error; they tend to attribute good results to their skills, but bad results to external factors.[10] In hypothetical situations, people assigned a particular advocacy position selectively recall information favorable to their side and make factual judgments that serve their side's interests.[11] A related tendency is what psychologist Lee Ross calls "naive realism"—people's beliefs that their own views are objective and based on reality, while contrary views are not.[12]

Other common biases in leadership contexts involve over-optimism, overconfidence, selective perception, and confirmation of prior beliefs. People tend to discount future risks and exaggerate their own ability to control them.[13] Individuals who consider themselves experts are especially prone to overconfidence and the errors that accompany it. In one study of some eighty thousand predictions, political and economic consultants made more errors than a random distribution would yield; monkeys throwing darts would have done better. Many of these experts resisted admitting they were wrong, or when forced to do so, resorted to excuses: unforeseen events had intervened, or they had been wrong for the right reasons.[14] Leaders are similarly susceptible to excessive self-confidence because they often have expertise and a history of success, and are surrounded by subordinates who feel pressure to agree with their supervisor.

Misjudgments also arise from individuals' disproportionate tendency to notice and remember information that is vivid or that confirms prior beliefs and values. People overvalue what is concrete, based on direct experience, and emotionally interesting; they fail to register changes that are small and incremental or facts that are inconsistent with their preconceived views and self-image.[15] Such biases can be particularly problematic in policy settings where immediate costs appear much more concrete and therefore salient than long-term consequences. That tendency is further compounded by pressure to please stakeholders who privilege the same short-term interests.[16] For example, such bias often distorts cost-safety tradeoffs. Leaders will spend vast sums to save identifiable victims, such as coal workers trapped in a mine, but are unwilling to invest proportionate amounts in safety measures to prevent such tragedies.[17] A related dynamic is "psychosocial numbing: people value lives less as the number of lives at risk increases."[18] As Joseph Stalin famously put it, "the death of a single Russian soldier is a tragedy. A million deaths is a statistic."[19]

A celebrated case study of how cognitive biases can affect leaders' behavior involves Henry Louis Gates, a Professor at Harvard and an eminent scholar of African-American studies. In 2009, on returning home around noon from an international flight, Gates found the front door to his Cambridge home jammed.[20] Gates, who was then 58, asked for help in forcing the door open from his cab driver, a dark-skinned Moroccan. A concerned neighbor who saw the men struggle with the door called the Cambridge police to report a possible burglary. In the preceding six months, the neighborhood had experienced twenty-three break-ins, many of which had occurred during the day. The first on the scene was Sergeant James M. Crowley, an officer with eleven years of experience and an instructor on methods to avoid racial profiling. He saw Gates in the foyer and asked him to step outside. Gates refused.

What happened next is a matter of dispute. Gates's version of events is that he explained that the house belonged to him and showed Crowley his Massachusetts and Harvard identification cards.[21] When Crowley questioned the explanation, Gates grew frustrated and asked for the sergeant's name and badge number. Crowley's account, reflected in the police report, is that Gates initially refused to show identification. Crowley explained to Gates that he was investigating a possible break-in, and Gates exclaimed, "Why, because I'm a black man in America?" and accused Crowley of racism.[22] The encounter escalated, and a video showed Gates responding belligerently as he was charged with disorderly conduct and led in handcuffs from the house.[23] Charges were subsequently dismissed. A joint statement by Gates's lawyer, Cambridge police and city officials, and the county district attorney's office called the incident "regrettable" and emphasized that it "should not be viewed as one that demeans the character and reputation of Professor Gates or the character of the Cambridge Police Department."[24]

Six days after Gates's arrest, President Obama was asked about the incident at the close of a press conference on health care. He responded:

> Now, I don't know, not having been there and not seeing all the facts, what role race played in that, but I think it's fair to say, number one, any of us would be pretty angry; number two, that the Cambridge police acted stupidly in arresting somebody when there was already proof that they were in their own home; and, number three, what

I think we know, separate and apart from this incident, is that there is a long history in this country of African-Americans and Latinos being stopped by law enforcement disproportionately. And that's just a fact.[25]

Obama's comments triggered widespread controversy. Critics claimed that he had prejudged the situation and had further "fuel[ed] the controversy" by charging the police with acting "stupidly."[26] According to Ben Heineman, a former general counsel and commentator on lawyers' leadership, Obama missed a "teaching moment."[27] By not stressing the need to make judgments based on facts rather than assumptions, he undercut his own position on racial profiling. He also diverted attention from the theme of his press conference—the urgency of health care reform.[28]

In the wake of public criticism, Obama made another statement to the press indicating that he "could have calibrated" his words more carefully.[29] However, he also stressed his conviction that the incident was "a sign of how race remains a factor in this society."[30] When the controversy persisted, Obama invited Gates and Crowley to the White House for a beer. The gesture attracted parodies from all quarters, including this from the Borowitz report:

> President Obama today named this Thursday, Drink a Beer With Someone Who Arrested You Day. Explaining his decision, the President told reporters, "When tempers run a little high, there's one thing that always helps people think more rationally: beer." The President said he hoped that his proclamation would result in thousands of friendly get-togethers around the country between police officers and the innocent people they recently arrested.[31]

Considerable media attention focused on the types of beer chosen and whether Obama's beer selection (Bud Light) was "a safe political choice." After all, Jon Stewart noted, the parent company of that beer was Belgian. Wasn't this a moment to "Buy American?"[32]

The meeting failed to shed light on the substantive problems that the incident exposed. In a public statement following the "beer summit," Crowley stated that he and Gates had "agreed to disagree" and "decided to look forward."[33] Their disagreement highlights the many roles that cognitive bias can play in decision making. The most obvious is the influence of race-based schemas in structuring interpretations of the event by Gates, his neighbor, Crowley, and Obama. The president's reaction is also an illustration of bounded rationality. By his own account, he did not know all the facts, yet he was willing to express an intuitive reaction to police conduct. That reaction was doubtless colored by the information that was for him most vivid, which was based on his personal knowledge of Gates, and his own experiences of racism. The decision to hold the beer summit may also have reflected what experts label "action bias," a desire to make some response to a problem without adequately considering the possible consequences.[34] If the desire was to minimize public criticism and draw attention to racial profiling, the choice of a beer summit was not well-suited to that end.

According to a *New Yorker* account of the incident, the takeaway for Obama was that "talking about race, especially extemporaneously, was just not worth it."[35] But in a nation where race still plays such a foundational role, leaders can ill afford to duck the issue completely. Rather, the lesson should be that a deliberative, not simply intuitive response is essential when talking about volatile issues. Obama and his advisors should have anticipated that he would be asked about the incident, and he could have made a more carefully calibrated statement along the lines that Heineman suggests: "I don't know the facts of this local police matter. But there is a potential question of racial profiling. Without passing judgment on Professor Gates' arrest, let me address that larger problem which, in my judgment, clearly continues to exist in America today."[36] A leader who makes an ill-considered initial remark may do best by apologizing and moving on, rather than prolonging the controversy by a public relations ploy that risks trivializing the substantive concerns.

Group Decision Making

Our image of leaders as decision makers tends to involve solitary individuals, who, like President George W. Bush, present themselves as the "decider." Yet their judgments are often the product of collective processes. The reasons are obvious. Decision making benefits from different perspectives that group members bring to the table.[37] Their involvement can also increase the legitimacy of the process and enhance the commitment of those who need to live with the outcomes. But group involvement can also result in poor decisions if participants lack sufficient expertise; if they have conflicting goals and values; if disagreements and disparities in power are not well managed: and if tendencies to conformity are not controlled. Social psychologist Irving Janis coined the term "groupthink" to describe the ways that highly cohesive groups suppress independent views and too quickly converge on ill-conceived decisions.[38]

Several decades of research has illuminated the circumstances under which groups can enhance or impair decision making. In their book *Problem*

Solving, Decision Making, and Professional Judgment, law professors Paul Brest and Linda Krieger summarize the conditions under which collective processes add value.

- The "group" must reflect a *diversity* of skills, opinions, information, and perspectives.
- Each member's judgments must be *independent* from the others. That is, an individual's knowledge and opinions cannot be influenced by the knowledge and opinions of other group members.
- The members must make and report their "sincere" judgments rather than skewing them for strategic purposes.
- The decision maker needs a mechanism for *aggregating* the individual judgments to turn large numbers of private judgments into a single one.[39]

By contrast, groupthink is likely to occur where members are homogenous, share information and values, and believe in their own morality and unanimity. The result is to censor or self-censor deviant views.[40]

Leaders can use a variety of strategies to improve collective decision making. One is to avoid disclosing their own preferences and to encourage members to voice objections and doubts. Leaders can reinforce candor by welcoming criticisms of their own judgments or by designating a devil's advocate to challenge group views. They can diminish insularity by assigning different members the responsibility to supply new information on key issues or by inviting comment by outside experts. Organizational theorists have also developed sophisticated strategies that mitigate tendencies toward premature consensus. One is the "step ladder" technique, in which each group member considers a problem alone. After the first two members discuss it, new members join the group one at a time and present their views before hearing what others think.[41] An alternative is the "Delphi technique," which relies on groups that do not meet face to face. Instead, members send ideas to a central coordinator, who then circulates them for comment and refinement.[42]

Groupthink is common in both the public and private sector. Some observers have argued that the Bush administration's decision to invade Iraq was an example. Among the conclusions of a Senate Intelligence Committee report were that:

> The Intelligence Community (IC) suffered from a collective presumption that Iraq had an active and growing weapons of mass destruction (WMD) program [based on Iraq's prior deception and refusal to

cooperate fully with UN inspectors]. This "group think" dynamic led Intelligence Community analysts, collectors, and managers to both interpret ambiguous evidence as conclusively indicative of a WMD program as well as ignore or minimize evidence that Iraq did not have active and expanding weapons of mass destruction programs. This presumption was so strong that formalized IC mechanisms established to challenge assumptions and group think [such as devil's advocacy] were not utilized....IC personnel involved in the Iraq WMD issue demonstrated several aspects of group think: examining few alternatives, selective gathering of information, pressure to conform within the group or withhold criticism, and collective rationalization.[43]

Other commentators noted that confirmation biases may also have inclined decision makers to interpret evidence in ways consistent with political interests.[44]

Some leaders, most famously Abraham Lincoln, resisted perils of insular thinking by appointing a "team of rivals," including formidable opponents, to top positions.[45] Mitt Romney is known for being a "decision maker by devil's advocacy," who will ask staff to argue all sides of contested issues.[46] Partway through his presidency, Bill Clinton invited Republican pollster Dick Morris into his inner circle to broaden the perspectives available. In applauding the decision, which was highly unpopular with some advisors, Hillary Clinton noted, "[i]n a rarified atmosphere like the White House, I don't think you can afford to surround yourself with people whose temperaments and views are always in sync. The meetings might run on schedule, but easy consensus can lead over time to poor decisions. Throwing Dick Morris into the mix of egos, attitudes and ambitions in the West Wing ratcheted up everyone's performance."[47] President Obama has also seemed sensitive to the potential pitfalls of group decision making. In 2008, after appointing his national security team, which included Hillary Clinton, he was asked about how he would ensure that the group would function as a team of rivals. He responded:

> I assembled this team because I am a strong believer in strong personalities and strong opinions. I think this is how the best decisions are made. One of the dangers in a White House based on my reading of history is that you get wrapped up in groupthink and everybody agrees with everything and there is no dissenting view. So I am going to be welcoming a vigorous debate inside the White House.[48]

Subsequent news reports indicated that Obama had, in fact, developed a "culture of debate" on major foreign policy decisions, such as expansion of the war in Afghanistan.[49]

However, on matters of domestic financial policy, he has been criticized for failing to build a sufficiently diverse team of advisors and regulatory officials, a criticism also leveled at his predecessor.[50] Many believe that leaders in both the public and private sector "got trapped in an echo chamber of conventional wisdom" about matters such as the ability of financial markets to police themselves.[51] A commitment to deregulation may also have led some political and regulatory officials to overlook abuses calling for greater oversight.[52] The combination of groupthink, overconfidence, and confirmation biases turned into a lethal combination of "contagious wishful thinking."[53]

In the private sector, a scandal that rocked Hewlett-Packard (HP) offers an illuminating example of dysfunctional decision making at the highest levels of leadership. In order to identify the source of leaks from the corporation's board of directors, the company's CEO, board chair, general counsel, and outside law firm all signed off on "pretexting"—deceptive investigatory methods, such as lying to telephone company employees, in order to obtain confidential information.[54] None of these leaders were well-informed about the pretextual methods involved, and most outsourced their responsibility for ethical oversight. The company's CEO didn't read the memo on the legality of the investigation; he deferred to the advice of the board chair.[55] She, in turn, relied on Ann Baskin, the general counsel, who delegated the issue to Ken Hunsacker, an employment lawyer who was in charge of ethical compliance.[56] Hunsacker did a cursory one-hour Web search and deferred to the private investigator. The investigator depended on an outside law firm, whose partner relied on memos by a summer associate and a paralegal.[57] None of this research apparently included obvious sources, such as position statements by the Federal Communications Commission or Federal Trade Commission, which considered pretexting illegal.[58] In responding to Hunsacker about whether the practice was lawful, the investigator concluded that although the individuals who were misled into giving out confidential information were in some sense "liable" for wrongfully doing so, the practice of deceiving them was "on the edge, but above board." Hunsacker's now infamous e-mail answer was "I should not have asked."[59]

After the investigation revealed that one of the board members was the source of the leaks, the board asked him to resign. One of his close colleagues on the board, unhappy with that decision, raised concerns about pretexting, both with a friend who was a law professor, and with Larry Sonsini, HP's outside counsel. Sonsini responded that pretexting was a "common investigatory method" and that "[i]t appears, therefore, that the process was well done and within legal limits."[60] The board member and his friend remained unconvinced, and when disagreements on this and other matters persisted, they reported the practice to the SEC, the California Attorney General, and the local U.S. Attorney. All of them launched investigations, which caused a national scandal and congressional hearings. Baskins and Hunsaker invoked their 5th amendment privilege, and along with the board chair, were forced to resign. Hunsaker, the chair, and some of the investigators faced felony charges that were later dismissed. In response to public criticism, Larry Sonsini maintained that his response to the board member was not a "legal opinion."[61] His firm was nonetheless replaced as outside counsel.[62]

What caused so many smart people to make such disastrous decisions? A number of the cognitive biases noted earlier were contributing factors. One was the inadequate framing of the problem. HP's leaders leaped immediately to the desired solution—stopping the leak—without addressing the board dysfunction that was responsible. Had they instead asked, "why is this problem a problem?" they could also have focused on the board's difficulties and involved its full membership in a solution. So too, framing the issue as whether pretexting was legal circumvented the broader issue of whether it was ethical and consistent with the company's internal code and values. Bart Schwartz, a former federal prosecutor hired to evaluate the company's conduct after the scandal unfolded, was struck by leaders' failure to consider ethical issues. "Doing it legally should not be the test; that is given. You have to ask what is appropriate and what is ethical."[63] Short-term concerns about the leak should not have obscured long-term reputational considerations.

Another cognitive failure in HP leaders' decision making was their insensitivity to incremental risks. The result was what psychologists term an "escalation of commitment," known colloquially as the "boiled frog problem."[64] A frog thrown into boiling water will jump out, but a frog placed in tepid water that gradually increases in temperature will calmly boil to death. In the case of HP, when accepted investigative techniques failed to identify the source of the leak, leaders authorized ever more intrusive and deceptive tactics.

A final contributing factor involved diffusion and displacement of responsibility. None of the leaders took it upon themselves to ensure that a highly sensitive decision—obtaining confidential records of board members' personal communications—was made after adequate research and full consideration of the ethical and legal concerns at issue. That failure is particularly problematic for the attorneys whose responsibilities included legal compliance. "Where were the lawyers?," asked one Congressman in hearings on the HP scandal. "The red flags were waving all over the place," but "none of the lawyers stepped up to their responsibilities."[65]

The same point has been raised about attorneys' complicity in other instances of corporate misconduct. Part of the explanation may involve how they perceive their role. Perceptions about identity help filter information ways that support individuals' self-image.[66] A survey of several hundred in-house counsel found that those who identified themselves more as employees than lawyers were more likely to interpret professional obligations in ways consistent with management's interests rather than with professional norms.[67] In the HP case, the desire to help corporate leaders solve the problem as they framed it may have eclipsed lawyers' broader fiduciary obligations to the organization and to the bar's ethical standards.

Influence

If, as chapter 1 suggested, the core of leadership is influence, a key issue is how best to achieve it. What strategies are most effective in motivating followers and how do followers influence—or circumvent—leaders? How do those in positions of authority foster innovation and manage conflict? How do they communicate most persuasively?

Strategies of Influence

The currency of influence comes in many forms. Leaders compel, intimidate, pressure, persuade, negotiate, model, and inspire. They exercise influence at personal, group, and organizational levels, through strategies that researchers place in four primary categories: authority, reciprocity, social influence, and association.

The most obvious source of influence stems from position, which confers authority to reward and punish. This power does not need to be explicit to be effective. Successful leaders rarely need to say "this is an order." Influence comes not only from benefits and sanctions, such as promotions, bonuses, dismissals, or discipline, but also from the credibility that is associated with a particular status. A notorious example of such authority is the obedience experiment pioneered by Yale psychologist Stanley Milgram and replicated hundreds of times since. Two-thirds of his subjects were prepared to deliver what they thought were life-threatening electric shocks when a person in

perceived events or individuals. So, for example, leaders who are seeking change within an organization or community can benefit from having well-respected "early adopters" speak in its favor; as experts note, "influence is often best exerted horizontally rather than vertically."[80] Pleasant experiences at events can also have positive effects, which is why so many leaders spend time and money on business entertainment. Negative influences can be equally powerful. Leaders have to worry about both being damned by association and being shielded from information by subordinates unwilling to deliver unwelcome messages. The significance of association emerges clearly in political campaigns. In 2008, Obama's efforts to distance himself from the radical racial pronouncements of Reverend Jeremiah Wright and to secure endorsements from popular mainstream figures like Caroline Kennedy were part of a strategy to reassure moderate white voters.

The effectiveness of different forms of influence varies by individuals and settings. For example, among those who take jobs in the public and nonprofit sectors, adjustments in compensation may be a less significant motivator than other factors such as recognition, challenge, job security, and a sense of contributing to a meaningful cause.[81] However, research on influence suggests some general insights that can guide leadership strategies across a wide range of contexts. One is that sanctions are more difficult than rewards to use effectively. Disincentives can lead to poorer performance by undermining confidence and self-esteem, and by provoking resentment, sabotage, and manipulation.[82] Experts emphasize the need to investigate thoroughly before resorting to sanctions, and to use them sequentially, beginning with coaching and warnings, before escalating to more serious penalties or dismissals. Recent research confirms Ovid's maxim that a leader "should be slow to punish and swift to reward." In summarizing this work, an influential *Harvard Business Review* article noted that a "kick in the pants" response to problems of motivation is frequently counterproductive. A better strategy generally involves job enrichment, such as providing greater opportunities for control and credit.[83] One reason is that rewards and sanctions are typically less effective than intrinsic motivation in promoting high performance.[84] Factors most likely to produce job satisfaction involve matters related to the work itself, including a sense of achievement, contribution, and opportunity for recognition.[85]

Relations with Followers

Analogous issues involve relations with followers, a topic too often neglected in the study of leadership. That inattention is, however, beginning itself to gain attention. Warren Bennis, one of the most prominent researchers in the field, points out that no matter who is memorialized as the leader, "followers do the heavy lifting of any successful enterprise."[86] Moreover, their power is increasing, partly due to the decline in command-and-control leadership styles and the rise of the Internet, which facilitates ground-up communication and organization. The result is often to blur the boundaries of leader and follower. Followers may lack formal authority, but they do not necessarily lack power. That is particularly true in law firms, where partners with a large book of business exert substantial influence. In some respects, all leaders are followers; to retain their authority, they have no choice but to "to follow their followers."[87] In the possibly apocryphal phrase of the French revolutionary leader Comte de Mirabeau, "There goes the mob, and I must follow them, for I am their leader."[88] Terms like "leading from behind" acknowledge the way that informal power structures may trump formal lines of authority.[89] Yet while all leaders may in some sense be followers, the converse is not necessarily true. Although in some circumstances, followers may be able to "lead up," such initiatives from the bottom are not always tolerated.[90] Hierarchies are real, and the boundaries between superiors and subordinates do not always blur.

To be effective, leaders need to understand why followers follow and what makes for productive relationships. Common motivations include rewards and sanctions; desires for stability, security and community; admiration, identification, and respect; and appeals to values and a vision of the future.[91] As Bennis notes, the qualities of the best followers are not so different from those of the best leaders; they are informed, engaged, and innovative.[92] Yet such qualities are not always what supervisors or organizational structures foster. Peer pressure and institutional rewards can produce dysfunctional conformity. Leaders can unconsciously compound the problem by discouraging dissent and rewarding ingratiation. Flattery by followers can easily become toxic; it reinforces leaders' narcissism and distances them from discomfiting realities.[93] The art of leadership is not simply what Dwight Eisenhower described: "getting someone else to do something you want done because he wants to do it."[94] Effective leaders also create channels for internal dissent, and invite constructive questions about what they *should* want done. The more leaders listen to followers, the more followers listen to them; trust is the most important factor affecting follower satisfaction and performance.[95] Sometimes, as Theodore Roosevelt reportedly put it, the "best leader is the one who has sense enough to pick good men to do what he wants done, and the self-restraint to keep from meddling with them while they do it." Common strategies for improving relationships with followers include offering them confidential opportunities to share critical feedback; providing positive rec-ognition and reinforcement for constructive criticism; creating a climate of transparency, responsiveness, and mutual respect; and involving individuals in key decisions that will affect their lives and their performance.[96]

The degree of appropriate involvement, of course, depends on the context. One of leaders' key tasks is to identify circumstances in which the best strat-egy is not to make a decision, but rather to engage stakeholders in adapting to difficult challenges and crafting the solutions they will have to live with. These are situations calling for what Harvard Professor Ronald Heifitz labels "adaptive leadership."

An example that Heifitz cites involved a copper plant owned by the American Smelting and Refining Company (Asarco) near Tacoma, Washington. The Asarco plant was the only one in the nation to use copper ore with a high content of arsenic, which was known to cause cancer. Under the Clean Air Act of 1970, the Environmental Protection Agency (EPA) had authority to determine whether the plant was operating with an "ample mar-gin of safety" to protect the public health. In 1983, the lawyer who headed the EPA, William Ruckelshaus, took an unprecedented action in deciding not to decide that question himself but rather to involve the community in the decision. The issue was both technically and politically complicated. Arsenic was one of the hazardous chemicals for which no clear threshold of safety had been determined. The plant was a mainstay of the local economy and the company claimed that the only ways to reduce arsenic emissions were prohib-itively expensive and would force the plant's closure. Ruckelshaus announced that the EPA would hold a series of public workshops on the issue. "For me to sit here in Washington and tell the people of Tacoma what is an acceptable risk would be at best arrogant and at worst inexcusable."[97] Few members of the community reacted positively. The prevailing view was "we elected peo-ple to run our government; we don't expect them to turn around and ask us to run it for them." Ruckelshaus persisted. "Listen," he told the *Los Angeles Times*. "I know people don't like these questions. Welcome to the world of regulation."[98]

The public workshops attracted broad attendance as well as local and national news coverage. EPA officials worked hard to present technical issues in an accessible fashion, and were surprised by community members' ability to understand the risks and to respond with constructive questions and sug-gestions for plant modifications. The meetings led to revisions of the EPA's original safety assessments and to further community-sponsored workshops focusing not just on trade-offs between jobs and safety, but also on the need to diversify the local economy.[99] A year later, while the EPA decision was still pending, Asarco closed the plant, primarily in response to depressed copper prices and shortages of high-arsenic copper ore. As a result of the process that Ruckelshaus had set in motion, the community was much better prepared to absorb the job loss and had already launched efforts to attract new industry and retrain workers. The Tacoma experience also improved EPA regulatory processes. In future disputes, the Agency began to sponsor forums among stakeholders and to learn from concerns generated at local levels. Regulators increasingly saw the importance of broadening analysis beyond narrow, technical estimates of risk. The Agency also needed to engage the public in hard questions about how much risk was reasonable to assume and how to cope with the economic consequences of reducing it. Such engagement in turn helped to increase public confidence in EPA regulatory processes.[100]

As this example makes clear, sometimes the most responsible decision by leaders is not to decide, and to shift responsibility to stakeholders. In other contexts, as the discussion below suggests, the challenge lies in anticipating change and positioning an organization or group to adjust.

Fostering Innovation and Managing Change

Former Army Chief of Staff Eric Shinseki observed that "If you don't like change, you're going to like irrelevance even less."[101] Any successful organization or movement needs to adapt to social, political, legal, economic, and technological developments. Estimates from the corporate sector suggest that most companies need moderate change at least once a year and major changes every four to five years.[102] No comparable projections are available for law firms or public sector and non-profit organizations; much depends on their relative exposure to competition. However, even government organizations that are most insulated from competitive pressures will pay a price if they fail to respond to changing circumstances. New initiatives may be necessary to ensure public legitimacy and to shore up political and financial support.[103] Yet those from whom change is expected may be subject to the status quo bias; people are naturally loss averse and tend to overvalue risks and undervalue benefits.[104] Moreover, for reasons noted in chapter 1, lawyers as a group tend to be particularly resistant to change, and those who reach leadership positions do not appear to be exceptions. In one recent survey, fewer than 20 percent of firm leaders described their philosophy as embracing innovation and change.[105]

Change comes in many forms, but much of the literature on leadership stresses innovation, defined as adaptation of an idea to a new setting.[106] Unlike invention and creativity, which refer to the development of something new, and may need only individual effort, innovation generally requires collective practices that produce adaptation.[107] Innovation is particularly important in contexts of rapidly evolving technologies or shifting stakeholder expectations. Many commentators believe that the contemporary legal profession is in such a context. Technology has displaced the role of lawyers in many routine tasks and the bar confronts escalating pressure to find new ways of delivering quality services at lower prices and greater efficiency.[108] Leaders need not themselves be the source of innovative ideas, but they do need to create a culture that anticipates and adapts to change. As Peter Drucker observed, "What brought you here won't get you there."[109]

The impetus for innovation varies. A crisis frequently dramatizes the need for change and creates the sense of urgency that makes it possible. An erosion of market power or public support can also propel organizations into action, as can mergers, technological developments, or financial and governance problems that defy conventional solutions.[110] Experts identify three stages at which leaders can guide change.[111] The initial phase requires overcoming inertia and creating a compelling vision for the future.[112] To this end, leaders must first identify the obstacles to change in their own organizations. Common problems include the "curse of complacency" and the "curse of homogeneity"; too many insiders are drinking the same Kool-Aid, or have too much personal investment in outdated strategies.[113] These dynamics are particularly apparent in law firms, where it has been difficult to convince well- off lawyers that their business model needs fixing.[114] To counteract these tendencies, leaders may need to develop strategic planning processes that identify serious problems or untapped opportunities. Getting perspectives from clients, peers, and outside experts can be helpful in identifying necessary reforms. Ronald Heifitz and Donald Laurie suggest that leaders try to look beyond their daily challenges as if they were on a balcony observing the field of play and seeking deeper patterns.[115]

Reaching people on an emotional level through direct experience or compelling narratives can also help create a sense of urgency that inspires action. For example, in health care, asking leaders to investigate examples of fatal but preventable mistakes at their own hospitals gave them a sense of the human tragedies that data spread sheets often mask; the result was a new commitment to remedial actions.[116] A corporate executive, who could not get his division presidents to see the waste created by inconsistent purchasing procedures, created a visual display to dramatize the problem, estimated to cost $200 million a year. The display featured 424 variations of one product—factory gloves—used in every division, with prices ranging from $5 to $17 for essentially the same item. That exhibit, coupled with benchmarking research showing how other competitors handled the issue, inspired the necessary commitment to change.[117] David Maister, an expert on professional services firms, suggests a powerful way of communicating through example. He proposes that a leader create standards for his own performance, ask others to rank him on those standards, publicly disclose the results, and pledge to step down if he doesn't achieve significant improvement in a year. It's a high-risk strategy, but the acceptance of accountability sends a powerful message about the organization's commitment to change.[118]

A second task for leaders is to develop a realistic strategy for moving forward and to enlist broad support in its behalf. Once proposals crystallize, leaders should solicit buy-in from key participants in order to minimize opposition later.[119] Meeting one-on-one can be critical in allaying concerns. Often the most effective approach is to seek short-term visible improvements that can lay foundations for broader transformations.[120] Professional service firms and non-profit organizations have had some success through comparing other organization's strategies and soliciting ideas for improvement from stakeholders.[121] Contrary to conventional wisdom, brainstorming sessions are not generally the best strategy for developing innovative ideas; groupthink tends to stifle creativity. However, electronic brainstorming appears to work more effectively; sharing at a distance allows people to be "alone together" and mitigates some pressures for conformity.[122]

Where people are the problem, leaders need to address their concerns and performance problems, or at least to work around resisters. To many individuals, the costs of change seem immediate and discomforting; the rewards lie in the future and may be organizational rather than personal. Typical reasons for opposing change are its threats to status, power, autonomy, competence, comfort, and job security.[123] Leaders can help allay such concerns by enabling employees to adapt, retool, or find other positions.[124] In *Crucial Confrontations,* experts on interpersonal dynamics emphasize the need for leaders to be sure that they are dealing "with the right problem" and addressing underlying causes.[125] What is holding individuals back? Is it primarily a matter of understanding, competence, or motivation? Are they aware of exactly how their performance is falling short? Do they have the skills and experience to respond? Is a lack of responsibility, training, or support standing in the way? Do they truly want to do what is necessary, see the need to do it, or believe they can do it and will be rewarded for their effort? Active listening, mutual problem solving, and a concrete plan are all essential to moving forward.[126] It is often essential not only to address individuals' dysfunctional behavior, but also to enlist the social pressure that can discourage it. For example, simply warning people that "AIDS kills" is less effective in reducing unprotected sex than convincing them that their peers approve of using condoms.[127] By analogy, it may not be enough to explain how a technological innovation could increase efficiency; lawyers may also need to hear that everyone else is embracing it.

A third leadership task is to assess and consolidate change. Here, the key is identifying the right time and metrics to evaluate progress. Premature assessment can stifle innovation. "Pulling up the radishes" to see how they're growing defeats the enterprise.[128] But once enough time has passed, leaders need to measure the outcomes of their strategic vision and to institutionalize what works. That requires creating reward structures that reinforce progress and that continue to reinvigorate the process.[129] Although straightforward in concept, institutionalization often founders in practice. In her Pulitzer Prize-winning book, *Join the Club*, Tina Rosenberg describes many change efforts that have bumped up against disabling political and cultural obstacles. For example, research has identified the advertising messages that are most likely to reduce teenage smoking. Contrary to conventional wisdom, it is not messages that focus on the health risks of tobacco.[130] Rather, what works are ads suggesting that tobacco companies are lying and trying to addict teens. Yet policy leaders are not acting on that knowledge; lobbying efforts have blunted reform efforts. As Rosenberg concludes: "change does not happen in a vacuum. Any decision on strategy must take into account the difficulties of building and maintaining political support, especially when the opponent is formidable."[131]

Leaders need to confront such obstacles to change not only in their own organizations but also in professional associations. The American bar has lagged behind other occupational groups in delivering professional services in part because it has refused to acknowledge the need for fundamental change in regulatory structures. For example, the bar's state-based standards of admission and ethical conduct are at odds with a world of increasingly national practice and lateral mobility among lawyers. Bar disciplinary processes also have been notoriously unresponsive to consumer complaints.[132] And bans on non-lawyers as financial investors or partners in multidisciplinary firms insulate the profession from valuable skills, perspectives, and capital. Other countries, including England and Australia, have been moving in the direction of greater non-lawyer involvement in bar regulation and investment structures. Yet leaders of the American legal profession have fiercely resisted such innovation.[133]

Ironically, the American Bar Association's 20/20 Commission, charged with recommending changes that would help lawyers adapt to the needs of 2020, described its mission as "preservation of core professional values, and maintenance of a strong, independent, and self-regulated profession." "Preserve" and "maintain," not innovate or adapt, set the Commission's tone. Unsurprisingly, as law professor James Moliterno notes, the reforms that the Commission has proposed are minor and do little more than formally acknowledge technological and global changes that have already happened. "This is management by looking backward and inward; management in service of the status quo."[134] Moliterno analogizes the bar's approach to that of Kodak, which developed the first digital camera in the 1970s, but determined not to enter the digital market for fear of jeopardizing its film business. By the time the company changed course, it was too late.[135]

By the same token, the bar's resistance to fundamental change and to non-lawyer involvement in the process ill-serves the interests of lawyers and their clients. Steven Johnson, in his pathbreaking book, *Where Good Ideas Come From*, reviews two hundred of the most important scientific breakthroughs from the past six centuries, and finds that significant innovation most often comes through interaction between those in different fields and networks.[136] The legal profession would benefit from more cross-disciplinary alliances, and its leaders need to become more engaged in efforts to permit them.

In *Switch,* psychologists Chip Heath and Dan Heath compare the process of leading change to riding an elephant. The rider holds the reins, but if the elephant doesn't want to go, they're both stuck. To make progress, the rider needs to know where to go, motivate the elephant, and clear the path of obstacles.[137] Many bar leaders, elected for a brief fixed term, dismount the elephant before identifying a strategy to move it forward. That needs to change to address the regulatory challenges of contemporary practice.

Conflict Management

Another critical leadership skill involves managing conflict. Leaders play multiple roles: negotiating and mediating disputes, advising disputants, and structuring processes for dispute resolution. Estimates suggest that business leaders spend between 15 and 40 percent of their time dealing with conflicts.[138] For lawyers holding leadership positions, the percentage may be even higher. Not only do they face problems in their own workplaces, they also may be advising clients involved in disputes. Failure to handle conflict effectively carries substantial costs. Unresolved workplace disputes can lead to stress, mental health difficulties, turnover, absenteeism, lack of cooperation and communication, litigation, and retaliation. Fear of conflict can inhibit constructive criticism. Mishandled disputes can cost millions, ruin reputations, and derail careers. In policy contexts, the social costs can be still greater.

Yet when managed effectively, conflict can be a source of necessary communication and change. It can provide a catalyst for innovation and challenges to received wisdom. There is truth in the quip that when two people always agree, "one of them is unnecessary."[139] Conflict can also signal problems in relationships or organizational practices that need attention. In short, conflict can be a source of leaders' best ideas as well as their worst failures.[140] A vast body of research explores conflict resolution in law-related contexts, including negotiation, mediation, international relations, alternative dispute resolution, and management. From this literature, lawyers who lead can derive some general insights about the dynamics of conflict and strategies for addressing it.

Dynamics of Conflict

A threshold issue is what exactly constitutes conflict. Some experts include any situation involving "apparently incompatible interests, goals, principles, or feelings."[141] Others define it as a struggle over values, resources, status, and power.[142] In some settings, it makes sense to distinguish between conflicts involving relationships and those involving tasks or issues. Of the disputes common in workplaces, employees express most frustration with those raising relational issues, such as conflicting work styles or personalities.[143] Many circumstances hold potential for conflict, but whether it develops depends on the importance of the issues at stake, the costs of fighting for them, the resources available, and the likelihood of success.

The causes of conflict obviously vary, but certain patterns are common. Often a history of unresolved differences and repressed animosity will flare up in response to some precipitating event or change in conditions. Root causes include objective circumstances, such as insufficient resources, incompatible interests, power disparities, and differences in race, ethnicity, gender, and culture. Subjective perceptions matter as well, particularly when fueled by incomplete information, miscommunication, and cognitive biases.[144] For example, a history of acrimony may result in attribution errors; parties may assign malicious motives to opponents' actions, rather than benign explanations. To reduce cognitive dissonance, parties may then selectively perceive information that confirms prior assumptions.[145] Antagonists may also engage

in "reactive devaluation"; their perception of the attractiveness of a proposal diminishes if it comes from an opponent.[146] In one telling example, a
researcher took peace proposals developed by Israeli negotiators and misla-
beled them as Palestinian proposals, and similarly misrepresented Palestinian
proposals as Israeli proposals. When he asked Israeli citizens to evaluate the
suggestions, they preferred those misattributed to Israelis.[147]

Responses to Conflict

Responses to conflict fall into common categories. Experts use different
labels, but generally identify six strategies: avoidance, contention, coercion,
appeasement, compromise, and collaboration. No single approach is consistently preferable, and research on relative effectiveness is mixed.[148] Although
context is critical, experts agree on certain general points.

Avoidance is many peoples' preferred response, and with reason.[149] Open
confrontation risks unpleasantness, stress, and retaliation, and may seem
pointless if the adversary has greater power and a history of unresponsiveness.
Leaders' desire for approval can also keep them from addressing difficult issues,
particularly if they do not seem critical to organizational performance.[150] Yet
while picking one's battles is critical, avoidance as a general strategy should
be avoided. Unresolved problems are likely to fester, impair productivity, and
lead to more costly confrontations later. During her presidential campaign,
Hillary Clinton "hated personal conflict [and] avoided it like the plague,"
which ended up perpetuating more conflict and confusion among staff
over who exactly was in charge.[151] Another famous example involved long-
suppressed disputes over control and credit between the NAACP's executive
secretary, Walter White, and its legal director, Thurgood Marshall. Marshall
orchestrated the campaign culminating in the Supreme Court's decision over-
turning segregation in *Brown v. Board of Education*. Yet at a press conference
following the victory, White dominated the discussion and announced "his"
future plans to attack discrimination in housing and transportation. Marshall,
feeling once again upstaged, uncharacteristically erupted in anger and point-
edly asked "what law school did you graduate from, Mr. White?"[152]

As that example illustrates, it often makes sense for parties to avoid confrontation until they have time to let their emotions cool and to carefully
consider their options.[153] Flight may be preferable to fight if it prevents public displays or hostilities that will be difficult to remedy later. But temporary
disengagement is no substitute for mutual problem solving under less volatile
circumstances.

step back
think
cool off
respond

Contention or coercion are more direct responses to conflict. Openly competing for control or imposing a solution may be necessary to reach closure or deter further hostile acts. But results that leave losers' fundamental needs unmet are likely to prove unstable, and to provoke resentment, resistance, or recurring confrontations.[154] Competitive and coercive approaches short-circuit opportunities for more creative, mutually acceptable solutions.

The same is true of appeasement. In some cases, if one side cares more about avoiding acrimony than achieving a particular outcome, a generous concession may seem prudent. Cultural differences may also push in that direction. In Asian societies, for example, conflict resolution tends to be relatively restrained, and harmonious relationships are highly valued.[155] But in most cultures, those who yield not because they believe the result is reasonable but because they see no viable alternative may nurse grievances that will erupt in more destructive fashion later. Moreover, capitulation may encourage even more oppressive behavior from a victorious bully. As experts note, "the leader who always appeases is like someone who feeds crocodiles hoping that they'll eat him last."[156]

Compromise is often preferable. Splitting differences may be productive particularly in contexts involving zero-sum trade-offs, in which no party can be made better off without the other party suffering. But that approach risks leaving both sides dissatisfied, and it may fail to promote a fair outcome if the starting point for division is skewed toward one party.[157]

The alternative that most experts promote is collaboration, or what some label integrative problem solving. Under this approach, parties work together to identify win/win outcomes that build on shared concerns and mutual respect.[158] This requires exploration of underlying needs, objectives, and expectations. Although this process has obvious advantages, it is generally time-consuming, and unlikely to work if the differences between the parties are too great.

Strategies

Leaders play multiple roles in conflict management. They negotiate, mediate, facilitate, and advise on particular disputes. They also create organizational structures designed to prevent, resolve, or creatively use conflict. Each of these roles presents distinct challenges. Each also calls for common skills and strategies.

Leaders' first requirement is knowledge, both of themselves and others. To resolve conflicts in which they are personally involved, leaders need to be aware of their own "hot buttons," their underlying interests and needs, and their "best alternative to a negotiated agreement."[159] Individuals who feel themselves losing control can ask for a time out, begin writing down constructive points that they wish to discuss later, or attempt to "freeze frames" by imagining a situation in which they felt calm and self-confident.[160] An effective resolution often depends on learning as much as possible about the goals and concerns of everyone involved in the conflict. Seeking information from multiple sources is often critical, as is active or "empathic" listening. Productive techniques involve listening without interrupting; restating points to be sure that the other parties' meaning is understood; paying attention to body language and to what is unsaid as well as said; avoiding accusations, blame, moral judgment, or inflammatory rhetoric; and probing for underlying reasons, concerns, and creative solutions.[161] It is often helpful for leaders to identify the effects that the other person's behavior is having, and how those might be inconsistent with that person's goals.[162] Once parties have identified a solution, they need to agree on specific remedial steps, which may include strategies for avoiding problems in the future. Productive dialogue is most likely when leaders have carefully selected the time, place, and manner of the conversation. In advising general counsel about "how to say no to your CEO," former General Electric counsel Ben Heineman reminds his audience that "for obvious reasons, CEOs view their authority as being very important. They don't want it directly challenged. So, saying no in a big group...sometimes needs to be done, but it's sometimes better if you can go in afterwards or find a place where you can be one on one to express the concern...You have to disagree without being disagreeable."[163]

In their landmark negotiation primer, *Getting to Yes,* Roger Fisher and William Ury suggest other strategies for managing conflict: focusing on interests not positions, insisting on objective criteria for assessing those interests, and inventing options for mutual gain.[164] Although the book also proposed separating "the people from the problem," Fisher has subsequently acknowledged that "[i]n some cases the people *are* the problem; negotiating a good relationship with them may be more important than the subsequent outcome of any one negotiation."[165] To that end, other experts advise leaders to be willing to reach out to restore productive communication. An apology that is genuine and does not make unwarranted concessions of fault may be a first step toward building trust and empathy. In short, the overarching goal should be to reframe the conflict as an opportunity for collaborative problem solving and to create the conditions that will enable this to occur.

That same approach is useful for leaders who are mediating conflict among others or facilitating its resolution through advice and coaching. This role typically involves:

- establishing credibility and rapport by expressing concern for all parties and maintaining impartiality;
- getting parties to remain civil, respectful, and committed to creating a productive working environment;
- assisting parties to identify shared values and objectives, to express underlying needs and concerns, and to see multiple sides of the same issue;
- providing a disinterested and reliable source of information; and
- helping parties to develop solutions and to agree on a specific plan for action that avoids toothless promises.[166]

In her manual, *Power and Influence for Lawyers,* Susan Letter notes that one of the hardest skills is to "stay in the attentive listening phase for a sufficient amount of time.... Listening takes time and time is money for lawyers."[167] As chapter 1 noted, lawyers as a group tend toward impatience, and leaders who are juggling many competing demands are understandably interested in moving the conversation to closure. Often they fail to appreciate the facial expressions and body language that signal frustration.

Leaders who are most noted for their conflict resolution skills have cultivated capacities for responsive listening and for keeping channels of communication open long enough to identify opportunities for consensus. Louis Brandeis famously described his role in a dispute as a "lawyer for the situation," and was known for what legal historian Robert Gordon describes as "extraordinary charm" in conflict management. In brokering the end of acrimonious garment workers strikes, "with all the parties screaming at each other across the table, Brandeis would listen intently to all the parties, beaming and nodding as each scored a point, and then would come in at the end with a summary of what seemed [to be] underlying points of agreement."[168]

Lawyers as leaders can also play a crucial role in creating "conflict competent" organizations. That requires fostering cultures that value trust, civility, and constructive disagreement; that provide multiple channels for dispute resolution; and that offer support, training, and mediation for those involved in conflict.[169] Research makes clear that people's sense of the fairness of dispute-resolution processes is even more important than substantive outcomes in promoting overall satisfaction and confidence.[170] Leaders should be sure that organizational structures are meeting participants' expectations of equity and legitimacy.

In *Leading Through Conflict*, Mark Gerzon describes a situation that is common in many legal organizations with branch offices, including law firms, government agencies, and corporations.[171] In Gerzon's example, disputes among leaders of offices of a multinational company repeatedly surfaced around issues of compensation and priorities, and meetings degenerated into recitations of what others were doing wrong and needed to change. With the help of a consultant, the CEO began structuring the meetings differently. Participants were placed on teams charged with taking responsibility for the organization's problems and proposing solutions. The result was to force department heads out of their self-interested positions and to make them address the big picture.

Values

In many conflict settings, one of the most difficult challenges for leaders involves knowing how much compromise to accept when matters of principle are at stake. Archibald Cox faced that dilemma during a leave from Harvard Law School to head the Truman administration's Wage Stabilization Board. Under the federal law then in force, Cox believed that the Board had no choice but to veto a wage increase for coal miners that had been reached through collective bargaining. Within a day of that decision, 300,000 of the nation's 375,000 soft coal miners went on an unauthorized walkout. Cartoons appeared in newspapers across the country featuring Cox as an ogre stealing milk from the bottles of miners' infants.[172] Despite the political fallout, Cox felt that allowing wages to rise would set an unacceptable precedent. As a matter of principle, labor should not be allowed to muscle its way to preferential treatment. While an appeal of the Board's decision was pending, Cox had a fifteen-minute meeting with President Truman in which to convince him not to back down. As Cox later recalled the experience, the President "began talking about the weather, the furniture, and every irrelevancy for thirteen minutes and then [excused himself with] 'Sorry, I have no more time.'"[173] Truman, then a lame-duck president, had realized that wage controls would be lifted under the new administration, and had determined that it made political sense to end the dispute. He overturned the Board's decision. Cox decided to resign, and against the administration's wishes, to issue a public statement explaining why. In his view, to allow an exception for miners would violate "the democratic ideal of equality and pu[t] a premium on the use of economic power"; to allow similar wage increases for other workers would "preserve the forms of stabilization without the substance." Many viewed this statement as a pointless and professionally imprudent gesture. It suggested that he was an "academic stickler lacking sufficiently thick political skin."[174] Cox himself was comfortable with his choice. And as it turned out, his willingness to stand by principle was part of what earned him a distinguished reputation and brought other public service opportunities, including appointment as Solicitor General.

Communication

A final way that leaders exercise influence is through communication. In both public and private settings, leaders try to persuade followers, clients, allies, adversaries, and the broader public. A key to that process is listening, which many law firm leaders rank as their most important skill.[175] Another critical capability is oral advocacy. Although it is taught in law school and continuing legal education programs and honed in some practice settings, surprising numbers of leaders fall short.

What goes wrong? For some lawyers, public speaking is a stressful experience, and anxiety often interferes with performance.[176] Even those who are comfortable with public speaking often misjudge what their audience would find most persuasive. In *Made to Stick: Why Some Ideas Survive and Others Die,* Chip and Dan Heath explore the problem by describing an example from a Stanford graduate school course. Students receive material from a government crime report and are asked to make a one-minute speech to persuade their classmates that nonviolent crime is or is not a serious problem. Students then rate the speeches. Almost all are good, but the top scores go to speakers who are most poised, smooth, and charismatic. The exercise appears over, and the class goes on to other matters. Then, after ten minutes, students are asked to write down everything they remember from each speech. They are shocked to discover how little they recall. Some draw a complete blank on certain speeches; at best, they remember one or two ideas from a speech they just heard. Almost no correlation appears between the speakers rated most accomplished and those most able to make their messages stick. Part of the reason is the disconnect between what speakers stress and what listeners find easiest to recall. Although the students used an average of two to three statistics per speech, only 5 percent of their audience remembered any. And although almost two-thirds of the students remembered stories, only one in ten speakers used them.[177]

Heath and Heath point out that these students are similar to many leaders who "seem to believe that, once they've clicked through a PowerPoint presentation showcasing their conclusions, they've successfully communicated their ideas. What they've done is share data. If they're good speakers, they may even have created an enhanced sense...that they are 'decisive' or 'managerial' or 'motivational.'" But if the audience were tested, leaders would discover that what they had *not* done was convey "ideas that are useful and lasting. Nothing stuck."[178] To be effective, leaders need to pay attention to a number of key factors: objectives, audience, substance, presentation, and preparation. The discussion that follows focuses on public speaking, but the same points are relevant for other forms of communication.

Objectives

Leaders' first task is to be clear about their objectives. Speakers frequently have multiple agendas that pull in different directions. For example, politicians need to consider whether a particular speech is primarily intended to mobilize their base, persuade uncommitted voters, attract favorable media coverage, shore up their legacy, or send a message to other leaders. Heads of law firms may want to convey information, build relationships, sell an idea, or motivate change. What speakers most hope to accomplish needs to guide both style and substance. The importance of such choices is captured in Roman historian Cato's famous observation: "When Cicero spoke, people marveled. When Caesar spoke, people marched."

The need for clarity of purpose may seem obvious, but even seasoned speakers can lose sight of their main objective. Robert Reich, former secretary of labor in the Clinton administration, wryly recalls his own naiveté in preparing for his Senate confirmation hearing. When asked in practice sessions about any significant—and therefore potentially divisive—issue, his tendency as a professor of public policy was to elaborate his views. But as senior administration officials explained, this was a mistake. "You have to respond to [Senators'] questions. You don't have to answer them. You *shouldn't* answer them. You're not expected to answer them." The main objective of confirmation hearings, from the point of view of most senators, was to give them, not the nominee, an opportunity to look learned and wise. The main objective from the point of view of the nominee was to gain support, which called for exuding deference and dodging controversy. An ideal answer would be something like, "Senator, you know far more about that issue than I do and I look forward to hearing your views in the months to come."[179] Lawyers who are accustomed to adversarial settings often fail to adapt to circumstances calling for more diplomacy. If leaders' primary objective is to win an audience's support, it doesn't help to show how much smarter they are than those asking the questions.

If another goal is media coverage, that too may require strategies that go against lawyers' natural inclinations. In his autobiography, Warren Christopher describes his own difficulties:

> I was not what reporters were looking for, a colorful talker who dispensed quotable tidbits as he went. Perhaps because of my background as a lawyer, I am hyperconscious of the ease with which words can be misunderstood or distorted. As a result, I used them sparingly. This is not, and was not, grist for inspired prose or punditry.[180]

By contrast, Joseph McCarthy achieved enormous power by giving the press exactly what it wanted: sensationalized sound bites, alarmist accusations, and clear villains. By holding closed door hearings and refusing to allow witnesses and lawyers to make exculpatory statements, he was also able to avoid exposing inconvenient facts that might undercut his narrative.[181] If reporters ultimately discovered those facts, McCarthy was ready with new charges to divert public attention.

Leaders not only need to be clear about their objectives, they also need objectives that are worthy of support. In the end, McCarthy grossly misjudged the public's tolerance for intimidation and reckless disregard of the truth. His abusive treatment of witnesses and other lawyers during hearings on Army security, along with ludicrous charges during hearings on his own censure, proved his undoing. His suggestion that the Senate itself had become the "unwitting handmaiden" of communism helped deprive him of the influence that he craved.[182]

Audience

As McCarthy's experience makes clear, understanding the audience is always critical. How many members will be informed on the subject under discussion or sympathetic to the leaders' position? How engaged or distracted will they be? What kinds of arguments will be most persuasive? How much time should be spent on prepared remarks and how much on dialogue? Finding the right person to ask the right questions in advance of a presentation can be as important as the performance itself. If in doubt, a safe assumption is that less is more. Lincoln's Gettysburg address took three minutes. Often it is more work to pare a speech down to essentials, which is what makes it particularly compelling. Woodrow Wilson made the point when asked how long it would take him to write a five-minute speech. "About a week," he answered. He was then asked about a half-hour speech. "Two days," was his response. "How about an hour speech?" "That one I can deliver right now."[183] Erring on the side of brevity is also prudent when it comes to showcasing personal experience. Too much self-referential material can leave captive audience members feeling like the P. G. Wodehouse character, who complained: "The Agee woman told us for three quarters of an hour how she came to write her beastly book when a simple apology was all that was required."[184]

Another rule of thumb, ignored with surprising regularity even by accomplished leaders, is that no one wants anything dull, particularly after dinner. The reasons why were amply demonstrated at a recent fundraising event at which I was making remarks. When I declined wine with the observation that at least the speaker needed to be sober, the host responded, "Why? No one else will."

A further problem involves the leader whose role is to introduce or celebrate another individual, and who forgets that the occasion is "not about you." In a typical recent example, a woman charged with introducing me decided to put my remarks "in context" with an extended digression on her own experiences concerning the topic. She finally began her appointed task with the comment, "And now for our speaker, Debbie Rhodes." I winced, not because I particularly care how my name is mangled, but because others will assume I do, and such easily preventable errors make the introducer look negligent, indifferent, or both.

Leaders also need to look for ways to establish credibility and "presence"— an authentic connection with audience members, collectively or individually.[185] It helps to make visual or verbal contact with as many people as possible, before, during, and after any presentation. The best credentials are not necessarily titles or accomplishments. As Richard Nixon noted, they often instead involve some personal bond or shared interest with those present, which is why so many politicians develop fondness for corn dogs in Iowa.[186]

Physical presence is not always necessary to forge connections, as has been clear since President Franklin Delano Roosevelt's "fireside chats" in the 1930s and early 40s. In these radio broadcasts, FDR spoke about complex challenges in simple language accessible to the average listener. Will Rogers said of the first broadcast, "our president took such a dry subject as banking and made everybody understand it, even the bankers."[187] Roosevelt's language of inclusion created bonds of intimacy and unity. His initial broadcast concluded that the nation's economic depression was "your problem, my friends, your problem no less than it is mine. Together we cannot fail."[188] People listened from homes, churches, theaters, and parks, and felt as if the President was "sitting by [their] side" and sincere when he invited them to "tell me your troubles." The volume of letters that the White House received grew from eight hundred a day to eight thousand, and the president not only insisted that they all be answered, but looked at samples himself to keep in touch with public concerns.[189] Contrary to conventional wisdom, the broadcasts did not significantly boost FDR's personal approval ratings, but they were effective in building support for administration policies, and in countering negative editorials in major newspapers largely controlled by Republicans.[190]

For contemporary leaders, the Internet and online social networks have provided further capacity to connect directly with audiences. In *Open Leadership: How Social Technology Can Transform the Way You Lead*, Charlene Li analyzes the many uses of virtual communication and cites Barak Obama's 2008 presidential campaign as an effective example. It relied on social network sites and Internet videos to build widespread support, particularly among younger voters, and to raise a record $745 million from three million donors.[191] By 2011, Obama had more than eight million followers on Twitter, and more than twenty-one million on Facebook.[192] The White House has developed an official app for iPhones and Androids in order to deliver news, often through live video streaming, and has posted an interactive video of speeches such as the 2012 State of the Union address to Congress. Other leaders in both the public and private sector are following suit and developing approaches that merge entertainment with substance.[193] But as the discussion of scandal in chapter 6 notes, the enormous instantaneous reach of the Internet carries risks as well as opportunities. Congressman Anthony Weiner's single tweet made his private parts no longer private and his political position no longer viable.

Content

For most leaders, crafting an effective presentation requires coping with the "curse of knowledge."[194] Often they will be so steeped in a subject that the challenge lies in deciding what not to discuss. Many otherwise impressive presentations suffer from one fact too many, or maybe more than one. For main points, communication experts suggest a rule of three. The goal is to provide enough to support the main theme but not to exceed the audience's attention span. In *Made to Stick*, Chip and Dan Heath offer a framework for communicating messages that will be retained: they should be simple, unexpected, concrete, credible, emotional, and tell a story (SUCCESs).[195] Other research emphasizes colorful language, metaphor, repetition, appeals to common values, and terms of inclusion (we and our).[196] As noted earlier, stories are generally better retained than statistics, but a single dramatic number can be powerful, as reflected in Occupy Wall Street's refrain of 99 percent.[197]

A compelling start and close are crucial, and they are particularly effective if tied together in a way that completes a circle and enhances coherence. A successful opening is often a personal anecdote, an amusing quotation, or a surprising, counterintuitive claim that will attract audience interest. Nora Ephron makes the point with a story about her first day in a high school journalism course. The class was asked to write the lead for an article in the school newspaper about an upcoming conference. The entire faculty was to participate in an all-day program the following week in the state capitol, led by speakers including then California governor Pat Brown and the world-renowned anthropologist Margaret Mead. Ephron recalled that she and most of her classmates produced opening sentences explaining "who, what, where, and when." No one spotted the lead that their teacher suggested: "There will be no school next Thursday."[198]

The most famous speeches by lawyer leaders reflect characteristics that experts have recommended. Perhaps the best known, Lincoln's Gettysburg Address, began with an unexpected turn. Lincoln noted that the audience had come for a dedication but that he could not provide one. He then reinterpreted the concept of dedication as a responsibility of the living to continue the efforts of the dead, not simply consecrate their memory.

> We are met here on a great battlefield of war. We have come to dedicate a portion of it as a final resting place for those who here gave their lives that that nation might live. It is altogether fitting and proper that we should do this. But in a larger sense we can not dedicate—we can not consecrate—we can not hallow this ground. The brave men, living and dead, who struggled, here, have consecrated it far above our poor power to add or detract. The world will little note, nor long remember, what we say here, but can never forget what they did here.
>
> It is for us the living, rather to be dedicated here to the unfinished work which they have, thus far so nobly carried on.... [W]e here highly resolve that these dead shall not have died in vain; that this nation shall have new birth of freedom; and that this government of the people, by the people, for the people shall not perish from the earth.[199]

Lincoln was, of course, wrong in one respect. The world did note and has long remembered this address, for its eloquent message of resolve in pursuit of a united nation.

Two other presidential speeches by lawyers are noteworthy, not for the power of their prose, but for their masterful use of stories. The first is one of Franklin Delano Roosevelt's appeals for a controversial fourth term as president.

> These Republican leaders have not been content with attacks on me or my wife or my sons. No, not content with that they now include my little dog Fala. Well of course, I don't resent attacks and my family doesn't resent attacks but Fala does resent them. You know, Fala is Scotch and being a Scottie, as soon as he learned that the Republican fiction writers in Congress and out had concocted a story that I left him behind on the Aleutian Islands and had sent a destroyer back to find—at a cost to the taxpayers of two or three, or eight or twenty million dollars—his Scotch soul was furious. He has not been the same dog since. I am accustomed to hearing malicious falsehoods about myself,—such as that old, worm eaten chestnut that I have represented myself as indispensable. But I think I have a right to resent, to object, to libelous statements about my dog."[200]

The emotional impact of this story was extraordinary, and the administration capitalized on its influence by coupling it with the tune "They Gotta Quit Kicking my Dawg Aroun," for radio broadcasts. Not only did the speech underscore Republicans' irresponsible attitude toward truth, it presented FDR in full fighting force, capable of another term.

The Fala speech inspired another classic of American oratory, Nixon's Checkers' speech, which saved his position as Eisenhower's running mate in 1952, and positioned him for a later presidential campaign. The speech was a response to claims that he had received $18,000 for personal expenses from backers, which was not illegal but which conveyed a sense that his support could be bought. Press editorials were running about two to one in favor of his resignation from the ticket, and Eisenhower's aides wanted to replace him.[201] The speech turned public opinion around. Some sixty million viewers tuned in—at that point the largest television audience in American history. Nixon began with assurances that all the funds were used for political, not personal expenses, and then offered an emotional accounting of his modest financial circumstances, which made outside support necessary. The audience learned that the family had two mortgages and no investments, and that "Pat doesn't have a mink coat." But, Nixon added, "she does have a respectable Republican cloth coat, and I always tell her, she would look good in anything." The only personal gift that the family had accepted was a cocker spaniel named Checkers, and, Nixon concluded, "regardless of what they say about it, we are going to keep it."[202] Today, audiences accustomed to full disclosure about candidate finances tend to find the speech unexceptional, except for its somewhat cloying sentimentality. But in Nixon's era, that kind of personal candor was unexpected, and his message resonated with the average voter. After the broadcast, some four million sent letters to the Republican national committee, running 75 to 1 in favor of keeping Nixon on the ticket.[203]

Barack Obama's 2008 presidential campaign offers a final example of deft communication strategies: vivid narrative tied to expressions of hope and appeals to common values. When announcing his candidacy from Springfield, Illinois, his location and rhetoric evoked Abraham Lincoln's calls for a "more perfect union." Subsequent speeches invoked Martin Luther King's references to the moral arc of the universe "bending toward justice."[204] Obama's speech before the 2004 Democratic Convention referred to his father's childhood herding goats in Kenya and maintained that "my story is part of the larger American story...and that in no other country on earth is my story even possible."[205] In his inaugural address, he made similar references to the "meaning of our liberty and our creed," which explained "why a man whose father less than 60 years ago might not have been served at a local restaurant can now stand before you to take a most sacred oath."[206]

Obama is also credited with being a "'shape shifter,' with a remarkable ability to come across differently to disparate constituencies" and to adjust his rhetorical style to audiences in church basements, huge stadiums, backyard barbeques, and elite policy forums.[207] He is not unique among lawyer leaders in that respect. Bill Clinton had similar skills:

> He seemed to sense what audiences needed and [to] deliver [it] to them—trimming his pitch here, emphasizing different priorities, there, always aiming to please. This was one of his most effective, and maddening, qualities in private meetings as well. He always grabbed on to some points of agreement, while steering the conversation away from the larger points of disagreement, leaving his seducee with the distinct impression that they were in total harmony on just about everything.[208]

Unlike Clinton, however, Obama faced some difficult racial challenges that could not be readily evaded. Initially, he confronted concerns that he was both "too black" and "not black enough."[209] His multiracial background and elite education distanced him from some African Americans, who initially had thrown their support to Hillary Clinton. At the same time, he could not afford to alienate white voters by seeming too out of the mainstream on race-related issues. The difficulty came to a head with exposure of incendiary statements by Reverend Jeremiah Wright, the pastor of Obama's Chicago church. As Harvard Law Professor Randall Kennedy notes, Obama's masterful Philadelphia speech on race managed to finesse divisive issues as much by what it did not say as for what it did. After distancing himself from Wright, Obama discussed racial oppression but without "identifiable perpetrators....Blacks are acted upon but no one is doing the acting." The passive voice seemed part of a deliberate effort "to discuss racial affairs without being accusatory...without affronting the sensibilities of the white audience."[210] Stanford Law Professor Richard Ford agrees, and points out that part of the way Obama "navigated the minefield of race relations" was by "steering safely clear of specific proposals."[211] Once elected, Obama tended to avoid the problem by avoiding the subject. A review of his first two years in office found that Obama discussed race less often than any Democratic president in fifty years.[212] As one commentator noted, "it seems that the President feels boxed in by his blackness."[213] No matter what position he takes, he risks criticism by the right for racial favoritism and by the left for inadequate responses to racial justice.

During his first term, Obama's rhetoric in general seemed to lose much of the appeal that had propelled him to victory. George Lakoff, an expert on political rhetoric, criticized Obama's early health care messages as a "policy speak disaster." Policy speak is the assumption that "If you just tell people the policy facts, they will reason to the right conclusion and support the policy..."[214] As examples, Lakoff cited the Obama Administration's Reality Check website, which set out key facts on the president's health care proposal, and an e-mail letter from advisor David Axelrod, which offered 24 points responding to Republican mischaracterizations. Lakoff questioned whether either the e-mail or the Reality Check website had itself "had a reality check." "Ask yourself which is more memorable: 'Government takeover,' 'socialized medicine,' and 'death panels,' or Axelrod's 24 points."[215] Relying on recent neuroscience and cognitive research, Lakoff noted that much of our reasoning process is unconscious and based on emotion rather than logic. As a consequence, evocative sound bites from the right can have more resonance and staying power than liberal policy analysis.[216]

Bill Clinton's health care proposal encountered similar difficulties. The president's six major principles and five key catchphrases added rather than reduced complexity. Public opinion polls consistently revealed that large numbers of Americans had relatively little understanding of what exactly the administration's plan would provide.[217] As Clinton himself later recognized, the administration had failed to present the proposal in a coherent positive way, "over and over again…[so as to invite] people to compare the alternatives."[218]

Although Obama, unlike Clinton, managed to rescue his health care proposal, many commentators believed that his administration's other policies suffered because of poor presentations. "Still Waiting for the Narrator-in-Chief," ran the title of a 2012 *New York Times* article.[219] Amitai Etzioni criticized Democratic leaders' "platformlike statements" that lacked mobilizing power and a "clear concise explanation of why we are in difficulty and what will get us out."[220] George Packer summarized similar criticism by congressional representatives and staff concerning Obama's handling of the financial crisis. They viewed his efforts to have sophisticated conversations on issues like foreclosure as "tone deaf." "You can't say to people whose homes are in foreclosure, who are losing their businesses, 'It's a complicated situation.' The President is having a very eloquent one-sided conversation. The country doesn't want to have the conversation he wants to have."[221] House Democratic Congressman Barney Frank agreed that Obama's "technocratic style" had been ineffective and that he would have been better off with a more "adversarial approach" toward insurance companies and banks.[222]

The difficulties came to a head during Obama's first presidential debate in the 2012 campaign. Pundits and polls agreed that he lost badly. Bill Keller, writing in the *New York Times*, described Obama as "like a professor who has forgotten his course outline and grown bored with his subject."[223] *Times* columnist Gail Collins agreed. "The president thinks these debates are ridiculous and he may well be right. But truly it would have been a better idea to keep the thought to himself."[224]

At least some of the difficulties Obama faced speak to a deeper dilemma in this age of what political scientists have termed "rhetorical leadership." "You don't win a presidential debate by being a policy wonk," noted George Lakoff.[225] But neither can you adequately address complicated issues through simple sound bites. Still, as Bill Clinton noted, on a complex problem, "Americans don't want me to help them understand. They just want me to do something about it."[226] Moreover, the kind of inspirational, unifying language that is necessary to engage broad-based support may also raise expectations beyond what the leader is able to deliver.[227] Nowhere has the disconnect been more apparent than Obama's 2008 campaign promise, "yes we can," and the policy paralysis that marked much of his first term and sent congressional approval ratings into single digits. Yet the answer is surely not for leaders to abandon the rhetoric that can help them win positions where progress is at least possible. Rather, it is to adapt to the particular setting and to remain conscious of the tradeoffs involved.

Presentation

The effectiveness of a leader's message often depends as much on the manner of presentation as the content. First impressions tend to be lasting.[228] If speakers don't know enough to look the part, the audience wonders, what else don't they know?

Of course, some gifted leaders can be forgiven. Thomas Jefferson was known for "slovenly clothes" and for wearing his shoes "down at the heels."[229] But appearance can be a problem, particularly for women, who face more intense scrutiny than men and more severe consequences for falling short.[230] It speaks volumes about the persistent double standard for leaders that the most highly paid member of Sarah Palin's vice presidential campaign was her makeup artist, and that Hillary Clinton was criticized on Larry King live for being "bottom heavy."[231] Yet what is "too feminine" or not "feminine" enough may be open to dispute, and the disproportionate attention to women's appearance diverts attention from performance. Secretary of State Hillary Clinton, after years of fielding one too many questions about her choice in fashion, finally responded: "would you ask a man that question?"[232] Women of color often face additional challenges in choosing a look that feels authentic to them but that fits within their workplace culture and conveys a leadership "presence."[233]

At the same time, however, leaders of either sex who seem too concerned with appearance risk seeming vain, shallow, or even pathetic. During his presidential campaign, John Edwards was ridiculed for spending $400 on a haircut, and mocked by a YouTube video showing him fussing with his hair to the tune of "I Feel Pretty." Washington power broker Lloyd Cutler, known as a fastidious dresser, was jokingly said to have pushed for a firm office in London rather than Paris because he preferred English tailors.[234] A *Boston Herald's* description of a highly made-up female politician began, "There seemed to be something humiliating, sad, desperate and embarrassing about... [this] woman of a certain age trying too hard to hang on."[235] That age was forty-three.

Yet however unfair the standards, this is the world that leaders and aspiring leaders inhabit. To avoid the issue, the simplest strategy is to avoid the unconventional. Research on mentoring suggests that many individuals are reluctant to volunteer criticism of appearance, particularly to women.[236] So if the dress code isn't self-evident, it makes sense for them to find someone safe to ask.

Effective leaders give thought not only to their own appearance but to also to graphics and special effects that can help make their messages stick. Heath and Heath offer an example from leaders of the Center for Science in the Public Interest. It was launching a campaign to reduce consumption of popcorn popped in coconut oil, which movie theatres used because it provided an appealing texture and aroma. However, it also was extremely high in saturated fats; one typical popcorn carton had almost twice the U.S. Department of Agriculture's recommended average for the entire day. Center leaders recognized that a campaign based on that fact would "have zero appeal. It's dry, it's academic, who cares?"[237] Instead they staged a press conference with the following message: "A medium-sized 'butter' popcorn at a typical neighborhood movie theatre contains more artery-clogging fat than a bacon and egg breakfast, a Big Mac and fries for lunch, and a steak dinner with all the trimmings—combined." The conference included a buffet table with all the fatty foods mentioned. The press had a field day. Typical headlines read: "Popcorn Gets an R Rating," "Lights, Action, Cholesterol," "Theatre Popcorn is a Double Feature of Fat."[238]

Effective communication often relies on such dramatic strategies. Nelson Mandela, at his inauguration as South Africa's first post-apartheid president, had one of his former white prison guards sit in the front row to underscore his commitment to racial reconciliation.[239] Margaret Thatcher won election as Britain's first female prime minister using clever visual campaign ads, such as a poster featuring a long queue outside a British unemployment office and a caption reading: "Labour isn't working."[240]

The growing influence of the mass media and Internet have amplified the importance of graphic presentations. Environmental leaders have brought public consciousness to new levels by showing footage of ice caps melting, polar bears stranded, and mockups of the potential disasters of uncurbed temperature changes. Earth Island Institute's video of dolphins killed by tuna nets helped achieve customer boycotts, federal legislation, and corporate pledges to alter fishing methods.[241] PowerPoint now makes such visual material available to any speaker, but too few take full advantage of the possibilities. Many make the mistake of simply presenting text, often in dense, list-like formats, rather than relying on compelling visual images.²⁴² These death-by-PowerPoint presentations leave many audiences if not half-asleep then otherwise engaged—catching up on messages and busywork. The problem is compounded when speakers encounter technical delays, or misjudge the length of their material, yet insist on getting through the entire slide collection either by speeding up or spilling over their allotted time.

These misjudgments are, of course, not unique to PowerPoint presentations. Leaders who are accustomed to controlling the agenda too often feel entitled to extend their remarks. Yet such sharing-impaired behavior can be profoundly irritating to other speakers, not to mention audience members ready for closure. The final impression a leader leaves should not be the one Samuel Johnson reportedly expressed about *Paradise Lost*: "No one ever wished it longer...."²⁴³

By contrast, tasteful humor tailored to the occasion is always welcome. Spontaneous wit can be devastating, particularly in response to hecklers. Flo Kennedy, the African-American lawyer who often shared a podium with Gloria Steinem, charmed audiences when men called out, "Are you a lesbian?" Her response was "Are you my alternative?"²⁴⁴ For leaders less gifted at spontaneous exchanges, careful preparation is a good substitute. Abraham Lincoln is widely revered as a master storyteller, but by his own account, "I never invented anything original. I am only a retail dealer."²⁴⁵ He began collecting early. Growing up, he kept a scrapbook of quotations and during his presidency, he read humor collections.²⁴⁶ He was also known for wry comments such as his famous note to one Civil War general: "My dear McClellan, If you don't want to use the Army, I should like to borrow it for awhile."²⁴⁷ Margaret Thatcher and Adlai Stevenson were also collectors. Thatcher kept in her purse 3-by-5 cards with quotes from Kipling, Shakespeare, and Disraeli.²⁴⁸ For four decades, Stevenson kept a notebook with quotations from a wide range of sources: the Bible, Will Rogers, an eleventh-century Chinese sage, and obscure wits like John Billings, who remarked that "scarce as truth is, the supply is greater than the demand."²⁴⁹ By the same token, inappropriate humor can seriously damage a lawyer's credibility. A famous example involved Jay Floyd, the lawyer who began his opening argument in *Roe v. Wade* with "Mr. Chief Justice, and may it please the Court. It's an old joke, but when a man argues against two beautiful ladies like this, they are going to have the last word."²⁵⁰ Floyd waited for a laugh that failed to materialize, and never quite recovered from his botched attempt at courtroom comedy.

Today's leaders have enormous advantages in assembling appropriate material. Some have writers on staff and others have access to a boundless supply of printed and online collections. But whatever the source, the most successful uses of humor are those adapted to a particular occasion, and that make a point not simply a joke. An example comes from one of Bill Clinton's Gridiron Club speeches before Washington journalists and politicians. At a point in his presidency after his wife had taken enormous criticism for her role in health care reform and the Whitewater real estate scandal, Clinton opened his speech by expressing her regret: "the First Lady is sorry she can't be with you tonight," he told an audience full of critics. "If you believe that, I've got some land in Arkansas I'd like to sell you."[251]

Preparation

Preparation is almost always critical to performance. For those who are not entirely comfortable at a podium, rehearsal of the material and familiarity with the venue and audience is especially critical.[252] Even for accomplished communicators, it rarely makes sense to "speak from the heart," even if that is what the occasion seems to demand. Effective speakers plan their remarks, even if they abandon or adapt their message in light of the circumstances. Contrary to popular myth, Abraham Lincoln did not compose the Gettysburg address on an envelope on the train to the burial ground. The best evidence is that he went through several drafts in the days before the speech.[253] FDR's seemingly simple conversational chats took three to ten days to prepare and sometimes went through as many as a dozen versions.[254] If the presentation needs to look unrehearsed, that often requires rehearsal. Speaking without notes is always impressive but doing it effectively generally requires preparation. Even the ablest speakers recognize as much. According to his son, Winston Churchill "spent the best years of his life writing his extemporaneous speeches."[255] He reportedly practiced in his bath, and when a startled valet once came rushing to the door, Churchill explained: "I was not speaking to you Norman, I was addressing the house of Commons."[256]

Crafting truly effective presentations can be time-consuming, so knowing how and when to delegate the drafting task is critical. To take an obvious example, American presidents can ill afford to labor over what White House insiders label "Rose Garden rubbish"—platitudes to accompany ceremonial occasions. But leaders can issue clear instructions, along the lines of one of Dwight Eisenhower's directives: "tell them to go to hell but put it so they won't be offended."[257] For most leaders, however, particularly those who do not have expert assistance, there are limits to what can be outsourced. Staff can help in finding the right visuals and turn of phrase, and in offering research and feedback. But at least for important occasions, speakers need to be sure that the material they are presenting reflects their own voice, vision, and values.

TAKEN TOGETHER, THE skills noted in this chapter make for a challenging agenda. It is, of course, not essential for all leaders to be gifted in all the respects described. What is necessary, as chapter 2 suggested, is for leaders to find a good match between the capabilities they have and the positions they occupy. However, the needs of an organization can change over time. Innovation or conflict management may, for example, be more critical during some periods than others. Leaders need to be prepared to develop skills that become crucial and to invite constructive feedback about when they fall short.

Constant, deliberate growth

5

Ethics in Leadership

IN PRINCIPLE, EVERYONE agrees about the need for ethical leadership. But in practice, controversy arises over what it requires and how it can be achieved. Serious discussion is in surprisingly short supply. Leadership publications aimed at popular audiences typically treat the issue in perfunctory or platitudinous terms. Often they just list a few qualities of ethical leadership that have "stood the test of time," such as integrity, honesty, fairness, and compassion, without acknowledging any complexity or potential conflict in their exercise.[1] Other commentators simply add "moral" as an all-purpose adjective in the mix of desirable characteristics that leaders should have: "moral imagination," "moral courage," "moral excellence," and, of course, a "moral compass."[2] Only rarely does a note of realism creep in, typically by way of acknowledgment that values may be in tension, or that leaders may have mixed motives, not all of them disinterested. Rarer still are any real insights about how to balance competing concerns. When examples appear, they are generally dumbed-down, gussied-up morality plays in which virtue is its own reward. The popular how-to publication, *If Aristotle Ran General Motors*, offers a representative sample of reassuring homilies: a "climate of goodness will always pay," and "unethical conduct is self-defeating or even self-destructive over the long run."[3] Would that it were true. But Aristotle would need to be running more than GM for goodness always to pay.

The literature on lawyers' ethics offers a less uplifting picture than the happily-ever-after portraits in "leadership lite." Less than a fifth of Americans rate attorneys' honesty and ethical standards as high or very high.[4] Even fewer have confidence in lawyers who lead law firms or who occupy positions of political leadership.[5] For over a century, bar leaders themselves have lamented the loss of professionalism and lawyer statesmen. In 1914, Louis Brandeis chastised prominent attorneys for becoming "adjuncts" of the wealthy and

how to overcome stigma.

neglecting "to use their powers for the protection of the people."[6] Two decades later, Supreme Court Justice Harlan Fisk Stone similarly warned that the "learned profession of an earlier day [had become] the obsequious servant of business... tainted with the morals and manners of the marketplace in its most antisocial manifestations."[7] Contemporary bar leaders have painted the profession as "lost," "betrayed," in "crisis," and in "decline."[8] The discussion that follows seeks to understand the basis for that concern and the leadership strategies that might address it. What challenges do leaders face in regulating their own conduct and that of their subordinates?

The Role of Ethics

"Ethical leaders" are what everyone wants more of, but what exactly the term means is not always self-evident. Here, the term refers to leaders who exemplify integrity and social responsibility in their personal conduct and who institutionalize practices that encourage such conduct by others. The concept entails not only compliance with formal ethical rules, but also adherence to widely accepted norms of honesty, fairness, civility, and respect for societal interests.

[margin note: ethical leaders]

A related definitional issue is whether all leadership has such an ethical dimension. An increasingly common position in both scholarly and popular literature is that the essence of effective leadership is ethical leadership. Historian James McGregor Burns advocated a "transformational" understanding of leadership, in which leaders and followers "raise one another to higher levels of motivation and morality," beyond "everyday wants and needs." They aspire to reach more "principled levels of judgment" in pursuit of values such as justice and self-fulfillment.[9] Similarly, John Gardner, in *The Moral Aspect of Leadership*, argued that effective leaders "serve the basic needs of their constituents," defend "fundamental moral principles," seek the "fulfillment of human possibilities," and improve the communities of which they are a part.[10] Yet this definition is inconsistent with conventional usage, which presents leaders such as Hitler, Stalin, and Saddam Hussein as demonstrably effective in inspiring followers in pursuit of a common mission. In law, leaders such as Joseph McCarthy and Richard Nixon were highly successful for a time in enlisting others in unethical action, and many other prominent leaders have simply been indifferent to moral concerns. As Harvard Professor Barbara Kellerman notes, it is unproductive to exclude from definitions of leadership those whose means or ends are ethically problematic: "How can we stop what we don't study?"[11]

[margin note: learn from the good and bad]

A related threshold question involves the "value" of values: to what extent does morality pay? Research on the economic rewards of ethical leadership is plagued by methodological challenges. One is the absence of consistent definitions or metrics of ethical responsibility. Another challenge involves the impossibility of drawing causal inferences from correlations between ethical and financial performance. However, most studies suggest some positive relationship between ethics and financial results.[12] People care deeply about "organizational justice" and perform better when they believe that their workplace is treating them with respect and ensuring basic rights and equitable reward structures.[13] Workers also respond to cues from peers and leaders. Virtue begets virtue, and observing moral behavior by others promotes similar conduct.[14] Employees who believe that their organization's leaders support fair and ethical conduct and care about ethical issues observe less unethical behavior and perform better in their jobs.[15] Workers who feel justly treated also respond in kind; they are less likely to engage in petty dishonesty, such as fudging on hours and expenses, or misusing business opportunities.[16] The payoffs are obvious: improved morale, retention, and client satisfaction; greater workplace trust and cooperation; and less employee misconduct and less need for costly surveillance to prevent it.

Moreover, a focus on values other than profits can enhance reputation and loyalty. Large-scale surveys indicate that what people want most from a leader is honesty; they also want someone with a vision that will unite them in a larger purpose than economic self-interest.[17] Studies of consistently high-performing companies find that they "make meaning, not just money."[18] Their leaders pursue values and principles and "consider the public interest along with business priorities."[19]

Yet it would be naive to suggest that market forces always provide enough incentives for ethical conduct. As the following discussion suggests, a range of individual self-interests, cognitive biases, and organizational dynamics can often trump moral concerns. Each of these characteristics calls for closer scrutiny.

Influences on Ethical Conduct

In his influential analysis of personal ethics, psychologist James Rest identified four characteristics:

- moral awareness—recognition that a situation raises ethical issues;
- moral reasoning—determining what course of action is ethically sound;

- moral intent—identifying which values should take priority in the decision; and
- moral behavior—acting on ethical decisions.[20]

Moral Awareness

Moral awareness, the first element, reflects both personal and situational factors. One involves the moral intensity of the issue at stake. Intensity is, in turn, affected by both social consensus about the ethical status of the acts in question and the consequences that result. Organizations that place overwhelming priority on bottom-line concerns encourage individuals to "put their moral values on hold."[21] Conventional understandings of the lawyer's neutral partisan role push in a similar direction. James St. Clair, counsel to President Nixon during the impeachment proceedings, voiced a widespread view in claiming that "Lawyers' private opinions of the people and principles in any lawsuit are not material."[22] This attitude may help explain why most research finds a relatively low "baseline level of ethical awareness and dialogue" in law firms, and why less than a fifth of surveyed lawyers have ever turned down a case for ethical reasons, and less than 3 percent have reported giving advice that addressed concerns of social responsibility.[23]

A second influence on moral awareness involves the "feeling of nearness (social, cultural, psychological, or physical)" that the decision maker has for victims or beneficiaries of the act in question.[24] Individuals' capacity for empathy and sense of group solidarity affect ethical sensitivity. This sensitivity, in turn, encourages altruistic action and receptiveness to principles of justice, equality, and fairness. Conversely, leaders' capacity to distance or devalue victims leads to moral disengagement and denial of moral responsibility.[25] In adversarial settings, a tendency to demonize opponents may blunt ethical awareness and escalate abuse. Joe Flom, one of the nation's premier litigators, known for his hardball tactics, was once told that he was called a "cellar rat." He responded, "I can live with that."[26] A leader of his firm wore a similar label as a badge of honor: "We pride ourselves on being assholes. It's part of the firm culture."[27] In high stakes litigation, that mindset can lead to chronic problems of evasion and delay, which come to be seen as matters of tactics rather than principles.[28] Lawyers who lead litigation departments and teams can become habituated to a process in which "one party sends the other party a piece of paper, and the other party sends the first party a piece of paper...and nothing ever happens."[29] The result is what psychologists describe as "ethical fading," in which the moral implications of decisions become invisible with repeated violations of ethics rules.[30]

Workplace incentives can also have a significant effect on ethical sensitivity.[31] So, for example, Enron's plummet from the nation's seventh largest corporation to a bankrupt shell has been partly attributed to its relentless focus on "profits at all costs."[32] The message conveyed by leaders was that ethics rules were niceties made to be stretched and circumvented when necessary. Those who advanced were those able to "stay focused" on financial objectives "unburdened by moral anxiety."[33] That untroubled state could often be reached only by willful ignorance, a deliberate avoidance of morally compromising information.[34]

Moral Reasoning

A second element in moral leadership is moral reasoning. Most evidence suggests that individuals have a relatively poor grasp of their own reasoning processes and understate the role that intuition, situation, and cognitive biases have on their decision making.[35] As noted in chapter 4, most decision making is intuitive and not under individuals' conscious control.[36] However, reasoning supplies an important check on those intuitive judgments. In some instances, such reflective analysis allows individuals to step back and consider the moral consequences of impulsive self-interested behavior; in other contexts, such reflection provides an opportunity to rationalize behavior that their initial instinct suggests is wrong.[37]

Many of the cognitive biases described earlier can skew this reasoning process. Those who obtain leadership positions often have a high confidence in their own capacities and judgment. That can readily lead to arrogance, overoptimism, and an escalation of commitment to choices that turn out to be morally problematic. As a result, individuals may ignore or suppress dissent, overestimate their ability to rectify adverse consequences, and cover up mistakes by denying, withholding, or sometimes destroying information. Demonization of opponents and self-serving rationalizations or euphemistic characterizations of harms and motives can also skew individuals' moral compass.

Such cognitive biases are common where firms have been involved in conflicts of interests or billing abuses. In "Fatal Arrogance," former *American Lawyer* editor Steven Brill describes one prominent Wall Street firm whose leaders treated conflicts rules as "meant for others" and viewed criticism of firm ethics with "indignation rather than introspection."[38] So too, John Gellene, one of New York's leading bankruptcy lawyers, ended up with criminal penalties for failing to disclose a conflict of interest in a bankruptcy proceeding. This ethical violation was part of a broader pattern that firm leaders failed adequately to address. Gellene had a history of ignoring firm billing rules and mentoring assignments, and of misrepresenting his bar membership status.[39]

Other case histories of billing fraud find similar failures by firm leaders and rationalizations by prominent lawyers responsible for deception. Webster Hubbell, former Arkansas Chief Jjustice and Associate Attorney General in the Clinton administration, acknowledged some four hundred instances of fraudulently padding bills and charging personal expenses as business expenses, but characterized the matter as a "private financial dispute" within the firm.[40] When asked if he inflated hours, Hubbell responded, "Yes I did and so does every lawyer in the country."[41] Other lawyers have rationalized meter running on grounds that the work really was worth more than hourly charges, or that upward "adjustments" were legitimate ways to compensate for unclaimed expenses.[42] Firm leaders who are aware of billing abuses often engage in their own rationalizations; most fail to report such misconduct to bar disciplinary authorities or to acknowledge failures of organizational oversight.[43] According to the managing partner of Hubbell's firm, "We thought and believe still we had good systems in place at the firm…but there is no system tight enough to prevent abuse by someone in a position of trust."[44] Experts, however, view that attitude as part of the problem, and fault bar leaders for "institutional ineptitude" and willful blindness.[45] Only a minority of surveyed lawyers report that their firm has written guidelines on billing practices, and most lawyers receive minimal or no training on the subject."[46] Abuses by powerful partners often go unchecked because "[n]obody wants to kill a rainmaker."[47]

Moral Intent

Moral reasoning, and its distortion by cognitive biases, is only part of what explains moral conduct. "Moral intent" also matters: are individuals willing to give priority to moral values over other interests such as power, status, money, job security, and peer approval? Moral motivations are in part a reflection of the centrality of moral concerns to individuals' identity and self-esteem.[48] Much depends on how they weigh these concerns in relation to competing considerations.

The tendency to privilege personal interests over moral values helps account for lawyers' complicity in some of the nation's most serious health, safety, financial, and law enforcement abuses. The firms that taught "the robber barons how to rob," that helped asbestos and tobacco companies suppress information on product risks, and that facilitated fraud by financial institutions, may have turned a tidy profit, but at enormous public expense.[49] So too, prosecutors' desires to win have resulted in chronic problems of suppression of evidence and prejudicial statements. A textbook example is *Connick v. Thompson,* in which the prosecution failed to turn over blood sample evidence exonerating Thompson from a murder charge. As a result, Thompson spent fourteen years on death row before an investigator happened to discover on microfiche a blood sample from the crime scene that failed to match Thompson's. His conviction was overturned and he was acquitted on retrial. He then sued the district attorney for failing to train prosecutors in their disclosure obligations. In the decade preceding the trial, Louisiana courts had overturned four convictions because prosecutors in that office had failed to disclose exculpatory evidence. The Supreme Court nonetheless reversed a multimillion-dollar civil liability judgment against the municipality on the ground that the district attorney should not be accountable for the misconduct of subordinates. In a *New York Times* op-ed following the decision, Thompson noted that none of the prosecutors involved in violating disclosure rules or in covering up the violation had faced criminal or ethics charges. "No one was fired and now, according to the Supreme Court, no one can be sued.... A crime was definitely committed in this case, but not by me."[50]

Socialization and peer pressure can also undermine moral intent. Under circumstances where bending the rules has payoffs for the group, at least in the short term, members may feel the need to put their moral convictions on hold. That is especially likely when organizations place heavy emphasis on loyalty and reward team players. Strategies of disengagement, such as euphemistic labeling, reattribution of blame, and denigration of victims, enable individuals to deny problematic aspects of their collective conduct.

A case study in peer pressure involves Edward Ennis, director of the Alien Enemy Control Unit in the Justice Department during World War II. Ennis had primary responsibility for presenting the Department's position supporting internment of Japanese Americans in two major Supreme Court cases, *Hirabayashi v. United States* and *Korematsu v. United States.* Ennis had opposed the policy but was prepared to defend it. However, during the course of his work on *Hirabayashi,* he discovered a crucial internal memorandum by staffers in the Office of Naval Intelligence. That memo, by the military unit most knowledgeable on the issue, undercut the rationale for wholesale evacuation. In particular, the memo concluded that the "Japanese Problem" had been magnified out of proportion, that the small number of Japanese Americans who posed potential threats were in custody or were already known and subject to apprehension, and that case-by-case determinations of dangerousness were preferable to a mass evacuation. Ennis believed that this report should be called to the Supreme Court's attention. He so advised the Solicitor General, but without success, and reluctantly signed a brief that made no such disclosure.[51]

A similar issue resurfaced a year later in *Korematsu*. Ennis was skeptical of certain assertions in the military's final report justifying the evacuation. At his request, the Attorney General authorized FBI and FCC investigations of allegations regarding Japanese espionage efforts on the West Coast. Both agencies concluded that certain assertions in a report justifying evacuation were false. It also appeared that the general who had authorized the report and supported the evacuation knew of the errors. Ennis and one of his staff members were determined to avoid reliance on the final report in presenting the government's case. They added a footnote acknowledging that certain facts in the report, particularly about espionage, were "in conflict with information in possession of the Department of Justice." Accordingly, the Court should not "take judicial notice" of those facts. The Solicitor General opposed this footnote and authorized an alternative. It eliminated any reference to espionage allegations in the report. Instead, it stated:

> We have specifically recited in this brief the facts relating to the justification for the evacuation, of which we ask the Court to take judicial notice; and we rely upon the Final Report only to the extent that it relates to such facts.[52]

Again, Ennis signed the brief. In a subsequent interview reflecting on these incidents, Ennis explained, "I really believe we didn't [quit our jobs] ... because we didn't want to put [the case] in the hands of Justice Department lawyers who were gung-ho for the Army's position. I think we felt that we'd just stay with it and do the best that we could, which wasn't a hell of a lot."[53] Yet Ennis was also uncomfortable with that justification, perhaps for reasons philosopher Bernard Williams once noted. The rationale of "working from within" has kept many "queasy people tied to many appalling ventures for remarkably long periods."[54] "When I look back on it now," Ennis stated, "I don't know why I didn't resign."[55]

In "The Inner Ring," C. S. Lewis suggests an answer to that question. He describes the process by which the need to belong to a favored circle undermines moral commitments:

> Just at the moment when you are most anxious not to appear crude, or naif, or a prig—the hint will come. It will be the hint of something which is not quite in accordance with the rules of fair play: something which the public, the ignorant, romantic public would never understand...but something, says your new friend, which "we"—and at the word "we" you try not to blush for mere pleasure-something "we" always do." And you will be drawn in, if you are drawn in, not by desire for gain or ease, but simply because at that moment you cannot bear to be thrust back again into the cold outer world....And then, if you are drawn in, next week it will be something a little further from the rules, and next year something further still....It may end in a crash, a scandal, and penal servitude; it may end in millions [and] a peerage....But you will be a scoundrel.[56]

Moral Behavior

Individuals need not only to identify the right course of action and intend to act accordingly. They must also have the capacity to follow through on that intent. What psychologists label "ego strength" will help determine whether individuals are able to put their moral values into action.[57] Factors include the person's ability to work around impediments, cope with frustration and pressure, and remain focused on moral objectives. Research generally confirms what common sense suggests; that there is often a gap between ethical reasoning and behavior.[58]

A variety of forces helps explain that gap. Group pressure and diffusion of responsibility are among the most powerful. Individuals are more likely to engage in unethical conduct when acting with others. Peer influence and the erosion of individual accountability can "protect people from their own conscience."[59]

A famous simulation by Wharton professor Scott Armstrong illustrates the abdication of moral responsibility that too often plays out in real life. The experiment asked groups of executives and business students to assume the role of an imaginary pharmaceutical company's board of directors. Each group received a fact pattern indicating that one of their company's most

profitable drugs was causing an estimated fourteen to twenty-two "unnecessary" deaths a year and would likely be banned by regulators in the company's
home country. The drug accounted for some 12 percent of the company's sales
and a larger percentage of its profits. A competitor offered an alternative med-
ication with the same benefits at the same price but without the serious side
effects. More than 80 percent of the boards decided to continue marketing the
product both domestically and overseas and to take legal and political action
to prevent a ban. None of the boards decided to recall the drug. By contrast,
when a different group of individuals with similar business backgrounds was
asked for their personal views on the same hypothetical situation, 97 percent
believed that continuing to market the product was socially irresponsible.[60]

A highly publicized case involving a similar diffusion of responsibility
concerned proceedings by the Securities and Exchange Commission (SEC)
against the CEO, top officers, and general counsel of Salomon Inc., one of
Wall Street's leading investment companies. The action arose from the firm's
failure to discipline and disclose securities law violations by one of its top trad-
ers, Paul Mozer. To settle the case, the firm ended up paying almost $300 mil-
lion in fines, which at the time was the second largest penalty ever imposed
on a financial institution. During a brief suspension, Salomon lost major clients and over $4 billion in trades, and its stock price and market share sub-
sequently plummeted. According to Deryck Maughan, the CEO who took
office n after the SEC charges, the events constituted a "billion-dollar error
of judgment."[61] How that error occurred provides an illuminating case history
of failed leadership.

The culture at Salomon was highly competitive. John Gutfreund, the
CEO at the time of Mozer's misconduct, sometimes "talked about values,... [but] his conduct often sent a contrary message. He ordered his staff
to arrive each morning ready to the 'bite the ass of a bear.' "[62] He was known
for getting rid of individuals and divisions without warning if they failed to
meet his bottom-line expectations. Mozer met those expectations. He was
a thirty-four-year-old trader whose aggressive style fit the Salomon culture.
He was very rich, but from his perspective, not rich enough. To increase his
earnings, he exceeded Treasury limits on bids for government securities by
placing a false bid in someone else's name. When the matter came to light,
his supervisor, Vice President John Meriwether, discussed the matter with
General Counsel Donald Feurstein, President Thomas Strauss, and CEO
John Gutfreund. Without further investigation of some other red flags, the
group accepted Mozer's characterization of the bid as an isolated incident.
However, Feurstein believed that the conduct was probably criminal and the

group agreed it should be reported to the New York Federal Reserve Bank.[63] A subsequent SEC report described the decision making as follows:

> [E]ach of the four executives who attended meetings…placed the responsibility for investigating Mozer's conduct and placing limits on his activities on someone else. Meriwether stated that he believed that once he had taken the matter of Mozer's conduct to Strauss and Strauss had brought Feuerstein and Gutfreund into the process, he had no further responsibility to take action with respect to the false bid unless instructed to do so by one of those individuals. Meriwether stated that he also believed that, though he had the authority to recommend that action be taken to discipline Mozer or limit his activities, he had no authority to take such action unilaterally. Strauss stated that he believed that Meriwether, who was Mozer's direct supervisor, and Feuerstein, who was responsible for the legal and compliance activities of the firm, would take whatever steps were necessary or required as a result of Mozer's disclosure. Feuerstein stated that he believed that, once a report to the government was made, the government would instruct Salomon about how to investigate the matter. Gutfreund stated that he believed that the other executives would take whatever steps were necessary to properly handle the matter. According to the executives, there was no discussion among them about any action that would be taken to investigate Mozer's conduct or to place limitations on his activities.[64]

After that discussion, Meriwether admonished Mozer and told him that the firm would report his conduct to the government. However, the firm failed to do so. Some speculated that Gutfreund was concerned that public disclosure might trigger fines, lawsuits, and adverse publicity and jeopardize his already precarious leadership position.[65] According to one insider, Gutfreund "went to sleep hoping it would just go away."[66] It did not. Mozer submitted further illegal bids which finally triggered an internal investigation. But it took three months for the company to notify the SEC and to issue a press release acknowledging the misconduct. That release did not disclose management's prior awareness of the incident. No one lived happily ever after. Gutfreund, Strauss, and Meriwether resigned and settled securities charges by accepting fines and suspensions. Mozer was fired and pled guilty to lying to the Federal Reserve Bank. He served four months in prison and was banned from the securities industry for life. The case illustrates the pathology that Hannah

Arendt described as "rule by Nobody." To Arendt, this form of bureaucracy was the most dangerous of all, "since there is no one...who could even be asked to answer for what is being done."[67]

Organizations

Organizational structure and climate can be similarly corrosive and can add a further dimension to the personal decision-making frameworks that theorists such as James Rest describe. One organizational characteristic involves the fragmentation of information. The size and structure of bureaucratic institutions and the complexity of issues may work against informed ethical judgments. In many of the recent scandals, as well as earlier financial, health, safety, and environmental disasters, large numbers of leaders were not well-informed.[68] Lawyers often lacked knowledge about matters, raising both moral and legal concerns. In some instances, the ignorance may have reflected willful blindness, but in other cases, the problem had more to do with organizational structures and practices. Work was allocated in ways that prevented key players from seeing the full picture, and channels for expressing concerns were inadequate. Shooting the messenger was the standard response to unwelcome tidings in companies like Enron, and ultimately, it was not just the messenger who paid the price.[69]

Additional aspects of organizational culture can play a critical role. As earlier discussion indicated, a key factor is ethical climate: the moral meanings that employees place on workplace policies and practices. Organizations signal their priorities in multiple ways: the content and enforcement of their ethical standards, their criteria for promotion and compensation, their treatment of employees, and their commitment to social responsibility. In prosecutors' offices, for example, the focus on conviction may cause lawyers to filter evidence in a way that screens out competing information. The result is a form of tunnel vision in which prosecutors convinced of guilt fail to perceive or produce exculpatory evidence.[70] In many moral meltdowns in both the public and private sector, participants did not appear intentionally immoral. Rather, they were caught in corrosive cultures that left them insufficiently attentive to ethical concerns.

Watergate as a Case Study

The Watergate scandal offers a particularly illuminating case history of how the good go bad, in part because of the sheer number of lawyers involved. The scandal owes its name to a Washington D.C. apartment complex, the site of the bungled burglary of the Democratic National Committee headquarters orchestrated by Nixon administration officials. Almost every major participant in the cover-up was an attorney, and twenty ended up on the wrong side of the law.[71] Lawyers who occupied leadership positions in the Nixon administration and his reelection campaign, including two Attorney Generals, were convicted of crimes including perjury, fraud, obstruction of justice, burglary, and conspiracy.[72] Nixon, also a lawyer, resigned to avoid impeachment for obstruction of justice and abuse of power. In testimony before a Senate Select Committee, John Dean, then Counsel to the President, recalled that he had "prepared a list of who was likely to be indicted as the investigation proceeded.... [M]y first reaction was... how in God's name could so many lawyers get involved in something like this."[73] Answers to that question reflect failures in moral awareness, reasoning, intent, and behavior along the lines just described.

Willful Ignorance

The moral myopia of many lawyers was in part a matter of willful ignorance. In *Blind Ambition*, Dean recounts his own efforts at selective perception. Shortly after arrival at the White House, the president asked him to have the Internal Revenue Service investigate a magazine that had published a parody of a vice presidential memo. Feeling "squeamishness" about the assignment, Dean consulted another staffer who offered to "take care of it."[74] Dean elected not to ask any questions, and recalled that "the fact that I had not carried out the assignment myself eased my conscience slightly."[75] Campaign finance chairman Maurice Stans pursued a similar strategy. When asked by the campaign treasurer why the campaign general counsel wanted $83,000, Stans responded, "I do not want to know and you do not want to know."[76] Presidential advisor Chuck Colson "repeatedly insisted that he knew nothing about Watergate and wanted to keep it that way."[77] Attorney General Richard Kleindienst, on being approached about the Watergate burglars, responded, "You get the hell out of here... Whatever you have to say, just say [it] to someone else."[78] This strategy of selective ignorance, however, came at a cost. By his own account, it "never occurred" to Dean that he and other lawyers were obstructing justice until "long after we had crossed the line."[79]

Cognitive Bias

Various cognitive biases also contributed to the moral meltdown among Watergate lawyers. Demonization of the opposition and self-serving characterizations of their own motives distorted moral reasoning. After Daniel Ellsberg leaked the Pentagon Papers to the *New York Times*, Nixon told Colson, "We've got a counter-government here and we've got to fight it. I don't care how."[80] In a discussion with his chief of staff, H. R. Haldeman, the president stated, "We're up against an enemy. A conspiracy. They're using any means. We are going to use any means. Is that clear?"[81] Nixon never expressed any qualms about authorizing IRS investigations of political opponents. As he explained in his memoirs, "When Democrats controlled the White House, I was routinely subjected to politically instigated IRS audits.... I was simply trying to level the playing field... In any case, I see nothing wrong with getting wealthy people to pay their taxes."[82]

Nixon's views were contagious and helped to create a bunker mentality within his administration. "It was us against them," Colson recalled.[83] "Them" was an inclusive category, including anti-war protestors, Democratic party leaders, media critics, and assorted political opponents. A memo by Dean, titled "How We Can Use the Available Political Machinery to Screw Our Enemies," included two hundred names.[84] Presidential advisor Murray Chotiner echoed Nixon's views on IRS investigations. Recalling Lyndon Johnson's use of tax audits that "damn near ruined a few [good Republicans,]" Chotiner told Dean, "It's the way the game is played."[85]

When it came to their own motivations, leaders' self-serving biases kicked in. Illegal activities were rationalized as necessary to "protect the presidency" or national security.[86] Earl Krogh, the Deputy Assistant to the President, recalled his justification for planning the break-in at the office of Daniel Ellsberg's psychiatrist:

> I see now that the key is the effect that the term "national security" had on my judgment. The very words served to block my critical analysis.... [T]o suggest that national security was being improperly invoked was to invite a confrontation with patriotism and loyalty and seemed to be... in contravention of the faithful performance of the duties of my office.[87]

Many other Watergate participants spoke in terms of loyalty to the presidency, but frequently confused the interests of the incumbent with the interests of the institution.[88] Nixon himself seems to have suffered from that confusion. In a television interview, when David Frost asked whether the president could

"decide that it's in the best interests of the nation, and do something illegal,"
Nixon famously responded, "Well, when the president does it, that means it's
not illegal."[89]

Group Pressure

A final factor that sabotaged moral sensitivity was group pressure. Its signals
were not subtle. Dean recalled being told by Chotiner that if "Richard Nixon
thinks it's necessary, you better think it's necessary. If you don't, he'll find
someone who does."[90] Earl Krogh similarly warned Dean that "there are some
people around here who think you have some little old lady in you."[91] Dean
concluded that "If I was going to play ball in Richard Nixon's league, I would
have to get over my squeamishness."[92] Dean's view was widely shared. In an
interchange during the congressional hearings, Paul Porter described feeling
that certain espionage activities were not "quite right." His failure to act on
that belief was due to "the fear of group pressure that would ensue of not
being a team player."[93]

Yet not every lawyer involved in Watergate succumbed to group pressures. Archibald Cox, the first Watergate special prosecutor, sought to
compel Nixon to produce tapes of White House conversations, despite the
President's claim of executive privilege. When Nixon asked Attorney General
Elliot Richardson to fire Cox, Richardson instead resigned, as did his deputy
William Ruckelshaus. The official next in line then followed the President's
orders and abolished the office. The public was outraged over what became
known as the Saturday Night Massacre. Nixon's approval ratings dropped to
17 percent, and he yielded to pressure to reinstate the special prosecutor.[94]
The steadfast adherence to principle by Cox, Richardson, and Ruckelshaus
was critical in keeping the Watergate investigation alive. As their examples
suggest, distinguished leaders often are remembered not only for what they
do, but also for what they refuse to do.

With four decades hindsight, Watergate offers some lasting leadership
lessons. One is that the combination of insecurity, ambition, and arrogance
can be toxic. The Nixon administration's insatiable desire for political intelligence and retaliation also reflected a particularly irrational form of groupthink. The president had no real need to risk so much for so little. As he later
acknowledged, "in view of the 30 percent lead I had in the polls it made no
sense to take such a risk [in burglarizing opposition headquarters] because
the likely Democratic nominee, Senator George McGovern, stood virtually no chance of winning.... To paraphrase Tallyrand, Watergate was worse

than a crime—it was a blunder."[95] But as Colson put it, "we wanted a corona-tion," not just a victory.[96] Ironically, that same ambition and concern for his historical legacy contributed in other ways to Nixon's downfall. He created the White House taping system to assist him in writing memoirs that would secure his place in the pantheon of great presidents. Yet it was the material on those tapes, including his instructions to halt the FBI's Watergate investiga-tion, that forced his resignation and marred his legacy.

For other members of his staff, the ambition to move up also ensured a move down. As Dean realized, "advancement would come from doing those things which built a common bond of trust—or guilt—from my superi-ors…Slowly, steadily, I would climb toward…the President's inner circle until I finally fell into it, thinking I had made it to the top just as I began to realize I had actually touched bottom."[97]

The Legacy of Watergate

From the bar's standpoint, one lasting legacy of Watergate is the field of pro-fessional responsibility that it helped to create. In response to public back-lash against lawyers, the American Bar Association decided to require ethics courses in law schools. In 1974, the Association mandated that accredited schools "require for all student[s]…instruction in the duties and responsi-bilities of the legal profession, including the history, goals and responsibil-ity of the bar and its Code of Professional Responsibility."[98] Not everyone applauded. To many faculty, it seemed ludicrous to suppose that the mas-sive misconduct of lawyers in the Nixon administration was due to lack of familiarity with the bar's history, goals, and rules of ethics. As one observer put it, the "morality of John Ehrlichman or John Mitchell would have been improved by the study of the Code of Professional Responsibility about as much…as study of Robert Louis Stevenson's Essay on Sportsmanship would improve the tennis court behavior of Ilie Nastase."[99] On the rare occasions when anyone asked a Watergate defendant whether a course in ethics would have mattered, the answer was no more encouraging.[100] Dean in fact had taken an elective course, which in that era was a quarter unit credit that boiled down to "Don't lie, don't cheat, don't steal, and don't advertise."[101]

Yet several decades of research on ethics instruction suggests a more hopeful assessment. A substantial body of evidence indicates that significant changes occur during early adulthood in individuals' basic strategies for deal-ing with moral issues.[102] Through interactive education, such as mentoring, problem-solving and role-playing, students can enhance their skills in moral analysis and gain awareness of the situational pressures and regulatory failures that encourage misconduct.[103] Moreover, the growth of ethics instruction after Watergate spurred a corresponding growth in ethics scholarship that in turn has provided a clearer understanding of why such scandals occur and how best to prevent them.

Dilemmas of Dirty Hands

One context in which greater understanding is essential involves what philosopher Michael Walzer has famously labeled "dilemmas of dirty hands." Walzer takes the phrase from Sartre's play, *Dirty Hands*, in which a communist leader acknowledges, "I have dirty hands right up to the elbows.... Do you think you can govern innocently?"[104] Walzer uses the term to refer to political contexts in which immoral means appear essential to achieve moral ends. Other commentators have used dirty hands more broadly as a shorthand for any situation that requires such trade-offs and demands suspension of moral principles in pursuit of morally justifiable objectives.

To the question posed by Sartre's communist, Walzer's own answer is "no, I don't think I could govern innocently; nor do most of us believe that those who govern us are innocent... —even the best of them. But this does not mean that it isn't possible to do the right thing while governing. It means that a particular act of government... may be exactly the right thing to do in utilitarian terms and yet leave the man who does it guilty of a moral wrong." Dilemmas arise when the only way for a leader to remain "morally innocent" is to do the wrong thing in terms of ultimate results, and thus "fail to measure up to the duties of his office."[105] The "moral" politician, according to Walzer, is one who acknowledges his personal wrong and feels the appropriate anguish. It is, as Walzer puts it, "by his dirty hands that we know him. If he were a moral man and nothing else, his hands would not be dirty; if he were a politician and nothing else, he would pretend that they were clean...."[106]

Trade-offs between moral means and moral ends appear particularly necessary in government, because success is often "measured by a historian's yardstick" and undue insistence on principle can prevent compromises that are in society's long-term interests.[107] As Richard Nixon observed,

> [A] leader has to deal with people and nations as they are, not as they should be. As a result, the qualities required for leadership are not necessarily those that we would want our children to emulate—unless we wanted them to be leaders... Guile, vanity, dissembling—in other

circumstances these might be unattractive habits, but to the leader they can be essential....Roosevelt talked of keeping America out of war while maneuvering to bring it into war.[108]

Huey Long, Louisiana's legendary governor and senator, is one of the most celebrated examples of lawyer politicians who retained a commitment to democratic ideals but operated under no illusion that he could realize his populist reform agenda through democratic processes. "They say they don't like my methods," Long noted. "Well I don't like them either....I'd do it some other way if there was one." But, he believed, "[y]ou've got to fight fire with fire."[109] As a youth his favorite biography was *The Count of Monte Cristo*, which he reread every year. From one of its main characters, he took an important political lesson. "The man in that book knew how to hate, and until you learn how to hate you'll never get anywhere in this world."[110] Long learned that lesson early, and when someone hates an enemy, much that might otherwise seem unthinkable becomes just another way of "get[ting] things done."[111] Long wanted not just to beat his opponents, but to annihilate them, and bribery, patronage, and smear tactics became a necessary cost of consolidating control to achieve policy objectives that he believed were "for the benefit of the people."[112]

In contemporary legal and political contexts, a recurrent dirty hands dilemma involves when to compromise convictions for the sake of obtaining, or retaining power. George Bernard Shaw captured the dilemma in commenting on a Labour Party colleague who lost his seat in Parliament after refusing to compromise on an issue:

> When I think of my own unfortunate character, smirched with compromise, rotted with opportunism, mildewed by expediency...I do think Joe might have put up with just a speck or two on those white robes of his for the sake of the millions of poor devils who cannot afford any character at all because they have no friend in Parliament. Oh, these moral dandies, these spiritual toffs, these superior persons. Who is Joe anyhow, that he should not risk his soul occasionally like the rest of us?[113]

Clearly, Shaw's view has resonated with many leaders. Franklin Roosevelt reversed course on key issues, including the League of Nations and prohibition, and when challenged, noted that "there is a difference between ideals and the methods of obtaining them."[114] Although he believed that the "presidency is preeminently a place of moral leadership," he was pragmatic about the shifts in principles that it sometimes entailed.[115]

Sandra Day O'Conner took a similar approach. She began her legislative career in the Arizona Senate with a commitment to women's issues. Her early focus was equal pay for equal work, and one of her first priorities was the repeal of protective labor legislation that prevented women from working more than an eight-hour day. Yet in debates over ratification of the federal Equal Rights Amendment she remained on the sidelines. Although she voted to bring the Amendment to a floor vote, she did not use her powers as majority leader on its behalf, nor did she speak out publicly in its favor.[116] Whatever O'Connor's motives, she was held responsible for the Amendment's defeat in Arizona, which turned out to be a blessing for her career. As one biographer notes, "it made O'Connor less of a threat to the male GOP movers and shakers who were in power.... and who become her main supporters in 1981" when she was nominated for the Supreme Court.[117] Her position on abortion evolved in similarly helpful directions. In the Arizona Senate she voted for a bill to decriminalize abortion. A decade later, while being vetted for the Supreme Court, she had "no recollection of how she voted."[118] Nor had she ever spoken out on abortion, and that proved sufficient to secure her nomination and confirmation. Once appointed to the Court, she voted to preserve *Roe v. Wade* and women's right to choose, which surprised and frustrated many of her original supporters.

When leaders have taken public positions that later become politically unsustainable, they face some hard choices. The dilemmas are not unique to politicians. They confront any leader who makes pledges in the course of seeking office that turn out to be unwise in discharging it. One option is to simply admit the change in position, explain the reasons, and trust people to understand. That was Obama's strategy in defending his decision to take "Super PAC" campaign funds after strongly condemning the *Citizens United* Supreme Court decision that made such contributions possible. A statement by his campaign explained:

> With so much at stake, we can't allow for two sets of rules in this election whereby the Republican nominee is the beneficiary of unlimited spending and Democrats unilaterally disarm. Therefore, the campaign has decided to do what we can, consistent with the law, to support Priorities USA in its effort to counter the weight of the GOP Super PAC.[119]

In a press conference following that statement, Press Secretary Jay Carnay faced a tough question on Obama's change in position.

> As you know, [the President] is on record as seeing that these PACs and the way they allow money to drive elections are a threat to democracy; now he's given his stamp to exactly that kind of organization so that the Democratic PAC can keep pace with Republican ones.... [W]hat is the point of taking a principled stand and campaigning against something if then you switch course and abandon it for the sake of strategy?

Carnay responded:

> Well... first of all the President's views of the influence of the *Citizens United* decision haven't changed. He strongly opposed it, as you know. And he holds those views today....The fact is... that he has been committed to working with Congress to eliminate the corrosive influence of money in Washington, and he proposed new ideas along those lines in his State of the Union address....But the campaign... cannot compete effectively if there are two sets of rules... [120]

Judging from the lack of public controversy over the decision, most Democrats appear to have accepted the justification that the president had not so much altered his ethical principles as accepted political realities. Obama had never condemned any politician who took advantage of Super PACs; he had deplored their existence, and that position remained unchanged.

His opponent, Mitt Romney, had greater difficulty walking back his positions, in part because there were more that required recanting. *New York Times* editorialist Nicholas Kristoff chronicled Romney's flip-flops on abortion, assault weapons, health care, tax pledges, and the legacy of Ronald Regan and concluded, "The reassuring thing about Mitt Romney is that for most of his life he probably wouldn't have voted for today's Mitt Romney." [121] For some conservatives, however, the consistent inconsistency was anything but reassuring, particularly given Romney's explanations of how his positions have "evolved." [122] "It's not every single issue I look at in my entire life I've...changed my views on," Romney told a New Hampshire town meeting. [123] But some of the issues on which his positions had "evolved" seemed to defy any principled explanation. One involved his attempt to reconcile his 1994 statements to Log Cabin Republicans on gay rights with his later opposition to gay marriage, gay adoption, and gay service in the military. Having originally promised to be more effective than Ted Kennedy in reaching "full equality" for gays and lesbians, he became a crusader against same-sex marriage. "Now someone will say, 'Yes, but look what you wrote in 1994 to the Log Cabin Club,'" Romney explained. "Well, okay, let's look at that in the context of who it's being written to."[124]

Yet from critics' perspective, that is precisely the point. Romney's ethical convictions appeared to shift with the audience he is trying to court. The sheer number of inconsistencies made him the target of comedians and cartoonists, as well as political opponents. "Mitt Romney will face his fiercest ideological opponent," Conan O'Brien once quipped. "Himself from four years ago."[125] A *Washington Post* cartoon similarly pictured a child-sized Romney sitting on the lap of a Republican elephant with a Santa Claus hat. The caption read, "What would you *like* me to ask for."[126]

At some point, what seems to be a shortage of settled convictions raises obvious ethical concerns. Whether Romney's changing views reached that point is clearly a matter for debate. Much will, of course, depend on whether one believes that the evolution has been in the right direction. But however one comes down in particular cases, Walzer is surely correct that a defining feature of moral leaders is that they never lose touch with the compromises that they have made and they constantly assess the price they have paid. British philosopher Bernard Williams similarly suggests that "the good need not be pure, so long as they retain some active sense of moral costs and moral limits and [the culture] has some genuinely settled expectations of civic respectability."[127] *awareness of moral costs > moral perfection*

Strategies of Ethical Leadership

Individuals committed to ethical leadership in practice as well as principle face two challenges. The first is to make ethical conduct a central priority in their own lives. The second is to promote cultures that make it a priority for others.

A leader's own ethical commitments are important in several respects. Those in positions of power set a moral tone and a moral example by their own behavior.[128] As noted earlier, employees take cues about appropriate behavior from those in supervisory positions. Whether workers believe that their leaders care about principles as much as profits significantly affects the frequency of ethical conduct. Moreover, leaders' demonstrated integrity, as well as consistency in matters of principle, build trust and enhance the legitimacy of decision-making processes. It is, however, not enough for leaders to exemplify ethical values in their own conduct. They also need to sustain cultures in which such values shape daily practices.

Creating Ethical Cultures

A true commitment to ethical leadership requires the integration of ethical concerns into all organizational activities. That means factoring moral considerations into day-to-day functions, including compensation and performance evaluations. Obvious though this seems in principle, many leaders appear oblivious to how it plays out in practice; neither the formal nor informal reward structures of many organizations reflect serious attention to the ethics of upper-level personnel or of the culture that they supervise. Performance assessments that focus only on short-term, bottom-line outcomes are particularly likely to skew moral decision making. Most of the scandals discussed earlier were partly attributable to reward structures that encouraged pushing the boundaries of ethical conduct.

To sustain an ethical culture, leaders also need to institutionalize best practices and to invite critical feedback from others. To counter self-serving biases and corrosive peer pressure, individuals in positions of power should actively solicit diverse perspectives and dissenting views on ethical issues. That will require more channels for dialogue and more effective protection for whistle-blowers. Individuals who seek to expose misconduct typically encounter harassment, ostracism, and retaliation.[129] Lawyers who take such actions do not appear to be exceptions.[130] And all too often, internal disclosures are largely ignored or produce no lasting change. As one whistleblower wryly predicted, "If you have God, the law, the press, and the facts on your side, you have a 50-50 chance of [victory]."[131] Fear of reprisals, along with lack of confidence that reports would be productive, are the major reasons that employees give for not disclosing abuses or airing ethical concerns.[132]

Those who are seriously committed to ethical leadership need to create more safe spaces for moral disagreements in general and reports of misconduct in particular. The problem in too many organizations is that "not only does no one want to listen but no one wants to talk about not listening."[133] Of course, some whistleblowers are vindictive employees with meritless or self-serving grievances. But creating adequate internal channels even for these reports is the best way to prevent the adverse consequences of external whistle-blowing. And even those whose motives are tainted may have valid concerns. A case in point is the disgruntled Texaco employee who, in order to protect his own job during restructuring, leaked tapes of racist slurs and plans for document destruction.[134] Whatever the costs of coping with self-serving internal dissent, the price paid for suppression is likely to be greater.

Ethics and Public Officials

Ethical leadership is particularly important in public sector organizations, given their need for public confidence. For example, the legitimacy of law enforcement processes depends on prosecutorial offices that are designed to serve justice and to hold lawyers accountable when they fall short. Yet all too often, leaders of these offices and of bar disciplinary agencies have failed to institutionalize such accountability. Almost never do prosecutors who commit misconduct face sanctions. In one study by the Center for Public Integrity, which reviewed 1,200 cases alleging abuse and 277 finding reversible error, none resulted in discipline.[135] Another study found only about a hundred cases of reported disciplinary action against prosecutors in the last century.[136] Leaders of prosecutorial offices need to establish better internal channels of oversight and accountability, and external disciplinary agencies should investigate every case in which courts find abuses, including failures of supervision.[137] A case study in such failures involved the recent prosecution of Alaska Senator Ted Stevens, in which Department of Justice lawyers did not disclose exculpatory evidence. An independent review of the case revealed numerous leadership missteps, including the absence of clear allocation of supervisory authority and the lack of formal policies or standardized procedures governing core prosecutorial functions.[138]

Creating opportunities for candid dialogue about ethical issues and causes of misconduct is equally critical. Every leader's internal moral compass needs to be checked against external reference points and opposing views. These were notably lacking in the memos on torture prepared for the Bush administration by lawyers in the Office of Legal Counsel (OLC). A review by the Department of Justice's Office of Professional Responsibility found that two senior lawyers in the OLC had committed misconduct by failing "to exercise independent legal judgment and render thorough, objective, and candid legal advice" as required by bar ethical rules.[139] In the view of the Office of Professional Responsibility (OPR), the "torture memo" by John Yoo fell short in several respects. It took its definition of torture from the use of "severe pain" in a medical benefits statute rather than directly applicable precedents, failed to consider adverse authority, and misstated supporting authority.[140] Jay Bybee, the OLC leader who approved the memo, was faulted for inadequate supervision and failure to consider relevant material, such as the military's determination that waterboarding constituted torture. Yoo's conduct was considered intentional, based both on the extent of his errors and on evidence that the CIA officials who had asked for the opinion were not interested in objective analysis, but rather in language that would protect interrogators from subsequent prosecution.[141] Accordingly, the OPR concluded that Yoo and Bybee should be referred to appropriate bar disciplinary agencies.

By contrast, David Margolis, the Assistant Attorney General with authority over the OLC, determined that although both lawyers had exercised "poor judgment," they had not violated rules of professional conduct. The "memos contained some significant flaws," and constituted "an unfortunate chapter" in the history of the office, but in Margolis's view, they did not rise to the level of reckless or intentional misconduct.[142] Yet, as a *New York Times'* editorial noted, "poor judgment" seemed an "absurdly dismissive" way to characterize facilitation of torture.[143] However one assesses the decision not to refer Bybee and Yoo for discipline, Margolis' conclusion seems less a vindication of their conduct than an indictment of oversight structures. According to many commentators, the case underscored the need for a more "credible" framework of accountability.[144] The stakes in having the OLC function appropriately are substantial. George W. Bush left no doubt that he had relied on the torture memo in formulating policy. In an interview following publication of his memoir, television commentator Matt Lauer asked Bush: "Why is waterboarding legal in your opinion?" Bush responded: "Because the lawyer said it was legal. He said it did not fall within the Anti-Torture Act. I'm not a lawyer, but you gotta trust the judgment of people around you and I do."[145] That trust was misplaced in the context of the torture memos, and lawyers heading the OLC and the Justice Department bear some of the responsibility.

Promoting Pro Bono Service

Another mark of ethical leadership is commitment to service pro bono publico. The tradition of representing parties without pay has deep historical roots, which extend to Roman tribunals, medieval ecclesiastical courts, and thirteenth-century English legal proceedings. In the United States, courts have intermittently exercised inherent authority to appoint counsel for indigents, and some bar leaders have been noted for their pro bono cases. Louis Brandeis was among the most celebrated examples. As he told one pro bono client, he considered it his duty to "help protect...public rights,...[and] he resolved early in life to give at least one hour a day to public service."[146] That commitment earned Brandeis the nickname of the "people's lawyer," and he was unique among leaders of the bar both for the extent of his contributions and for his insistence on compensating his firm from personal funds for the time he spent on charitable works.[147]

Until the 1970s, however, such significant pro bono commitments were relatively rare. Bar ethical standards included no obligation to provide service. Aspirational provisions of the ABA Canons of Professional Ethics advised only that lawyers should not refuse a court appointment to defend an indigent prisoner for any "nontrivial reason"; that a client's poverty might require a reduced fee or "no fee at all"; and that "reasonable requests of brother lawyers [for assistance], and of their widows and orphans without ample means should receive special and kindly consideration."[148] Whatever their response to widows and orphans, leaders' solicitude for other indigent clients was largely noticeable for its absence. One survey found that lawyers in even the most public-spirited firms contributed on average only about five hours a year.[149] Most assistance went not to indigent clients or law reform but to friends, relatives, and employees of lawyers or their clients, or middle-class organizations such as garden and Rotary clubs.[150]

Beginning in the 1970s, however, a heightened commitment to public service took hold. The ABA Model Rules of Professional Conduct, adopted in 1985, included an aspirational standard calling for fifty hours a year in unpaid or reduced-fee work, predominantly for persons of limited means or organizations that served them. Legal periodicals began showcasing exemplary pro bono commitments, and the *American Lawyer* began ranking large firms on the number of hours contributed. Yet although most bar leaders now endorse an ethic of service, a wide gap persists between their public pronouncements and actual practices. Only a quarter of lawyers meet the ABA standard of an hour a week.[151] Fewer than half of the lawyers in America's two hundred most profitable law firms provide over twenty hours a year in pro bono assistance.[152]

Leaders' failure to make pro bono work a higher organizational priority is a missed opportunity for both the profession and the public. A wide range of evidence suggests that volunteer work promotes both physical and mental health. People who regularly volunteer in public interest activities have longer lives, less pain, stress, and depression, and greater self-esteem than the general population.[153] Pro bono work can also offer valuable experience, training, visibility, and community contacts. Selfless action is, in short, good for the self, and charitable involvement often expresses the values of social justice that led many lawyers to legal careers in the first instance.[154] Part of leaders' own public service contribution should be to institutionalize an ethic of pro bono work.

At a minimum, that means ensuring that every lawyer in their organization receives sufficient time, support, and incentives to meet the ABA standard of at least fifty hours a year of public service.

Not only should leaders do more to ensure broad pro bono participation, they should also do more to monitor the effectiveness of assistance. The most comprehensive survey of pro bono programs found that none made formal efforts to assess the impact of aid or the satisfaction with services among clients and non-profit organizations that referred or co-counseled cases.[155] Nor did the vast majority of firm leaders monitor quality in any rigorous fashion, and none engaged in systematic analysis of cost-effectiveness and social impact.[156] Many leaders take a "pray and spray" approach to aid; their organizations spread assistance broadly and trust that something good will happen as a result. Something usually does, but it is not necessarily the most cost-effective use of services. Equally problematic is the assumption that that any unpaid service is a good in itself, and that its quality need not be questioned unless someone actually complains. Yet this reactive approach is better suited to commercial practice, where dissatisfied clients can vote with their feet. In charitable settings, recipients of aid may lack the knowledge or sense of entitlement to express concerns. Under the current system, performance problems are not always adequately addressed. In a recent survey of leaders of major public interest legal organizations, about three-fifths expressed concerns about the quality of pro bono assistance that they received from the private bar.[157]

A true commitment to public service requires more strategic direction and oversight from law firm leaders and in-house counsel. Often the best approach is to target compelling unmet needs that fit the organization's particular capabilities. Ongoing partnerships with groups working in the field can help identify appropriate projects and leverage assistance. A key to success is evaluation. To be sure, the "social return on investment" is often hard to quantify for pro bono work. But firms that want to make a difference cannot simply assume that good intentions inevitably lead to good results. Some metrics of performance are essential. American Bar Association standards for pro bono programs suggest collecting data on individuals served, results obtained, and evaluations from participating lawyers, clients, and referring or collaborating organizations.[158]

In short, leaders' focus needs to extend beyond the bottom line. Too often, they tend to view pro bono work in largely instrumental terms; how much does it contribute to training, recruitment, and reputation. Such assessments should, of course, play a role. Demonstrating that law firms can do well by doing good is a key strategy in sustaining charitable commitments. But to present public service programs purely in those terms is to compromise what makes them a *public* service. When leaders talk about pro bono, they generally speak in shorthand. "Publico" has dropped out of the discourse. Leaders can afford to lose the Latin, but not the concept. It is not enough for lawyers to label their assistance "pro bono." They also need to know how much the public is actually benefitting.

PHILOSOPHER KURT BAIER began his celebrated book, *The Moral Point of View*, with the observation that "Moral talk is often rather repugnant. Leveling moral accusations, expressing moral indignation, passing moral judgment,...administering moral reproof, justifying oneself, and above all moralizing. Who can enjoy such talk? And who can like or trust those addicted to it?"[159] The lesson for leaders is to focus on action rather than talk. It is easy to draft policies or sermonize at official functions. The test of true leadership lies in priorities and practices.

6

Leadership Scandals

SCANDALS, NOTES LAURA Kipnis, will always be with us, "sniffing at the back door, nosing around for cracks in the façade." Because the "human personality is helpless against itself," we will always see leaders "orchestrating their own downfalls, crashing headlong into their own inner furies."[1] And we, the public, the "collective superego" cannot resist the spectacle. Nor can we sometimes help but relish the satisfaction of seeing the privileged brought down to size for violating norms that inconveniently constrain our own behavior.

What is, however, distinctive about the modern era is that social, economic, and technological forces have publicized conduct that might once have remained private. Most obviously, the public's increased comfort in discussing sex has created a market for scandal that the press has been all too willing to supply. Competition among media has pushed in similar directions. As Ari Adut notes in *On Scandal*, the proliferation of news sources and "the establishment of the round-the-clock cable news cycle have stoked the demand for scandal and facilitated its publicization process. The effects of the citizen-journalism of YouTube, which allows almost anyone to put any kind of compromising images about elites into the public domain, are obvious...."[2] The rise in watchdog groups that trade in publicity, and communications strategists that specialize in spin, has also heightened the visibility of leadership missteps. Technology has provided more ways to obtain information and to make it instantly accessible. It is one thing to disclose that a congressman has sent prurient photos to a woman he met online. It is another to circulate his crotch shot to millions. Those in positions of power are increasingly vulnerable to exposure of their own frailties, as well as increasingly responsible for organizational scandals not of their own making. According to recent studies, chief executive officers believe that reputational loss is the second greatest hazard they confront.[3] This chapter explores the dynamics of scandal. What enmeshes lawyers in political, financial, and sexual misconduct? When and why does their private conduct become a subject of legitimate public concern? How important is hypocrisy, and how important should it be? How can leaders effectively manage reputational crises?

Hypocrisy

Hypocrisy is at the foundation of many leadership scandals. This should come as no surprise. If, as conventional usage suggests, hypocrisy means assuming a false appearance of virtue, or failing to practice what one preaches, it is endemic to public life. Leaders are subject to normal human frailties, exposed to the temptations of power, and expected to rise above both. As philosopher Judith Sklar notes, charges of hypocrisy are especially pervasive in politics because

> It is not difficult to show that politicians are often more interested in power than in any of the causes they so ardently proclaim. It is, therefore, easier to dispose of an opponent's character by exposing his hypocrisy than to show that his political convictions are wrong. ... The paradox of liberal democracy is that it encourages hypocrisy because the politics of persuasion require ... a certain amount of dissimulation on the part of all speakers. On the other hand, the structure of open political competition exaggerates the importance and the prevalence of hypocrisy because it is the vice of which all parties can and do accuse each other.[4]

Psychologists have identified two cognitive biases that contribute to hypocrisy at leadership levels. One is people's tendency to see themselves as unique and superior to others, particularly concerning moral conduct.[5] This uniqueness bias is exacerbated by conditions of power. Leaders live in what consultant Eric Dezenhall labeled a "mental aquarium," an environment of admiration that leads to an inflated sense of self-confidence and self-importance.[6] A second cognitive bias is individuals' tendency to view their own transgressions as less objectionable than identical actions by others.[7] Power again increases the likelihood of such bias.[8] Although social disapproval normally helps check self-interest, feelings of power tend to reduce sensitivity to that constraint.[9] The result is often for leaders to project a false image of moral superiority.

Although almost no one doubts the pervasiveness of hypocrisy, commentators divide on its significance. In sorting through their arguments, it is useful to distinguish between individual and institutional hypocrisy. Leaders can be criticized either for failing to live up to *their* principles, or for failing to keep an organization or institution living up to *its* principles. So for example, Thomas Jefferson can be faulted for violating his professed commitment to liberty and equality because he owned slaves, or for designing a constitutional system that proclaimed adherence to those values but ignored their meaning for African-Americans.[10] Some commentators also distinguish between hypocrisy and moral weakness. As political theorist Ruth Grant argues, "to profess principles that one has no intention of following is hypocrisy: to be unable to live up to our best expectations of ourselves is human nature."[11]

Grant and Sklar both argue that hypocrisy is appropriate where leaders need to persuade others through rational argument. "The frank exposure of self-interested motivations is often a threat to that process," Grant notes. Sklar similarly observes that "[o]ften our public manners are better than our personal laxities. That 'sugary grin'…is a very necessary pretense, a witness to our moral efforts no less than to our failures…Honesties that humiliate and a stiff-necked refusal to compromise" are generally counterproductive.[12] Grant describes a paradox in politics that is true in many other leadership contexts as well.

> Some sorts of hypocrisy…sustain the public conditions for…integrity. Every act of hypocrisy involves a pretense of virtue, which necessarily includes public acknowledgement of moral standards for political action, and sometimes that public statement is the best that can be done. Moreover, even the pretense can serve as a genuine constraint.…In sum, the paradoxical truth is that there will be more genuine virtue and integrity in politics where there is a judicious appreciation of the role of political hypocrisy than where there is a strident and wholesale condemnation of it.[13]

Other commentators worry that a focus on hypocrisy will divert attention from the substance of the conduct at issue and discourage too many potential leaders from entering public life.[14] Many talented individuals who are basically "decent and well meaning" have also made some "significant missteps they would rather not read about in the morning paper."[15] By the same token, newspapers often end up in an "appallingly wasteful" diversion of scarce resources by duplicating each others' efforts to "sniff out the latest scandal."[16]

Yet exposure of hypocrisy can also serve legitimate functions. When leaders who advocate "morally demanding principles fail to live up to them," that

failure can spark a useful debate about the "practicability" of those principles.[17] Concerns about hypocrisy can also discourage overreaching, unprinci-
pled, or self-righteous conduct that undermines leaders' legitimacy. Context
matters. In determining whether condemnation is appropriate, it makes sense
to ask why leaders have violated professed principles, and what will be the
likely consequences of their actions.[18]

Consider John Edwards's much mocked $400 haircuts during the
2008 presidential campaign. After a YouTube video went viral, showing
him fussing with hair and makeup, to the tune of "I Feel Pretty," Edwards
reimbursed his campaign $800 for two Beverly Hills salon visits while
insisting that he hadn't known how much they cost.[19] His gesture did little
to quiet critics. As Maureen Dowd noted in the *New York Times*, "someone who aspires to talk credibly about [poverty and] the two Americas
can't lavish on his locks what working families may spend on electricity
in a year. You can't sell earnestness while indulging in decadence."[20] Dowd
also pointed out that Edwards at the time was living in a 28,000 square
foot North Carolina mansion with a basketball court, squash court, and
swimming pool, which scarcely enhanced his credibility as a spokesman
for the poor.

So too, high-profile politicians and their families are routinely advised
to give up preferences that seem too upscale. First Lady Michelle Obama
was widely criticized for heading to a five-star European beach resort with
a cavalcade of taxpayer-subsidized staff and security agents, even as most of
the country was "pinching pennies" and "sliding into a double-dip depression," and the president was "campaigning against the excesses of the rich."
If Obama had wanted an ocean vacation, why not the Gulf Coast where she
and her daughters could have "cleaned a few pelicans"?[21] Jay Leno quipped
that Obama had a new book out: "Spain on $75,000 a day."[22] When asked to
comment on the expenditure, part of which was financed by taxpayers, White
House advisor David Axelrod responded that "[f]olks in the public eye are
also human" and shouldn't have to defer all the opportunities that come with
office.[23] But no one was demanding "all," just the ones that seemed grossly
excessive, especially during a recession.

Romney was another leader whose gaffes about wealth brought widespread criticism, though on grounds of political insensitivity rather than
hypocrisy. His offhand offer of a $10,000 bet, his casual references to friends
who owned sports teams, and his implausible claim of concern about getting
a pink slip, all served to highlight his distance from the average voter.[24] His
insistence that he "worked hard" for his money and wouldn't "apologize for

being successful" grated on those who worked hard as well and hadn't had the advantages with which Romney started.

Those examples also highlight a public ambivalence about authenticity: voters want a candidate that looks, acts, and thinks like them, and then are disappointed when the pretense is revealed. But the takeaway is not that wealthy leaders will always be punished for focusing on poverty and economic inequality. As examples like FDR and Ted Kennedy suggest, people do not expect politicians to take a vow of poverty before speaking out on the issue. If their compassion seems genuine and their lifestyle is not overly opulent, then leaders are unlikely to be branded as hypocrites if they advocate redistributive policies. What got Edwards in trouble was more his vanity and ostentation than his affluence. Leaders occupying positions of privilege need to be sensitive to symbolism, and should draw attention to their commonalities, not their differences, with their followers.

Public and Private

At what point does a leader's private conduct become a matter of legitimate public concern? If a national political leader hires a hooker, has an affair, or tells a racist story at a private party, does that call into question his leadership capacities? Those who believe it does generally make two claims. One is that character cannot be compartmentalized and that the qualities that individuals display in their personal lives spill over to their professional lives. In suggesting that South Carolina Governor Mark Sanford was unfit for office because of lies about an extramarital affair, former cabinet member and conservative commentator William Bennett maintained that: "Someone who lies in private is going to lie in public and you can't trust someone who does that."[25] A second reason for caring about private conduct involves issues of public credibility. Leaders charged with making or enforcing standards of ethical conduct should follow them as well. In order to maintain respect and serve as appropriate role models, leaders should behave responsibly in their personal as well as their professional lives.

Such categorical claims are problematic on several grounds. A threshold difficulty involves the assumption that character reflects consistent personality traits, and that individuals who exhibit dishonesty or disrespect for ethical standards in one context will do so in another. A vast array of social science research suggests that this assumption is, to a large extent, a "figment of our aspirations."[26] Context plays a critical role in shaping moral behavior, and little correlation is apparent between seemingly similar character traits, such as lying and cheating.[27] Although individuals clearly differ in their responses to temptation, even slight changes in situational factors can substantially affect tendencies toward deceit. For example, studies of students indicate that it is impossible to predict cheaters in French from cheaters in math.[28]

If we cannot reliably make those sorts of predictions, it is hard to defend the far more attenuated inferences about matters such as sexual behavior spilling over into other domains. Whatever else one may say about infidelity in marriage, history does not disclose it to be a particularly accurate predictor of leaders' ethics or effectiveness in office. Compare, for example, Richard Nixon, who was faithful and Franklin Delano Roosevelt, who was not. John F Kennedy lied frequently about his sexual affairs but was honest with the public about the botched invasion of the Bay of Pigs.

A second problem with drawing inferences from personal conduct is that it encourages a kind of Gresham's law of journalism. All it takes is one reporter with a peephole perspective. As soon as a scandal breaks in any major media outlet, it becomes difficult for other members of the press to remain above the fray. The kind of "let the public decide" philosophy that currently guides character investigation encourages the media to pander to our worst instincts, and to divert its attention from more substantive issues. As Warren's and Brandeis's celebrated article on privacy noted, gossip about scandal "both belittles and perverts....It usurps the place of interest in brains capable of other things."[29] Details about the sexual conduct of Bill Clinton, Eliot Spitzer, Mark Sanford, Michael McGeevy, and David Vitter demeaned not only the leaders but ourselves.

The costs of such coverage are not born by leaders alone. Society also suffers when its choices for leadership narrow to those willing to put their entire life histories on public display. Under the watchful eye of reporters scrambling for a scoop, almost everyone has something frayed around its ethical edges. Our nation has a limited supply of gifted leaders and many are either unwilling or unable to withstand our increasingly intrusive media coverage.

The point is not that personal conduct should be irrelevant in assessing qualifications for leadership. It is rather that, here again, context matters. Much depends on the nature and consequences of the conduct and how the leader responds. A case in point involves Gary Hart, whose extramarital affair derailed his presidential candidacy. The information that emerged about his sexual liaison aboard a yacht named Monkey Business was relevant to his candidacy in two respects. The first had to do with qualities of honesty and judgment that became apparent in the way Hart publicly responded to personal inquiries. Rather than refusing to discuss charges of extra-marital relationships, Hart flatly denied them and challenged reporters to verify his denials. Yet once having proclaimed his marital rectitude, Hart failed to display it even for a few months, a fact that inevitably raised doubts about his judgment and self-control. Moreover, in the face of mounting evidence about his frequent contacts with model Donna Rice, Hart denied that they had any "personal relationship." As a *New York Times* editorial wryly inquired, "would 'political' or 'business' relationship better describe it?"[30] Hart's lack of discretion at a critical juncture in his career is reminiscent of a possibly apocryphal anecdote about a former president of U.S. Steel. When forced to resign after his liaison with actress Lillian Russell became public, the president objected to his board of directors that he was being penalized for doing publicly what many of them did behind closed doors. To which the response was, "that's what doors are for."

The problem with Hart's conduct was not simply his lack of honesty. Suppose he had been utterly candid about his personal life and insisted that it had no bearing on his fitness for public office? Guido Calabresi, then-Dean of Yale Law School, suggested that Hart should have said something like the following:

> I have a problem. I have a weakness for beautiful women. It's not something I'm proud of. It's not something that's good. It's a weakness. It's made strains on my marriage. If I were to tell you I would never do that kind of thing again, that would be foolish. You never know. If that is so much of a problem for you that you cannot vote for me on it, so be it. That is what I am.[31]

Yet to present Hart's conduct in these terms risks trivializing its significance. His habitual weakness for casual affairs was not like a weakness for chocolate. It signified a lack of concern and respect for the wife to whom he owed some ongoing responsibility. In an age in which divorce is readily available and acceptable, a leader's choice to remain married, while repeatedly violating marital commitments, raises questions about character. For positions involving moral leadership, those questions are relevant.

But neither are they conclusive. How candidates treat women in private life is not, of course, more critical than how they treat women's concerns in a political capacity. Bill Clinton had an abysmal record on marital fidelity but an excellent one on gender issues. What makes for personal goodness is not always the same as what makes for the common good. Nor will private conduct reliably predict public performance. Rather, the point is simply that when an important aspect of an important job involves upholding ethical standards, it makes sense to consider whether a leader exemplifies those standards in his own life.

The Corrosion of Judgment

Leadership scandals invite attention not only because they offer the perverse pleasure of seeing the mighty fallen, but also because they often present such a curious paradox. How could leaders who seemed so smart in other aspects of their lives be so clueless in the matters that could cost them their positions? Why have such ambitious individuals risked so much for gratification that seems trivial by comparison? Social scientists see this behavior as one of the paradoxes of power, which is rooted in the cognitive biases and structural conditions noted earlier: leaders' tendencies to see themselves as unique and invulnerable, and to have those perceptions reinforced by the perks and deference that accompany powerful positions.[32] Leaders are often risk takers, and those individuals "tend to believe they control their destiny."[33] Recent research also suggests that individuals who need to exert a great deal of control in their working lives may have less ego strength to regulate their private lives.[34] These dynamics bear closer examination in leadership scandals that are most common, those involving money and sex.

Money

Money may not be the root of all evil, but it lurks around the edges of a good bit of it. Although it might seem that affluence should insulate most leaders from temptation, in fact, research indicates that the rich are more susceptible to financial misconduct. Social psychologists hypothesize that increased wealth and independence from others is associated with increased willingness to prioritize self-interest and more favorable attitudes toward greed.[35] Whatever the causes, many leaders' careers have been derailed or tarnished by corruption in an amount that seems trivial given their economic status. Ethical problems take a variety of forms, some more serious than others. One category involves acceptance of money to which leaders are not entitled, such as use of campaign funds or government transportation for personal purposes. A second form involves abuse of status to secure money, and a third involves use of money to secure status, or more money. What many of these lapses have in common is a lack of clear or premeditated intent to violate the law. Rather, many of the leaders backed into their difficulties because the rules were murky, the initial violations were minor or readily rationalized, or an opportunity presented itself before they had time to think it through clearly.

The bribery conviction of Dickie Scrubbs, a leader of the plaintiff's bar, is an example of the last problem. Scrubbs was a multimillionaire who made his fortune suing asbestos and tobacco companies. According to a *New Yorker* profile, he had "more money than he could spend, and was fully stocked with yachts, planes and vacation homes."[36] But his affluence didn't keep him from haggling over some three million dollars in fees with co-counsel in a fraud case against State Farm Insurance. Scruggs had a history of such fee disputes and was not a gracious loser. So he readily accepted an offer by a fellow lawyer, Tim Balducci, who said he might be able to help with the trial judge in the case, a friend and mentor. Balducci, who was hoping for a share of the disputed fee, approached the judge and suggested that it would be helpful if he thought that Scruggs had the right side in the fee dispute. Later in the conversation, Balducci said that he knew that the judge meant to retire soon and that he would be welcome to join Balducci's firm on an of-counsel basis. The judge considered the request grossly improper and agreed to tape his next conversation with Balducci. During that conversation, he told Balducci that he had gotten himself into a fix and needed $40,000 to "get me over a hump." Balducci agreed, and then approached the Scruggs firm to cover the cost. Although accounts of what then happened differed, there is no dispute that Scruggs issued a check to Balducci's firm for $40,000, ostensibly as payment for legal work on an unrelated case. After Balducci delivered the payment to the judge, he was arrested and persuaded to tape a conversation with Scruggs. In that conversation, Balducci requested another $10,000 for the payoff. Scruggs said he would "take care of it."[37] That statement became the basis for a charge of conspiracy to bribe a judge.

Scruggs pled guilty to that charge although he was at pains to point out at his hearing on the plea that at least initially he had "no intent to bribe the judge." His original understanding was that Balducci would "earwig the judge," a term that refers to casual ex parte conversations about a case. Although these are technically violations of ethical rules, they usually involve no bribery or other undue influence. But like the proverbial frog, who doesn't jump out of the pot when the water gradually approaches a boil, Scruggs did not distance himself from the scheme when the topic turned to cash. To many observers, it seemed inexplicable that a man worth close to a billion would risk his freedom for a few million that he couldn't possibly need. But as one colleague put it, "Dick didn't get where he got by asking permission. He got where he got by counting on asking for forgiveness, if he needed to."[38] At some point in the process, he lost sight of the point at which forgiveness would stop.

Other lawyers have proven similarly insensitive when on the receiving end of illegitimate or excessive payments. In 1969, Supreme Court Justice Abe Fortas was disgraced by receipt of an exorbitant payment from former business clients for a summer seminar program, and by acceptance of $20,000, intended as the first installment of a lifetime honorarium from the foundation of a former client whom he continued to advise regarding a fraud investigation.[39] Unable to reconcile his salary with his lifestyle, Fortas found the financial aspects of his move to bench "oppressive and depressing."[40] In resigning under pressure, Fortas continued to deny wrongdoing.[41] Kwame Kilpatrick, while mayor of Detroit, made similar denials when accused of using city funds to lease a car for his family, and charging a city credit card thousands of dollars for spa massages, extravagant dining, and expensive wine.[42] Although Kilpatrick paid back some $9,000, he also denounced ethics-related criticisms as part of a "hate-driven bigoted assault" and "illegal lynch-mob mentality."[43]

Other lawyers have faced substantial criticism for using institutional funds to gratify personal preferences. In 2010, Mark Yudof, President of the University of California, used some $700,000 to renovate his private residence. At a time when the university was facing massive financial cutbacks, many observers were outraged at the expenditure of large amounts of money and staff time on the upkeep of a palatial rental home that wasn't even the official president's house.[44] Similar controversies led to the resignation of Abe Goldstein as the provost at Yale. Cost overruns on redecorations for the Provost's house ran to five times the amount budgeted for the project, totaling about $313,000 in current dollars. Those costs included repainting several rooms when Mrs. Goldstein decided she preferred a different color.[45]

In some instances, misconduct has stemmed from the pursuit of status rather than money. In 2010, the U.S. House of Representative censured Charles Rangel based on findings of its ethics committee that the congressman had committed eleven violations of House Ethics Rules. The violations included sending letters on congressional stationary seeking donations to New York City College's Charles B. Rangel Public Service Center. The letters went to individuals and organizations with interests that could be affected by legislation before the House Ways and Means Committee, which Rangel chaired. The committee also found that Rangel had used House resources, including staff and supplies, to support his fundraising.[46] The quid pro quo that Rangel's efforts implied is well-captured in a famous story about congressional power broker Russell Long. A businessman interested in having Long introduce a rider to a tax bill in exchange for a generous campaign contribution balked at the amount requested. When he asked what he would get for a smaller contribution, Long reportedly responded: "Good government."

Abuse of office can also stem from efforts to defend or conceal misconduct. A Senate Ethics Panel found that Larry Craig improperly used $213,000 in campaign funds to pay legal fees and public relations costs connected with charges of soliciting sex in an airport restroom. Campaign funds may only be used to pay legal expenses related to a senator's official duties.[47] New York Governor David Patterson was fined by the Commission on Public Integrity for lying about the solicitation of free tickets from the Yankees for the World Series.[48]

Underlying all of these scandals is a sense of entitlement and invulnerability that often accompanies power. Stanford psychologist Roderick Kramer labels this *"genius-to-folly syndrome—*a swift and steady rise by a brilliant, hard-driving, politically adept individual followed by surprising stints of miscalculation or recklessness."[49] In accounting for this syndrome, Kramer resists attributing it simply to "personal failings or lack of moral fiber," because those flaws didn't emerge earlier in leaders' careers. Rather, he sees such misconduct as a byproduct of the pursuit of power. Leaders sometimes advance by bending rules and focusing relentlessly on their ascent to the top; by the time they arrive, they have come to believe that they no longer have to sweat the small stuff and that it doesn't much matter what others think. With that mindset, minor misconduct can easily mushroom into a major scandal.

A case study involves Mark Drier, once the head of a prominent New York law firm with multimillion dollar clients. He is now a convicted felon serving a 20-year term for defrauding hedge funds of some $380 million dollars and stealing another $45 million from client escrow accounts. It was an unlikely career path for someone who started out with degrees from Yale College and Harvard Law School, and then made partner in an established Manhattan firm. Neither that firm, nor two others to which he moved, provided the status and recognition he desired, so he struck out on his own. In a *Vanity Fair* profile, Dreier reflected on the process that ended in federal prison. It started with his sense that "I needed to give people the idea I was doing very well. That was the first step in a pattern toward living above my means."[50] He moved his office to a Park Avenue building designed by I. M. Pei, but remained disappointed. Feeling that "life was passing me by," he made two resolutions. One was that he would buy himself a bigger house on the beach. The other was that he would get the money to support his lifestyle by dramatically expanding his firm, a solely owned business, Dreier LLP. To lure teams of all-star lawyers, Dreier guaranteed high salaries, plus a bonus based on performance. That required a good deal of money up front.

Dreier didn't recall the moment at which he considered solving his cash flow problems through fraud, but acknowledged that the decision was made easier by a long track record of "cutting corners" on matters like expense reports and tax returns. He discovered that "once you cross a gray line, it's much easier to cross a black line." He rationalized fraud as something he could "get out of…relatively quickly" once he had subsidized his expansion. "I'd like to say I have a clear recollection of going through some great ethical analysis and agonizing over it. But I don't believe I did. I should have. I just don't remember that kind of angst." To finance his expansion, Dreier created a fictitious real estate development company and borrowed $20 million. Further fraudulent loans eventually totaled $200 million. Then, when one of his bogus financial statements and an escrow fund shortfall were discovered, Dreier created an elaborate ruse to replace the cash. His impersonation of the executive of a former client triggered suspicions that led to his arrest.

In reflecting back on the debacle, Dreier noted:

> Many people are caught up in the notion that success in life is measured in professional and financial achievements and material acquisitions, and it's hard to step back from that and see the fallacy…. I see people my children's age first coming into finance, the working world, as having to make basic choices about how to define happiness and success. Obviously, I made the wrong choices. But they don't have to.[51]

How can leaders protect themselves from such choices? Psychologists suggest several strategies. One is to "keep your life simple," guard against greed, and "remember what really matters."[52] A second strategy is to "sweat the small stuff."[53] Avoid the venial sins that make the serious ones easier to commit. Willpower is strengthened through practice.[54] A third strategy is to learn to be reflective, particularly about weaknesses. Have people in your life whom you can trust for candid assessments. John Ensign echoed that view in his farewell message to the Senate while under investigation for ethics violations: "My caution to all of my colleagues is to surround yourself with people who will be honest with you about how you really are and what you are becoming."[55] Such honesty is easier to achieve if the leader's organization imposes meaningful oversight processes and bottom-up performance evaluations. Dreier's workplace was structured to avoid such oversight. He lacked partners who could have asked awkward questions about the organization's finances before it was too late.

Similar results can occur in more traditional partnership structures if too much power is concentrated in a single leader who faces too little pressure for transparency. Scott Rothstein, the CEO and managing partner of a Fort Lauderdale firm, Rothstein, Rosenfeldt, Adler, orchestrated a $1.2 billion Ponzi scheme that lured investment in non-existent settlements of employment cases.[56] Like Dreier, Rothstein used the funds to support an ostentatious lifestyle, complete with yachts, exotic cars, expensive art, and generous political and charitable contributions. Also like Dreier, his conduct reflected a toxic combination of over-optimism and narcissism. As he put it in a suicide text message to his partners, "I am a fool. I thought I could fix it but got trapped by my ego and refusal to fail."[57] His partners, for their part, engaged in willful ignorance. The signs of problems were clearly visible. Rothstein was obsessively secretive, and isolated himself in an office protected by a bulletproof door, special entry key card, and security guard.[58] In the year before the fraud was discovered, Rothstein paid himself $10 million and one of his partners $6 million. In a firm that was generating only about $8 million in genuine business, that should have triggered internal inquiries.[59] Although it is easy to dismiss this case as aberrational, it is also clear from the discussion of firm meltdowns in chapter 8 that Dreier's and Rothstein's cases reflected in extreme form more common patterns of outsized aspirations and partner passivity. Particularly in organizational structures with highly centralized governance authority, some checks and balances are critical to ensure oversight and deter overreaching.[60]

Sex

On the whole, as George Orwell observed, "human beings want to be good, but not too good, and not quite all the time."[61] Lawyers in leadership roles are no different, particularly when it comes to sex. But what is different is the distance between their public posture and private conduct, and the amount of popular attention that focuses on the gap. "What were they thinking"— or not thinking—is often the public's first response. The answer again lies mainly in the high-risk combination of entitlement and invulnerability that accompanies power.[62] Eliot Spitzer, the New York governor who resigned after patronizing a high-priced call girl, found such sex convenient and thought he would never get caught. "Stupid hubris" was how he described it.[63] John Edwards similarly attributed his extramarital affair to an "egotism, a narcissism" fed by national acclaim, "that leads you to believe that you can do whatever you want. You're invincible. And there will be no consequences."[64]

The murkiness of moral boundaries also plays a role. Americans have long been ambivalent about promiscuity, at least among men, and the leaders involved in sex scandals are almost entirely men. The public wants to see a public posture of rectitude, but is often tolerant of the leader who strays. Grover Cleveland admitted fathering an illegitimate child, but was elected president nonetheless. A slogan coined to defeat him, "Ma, Ma, where's my Pa?" was later modified by supporters to conclude "Gone to the White House, Ha! Ha! Ha!"[65]

Ambivalence about extramarital activity was clearly on display during the scandals involving Bill Clinton. Although only 14 percent of the public said that they would not vote for an adulterer, 47 percent said that if Clinton had lied under oath about his affair with Monica Lewinsky and asked her to do so, he should be removed from office. [66] But by the close of his term, even though a court found that he had lied under oath, his approval ratings remained high, upwards of 60 percent. Such inconsistent attitudes may help explain why leaders often believe that they can get away with extramarital sex, and why they are sometimes mistaken.

Multiple factors affect the outcome of sexual scandals. The most obvious is the nature of the conduct. Was the sex criminal or did it lead to related offenses? Soliciting a minor, or in Congressman Larry Craig's case, an undercover male police officer, is political suicide. The misuse of campaign funds or taxpayer dollars to finance an affair can also play a role, as was the case with Larry Craig and John Edwards. New Jersey Governor Mike McGreevy resigned after disclosures of a closeted gay affair with a partner whom he had put on the state's payroll.[67] Senator John Ensign also resigned in the wake of an investigation for violating tax and lobbying laws while covering up an affair with a campaign aide.[68] Ohio representative Wayne Hays inflamed voters by employing a secretary whose primary duty was sex; Elizabeth Ray, by her own admission, didn't know how to type.[69]

Gender also plays a role, not only in the frequency of sexual scandals but also in how they are perceived. A number of reasons have been suggested for why so few women leaders have been embroiled in such scandals. One is that they appear more risk averse, partly due to lingering double standards of morality, which make promiscuity more costly for women than men (particularly if they are married and have children).[70] Lionel Tiger has argued further that women have fewer sexual opportunities because power is not as alluring in women as in men.[71] Others have suggested that women in positions of leadership have less time for, less interest in, or less sense of entitlement to extramarital sex. Whatever the reason, it is clear that women have a different attitude with respect to sexual scandal, and that their increased involvement in leadership positions may reduce its frequency.[72]

Hypocrisy also matters. The greater the disparity between the public image and private conduct, the more judgmental the public is likely to be. Mark Foley resigned from the Senate in 2006 after sending sexually suggestive e-mails to former Senate pages. He had a record of support for anti-gay legislation and had criticized Clinton's relationship with a White House intern as "vile."[73] Eliot Spitzer, the New York governor who resigned after patronizing a high-priced call girl, had supported increased penalties for patronizing prostitutes and had cast himself as a moral crusader while attorney general. David Vitter, a Louisiana senator who purchased services from the "D.C. Madam," was pummeled by the press and his opponent (although not by voters) because of his prior stand on "family values," including his condemnation of then-president Bill Clinton as "morally unfit to govern."[74] By contrast, Barney Frank, a liberal Massachusetts congressman who was open about his sexuality, survived a scandal involving a gay prostitute with whom he lived and whose parking tickets he fixed. Many voters apparently agreed with Frank that "Everyone in public life is entitled to privacy but no one in public life is entitled to hypocrisy."[75]

The extent to which others rally around leaders can also be critical in determining whether they survive a sexual scandal. Vitter survived because his substantive positions continued to resonate with his conservative base. Bill Clinton benefitted from the continued support of feminists. However much they deplored his personal sexual history, women's rights activists felt that he had been good on their issues, and that his impeachment would set them back. By contrast, Eliot Spitzer's fall was partly attributable to a governing style that had alienated political colleagues.[76] The clenched-teeth stoicism of wives can often be crucial, while a tell-all memoir or interview invites further disaster.[77] Former wives can also precipitate a scandal. Jack Ryan's Illinois Senate race was derailed by his ex-wife's revelations that he had taken her to sex clubs and pressured her to have sex with patrons.[78] For some misconduct, however, spousal support may be inadequate. Spitzer's resignation, with his demonstrably mortified wife standing beside him, was "like watching someone swallow a hand grenade in real time."[79]

A final factor that affects survival of sexual scandals is how well they are managed. Decisions about whether to concede wrongdoing, what to say in an apology, and what corrective action to take can make a critical difference.

Crisis Management: Apologies and Corrective Action

Leaders confront crises based on their own conduct, their subordinates' conduct, or some combination. Whatever the context, the fundamental choices are similar. In terms of public statements, leaders have four main options: (1) a denial of wrongdoing, (2) a refusal to comment, (3) an expression of sympathy or regret (often termed a partial apology or non-apology apology), or (4) a full apology accepting responsibility. Each strategy has its advantages and limitations.

A credible denial is almost always the most effective response to a scandal, particularly if the conduct implicates integrity.[80] Part of the reason is that when evaluating ethical behavior, people tend to weigh negative acts more heavily than positive acts, so any statement that admits moral culpability is hard to remedy.[81] Such considerations doubtless figured in Clinton's initial insistence that "I did not have sex with that woman," and Larry Craig's announcement that "I am not gay. I have never been gay."[82] However, if the facts are not sufficient to support a denial, or at least to create reasonable doubts, then a refusal to acknowledge responsibility is counterproductive. Leaders "cannot win through spin."[83] When wrongdoing seems clearly to have occurred, the public expects conciliatory statements and corrective action. Excuses or denials under these circumstances fuel anger because they compound the misconduct and suggests the likelihood of future abuses.[84] John Edwards's bungled efforts to evade tabloid reporters and to have his campaign manager assume paternity of Edwards's own illegitimate child contributed to his political freefall. Bill Clinton was impeached not because of his sexual affair with White House intern Monica Lewinsky, but because he lied about it under oath in a sexual harassment suit.

Refusal to comment is another option. It makes sense when leaders believe that: evidence of culpability is unlikely to surface, the risks of creating potential legal liability by apologizing are too great, more time is necessary to gain information, or the issues are so personal that full disclosure seems unwarranted. However, in terms of public relations, silence is usually the least effective option. It is less reassuring than denial because it fails to disclaim guilt, and it is less reassuring than apology because it fails to signal remorse and promise corrective action.[85] If the goal is to convince others to withhold judgment, silence seldom succeeds, particularly when it is coupled with other evidence of culpability. A representative example involved Merrill Lynch's recommendation of stocks that analysts privately described in e-mails as "dogs," "trash," and "piece of s—." The purpose of the recommendations was to retain banking business from companies that issued these stocks. To settle charges, the firm paid a $100 million fine without admitting misconduct. But as New York's Attorney General pointedly noted, "You don't pay a $100 million fine if you didn't do anything wrong."[86]

Partial apologies that express sympathy without acknowledging responsibility present similar trade-offs but may have higher upside potential. As common sense suggests and psychological research confirms, they are never as effective as full apologies in suggesting that the speaker is "aware of the social norms that have been violated" and therefore likely to "avoid the offense in future interactions."[87] Ritualistic apologies can also backfire. Those who utter frequent statements of regret may end up appearing weaker, less confident, and less sincere than those who don't apologize at all.[88] Yet in some settings, expressions of sympathy are better than nothing or than an a full apology that acknowledges responsibility and increases the risk of litigation.[89] Some conciliatory statement may be necessary to avoid making the leaders or their organizations appear callous and unresponsive. Genuine expressions of concern and empathy can help reduce hostility, restore respect, and thus help to avoid or resolve disputes.[90] That seemed to be the motivating force behind an expression of regret by Citigroup's CEO: "Let me start by saying I'm sorry. I'm sorry that the financial crisis has had such a devastating impact for our country. I'm sorry about the millions of people, average Americans, who lost their homes. And I'm sorry that our management teams, starting with me, like so many others, could not see the unprecedented market collapse that lay before us."[91]

Full apologies are, however, more effective in defusing anger, rebuilding relationships, and encouraging confidence that the misconduct will not recur.[92] In politics, apologies by leaders have often served a largely symbolic role; they have expressed collective expiation for wrongdoing ranging from the internment of Japanese Americans to abusive practices by the Internal Revenue Service.[93] In contexts involving legal liability, apologies have reduced financial demands and the chance of lawsuits.[94] To encourage such apologies, about two-thirds of states have statutes that limit or prevent the use of apologies as evidence of wrongdoing in subsequent litigation.[95] Even in cases that go to trial, apologies that accept responsibility can help mitigate guilt, and are much more likely to have a positive influence than those that simply express sympathy and remorse.[96]

The most effective apologies are ones in which leaders:

- promptly acknowledge responsibility;
- are specific about the wrongs inflicted;
- convey sincere emotions;

- ask for forgiveness;
- promise not to repeat the conduct; and
- indicate a desire to do what is necessary to put things right.[97]

Leaders can often amplify the persuasiveness of apologies through symbolic gestures. Holy Roman Emperor Henry IV set the gold standard in 1077 when apologizing to Pope Gregory VII for church–state conflicts by standing barefoot in the snow for three days.[98] Japanese leaders have perfected the contemporary equivalent. A rich literature is available to advise them on the art of the apology, complete with photographs comparing the angles of bows and tips on wardrobe. Suits in "sedate, calming colors" like black or navy are recommended.[99]

By contrast, many American leaders have badly bungled their apologies. Richard Nixon made the following statement:

> I regret deeply any injuries that may have been done in the course of events that have led to this decision [to resign]. I would say only that if some of my judgments were wrong, and some were wrong, they were made in what I believed at the time to be in the best interest of the nation.[100]

The passive voice construction avoided casting Nixon as the person responsible for injuries and glossed over their significance by asserting that they occurred in pursuit of a greater good. Bob Packwood's response to some two dozen women who alleged sexual abuse and harassment was stunningly vague: "I'm apologizing for the conduct that it was alleged that I did."[101] John Edwards accelerated his political downfall by suggesting that a mitigating circumstance during his affair was that his wife's fatal cancer was in remission.[102]

Bill Clinton botched several opportunities before managing an apology that sounded sufficiently apologetic. One of his early efforts attracted widespread criticism for attempting to shift some of the blame for the scandal:

> I did have a relationship with Miss Lewinsky that was not appropriate. In fact, it was wrong. It constituted a critical lapse in judgment and a personal failure on my part for which I am solely and completely responsible.... [However, the Independent Counsel investigation] has gone on too long, cost too much, and hurt too many innocent

people....Now this matter is between me, the two people I love most—my wife and our daughter—and our God. It's nobody's business but ours. Even Presidents have private lives.[103]

His next effort was not much better.

I have acknowledged that I made a mistake, said that I regretted it, asked to be forgiven, spent a lot of very valuable time with my family in the last couple of weeks, and said I was going back to work.[104]

As Clinton acknowledged in his memoirs, "my anger hadn't worn off enough for me to be as contrite as I should have been."[105] "Get over it," was his implicit message, and the public didn't.

Finally, at a White House Prayer breakfast, Clinton delivered the apology that most commentators felt he should have given at the outset. Part of what made it satisfying was his recognition that he had missed opportunities earlier.

I agree with those who have said that in my first statement after I testified, I was not contrite enough. I don't think there is a fancy way to say that I have sinned. It is important to me that everyone who has been hurt know that the sorrow I feel is genuine: first and most important my family; also my friends; my staff, my Cabinet; Monica Lewinsky and her family, and the American people. I have asked all for their forgiveness. But I believe that to be forgiven, more than sorrow is required, at least two more things. First, genuine repentance; a determination to change, to repair breaches of my own making. I have repented. Second what my Bible calls a "broken spirit": an understanding that I must have God's help to be the person that I want to be....[106]

Yet however adeptly handled, scandals can be costly to all concerned. And in this world of digital footprints and gotcha journalism, they are becoming harder to conceal.[107] Gone are the days in which the press could be counted on to exercise some restraint, as long as an affair was handled discretely. Leaders now need to anticipate that their conduct might make front page copy, and if that prospect is unthinkable, then they must adjust their behavior accordingly.

Leaders also need to assume responsibility for preventing scandals by others and for establishing reporting structures that will make it possible. Where were the lawyers at Penn State when university officials failed for over a decade to report an assistant coach's sexual abuse of young boys in a campus locker room?[108] And where were the lawyers during the years that Foley's improper advances were known to congressional leaders?[109] One of the distinguishing characteristics of leaders is a willingness to assume some accountability for addressing misconduct by others. Scandals may always be with us, but that does not absolve leaders from doing their best to minimize the causes and consequences.

7

Diversity in Leadership

WHEN I WAS INTERVIEWING with a prominent Chicago law firm in the late 1970s, the head of its hiring committee assured me that the firm had no "woman problem." One of its 70-some partners was female, and she had no difficulty reconciling her personal and professional life. The past year she had given birth to her first child. It happened on a Friday and she was back in the office the following Monday.

Over the last several decades, the demographic landscape has been transformed. Yet particularly at leadership levels, progress seems stalled. One irony of this nation's continuing struggle for diversity and gender equity is that the profession leading the struggle has so often failed to set an example in its own organizations. Although Blacks, Latinos, Asian Americans, and Native Americans constitute about a third of the population and a fifth of law school graduates, they account for only 6 percent of law firm partners and 9 percent of general counsel of Fortune 500 corporations.[1] Women constitute over a third of the profession but only about a fifth of law firm partners, general counsel of Fortune 500 corporations, and law school deans.[2]

Part of the problem lies in a lack of consensus on whether there is a serious problem, and if so, what strategies would effectively address it. In exploring these issues, it makes sense to focus on race, ethnicity, and gender. Although these are not the only relevant dimensions of diversity, they affect the most lawyers and have generated the most systematic research. The following discussion tracks conventional usage in referring to "women and minorities," but that should neither obscure the unique experience of women of color, nor mask differences within and across racial and ethnic groups. The point rather is to understand how key aspects of individual identity intersect to structure the leadership experience and what leaders can do to promote diverse and inclusive legal institutions.

The Historical Context

Until the past half century, almost no women or minorities reached leadership positions in law and almost no one in those positions considered this
a problem. Both formal policies and informal practices reinforced exclusion
on the basis of race, ethnicity, sex, and religion. As late as l960, when women
accounted for half of college graduates, they constituted less than 3 percent
of lawyers and were notable for their absence at the upper level in government, law firms, and the judiciary.[3] The same was true for lawyers of color,
who accounted for only 1 percent of the profession.[4] Not until 1964 did all
accredited law schools formally abolish discrimination on the basis of race in
admissions, and the last gender barriers did not fall until 1972.[5]

For women, the obstacles took two main forms. One involved women's
roles; the other involved men's preferences. For most of this nation's history,
the conventional wisdom was that women lacked a "legal mind" and legal temperament. An 1873 United State Supreme Court decision reflected such views
in upholding the exclusion of Myra Bradwell from the Illinois bar. According
to Justice Bradley, women's "natural and proper timidity and delicacy" made
them unfit for many vocations, including legal practice. The "law of the
Creator" dictated marriage and motherhood as their "primary destiny and mission," and this role was incompatible with a "distinct and independent career."[6]
Such views persisted well into the twentieth century. Public opinion polls in
the 1930s, '40s, and '50s found that between two-thirds and three-quarters of
men did not approve of their wives working.[7] Nor were the attitudes confined
to men. Almost half of female lawyers surveyed in 1920 believed that marriage
and career were incompatible.[8] In speeches and articles such as "I Gave Up My
Law Books for a Cook Book," women advised married colleagues, "if the man
objects, for the happiness of all concerned, give it up."[9] Many did. Surveys during the early twentieth century found that only a third to half of women lawyers
were married and only about a quarter had children.[10]

A second cluster of concerns involved not the role of women, but the dis-
traction and discomfort of men. Administrators at Harvard worried about
unchaperoned interchange in the library, at Hastings about the rustling
of female skirts in the classroom, and at Columbia, about the "cranks and
freaks" who would adversely affect the school's culture and competitive edge.[11]
Other law school and law firm leaders put the problem of prejudice in pragmatic terms. Given discrimination by clients and colleagues, and pressures
from family that would keep women from establishing successful careers, it
made little sense to waste a position on them. The fact of bias thus became a

sufficient reason for perpetuating it. In the absence of any accountability for restrictive policies, many decision makers saw no reason even to give a reason. When a woman barred from applying to Columbia Law School in 1922 asked Dean Harlan Stone (later Chief Justice of the United States Supreme Court) why the school wouldn't allow women, his response was "We don't because we don't."[12]

In the face of such discrimination, early women lawyers faced steep hurdles even obtaining a law degree or establishing a practice, let alone achieving leadership positions. Ignored by clients and excluded by employers and bar associations, these women encountered roadblocks in all the traditional paths to success. Even after they obtained the vote, they were almost never perceived as credible candidates for significant public or judicial office. Until the late twentieth century, the only political positions in which women were well-represented were library and school boards, and the only judicial positions were in family and juvenile court.[13] In major firms, the options for women were generally secretary or office cleaner; stated reasons were that staff wouldn't take orders from women lawyers, men's wives would object to their presence, and no one would have lunch with them.[14] "Girl Lawyer Has Small Chance for Success," ran the title of an early twentieth-century interview, and the barriers it recounted left little doubt why so many women lost the "ambition and courage" to persist in practice.[15]

Discrimination based on race, religion, and ethnicity could be similarly debilitating. Lawyers of color bumped up against all the stereotypes common in the culture generally: "ignorant," "uncouth," "slovenly," "lazy."[16] Recent immigrants and Jews were often seen as "shrewd," "shifty," "undeserving and unfit."[17] Their "unwholesome manner" and "eager quest for lucre" were thought to debase the profession in the eyes of the public.[18] Again, the issue was not simply the presumed inferiority of the racial and ethnic groups, but the status and comfort of their privileged counterparts. In 1912, when the American Bar Association unknowingly admitted three blacks, members voted to institute a racial restriction that would "kee[p] pure the Anglo Saxon race"; the policy remained in force until 1941.[19] Other local bars took similar actions in order to preserve the "dignity" of their organizations, and some extended the exclusion even to law libraries.[20] The problem was not only prejudice among whites but also its influence among blacks and other disadvantaged groups. Many clients of color were reluctant to hire lawyers of their own background out of concern that they would be ineffective in a biased legal system.[21] Making a living was often impossible; a 1920 survey found that half of black lawyers in the south not were practicing law.[22]

132   LAWYERS AS LEADERS

For women of color, the combined impact of racial and gender bias was particularly daunting. A 1940 survey revealed only 57 black women attorneys in the entire country.[23] The experience of the nation's first black woman lawyer in the United States was all too typical. Charlotte Ray gained admission at Howard Law School in 1868 by applying under her initials and persisting despite the "commotion."[24] Yet despite what contemporaries described as a "fine mind" and demonstrated expertise in corporate law, she found no one willing to hire her, and ended up barely making a living as a public school teacher.[25]

From a leadership standpoint, what bears emphasis is not simply the extent of discrimination but also the strategies that enabled some lawyers to mount successful challenges. While few obtained positions of prominence, they often played leadership roles in the struggle for equal rights. Although the strategies varied somewhat by group, given the different sources of prejudice that each confronted, there are some overarching patterns that shed light on contemporary challenges.

These early women and minority leaders became interested in law for a mix of reasons, many unrelated to aspirations of leadership. Women typically sought intellectual challenge and economic security beyond what was available in the limited female occupations available such as teaching, dressmaking, and secretarial work. Some wives began with a desire to support their husbands; others turned to law when their husbands failed to support them. Myra Bradwell started as a helpmate, but then established a prominent legal journal that her husband ended up assisting.[26] As chapter 3 noted, Clara Foltz, California's first woman lawyer, launched a highly successful career as courtroom advocate and social activist after being abandoned by the father of her five children.[27]

Lawyers of color similarly sought escape from the low-level menial jobs that were assumed appropriate to their abilities. Some stiffened their resolve in response to suggestions that law was an unrealistic aspiration. Antonia Hernandez, who worked in the fields as a child and later headed the Mexican American Legal Defense Fund, was told that despite her excellent grades, she was not "college material" and that law was out of the question because "You're a girl."[28] The teachers of one of Seattle's first Latino lawyers suggested that he train as an auto mechanic instead of an attorney.[29] Other experiences of discrimination also launched many of these early leaders on a path of activism. The virulent racism and petty indignities that were part of Charles Houston's daily life in segregated Washington and in the armed forces during World War I convinced him to enter law and then to inspire legions of civil rights lawyers during his deanship at Howard and his work for NAACP.[30] Cruz Reynoso, the son of farm workers who later became a justice on the California Supreme Court, observed the injustices of racism that went unchallenged because no Spanish-speaking lawyer was available.[31]

For most of these early leaders, the support of mentors, role models, and family members was critical to their success. Myra Bradwell, who ran a successful lawyer's journal in defiance of the "Law of the Creator," had the active assistance of her husband, and used her publication to profile the achievements of other women practitioners. Clara Foltz and Belva Lockwood relied on relatives to help with childcare and domestic tasks.[32] Constance Baker Motley received her college and law school tuition, as well as a wardrobe, from a white philanthropist.[33] Raymond Alexander, a civil rights activist in the 1920s and 1930s, met the nation's first African American Assistant General through his Baptist church, and became determined to follow in his footsteps.[34] Irma Rangel, the first Mexican American woman elected to the Texas legislature, was inspired to leave teaching and enter law through the influence of Cesar Chavez and a local farm workers' attorney.[35] Thurgood Marshall fell under the wing of Charles Houston while he was at Howard Law School and later at the NAACP, and then Marshall himself served many of the same mentoring functions for Motley and other civil rights activists.[36]

These leaders' responses to discrimination fell across a spectrum ranging from resistance to resilience. Some directly challenged policies of exclusion. Belva Lockwood, who became the first female attorney in the District of Columbia, attempted enrollment at four law schools before finally obtaining a diploma in 1873. Then, on being denied admission to the Court of Claims and United States Supreme Court, she drafted legislation authorizing women's practice and enlisted the local press in her campaign. "Patient, painstaking and indefatigable," was how she described her style and she saw it as part of a broader mission. "My cause," she noted, "is the cause of thousands of women."[37] When direct confrontation appeared fruitless, these early leaders established their own practices, law schools, and bar associations. Women joined firms with family members or occasionally with each other. Sadie Alexander, the first African American woman to earn a PhD, and to gain admittance to the Pennsylvania bar, found that neither her economics degree nor her law degree was a sufficient pedigree for any law firm but her husband's.[38] Women who were frustrated by exclusionary policies of law schools launched their own schools in Boston and the District of Columbia.[39] Women denied officer positions in the black National Bar Association formed a separate division and then the National Association for Black Women Attorneys.[40]

In an effort to bolster their credibility, these early leaders generally took particular care to conform their appearance to professional standards. White men could often afford to be indifferent, at least within reasonable bounds. Thomas Jefferson was known to greet company in a state of "undress, sometimes with his slippers on," Abraham Lincoln was famously "careless but not slovenly," and the legendary twentieth-century trial lawyer Edward Bennett Williams had the "rumpled" "baggy" look of an insurance adjuster.[41] By contrast, minorities and women could not afford indifference. Jewish lawyers who appeared too "ethnic" were advised to "think Yiddish, dress British."[42] Early women lawyers obsessed over details of decorum, such as whether to wear a hat in court.[43] Black women like Motley felt the need always to be "elegantly dressed."[44] Marion Wright Edelman, founding president of the Children's Defense Fund, recalled her embarrassment at the "crestfallen" reaction of some local Mississippi blacks who came to "look for and at me" when she was in jeans and a sweatshirt. After that experience, she "never wore jeans in public again in Mississippi and made it a point to try to meet the expectations of poor black Mississippians of how a proper lady lawyer should dress and act."[45] Bella Abzug wore a hat and gloves so as not to be mistaken as a secretary.[46] But even the most conservative wardrobe choices could help only so much. Supreme Court Justice Ruth Bader Ginsburg discovered the limits after tying for first place in her 1959 Columbia Law School class but being rejected for law firm and clerkship positions. Justice Felix Frankfurter refused to consider her. "I can't stand girls in pants. Does she wear skirts?" he wanted to know.[47] She did, but in the end, he still felt uncomfortable with the prospect of hiring a woman.

Many of these early pioneers attempted to conform to traditional norms in other ways as well. Bradwell avoided being a "shouter of women's rights"; she distanced herself from radical tactics and challenged claims that she was a "destroyer of domesticity" by presenting herself as a devoted wife and mother.[48] Lelia Robinson, who sued the Massachusetts bar for admission, advised the Equity Club in 1888: "Do not take sex into the practice.... Simply be lawyers and recognize no distinction...between yourselves and the other members of the bar."[49] Lavinia Goodell, who brought the case challenging Wisconsin's exclusion of women, made sure she exhibited "no other alarming eccentricity than a taste for legal studies." She taught "Sunday school, attend[ed] the benevolent society and [made] cake and preserves."[50] As an Arizona state legislator, Sandra Day O'Connor earned a reputation as "attractive," "feminine," and a "pretty little thing with a disconcerting load of expertise."[51] It was, in part, her conservative image and distance from the women's movement that helped win her an appointment to the Supreme Court.[52] That, in turn, gave her the platform and independence to speak out on women's issues.

For many aspiring leaders, however, no amount of conformity could enable them to break through gender and racial barriers. Even during the height of activism around civil rights and women's rights in the 1960s and 1970s, bar leaders frequently resisted seeing problems in their own organizations. In 1971, when only nine women figured among the 1,409 partners in Wall Street's largest firms, it took federal litigation and proceedings before the New York Human Rights Commission to force some accountability.[53] King and Spaulding, one of Atlanta's most respected firms, not only challenged the application of antidiscrimination statutes to law firm partnerships, it also staged a wet tee shirt contest during the litigation to identify the female summer associate whose "body we'd like to see more of."[54] Even the few women who attended elite law schools encountered significant obstacles. When federal judge Nancy Gertner graduated from Yale Law School, her mother urged her to take the Triborough Bridge toll takers exam, "just in case."[55]

As changes in the legal, social, and political climate eroded overt forms of bias, women and minorities faced challenges of a different order. With the rise of affirmative action, they had to prove that they "deserved" the positions at issue, and were not simply the beneficiaries of preferential treatment.[56] Hard work, long hours, and exceptional competence were the strategies of choice but as chapter 2 noted, a sense of humor could be useful as well. When asked how she felt about getting her job as assistant attorney general in the Carter administration because she was a woman, Barbara Babcock responded, "It's better than not getting your job because you're a woman."[57]

The Gap between Principles and Practices

Over the last several decades, opportunities for women and minorities have dramatically increased along with public acceptance of women and minorities in leadership roles. Women now account for about 47 percent of entering law students, and minorities about 20 percent. Recent surveys find that 96 percent of Americans feel comfortable with female members of Congress or heads of law firms, 86 percent feel similarly about a Chief Justice of the Supreme Court, and 75 percent about the presidency.[58] The presence of at attorneys of color such as Barak Obama, Eric Holder, and Sonia Sotomayor in leadership roles suggests similar progress in eroding racial barriers.

Yet significant inequalities persist. In the nation's major firms, women constitute 44 percent of associates but only about 15–16 percent of equity partners, a proportion that has not significantly improved over the last fifteen years.[59] As noted earlier, in large corporations, women constitute only a fifth of general counsels.[60] These gender gaps cannot be explained by differences in the pool of qualified lawyers. Attrition rates are almost twice as high among female associates as among comparable male associates.[61] In studies comparing the likelihood of making partner by gender, men's rate ranges from two to five times greater than women's, and substantial disparities persist even when controlling for other factors, including law school grades and time out of the work force or part-time schedules.[62] Women are also underrepresented in leadership positions such as managing partners and members of governing and compensation committees.[63] So too, although female lawyers report about the same overall career satisfaction as their male colleagues, women experience greater dissatisfaction with dimensions of practice relevant to leadership opportunities, such as level of responsibility, recognition for work, and chances for advancement.[64]

Research on minority lawyers is more limited, but as noted earlier, they too are underrepresented at leadership levels such as equity partner (6 percent) and general counsel (9 percent).[65] Although they are generally satisfied with the decision to become lawyers, minorities report higher levels of dissatisfaction than white colleagues with factors relevant to leadership opportunities.[66] Of some one thousand women of color in corporate counsel offices, about half said being a woman was a significant barrier, and a third indicated that race impeded advancement.[67] In a survey of Latino lawyers, half felt ethnic identity had caused difficulties.[68]

Rarely, however, do lawyers report examples of "blatant" or "overt" discrimination.[69] And the absence of such demonstrable bias often makes it difficult for leaders to perceive problems in their own workplaces. The tendency is to attribute racial, ethnic, and gender differences in leadership to differences in choices, capabilities, and commitment that organizations have limited ability or responsibility to influence.[70] In response to an article about women's absence in leadership positions, one reader responded:

> Oh jeez, here we go again. Ever stop to think that maybe more women aren't in power because they simply don't want it. Have you ever personally known people who are at the top of large organizations? They have extreme type A personalities, a lot of enemies, and a ruined home and personal life due to the…obsessiveness require[d] in order to maintain their position.[71]

One managing partner put a similar point more diplomatically. His firm had been unable to persuade women to take leadership positions. Those with families didn't want the travel and time commitments; others were unwilling to jeopardize their practice or give up control over their schedules and their lives.[72] As one senior woman put it, management roles involve "real work and much of it is administrative and invisible. It's not that I am opting out, it's that I'm making an intelligence choice with my time."[73] At a Women's Power Summit on Law and Leadership, participants also pointed to research underscoring many women's discomfort with the pursuit and exercise of power, which is inconsistent with traditional notions of femininity.[74] Studies summarized in Sheryl Sandberg's *Lean In* similarly document the gender gap in leadership ambition that can short circuit women's careers.[75]

In accounting for the underrepresentation of leaders of color, lawyers generally blame the small pool of qualified candidates, and believe that any responses involving special preferences would be counterproductive. Research by the Minority Corporate Counsel Association finds widespread concern that affirmative action can cause resentment and "undermine....acceptance of diversity and inclusion."[76] As one white male attorney put it, giving opportunities to lawyers "based upon race, gender, or sexual identity is forcing us apart not bringing us together....I can think of few things worse for an ostensibly color blind and meritocratic society."[77]

Such attitudes help account for the relatively low priority that most legal employers attach to leveling the playing field for women and minorities. In a survey by the ABA Commission on Women in the Profession, only 27 percent of white men felt strongly that it was important to increase diversity in law firms, compared with 87 percent of women of color and 61 percent of white women.[78] A study by Catalyst similarly found that only 11 percent of white lawyers believed diversity efforts were failing to address subtle racial bias, compared with almost half of women of color.[79] Only 15 percent of white men felt that diversity efforts were failing to address subtle gender bias, compared with half of women of color and 42 percent of white women.[80] Given these views among the group that dominates leadership positions, it is scarcely surprising that many legal employers cut back their diversity efforts during the economic downturn.[81] Yet a vast array of evidence suggests that such perceptions understate the extent to which unconscious stereotypes, selective mentoring and support networks, and inflexible workplace structures disadvantage women and minorities as well as the institutions in which they practice.

Racial, Ethnic, and Gender Stereotypes

Racial, ethnic, and gender stereotypes play a well-documented role in American culture, and legal workplaces are no exception. The stereotypes vary across groups. For example, blacks and Latinos bump up against assumptions that they are less qualified. Many report that their competence is constantly questioned, and that even if they graduated from an elite law school, they are assumed to be beneficiaries of affirmative action rather than meritocratic selection.[82] Asian Americans are saddled with the myths of the "model minority"; they are thought to be smart and hardworking, but also "timid" and insufficiently assertive to command the confidence of clients and legal teams.[83] The result is that talented minorities lack the presumption of competence granted to white male counterparts; up and coming whites may be fast-tracked based on promise, while minorities need to demonstrate performance.[84] Even outstanding capabilities of a leader of color may do little to dislodge traditional assumptions. A classic example is the description that then Senator Joseph Biden offered of Barack Obama during the 2008 presidential campaign, as the "first mainstream African-American who is articulate and bright and clean and a nice-looking guy."[85] Psychologists refer to this as the "flower blooming in winter" effect.[86] Although this dynamic can provide special recognition for the exceptional leader, it does little to assist those aspiring to such roles.

Gender stereotypes also subject women to double standards and a double bind. Despite recent progress, women, like minorities, often fail to receive the presumption of competence enjoyed by white men.[87] In national surveys, between a third and three-quarters of female lawyers believe that they are held to higher standards than their colleagues.[88] A recent study of performance evaluations finds some support for those perceptions; it reveals that similar descriptions of performance result in lower ratings for women.[89] Mothers, even those working full-time, are assumed to be less available and committed, an assumption not made about fathers. In one representative study, almost three-quarters of female lawyers reported that their career commitment had been questioned when they gave birth or adopted a child. Only 9 percent of their white male colleagues, and 15 percent of minority male colleagues, had faced similar challenges.[90] Women leaders also report doubts from colleagues that they can give their all to leadership roles.[91] Yet women without family relationships sometimes face bias of a different order: they are viewed as "not quite normal" and thus "not quite leadership material."[92]

Women are also rated lower than men on qualities associated with leadership, such as assertiveness, competiveness, and business development.[93] Even though women are more likely to use effective leadership styles, people more readily credit men with leadership ability and more readily accept men as leaders.[94] An overview of more than a hundred studies confirms that women are rated lower when they adopt authoritative, seemingly masculine styles, particularly when the evaluators are men, or when the role is one typically occupied by men.[95] What is assertive in a man seems abrasive in a woman, and female leaders risk seeming too feminine or not feminine enough. Either they may appear too "soft" or too "strident"—either unable to make tough decisions or too pushy and arrogant to command respect.[96]

Self-promotion that is acceptable in men is viewed as unattractive in women.[97] In a telling Stanford Business School experiment, participants received a case study about a leading venture capitalist with outstanding networking skills. Half the participants were told that the entrepreneur was Howard Roizen; the other half were told that the individual was Heidi Roizen. The participants rated the entrepreneurs as equally competent but found Howard more likable, genuine, and kind, and Heidi more aggressive, self-promoting, and power-hungry.[98] Even the most accomplished lawyer leaders can encounter such biases. Brooksley Born, now widely acclaimed for her efforts to regulate high-risk derivatives while chair of the Commodity Futures Commission, was dismissed at the time as "abrasive," "strident," and a "lightweight wacko."[99] In commenting on those characterizations, a former aide noted, "She was serious, professional, and she held her ground against those who were not sympathetic to her position. I don't think that the failure to be 'charming' should be translated into a depiction of stridency."[100] Hillary Clinton has been subject to even more vitriolic descriptions: "power-hungry," "castrating," "Hitlerian," and "feminazi."[101] During her presidential campaign, she coped with sales of a "Hillary Clinton Nutcracker," charges that she reminded men of a scolding mother or first wife, and hecklers with signs demanding "Iron my shirt."[102]

Other cognitive biases compound the force of traditional stereotypes. People are more likely to notice and recall information that confirms their prior assumptions than information that contradicts those assumptions; the dissonant facts are filtered out.[103] For example, when lawyers assume that a working mother is unlikely to be fully committed to her career, they more easily remember the times when she left early than the times when she stayed late. Such selective recollection may help account for a study finding that where women and men worked similar hours, over a quarter of male lawyers nonetheless thought their female counterparts worked less, and a fifth rated the number of hours of these women as "fair to poor."[104] So too, when female and minority lawyers are assumed to be less effective, their failures will be recalled more readily than their achievements. Both women and minorities also receive less latitude for mistakes.[105] That, in turn, may make lawyers reluctant to seek risky "stretch assignments" that would demonstrate leadership capabilities.

Mentoring, Sponsorship, and Networks

A related set of obstacles involves in-group favoritism. Extensive research documents the preferences that individuals feel for members of their own groups. Loyalty, cooperation, favorable evaluations, mentoring, and the allocation of rewards and opportunities are greater for individuals who are similar in important respects, including gender, race, and ethnicity.[106] As a consequence, outsiders face difficulty developing "social capital:" access to advice, support, sponsorship, desirable assignments, and new business opportunities.[107] In law firms, racial and ethnic minorities often report isolation and marginalization, while many white women similarly experience exclusion from "old boys" networks.[108] In ABA research, 62 percent of women of color and 60 percent of white women, but only 4 percent of white men, felt excluded from formal and informal networking opportunities; most women and minorities would have liked better mentoring.[109]

Part of the problem lies in numbers. Many organizations lack sufficient women and minorities at senior levels who can assist others on the way up. The problem is not lack of commitment. Recent research finds little evidence for the Queen Bee syndrome, in which women reportedly keep others from getting ahead.[110] In one Catalyst study, almost three quarters of women who were actively engaged in mentoring were developing female colleagues, compared with 30 percent of men.[111] But the underrepresentation of women in leadership positions, and the time pressures for those juggling family responsibilities, leaves an inadequate pool of potential mentors. Although a growing number of organizations have formal mentoring programs, these do not always supply adequate training, rewards, or oversight to ensure effectiveness.[112] And they cannot substitute for relationships that develop naturally and that yield not simply advisors but sponsors—individuals who act as advocates and are in positions to open opportunities. Recent research on the corporate sector finds that men are substantially more likely to have such sponsors than women, and to have their help in promotions.[113] There is no reason to think law is different. As participants in one ABA study noted, many female leaders may have "good intentions," but are already pressed with competing work and family obligations or "don't have a lot of power so they can't really help you."[114] Concerns about the appearance of sexual harassment or sexual affairs discourage some men from forming mentoring relationships with junior women, and discomfort concerning issues of race and ethnicity deters some white lawyers from crossing the color divide.[115] In cross-racial mentoring relationships, candid dialogue may be particularly difficult. Minority protégés may be reluctant to raise issues of bias for fear of seeming oversensitive. White mentors may be reluctant to offer candid feedback to minority associates for fear of seeming racist or of encouraging them to leave. The result is that midlevel lawyers of color can find themselves "blindsided by soft evaluations": "your skills aren't what they are supposed to be but you didn't know because no one ever told you."[116]

Assumptions about commitment and capabilities also keep mentors from investing in female or minority subordinates who seem unlikely to stay or to succeed.[117] Such dynamics also put pressure on these lawyers to suppress their cultural identity and assimilate to prevailing norms. As one attorney of color put it, the "only way to succeed in a large firm is to make them forget you're Hispanic."[118] If a minority lawyer "just doesn't fit in," the assumption is that the problem lies with the individual, not the institution.[119]

In-group favoritism is also apparent in the allocation of work and client-development opportunities. Many organizations operate with informal systems that channels seemingly talented junior lawyers, disproportionately white men, to the leadership tracks, while relegating others to "workhorse" positions.[120] In the ABA Commission study, 44 percent of women of color, 39 percent of white women, and 25 percent of minority men reported being passed over for desirable work assignments; only 2 percent of white men noted similar experiences.[121] Other research similarly finds that women and minorities are often left out of pitches for client business.[122] Lawyers of color are also subject to "race matching"; they receive work because of their identity, not their interests, in order to create the right "look" in courtrooms, client presentations, recruiting, and marketing efforts. Although this strategy sometimes opens helpful opportunities, it can also place lawyers in what they describe as "mascot" roles, in which they are not developing their own professional skills.[123] Linda Mabry, the first minority partner in a San Francisco firm, recounts an example in which she was asked to join a pitch to a shipping company whose general counsel was African American. "When the firm made the pitch about the firm's relevant expertise, none of which I possessed, it was clear that the only reason I was there was to tout the firm's diversity, which was practically nonexistent. In that moment I wanted to fling myself through the plate-glass window of that well-appointed conference room…."[124]

Workplace Structures and Gender Roles

Escalating workplace demands and inflexible practice structures pose further obstacles to diversity and inclusion. Hourly demands have risen significantly over the last quarter century, and technology that makes it possible for lawyers to work at home makes it increasingly impossible not to. Expectations of constant accessibility have become the new norm, particularly for those in leadership positions. Law is the second most sleep-deprived profession, and long hours contribute to lawyers' disproportionate rates of stress, substance abuse, and mental health disorders.[125] These conditions of practice have made leadership positions unattractive to many lawyers, especially those with significant family responsibilities.

Despite some efforts at accommodation, a wide gap persists between formal policies and actual practices concerning work/life conflicts. Although over 90 percent of American law firms report policies permitting part-time work, only about 6 percent of lawyers actually use them.[126] Many lawyers believe, with good reason, that any reduction in hours or availability would jeopardize their leadership opportunities.[127] Stories of the "faster than a speeding bullet" maternity leave like the one that opened this chapter are still common. One woman who drafted discovery responses while timing her contractions saw it as a sensible display of commitment. If you are billing at six-minute intervals, why waste one? Those who opt for a reduced schedule after parental leave often find that it isn't worth the price. Their schedules aren't respected, their hours creep up, the quality of their assignments goes down, their pay is not proportional, and they are stigmatized as "slackers."[128]

These are not only "women's issues," but women bear their greatest impact. Despite a significant increase in men's domestic work over the last two decades, women continue to shoulder the major burden.[129] An MIT study found that only a third of male lawyers, compared with over two-thirds of female lawyers, had partners at home who were equally or more committed to their careers. Of men with children, 85 percent worked over 50-hour weeks, compared with just a third of women.[130] It is still women who are most likely to get the phone call that federal district judge Nancy Gertner received on the first day that she was about to ascend the bench: "Mama, there's no chocolate pudding in my [lunch box]."[131] An American Bar Foundation survey reported that women were about seven times more likely than men to be working part-time or to be out of the labor force, primarily due to childcare.[132] Only 2 percent of male lawyers take part-time status and many worry that taking significant time off will signal that they are no longer a "player."[133] Their fears are not without foundation. Male lawyers who make such choices suffer even greater financial and promotion costs than female colleagues who do so.[134]

These patterns are deeply rooted in traditional gender roles and cultural norms that give bragging rights to those willing to work sweatshop hours. Particularly in challenging economic times, there are no shortage of lawyers in that category. At large firms, where average billable hours are over two thousand, about three-quarters of midlevel associates described their workloads as manageable.[135] Of course those who reach such positions are a self-selected group and likely to exclude many of the most talented women that firms can ill-afford to lose. The problems are likely to increase. Millennial lawyers, defined as those from the generation born in the 1980s and 1990s, have expectations inconsistent with prevailing norms.[136] Growing numbers of men as well as women are expressing a desire for better work–life balance, and examples of those who insist on it are in increasingly visible supply at leadership levels.

Some of the nation's most prominent lawyer leaders have managed to carve out the time necessary for family commitments. As Governor of California, Earl Warren took no official calls or visitors on business while at home.[137] Bill Clinton, while president, once put off an important trip to Japan so he could help his daughter, then a high school junior, prepare for her midterms.[138] Barak Obama has refused to "do the social scene" in Washington even though it might have political payoffs because he and his wife "want to be good parents at a time that is vitally important for our kids."[139] A *New York Times* article titled, "He Breaks for Band Recitals," reported that Obama was willing to leave key meetings in order to "get home for dinner by 6 or attend a school function of his 8 and 11 year old daughters." According to senior advisor David Axelrod, certain functions are "are sacrosanct on his schedule—kid's recitals, soccer games…"[140] Yet one irony is that President Obama's commitment to a family-friendly schedule in his own life makes it harder for others to do the same. When he adjourns a meeting at 6 and resumes at 8 to allow his dinner break, other high-level officials who don't "live over the shop" end up extending their own workday well past their children's bedtimes.

Moreover, for every one of these leaders who has coped, there are countless others who lack sufficient control over their schedules to strike a manageable balance. For many lawyers, Ann -Marie Slaughter's departure from a high-level state department position because of family commitments struck a responsive chord. Her widely publicized account of "Why Women Still Can't Have It All" helps explain the persistent gender gaps at leadership levels.[141]

Although bar leaders generally acknowledge the problem of work/life balance, they often place responsibility for addressing it anywhere and everywhere else. In private practice, clients get part of the blame. Law is a service business, and their expectations of instant accessibility reportedly make reduced schedules difficult to accommodate. Resistance from supervisors can be equally problematic. Particularly in a competitive work environment, they have obvious reasons to prefer a subordinate willing to be at their "constant beck and call."[142]

Yet the problems are not as insurmountable as is often assumed. The evidence available does not find substantial resistance among clients to reduced schedules. They care about responsiveness, and part-time lawyers generally appear able to provide it.[143] In one recent survey of part-time partners, most reported that they did not even inform clients of their status and that their schedules were adapted to fit client needs.[144] Accounting, which is also a service profession, and anything but indifferent to the bottom line, has developed a business model that more than offsets the costs of work/family accommodation by increasing retention.[145] Considerable evidence suggests that law practice could do the same, and reap the benefits in higher morale, lower recruitment and training expenses, and less disruption in client and collegial relationships.[146] Although some leadership positions may be hard to reconcile with substantial family demands, many women could be ready to cycle into those positions as family obligations decrease. The challenge lies in creating workplace structures that make it easier for lawyers of both sexes to have satisfying personal as well as professional lives, and to ensure that those who temporarily step out of the workforce or reduce their workload are not permanently derailed by the decision.

The Limits of Law

Although antidiscrimination law provides some protection from overt bias, it is ill-suited to address contemporary racial, ethnic, and gender obstacles on the path to leadership. Close to fifty years experience with civil rights legislation reveals almost no final judgments of discrimination involving law firms.[147] The frequency of informal settlements is impossible to gauge, but the barriers to effective remedies are substantial. Part of the problem is the mismatch between legal definitions of discrimination and the social patterns that produce it. To prevail in a case involving professional employment, litigants generally must establish that they were treated adversely based on a prohibited characteristic, such as race, ethnicity, or sex.[148] Yet as the preceding discussion suggested, many disadvantages for women and minorities do not involve such demonstrably discriminatory treatment. Nor is it often possible for individuals to know or to prove whether they have been subject to bias, given the subjectivity of evaluation standards for professional positions. Evidentiary barriers in these cases are often insurmountable; much bias is unconscious, lawyers generally are smart enough to avoid creating paper trails of prejudice, and colleagues with corroborating evidence are reluctant to expose it for fear of jeopardizing their own positions.[149] Even those who believe that they have experienced discrimination have little incentive to come forward, given the high costs of complaining, the low likelihood of victory, and the risks of informal blacklisting.[150] Many women and minorities do not want to seem "too aggressive" or "confrontational," to look like a "bitch" or to be typecast as an "angry black."[151] Lawyers who do express concerns are often advised to "let bygones be bygone," or to "just move on."[152] The message in many law firm cultures is that "complaining never gets you anywhere.... [You are perceived as] not being a team player."[153]

Lawyers who persist in their complaints are putting their professional lives on trial, and the profiles that emerge are seldom entirely flattering. In one widely publicized case involving a gay associate who sued Wall Street's Sullivan and Cromwell for bias in promotion, characterizations of the plaintiff in press accounts included "smarmy," and a "paranoid kid with a persecution complex."[154] In an equally notorious sex discrimination suit, Philadelphia's Wolf, Block, Schorr & Solis-Cohen denied a promotion to Nancy Ezold, whom leaders believed lacked both analytic abilities and other characteristics that might compensate for the deficiency. According to one partner, "It's like the ugly girl. Everybody says she has a great personality. It turns out that [the plaintiff] didn't even have a great personality."[155] What she did have, however, was access to sufficient evidence to prevail at trial. At the time she was rejected for partnership, the firm's litigation department had just one woman out of 55 partners; nationally, by contrast, about 11 percent of partners at large firms were female.[156] Ezold had positive evaluations by the partners for whom she had worked, and a comparison with other male associates who had been promoted revealed performance concerns at least as serious as those raised about her. Characterizations of some of those men included: "wishy washy and immature," "more sizzle than steak," and "not real smart."[157] The record also revealed gender stereotypes, such as some partners' belief that Ezold was too "assertive" and too preoccupied with "women's issues."[158] Despite such evidence, the court of appeals found for the firm. In its view, the performance concerns of the two-thirds of partners who

voted against Ezold were not so "obvious or manifest" a pretext to show discrimination.[159] Yet, given the damage to the firm's reputation and recruiting
efforts, the victory was hardly a full vindication. In reflecting on the decision
not to settle the matter, one firm leader concluded: "This may have been a
case that wasn't worth winning."[160]

Similar evidentiary difficulties confront women who take reduced
schedules and find themselves out of the loop of challenging assignments
and career development opportunities. In dismissing a class action complaint brought by mothers against Bloomberg News, the district court
expressed widely prevailing views. The law "does not mandate work–life
balance." In an organization "which explicitly makes all out dedication its
expectation, making a decision that preferences family over work comes
with consequences."[161] Attorneys who experience such consequences seldom see options other than exit. One mother who returned from leave after
three years at a firm found her situation hopeless: "I was simply dropped
from all my work with no questions or discussion... It was as if I had fallen
off the planet."[162]

Not only does current antidiscrimination law provide insufficient remedies for individuals, it also offers inadequate incentives for institutions to
address unintended biases. Columbia Law Professor Susan Sturm's research
suggests that fear of liability can discourage organizations from collecting
information "that will reveal problems... or patterns of exclusion that increase
the likelihood that they will be sued."[163] Yet while law has supplied inadequate
pressures for diversity initiatives, other considerations are pushing strongly in
that direction. Both the moral and business case for diversity should inspire
leaders in law to do more to build inclusiveness in their institutions and in
their own ranks as well.

The Case for Diversity

Beginning in the late 1980s, bar leaders launched a series of initiatives designed
to increase minority representation and influence in the profession. Drawing
on arguments gaining influence in the corporate sector, they stressed the business case for diversity. As the Minority Corporate Counsel Association put
it, law firms must "commit to becoming diverse because their future, market
share, retention of talent, continuation of existing relationship with corporate
clients and performance depend on understanding and anticipating the needs
of an increasingly diverse workforce and marketplace."[164] A 2009 Manifesto

on Women in Law makes a similar business case for gender equity. Its core principles state:

A. The depth and breadth of the talent pool of women lawyers establishes a clear need for the legal profession to recruit, retain, develop and advance an exceptionally rich source of talent.
B. Women increasingly have been attaining roles of influence throughout society; legal employers must achieve gender diversity in their leadership ranks if they are to cultivate a set of leaders with legitimacy in the eyes of their clients and members of the profession.
C. Diversity adds value to legal employers in countless ways—from strengthening the effectiveness of client representation to inserting diverse perspectives and critical viewpoints in dialogues and decision making.[165]

Such claims draw on a wide range of evidence. Social science research suggests that diverse viewpoints encourage critical thinking and creative problem solving.[166] As Brooksley Born notes, women and minorities who are "not quite insiders" may find it easier to defy conventional wisdom and blow the whistle on high-risk transactions.[167] In a recent Pew Center study, of the traits most important to leadership, five were thought more common to women (honest, intelligent, compassionate, outgoing and creative), two were thought equally applicable to both sexes (hardworking and ambitious), and only one more common to men (decisiveness).[168] Some, although not all, studies also find a correlation between diversity and profitability in law firms as well as in Fortune 500 companies.[169] It is however, important not to undermine the credibility of diversity justifications by overstating the financial case. In studies finding correlations between diversity and profitability, it is unclear which way causation runs. It may well be that financial success sometimes enhances diversity rather than the converse; organizations that are on strong economic footing are better able to invest in diversity initiatives and in sound employment practices that promote both diversity and profitability.[170] Moreover, if diversity is poorly managed, it can heighten conflict and communication problems rather than enhance decision making.[171] Yet despite such qualifications, the combined moral and economic justifications for diversity remain compelling. In a profession where over half the incoming talent pool consists of women and minorities, it is reasonable to assume that firms will suffer some competitive disadvantage if they cannot effectively retain those groups and profit from differences in backgrounds and perspectives.

Moreover, an increasing number of clients are strengthening the business case for diversity by making it a factor in allocating work. Over a hundred companies have signed a Call to Action: Diversity in the Legal Profession, in which they pledge to "end or limit…relationships with firms whose performance consistently evidences a lack of meaningful interest in being diverse."[172] A growing number of clients impose specific requirements, including reports on diversity within the firm and in the teams working on their matters, as well as relevant firm policies and initiatives.[173] Wal-Mart, which has been the most public and detailed in its demands, specifies that firms must have flexible time policies and include as candidates for relationship partner for the company at least one woman, one lawyer of color, and one partner on a flexible schedule. It has also terminated relationships with firms that have failed to meet its diversity standards.[174] The Gap also inquires into flexible time policies, and sets out expectations for improvements with firms that fail to meet its goals.[175] Microsoft provides incentives for firms to hit its diversity targets.[176]

Again, it is important not to overstate the reach of these initiatives. Almost no research is available to evaluate the impact of these policies, to determine how widely they are shared, or to assess how often companies that have pledged to reduce or end representation in appropriate cases have actually done so. The only national survey on point, conducted in 2007, did not find that diversity was one of the most important factors in general counsels' choice of outside law firms, and it is unclear how much has changed in the intervening years.[177] Still, the direction of client concerns is clear, and in today's competitive climate, the economic and symbolic leverage of prominent corporations should not be discounted.

Nor should employers undervalue other considerations that underscore the importance of inclusiveness. Potential job applicants are becoming more informed about diversity and gender equity. Groups such as Building a Better Legal Profession rate firms based along these and other dimensions, and such information is readily accessible online. Moreover, apart from external pressure, workplaces have internal interests in reform. As the discussion below suggests, many practices that would improve conditions for women and lawyers of color serve other institutional objectives as well. Better mentoring programs, more equitable work assignment practices, and greater accountability of supervising attorneys are all likely to have long-term payoffs. The question then becomes how leaders can help institutionalize such initiatives and build cultures of inclusiveness. And equally important, what can women and minorities do to put themselves on a path to leadership?

Strategies for Aspiring Leaders

Women and minorities who seek leadership positions should be clear about their goals, seek challenging assignments, solicit frequent feedback, develop mentoring relationships, and cultivate a reputation for effectiveness. Succeeding in those tasks also requires attention to unconscious biases and exclusionary networks that can waylay careers.

So, for example, aspiring female leaders need to strike the right balance between "too assertive" and "not assertive enough." Surveys of successful managers and professional consultants underscore the importance of developing a leadership style that fits the organization, and is one that "men are comfortable with."[178] That finding is profoundly irritating to some lawyers. At an ABA Summit on Women's Leadership, many participants railed against asking women to adjust to men's needs. Why was the focus always on fixing the female? But as others pointed out, this is the world that aspiring women leaders inhabit, and it is not just men who find overly authoritative or self-promoting styles off-putting. To maximize effectiveness, women need ways of projecting a decisive and forceful manner without seeming arrogant or abrasive. As chapter 2 noted, experts suggest being "relentlessly pleasant" without backing down.[179] Strategies include frequently smiling, expressing appreciation and concern, invoking common interests, emphasizing others' goals as well as their own, and taking a problem-solving rather than critical stance.[180] Successful leaders such as Sandra Day O'Connor have been known for that capacity. In assessing her prospects for success in the Arizona state legislature, one political commentator noted that "Sandy...is a sharp gal" with a "steel-trap mind...and a large measure of common sense....She [also] has[a lovely smile and should use it often."[181] She did.

Formal leadership training and coaching can help in developing interpersonal styles, as well as capabilities such as risk-taking, conflict resolution, and strategic vision. Newly emerging leadership programs designed particularly for women or minorities provide particularly supportive settings for addressing their special challenges.[182] Profiles of successful leaders can also provide instructive examples of the personal initiative that opens leadership opportunities. These are not lawyers who waited for the phone to ring. Michele Mayes, one of the nation's most prominent African American general counsels, recalls that after receiving some encouragement from a woman mentor, she approached the chief legal officer at her company and "told him I wanted his job."[183] After the shock wore off, he worked up a list of the skills and experiences that she needed and recruited her to follow him to his next general counsel job. She never replaced him, but with his assistance she prepared to assume his role in other Fortune 500 companies. Louise Parent, the general counsel of American Express, describes learning to "raise my hand" for challenging assignments and being willing to take steps down and sideways on the status ladder in order to get the experience she needed.[184] Terry McClure, the General Counsel of United Parcel Service, was told she needed direct exposure to business operations if she wanted to move up at the company. After accepting a position as district manager, she suddenly found herself as a "lawyer, a black woman, [with] no operations experience walking into a...[warehouse] with all the truck drivers."[185] Her success in that role was what helped put her in the candidate pool for general counsel.

Setting priorities and managing time are also critical leadership skills. Establishing boundaries, delegating domestic tasks, and giving up on perfection are essential for those with substantial caretaking commitments. What aspiring leaders should not sacrifice is time spent developing relationships with mentors who can open doors at leadership levels.[186] To forge those strategic relationships, lawyers need to recognize that those from whom they seek assistance are under similar time pressures. The best mentoring generally goes to the best mentees, who are reasonable and focused in their needs and who try to make the relationship mutually beneficial. Lawyers who step out of the labor force should find ways of keeping professionally active. Volunteer efforts, occasional paying projects, continuing legal education, and reentry programs can all aid the transition back.

Strategies for Organizations and Their Leaders

Supporting aspiring leaders is itself a leadership skill, and one that has received inadequate attention in many legal workplaces. The most important factor in ensuring equal access to leadership opportunities is a commitment to that objective, which is reflected in organizational policies, priorities, and reward structures.[187] That commitment needs to come from the top. An organization's leadership needs to not simply acknowledge the importance of diversity, but also to establish structures for promoting it, and to hold individuals accountable for the results. The most successful approaches tend to involve task forces or committees with diverse and influential members who have credibility with their colleagues and a stake in the results.[188] The mission of that group should be to identify problems, develop responses, and monitor their effectiveness.

As an ABA Presidential Commission on Diversity recognized, self-assessment should be a critical part of all diversity initiatives.[189] Leaders need to know how policies that affect inclusiveness play out in practice. That requires collecting both quantitative and qualitative data on matters such as advancement, retention, assignments, satisfaction, mentoring, and work/family conflicts. Periodic surveys, focus groups, interviews with former and departing employees, and bottom-up evaluations of supervisors can all cast light on problems disproportionately experienced by women and minorities. Monitoring can be important not only in identifying problems and responses, but also in making people aware that their actions are being assessed. Requiring individuals to justify their decisions can help reduce unconscious bias.[190]

Whatever oversight structure an employer chooses, one central priority should be the design of effective systems of evaluation, rewards, and allocation of assignments and professional development opportunities. Supervising lawyers and department heads need to be held responsible for their performance on diversity-related issues, and that performance should be part of 360-degree evaluation structures.[191] Such accountability is, of course, far easier to advocate than to achieve, particularly given the absence of systematic research on what oversight strategies actually work. Our knowledge is mainly about what doesn't. Performance appraisals that include diversity but lack significant rewards or sanctions are unlikely to affect behavior.[192] However, we know little about what has helped firms deal with powerful partners who rate poorly on diversity, or whether incentives like mentoring awards and bonuses are effective in changing organizational culture. More experimentation and sharing of information could enable organizations to translate rhetorical commitments into institutional priorities. What research is available casts doubt on some interventions that are frequently part of diversity initiatives. One of the least effective is training. Surveyed lawyers tend to be at best "lukewarm" about the usefulness of diversity education, and experts who have studied its effectiveness are even less enthusiastic.[193] In a large-scale review of diversity initiatives across multiple industries, training programs did not significantly increase the representation or advancement of targeted groups.[194] Part of the problem is that such programs typically focus on individual behaviors not institutional problems, provide no incentives to implement recommended practices, and sometimes provoke backlash among involuntary participants.[195]

Another common strategy is networks and affinity groups for women and minorities. Almost all large firms report women's initiatives that include networking.[196] Many organizations also support groups for minority lawyers within or outside the firm. These vary in effectiveness. At their best, they provide useful advice, role models, and contacts.[197] Affinity groups for women of color can play a special role in reducing participants' sense of isolation. By bringing potential leaders together around common interests, these networks can also forge coalitions on diversity-related issues and generate useful reform proposals.[198] Yet the only large-scale study on point found that networks did not significantly assist career development; they may increase participants' sense of community but not do enough to put potential leaders "in touch with what or whom they ought to know."[199]

Among the most effective interventions is mentoring, which directly addresses the difficulties of women and minorities in obtaining the support necessary for leadership development. Many organizations have formal mentoring programs that match employees or allow individuals to select their own pairings. Well-designed initiatives that evaluate and reward mentoring activities can improve participants' skills, satisfaction, and retention rates.[200] However, most programs do not require evaluation or specify the frequency of meetings and goals for the relationship.[201] Instead, they permit a "call me if you need anything" approach, which leaves too many junior attorneys reluctant to become a burden.[202] Ineffective matching systems compound the problem; lawyers may end up with mentors with whom they have little in common.[203] Formal programs also have difficulty inspiring the kind of sponsorship that is most critical for aspiring leaders. They need advocates, not simply advisors, and that kind of support cannot be mandated.

The lesson for leaders is that they cannot simply rely on formal structures. They need to model, cultivate, and reward sponsorship of women and minorities, and to ensure that diversity is a significant dimension of leadership succession plans. Being proactive in identifying and nurturing high performers should be a high priority.[204] In building cultures of inclusion, it is important to emphasize the mutual benefits that can flow from mentoring relationships. Quite apart from the satisfaction that comes from assisting those in need of assistance, leaders may receive more tangible payoffs from fresh insights and from the loyalty and influence that their efforts secure. They can also take pride in laying the foundations for an organization that is reflective of, and responsive to, the diverse constituencies that it serves.

In building that legacy, leaders can also look beyond their own organizations and spearhead pro bono efforts to expand the pool of qualified minorities through scholarships and educational reform initiatives. For example, the law firm Skadden and Arps has pledged $10 million for a ten-year program offering law school preparation to students from disadvantaged backgrounds.[205]

As one ABA official notes, "this is the kind of money we need to make a difference.... Now we need just 500 other firms to take action."[206]

Women and minorities who are in positions of power should pay special attention to the not always intended messages that their example sends. A case in point involves a large firm's long-planned program on women's leadership that the firm's most prominent female partner did not attend. She did, however, supply all participants with one of her recent speeches, printed on expensive parchment and wrapped with firm-embossed ribbon. It was not a gesture calculated to sit well with other busy women who had made sacrifices to be present and who questioned the firm resources spent on a self-aggrandizing talk that few if any were likely to read.

By contrast, the most effective leaders are those who are personally invested in building a broad consensus for diversity, and in addressing any sources of inertia or passive resistance. This agenda needs to be seen not as a "women's" or "minority" issue, but as an organizational priority in which women and minorities have a particular stake. As consultants emphasize, "[i]nclusion can be built only through inclusion.... Change needs to happen in partnership *with* the people of the organization not *to* them."[207] Leaders are critical in creating that sense of unity and in translating rhetorical commitments into organizational priorities.

8

Leadership in Law Firms

LAW FIRMS DESERVE particular focus in a study of leadership because they are where the largest number of lawyers have opportunities to develop leadership skills and where the largest number suffer when those skills are absent. According to the most comprehensive data available, about a third of U.S. lawyers practice in law firms.[1] A majority work in firms with at least ten lawyers, and over a quarter are in firms of over a hundred lawyers, where leadership is especially critical.[2] Recent research finds that the most powerful predictor of large firm profitability is "the quality of partners' leadership skills."[3] Inept management is also at least partially responsible for growing numbers of law firm failures.[4] A further reason for focusing on firms is that although they pose some distinctive challenges, the leadership skills that they require are fairly typical of those necessary in other environments, and many lawyers use those skills in other settings. Moreover, because large firms have been the fastest growing and the most profitable and visible segment of legal practice, their leadership structures have served as models for smaller organizations.[5]

Generalizing about law firm leadership presents several challenges. The first is definitional. There is no single profile of the successful leader in part because there is no single definition of the successful firm. Indeed, one of the greatest difficulties of leadership in this setting is that those who need to be led often share no consensus about how, apart from profits, success should be measured. Although virtually all lawyers agree that profitability is important, they frequently disagree about how important it is, how profits should be distributed, and how other values should affect decision making. What importance should the firm assign to growth, diversity, work/life balance, and pro bono service, not just in principle but in practice? These disagreements reflect broader disputes within the profession and the culture generally about the priority of profit, and about size as a measure of status.

A second difficulty in talking about law firm leadership is the importance of context. Research on firms confirms the general finding, explored in chapter 2, that no single set of traits or styles works best in all circumstances. The key to success is leaders' adaptability to firm culture, goals, and market conditions. That, in turns, requires an ability to help firms capitalize on their distinctive strengths to meet the demands of their business environment.[6]

A third limitation in generalizing about leadership in firms is the inadequacy of research. The focus of most published work is on dysfunctional leadership, particularly when it leads to firm closures or ethical scandals.[7] Not enough attention has centered on success, and on fine-grained analysis of the leadership characteristics that sustain effective performance. Nor has systematic study centered on how management authority is allocated. In many firms, major influence is exercised not simply by the firm's chair or managing partner, but also by members of executive committees, and heads of local practice groups. We lack sufficient candid and corroborated accounts of the internal dynamics of enough firms to determine which governance structures are most effective across different circumstances.[8]

Despite these limitations, some general insights emerge from empirical research on law firms, and from the perspectives and career paths of prominent leaders. Although there is no single definition of effective leadership, there are some widely shared criteria, such as sustained profitability and satisfaction among stakeholders. There is also one clear measure of failure, and in-depth case histories have identified the leadership deficiencies that have contributed to law firm dissolutions. Taken together, the studies available offer some useful lessons about how lawyers can become more effective leaders.

The Historical Backdrop

To understand the challenges confronting law firm leaders, a brief historical overview is helpful. The structure of many mid- to large-size American firms has its origins in the early twentieth century, when Paul Cravath took command of Cravath Swaine & Moore. His system, which became the template for elite metropolitan firms, had several distinctive features.[9] It included an autocratic governance structure, a commitment to merit principles, and an insistence that every lawyer practice "solely as a member of the Cravath team."[10] The firm would hire recent law school graduates based on legal ability, not social or family connections.[11] After a prescribed number of years of training, young associates would move up or out. In the view of founding partners, job security for associates was unwise because a lawyer with no hope of promotion "tends to sink into a mental rut and to lose ambition; and loss of ambition invites carelessness."[12] Curiously, these leaders did not see a problem with life tenure for partners, or a lock step compensation system based on seniority not productivity.[13] Nor did Cravath founders or disciples worry about work–life balance. Sweatshop hours were common; the unstated assumption was that the exclusively male workforce would have spouses or hired help to deal with any domestic responsibilities. Swaine's history of the firm recounts a story about Moore that was probably apocryphal, but nonetheless apt. When approached by a partner who complained that the associates were being pushed too hard, Moore reportedly responded, "That's silly. No one is under pressure. There wasn't a light on when I left at two this morning."[14]

American lawyers often romanticize the early years of law firms as a time when private practice was a profession rather than a business. Compared with contemporary pressures, the challenges confronting early and mid-twentieth century firms seem to have been more manageable. Partners and clients were more loyal; "raiding" of rainmakers by rival firms was rare and information about others' compensation was not readily available.[15] Competition was less intense and threats from outside the profession or outside the United States were of little concern. In this relatively genteel environment, leaders who were obsessively legalistic on behalf of clients could be strikingly casual in dealings with each other. Many major firms did not even have written partnership agreements. "Everybody trusts everybody here," one Wall Street lawyer explained in Erwin Smigel's classic 1964 study.[16] According to a Cravath partner, "we don't want people for partners with whom we need written agreements."[17]

Yet from a leadership perspective, this environment also left much to be desired. Some firms were managed with the autocratic authoritarian style noted in chapter 1, with all the dysfunctional byproducts of disengagement and dependency.[18] An insistence on "total control" was sometimes pushed to extremes. Cromwell of Sullivan & Cromwell was notorious for fretting about whether paper clips were being reused and closet lights turned off, and he checked the cloakroom to determine if associates were in the office if they weren't at their desks.[19] Elkins of Vinson & Elkins personally made all major hiring, promotion, and compensation decisions even though in later years his choices were increasingly erratic.[20] He also believed that "Lawyers wear hats." "Therefore hats were worn."[21] After vowing that he would "be damned" if he complied, one hatless associate encountered a wrathful Elkins in an elevator. After Elkins stated the obvious, the associate ingloriously improvised: "I did have a hat but somebody stole it and I'm on my way right now to buy another one."[22] It was estimated that V& E lawyers accounted for about half the hats sold in Houston in the early 1960s.[23]

By contrast, other firm leaders were ignorant or indifferent regarding governance. In Smigel's study, the managing partner typically dealt with "everyday housekeeping problems," and exercised little real power.[24] An interviewer once asked Harrison Tweed for details about leadership issues: "You talked about the management of the firm…I don't understand that part of it." "Well," responded Tweed, "I don't either."[25] The result was often as one observer described the Phillips Nizer firm: "A good sized business that's administered as if it were still a candy store. It's a system of happy anarchy."[26] But not all the anarchies were happy and internal rivalries could be corrosive.

Even the most congenial of firms paid a price for their homogenous atmosphere. Despite their self-proclaimed myths of meritocracy, hiring and promotion systems were generally anything but. Elite firms looked for "lawyers who are Nordic, have pleasing personalities, and 'clean cut' appearances, are graduates of the 'right schools,' [and] have the 'right' social background…."[27] "Background" was the euphemism of choice for biases based on religion, race, sex, and class. As chapter 7 noted, two prominent victims were Sandra Day O'Connor and Ruth Bader Ginsburg. Both graduated at the top of their classes, O'Connor at Stanford and Ginsburg at Columbia, but found no firms willing to hire them. For Ginsburg, the problem was not just her sex. Rather, as she later noted, it was being "a woman, a Jew, and a mother to boot."[28] The firms most open to hiring female lawyers were seldom as willing to promote them, or to include them in social gatherings, many of which occurred at all male clubs.[29] "Beware of the firm looking specifically for a woman lawyer," warned one veteran. "They want you for work they cannot get any man to do."[30] Lawyers of color were notable for their absence. Some prominent southern firms like Vinson & Elkins had no blacks until the 1970s, and a 1973 survey of some 1,500 lawyers in leading Wall Street firms found only one partner who was black.[31]

Contemporary Challenges

The second half of the twentieth century brought substantial change to traditional firms. The push for diversity began in the aftermath of World War II, when anti-Semitism became less acceptable, and competition from firms with distinguished Jewish and Catholic lawyers brought home the price of bias. The civil rights and women's rights movement, together with anti-discrimination *but do they actually do this?*

legislation, lawsuits, and changes in the law school recruiting pool, also encouraged more inclusive employment practices. As chapter 7 notes, today's firms face new pressures from both lawyers and clients to attract and promote underrepresented groups, to ensure a more equitable working environment, and to address work/family conflicts.[32]

On the economic front, increases in competition, together with increases in globalization, technological innovation, and information about the legal market, have transformed the daily realities of law firm life. Technology has reduced demand for routine lawyers' services that can now be performed by computers or paralegals. Businesses facing heightened pressures in their own markets have become more sensitive to price and efficiency. Many have moved routine legal work in-house and shopped for outside counsel based on short-term concerns of price and expertise rather than long-term relationships. Corporate clients have often resisted paying for the training of junior associates, and insisted on discounts or write-offs of seemingly excessive fees.[33] Many no longer want to pay for customized legal work for routine matters. As Mark Chandler, General Counsel for Cisco put it, winners in this new environment will be "those who are able to standardize services to meet clients' cost management and predictability needs where very good is good enough."[34] Experts such as Richard Susskind have predicted that emerging technologies and outsourcing possibilities are radically transforming the delivery of legal services, and that traditional models will need to adapt accordingly.[35]

Competition inside law firms has also intensified. The increase in size, geographic dispersion, and preoccupation with short-term profits has brought less collegiality and more external and internal rivalry. Although few leaders would put it as crudely as a Finley Kumble managing partner, "[s]tealing lawyers and clients from other firms" has become "a keystone of…progress."[36] Partnership, especially in large firms, has become less accessible and less attractive. Fewer lawyers gain full equity status and it no longer promises life-time security or saner schedules.[37] To many attorneys, the struggle looks increasingly like a "pie eating contest where the prize is more pie."[38] High rates of associate attrition and lateral mobility and increased use of temporary contract attorneys give fewer lawyers a stake in serving organizational values. Partners are spending more time marketing their services and have less opportunity and incentive to mentor junior colleagues, most of whom likely to leave.

Increased compensation appears necessary to attract and retain rainmakers, which exacerbates economic inequalities and compromises collegiality. Billable hour expectations have escalated and overwork is a leading cause of inefficiency as well as disproportionately high rates of stress, substance abuse, and mental health difficulties.[39] Although the economic model of most law firms requires substantial attrition, current rates are not cost-effective. Firms report that about half of departures are unwanted, and most occur before the lawyer has generated substantial profits.[40] Excessive attrition imposes heavy recruitment and training expenses, and harder to quantify costs from disrupted client and collegial relationships.[41] Moreover, the lawyers who leave are not necessarily the ones firms want to lose; dissatisfaction rates are highest among those with the best credentials.[42]

The economic downturn that began in 2007 accelerated these challenges. Reduced demand for legal work and increased pressure to cut costs led to downsizing, layoffs, demotions of equity partners, and dissolutions of established firms.[43] Even after the economy started to recover, law firm leaders generally felt that increased price competition and pressure for efficiency were permanent changes.[44] As an Altman Weil survey concluded, the "traditional law firm profit model is under siege" and "there will be more scrutiny and accountability for lawyers at all levels."[45] In *Declining Prospects,* Michael Trotter paints a bleaker picture: "there are far more capable lawyers and law firms than there is work for them to do."[46] That situation is also unlikely to improve as long as law schools continue graduating far more students than available job openings.[47]

In this environment, experts agree that the central task of leaders is to promote a strategic vision for the firm that can attract consensus and serve its long-term values.[48] What those values are and how agreement can be achieved vary across firms, and a critical leadership skill is the ability to adapt to the organization's particular culture, capacities, and constraints. All firms, however, are necessarily focused on financial well-being, and when asked about their greatest concerns, law firm leaders generally mention economic issues: profitability, demand, pricing, and efficiency.[49] Underlying those concerns are more fundamental questions of how to reconcile financial priorities with other values that are necessary to sustain reputation and satisfaction.

In striking a balance, leaders confront challenges on several levels. Some difficulties arise from environments that are high in autonomy and low in trust.[50] Most equity partners perceive themselves as being "owners of the firm...not as employees to be managed."[51] They value independence and are often skeptical of governance structures based on shared credit, collaboration, and subordination of their own interests to the greater good. These challenges are exacerbated by lateral hiring, mergers, and branch offices.[52] The lack of face-to-face contact and shared norms makes consensus difficult. In times of "every man for himself" environment

stress, many lawyers are reluctant to make sacrifices that they are not confident will be reciprocated. As a wide range of research makes clear, individuals' willingness to make concessions for common goals is conditional on the belief that others will act similarly.[53] That confidence is often lacking in the contemporary law firm environment.

A related set of problems involves the devaluation of leadership skills and responsibilities. Lawyers often take a highly analytic view of management. They focus on financial scorecards and undervalue relational abilities. Lawyers typically rise to leadership positions because of their capabilities as lawyers and rainmakers, not as leaders, and some are difficult to work for or with.[54] As one managing partner put it, "It's like the Dutch philosopher Erasmus said, 'In the land of the blind, the one-eyed man is king.'"[55] For some leaders, no details, down to the office toilet paper, are too trivial for their attention; by contrast, others are too preoccupied with grand visions or their own practices to get essential details right.[56]

Even those who have strong managerial capabilities bump up against colleagues who do not, and whose tendency in evaluating proposals is to look for loopholes and counterexamples.[57] The result can be strategic paralysis and internal friction. Compounding these problems is the inadequate priority often given to leadership roles. Less than a third of surveyed firms make chairs among their highest-paid partners.[58] Many managing partners are not full-time managers, and their power base depends on client relationships that they are reluctant to give up.[59] Some partners with significant governance obligations bill only about 10 percent fewer hours than their peers, which leaves insufficient time for leadership responsibilities.[59] And because firms almost always fill chair vacancies from within, some lawyers are reluctant to invest too much effort in managerial roles because they will be unable to capitalize on their experience once they leave the position.

Leaders also confront more specific challenges on particular issues. Those relating to money are scarcely surprising, given the link between income and status in contemporary law firms and in the culture more generally. A *New Yorker* cartoon captures the prevailing climate. It pictures a limousine conversation in which one well-heeled professional tells his colleague "I may be overcompensated, but I'm not overcompensated enough."[61] Income expectations have risen dramatically in recent decades. In 1985, the average profits per partner for the fifty highest grossing firms was $623,000 in current dollars; today, it is more than $1.5 million.[62] Transparency has increased along with income. As Steven Brill, former editor of the *American Lawyer* has noted, once legal periodicals began publishing lawyers' salaries, "suddenly all it took for a happy partner...to become a malcontent was to read that at the firm on the next block a classmate was pulling down [$500,000] more."[63] If that partner has a valuable and transportable book of business, firms are under pressure to match any potential offer, which creates problems of lateral equity. At some large firms, top rainmakers earn ten times the income of other partners.[64] As the recent woes of Dewey LaBoef make clear, lavish compensation packages to lure laterals can become a major source of friction and instability when revenue projections fall short of expectations.[65] "Eat what you kill" compensation structures, which may seem necessary to reward rainmakers, also fuel internal rivalries, encourage hoarding, and undermine teamwork. As chapter 1 noted, consultants believe that powerful partners too often behave like warlords, "acting as temporary allies until a better opportunity comes along."[66]

Associates, for their part, have frequently demanded compensation beyond what a sensible business plan would justify. If a few firms substantially increase starting salaries or mid-level bonuses, others feel compelled to follow suit, even when, as Orrick's CEO observed, the raise has "no rational foundations."[67] Leaders worry that recruitment, retention, and morale will suffer if word goes out that their firm is "shortchanging" associates.[68] Yet whether this is always money well-spent is open to question, particularly given research that reveals no relationship between associates' satisfaction with their compensation and their expectation that they will remain at the firm for at least two more years.[69]

Related research also raises broader questions about the role of money in driving leaders' decisions. At lawyers' income level, wealth is not a good predictor of professional satisfaction.[70] Part of the reason is that satisfaction is most affected by relative, not absolute, income, and increases in pay are generally offset by changes in reference groups.[71] The increasingly public nature of lawyers' salaries has made the competition for relative status harder to resist and harder to win. There is, in fact, only so much room at the top, so this kind of arms race has few winners and many losers.[72] Moreover, attempts to attract and retain rainmakers largely through compensation miss what these partners themselves report as most important in driving decisions to move; support for their practice and law firm culture, reputation, and financial health.[73]

Leaders are caught in a vortex of competing demands with no easy solutions. Clients want to pay less, and partners and associates want to earn more, which makes it hard to invest adequately in collective goods such as mentoring, manageable hours, and public service, which affect workplace efficiency and satisfaction.[74] Surveys of law firm leaders reveal chronic difficulties on issues such as dealing with unproductive senior partners, evaluating non-financial contributions, promoting teamwork, dealing with work/life conflicts, and maintaining an "acceptable compensation ratio" across firm members.[75]

Some of these problems are likely to increase as the legal workforce ages. Over the next two decades, the number of attorneys age fifty or older will triple, and by 2020 they will account for almost half of the legal profession.[76] The increased life expectancy and improved health of this generation means that many senior lawyers will have a substantial period in which full- or part-time work is possible.[77] Their expectations often conflict with firm policies or practices that force senior attorneys into retirement. Recent surveys find that between 40 to 60 percent of firms with at least fifty lawyers have mandatory retirement policies.[78] About 40 percent of surveyed lawyers in management positions favor mandatory retirement, largely on the ground that it opens opportunities for younger colleagues, facilitates orderly transitions in leadership, and avoids awkward conversations with unproductive older partners.[79] However, most lawyers believe that such policies are too inflexible, and in 2007, the American Bar Association passed a resolution calling on firms to end mandatory retirement.[80]

Whether most firms will move in that direction remains unclear, but however they respond, the graying of the profession is likely to pose increasing challenge, including the possibility of age discrimination suits. In 2009, forty firms were subject to EEOC complaints alleging such bias.[81] Many leaders see a cautionary tale in the high-profile settlements of such cases involving Sidley & Austin and Kelley Drye.[82] Almost four out of ten Am Law 200 firms report that the treatment of senior lawyers is already a significant management problem.[83] It is likely to increase, given current demographic projections.

A final leadership challenge involves controversial clients. The recent dust-up concerning King and Spaulding is a case in point. In 2010, former Solicitor General Paul Clement committed the firm to represent Republican leaders of the House of Representatives in litigation challenging the federal Defense of Marriage Act (DOMA). That Act denies recognition to same-sex marriages even when sanctioned by state law, and the Obama Administration recently determined not to defend its constitutionality. In the wake of vehement protests by gay rights groups, King and Spaulding withdrew from representation. The firm's chair explained that "the process used for vetting this engagement was inadequate" and accepted full responsibility "for any mistakes that occurred."[84] Clement issued a public letter of resignation from the firm. It expressed his conviction that "representation should not be abandoned because the client's legal position is extremely unpopular in certain quarters.

Defending unpopular positions is what lawyers do." Many bar leaders and legal ethics experts agreed and condemned the firm for being willing to "fold like a cheap suitcase…" in response to protest.[85] The *New York Times* account quoted law professor Stephen Gillers's prediction that the firm's "timidity here will hurt weak clients, poor clients, and despised clients."[86]

To other commentators, such analogies missed the mark. The Republican leadership was scarcely "weak" or "poor" and was hardly prejudiced by this decision. Clement continued to represent them at Bancroft, his new law firm, for $520 hour. Moreover, to these observers, what made the King and Spaulding's representation particularly objectionable was a clause in the original retainer agreement. It prevented any member of the firm from "lobbying or advocacy for or against any legislation" that would "alter or amend" DOMA. Apparently Clement signed that agreement letter before submitting it to the firm's business committee for review.[87] Who among the firm's leaders knew of his action is unclear, but the statement by the firm's chair acknowledged at least his own responsibility. Certainly he and Clement should have anticipated the outcry that would be provoked by a clause attempting to muzzle their colleagues on such a fundamental issue. Acceptance of such a clause compromised the firm's public commitment to diversity and claims that it actively welcomed lesbian and gay lawyers. It was a public relations disaster for the firm's rejection of the case to be seen as a response to external pressure, rather than as a principled application of its own antidiscrimination principles.

Had the retainer agreement not included the restriction on speech, firm leaders would have faced a harder question: should they reject a client whose objectives were deeply offensive to many of their colleagues? In his letter of resignation, Clement stated that his "thoughts about the merits of DOMA are…irrelevant." Many firm members disagreed and saw no reason why the firm should lend its expertise to deny gays and lesbians a fundamental civil right. How lawyers should resolve such issues is a matter of longstanding dispute. Abraham Lincoln famously rejected a client seeking repayment of a questionable $600 debt from a poor widow with six children. Lincoln reportedly told the man that "some things legally right are not morally right. We shall not take your case but will give you a little advice for which we will charge you nothing. You seem to be a sprightly energetic man; we would advise you to try your hand at making $600 in some other way."[88]

A century and a half later, a similar issue arose when Cravath, Swaine & Moore agreed to represent Credit Suisse bank in an investigation of its complicity in laundering money that Nazis stole from victims of the Holocaust.

Prior to accepting the case, the firm held an unusual meeting of all partners to consider the question. After the meeting, the presiding partner wrote to all members of the firm acknowledging that its representation of the bank was a matter of "great moral consequence," and asserting that the firm's involvement could make a "terrible situation better" by helping to broker a "fair and just solution."[89] That explanation sat poorly with some associates who filed an open letter of protest and threatened to resign. In their view, it was "implausible that Cravath could both serve Credit Suisse and bring about the fair and honest resolution for those who suffered at the hands of the Nazis.... We suspect that, even with the best intentions, Credit Suisse's interest may be too closely connected with containing the financial consequences of scandal for justice to be served..." Under the circumstances, the firm should not lend "legitimacy" to the bank's position.[90] However, at least some prominent members of the New York bar and Jewish community disagreed. Arthur Liman argued that if responsible firms declined the case, it could end up in the hands of lawyers who saw only "dollar bills," and that "would be a disaster."[91] From a leadership standpoint, however, the important lesson is how the firm avoided having its own actions turn into a public relations disaster. By involving the full partnership in the decision, offering a principled reason for its representation, and standing firm in the face of protest, Cravath managed to avoid the kind of reputational damage that King and Spaulding suffered.

A related issue arises when one member of a firm wishes to take on a pro bono case that other members and clients may find offensive. Firm leaders vary in how they handle the issue. Some take the position that unpopular clients deserve representation; others see no reason to expend scarce resources on matters that could tarnish the firm's reputation and alienate current or potential sources of business. Either position is defensible. What is important is to have a consistent policy that is widely accepted within the firm, and to avoid taking a controversial case and then withdrawing after pressure arises.[92]

Leadership Strategies

As the title of recent *Economist* article noted, American law firms confront "A Less Gilded Future."[93] There are no universally successful responses to these challenges, but some leadership strategies are more effective than others. Strategic planning is among the most critical. Although many lawyers tend to be skeptical of the process, researchers and consultants underscore its importance.[94] Its point is to identify the firm's central mission and direction, to specify the steps necessary for achieving its goals, and to establish governance structures that advance those goals and ensure accountability for the results. When done well, the process requires leaders to face tough questions, consult widely, and forge consensus on a definition of success and measures to achieve it.[95] A realistic assessment of the firm's strengths, limitations, and market position, together with concrete initiatives and buy-in from stakeholders, are essential to such strategic planning. Leaders who try to achieve agreement by papering over differences generally find that "vague ambiguous mandates...result in vague ambiguous responses."[96]

Although the conventional assumption is that profit maximization will always be central to a firm's mission, its relative importance varies in light of other values.[97] As a presiding partner of Cravath once put it, "there has to be a lot more than money to hold a group of very smart Type A partners together."[98] Growth, reputation, public service, collegiality, quality of life, intellectual challenge, and diversity are among the other objectives that assume different priorities in different firms. Some firms thrive through a tradition of client and public service and a reward structure that is not narrowly focused on revenue production.[99] Paradoxically, leaders who focus most intensely on increasing profitability sometimes have the most difficulty achieving it. Research on corporate financial performance over a sustained period finds that companies that have made maximizing shareholder wealth the dominant concern do less well financially than businesses that have broader visions and goals.[100]

Developing and implementing a successful strategic plan generally depends on leaders' ability to "herd...factions" and forge agreement.[101] In one survey of firm leaders, almost twice as many described themselves as leading by consensus as by decree, and other research similarly finds that the characteristic they rate most highly is "builder of coalitions."[102] How leaders achieve agreement varies in light of their styles and their firms' size, culture, governance structure, and financial circumstances. Some partners receive deference because of their founding role and economic importance to the firm. "He built it. He made it. I may disagree with him but I trust his judgment" is a common view.[103] A *California Lawyer* magazine profile, *The Great Sonsini,* leaves no doubt that Wilson Sonsini operates on this principle.[104] Other leaders earn respect though their understanding of the culture and politics of the firm, and their willingness to consult widely, admit mistakes, and respond to others' concerns.[105] Particularly during their "honeymoon phase," leaders should listen to everyone, from clients to the mailroom staff, about what is working and what is not.[106] In that process, leaders need to be perceived as having not "a personal agenda," but rather a desire to do "what is best for the firm."[107]

Firms vary in how they allocate governance authority. Everything from benign dictatorships to direct democracy can work if adapted to meet evolving needs.[108] Whatever the structure, leaders should ensure that potentially divisive issues, such as compensation, promotion, or controversial clients, should be resolved through processes that are transparent, widely accepted, and responsive to competing concerns.[109] Research on organizational culture underscores the importance of making individuals feel that they are treated with fairness and respect.[110] As one chair noted, "It's much more important that your partners believe that what you're going to do is the product of an open inclusive discussion [than that]…they believe it is the right thing to do."[111] Soliciting and addressing associates' concerns can also be crucial for recruitment, retention, and engagement.

Personal example is equally important. In the 1980s, two founding partners of the Howry firm helped it weather the collapse of its antitrust practice by convincing the ten most highly compensated partners to take a steep pay cut. As one attorney recalled, "that bought a decade and a half of loyalty from junior partners," and enabled the firm to broaden its scope of practice.[112] When he was editing *The American Lawyer*, Steven Brill observed that the "leaders…of almost every successful firm that I have seen, have 'bought' their leadership role in part by sacrificing personal income for the sake of building the institution."[113] By contrast, a legacy to be avoided is that of Paul Cravath. When a committee of partners delicately raised the possibility of revisiting the compensation structure that gave him 50 percent of the firm's net proceeds, Cravath made it clear that any new arrangement was acceptable to him, provided that it left his share undisturbed.[114]

Leaders can also take innovative approaches in addressing a graying workforce. One is to better integrate senior lawyers into firm pro bono programs. Most surveyed lawyers report wanting to work after they reach retirement age, but income is not their primary motivation.[115] Many seek opportunities for meaningful service, and pro bono activities are an ideal way to give back to the community and to strengthen firms' charitable initiatives. Senior lawyers can provide valuable training and mentoring and help develop signature projects, including joint ventures with clients. Providing such opportunities can also encourage older lawyers to transition clients' paid work to younger colleagues. To that end, leaders can more actively encourage pro bono efforts by accommodating retired attorneys' substantive interests and ensuring adequate administrative support and malpractice coverage.[116]

A final, frequently neglected strategy involves cultivating future leaders and providing for orderly transfers of authority. Surveys find that only about a quarter of firms have succession plans, and only a fifth have formal leadership development programs.[117] A common assumption is that leaders will just "emerge naturally."[118] Yet as chapter 1 notes, this view understates the extent to which leadership skills can be consciously cultivated, and the value of formal programs in assisting that process. Not all lawyers who rise through the ranks "naturally" have the full range of necessary skills, and other lawyers with significant potential will not put themselves forward without direct encouragement. In recognition of that fact, a growing number of firms are creating structures to identify potential leaders and to provide the training, responsibilities, and mentoring that will support their professional development.[119] Leaders need to be proactive in grooming their own successors and in stepping aside when a transition would serve firm interests, if not necessarily their own. Organizations that have the most sustained financial performance have leaders with "ambition not for themselves but for their [organizations]."[120]

Leadership Failures

The breakdowns of prominent firms during the early twenty-first century provide further insights into leadership strategies, particularly those unlikely to be effective. When fistfights break out or vases are smashed on partners' doorsteps after hours, it seems fair to infer that "mistakes were made."[121] A Hildebrandt Institute study of some eighty failed law firms found that about half had "fundamental flaws... [stemming] from a lack of clear strategies, of clearly articulated and compatible goals among their partners, and of strong leadership to achieve their mutually shared strategic visions."[122] Problems fell into three main categories. The first was inadequate financial performance, typically involving unproductive partners, excessive borrowing to fuel growth or sustain profits, and poor "financial hygiene," such as failing to control partners' discounts on fees. A second category of problems involved internal dynamics, including the absence of a realistic strategic focus, loss of trust, and poorly conceived compensation structures. A third group of difficulties involved external competitive pressures, and leaders' failure to respond to market trends as well as to manage partner expectations in light of those dynamics.[123] Enough details are publicly available about some breakdowns to suggest more specific leadership lessons.[124]

At its height, Brobeck, Phleger & Harrison LLP (Brobeck) was one of the nation's most respected firms. It had over one thousand attorneys in offices across the nation and represented prominent global corporations such as Apple, Bank of America, and Chevron.[125] When the firm dissolved in 2003, some outsiders blamed it on the recession and the high-tech boom and bust cycle.[126] However, insiders also faulted leaders who were unable to forge consensus in an exceptionally competitive, combative, and Balkanized workplace. Longstanding differences over growth and compensation came to a head as the economy worsened. Some senior lawyers, including the firm's chair, Tower Snow, believed that the partners should take pay cuts during the downturn. To Snow, it seemed "only fair that the people who had benefited the most from the boom should absorb the shock of the bust. A partner who earned hundreds of thousands of bucks a year instead of $1.17 million would still be rich. A laid-off secretary or associate was in danger of losing every-thing."[127] As he put it to colleagues, "Do you really want to fire 100 people to put $10,000 in your pocket, $5000 of which will go to Uncle Sam?"[128] Many of his colleagues were put off by the implicit accusations of greed. In their view, "Partners are owners and [major dips in their] income are disconcerting and undesirable."[129] They circulated a no-confidence petition that triggered Snow's resignation as chair.

His replacements immediately began dismantling the firm's previous man-agement team and many day-to-day operations fell to inexperienced attorneys who were ill-equipped to handle them. Without strong central leadership, branch offices began running themselves and key partners began jumping ship with entire practice groups in tow. When the firm leadership heard that Snow and thirty colleagues were talking with British-based Clifford Chance, it summarily expelled him. By the end of 2002, some seventy partners had left and the firm had trouble paying bills, funding retirement accounts, and renegotiating leases.[130] To avoid reducing partner income, the firm also began drawing down its line of credit. The situation worsened when Citibank demanded repayment of the debt. Partners then agreed to compensation cuts, but another group of defections caused negotiations over leases and a poten-tial merger to collapse, and the firm filed for bankruptcy.[131]

Another prominent meltdown involved Wolf Block, a distinguished Philadelphia-based firm with nine offices. The precipitating cause of its 2009 collapse was the recession, particularly the downturn in the real estate mar-ket, which accounted for about 40 percent of the firm's revenues. Deeper problems reflected failures of leadership. For a decade, the firm was chaired by a "Troika" that reportedly "ruled by fear" and secrecy.[132] Its approach led to hoarding of clients, defections of partners, and a failure to diversify into profitable specialties. The chair who replaced the Troika was a pleasant and talented attorney, but an indecisive leader who was unwilling to make tough choices or pressure colleagues to do so.[133] When the firm faced difficulties in obtaining a necessary line of credit, many partners were reluctant to accept the loan out of fear that others would leave and those remaining would be stuck with the debt. The chair's equivocation about his own plan was the final straw.

After the antitrust and intellectual property powerhouse Howrey disbanded in 2011, its Chair Robert Ruyak blamed market factors and partners' willingness to offer flat, discounted, and contingent fee arrangements that yielded insufficient and irregular profits.[134] His colleagues identified a range of leadership failures: overly optimistic financial projections, excessive emphasis on growth, high-risk investments in contingent fee cases, lack of disclosure and consultation concerning the firm's financial difficulties, and an unwillingness to prune unproductive partners or to rein in problematic billing practices.[135] With the rapid acquisition of laterals and branch offices, the firm lost much of its "cultural glue"; new hires were not well-integrated into the organizational culture, and the governance structure was not designed to encourage collaboration and consensus.[136] Ruyak's focus on establishing new European offices diverted attention from other managerial concerns, and the process for acquisition lacked due diligence; no one was studying the factors likely to influence profitability, and the results were often disappointing.[137] Financial problems were increasing by the time of a 2008 partner's retreat, where Ruyak provided a pamphlet with an unintentionally prescient title: "Our Iceberg is Melting." Although his point was to underscore partners' need to pay attention to their market surroundings, Ruyak gave an unduly rosy account of the firm's overall position. "Howrey: Succeeding Against All Odds" was the title of his accompanying report.[138] In fact, it wasn't and members of the executive committee were playing a passive role. Ruyak's style was to present them with "prepackaged" plans and say "This is what I'm doing. Does anyone disagree?"[139] The deaths of two high-earning partners, unprofitable branches, and four straight years of declines in demand took their toll on compensation, and jeopardized a credit agreement with Citibank. No other partner was willing or able to replace Ruyak, and heads of profitable practice groups began to depart rather than do the "heavy lifting" necessary to keep the firm together.[140] In a comment that speaks volumes about the lack of insight that led to the failure, Ruyak looked back on his own performance and concluded "I have no regrets."[141]

Coudert Brothers, an international pioneer with a 150-year legacy and twenty-eight offices around the world, confronted similar difficulties. It declared bankruptcy in 2005 and years of infighting followed about who owed what to whom.[142] By all accounts, the firm's demise was attributable to overly ambitious expansion. Coudert prided itself on being the first American firm in distant locations like Singapore and Moscow, whether or not they were profitable. As one former partner noted, its overseas offices were based on "opportunity and impulse, rather than thorough analysis of business potential..."[143] Faced with growing global competition and an inadequate domestic client base to feed its international offices, the firm began to curtail compensation and lose partners. Rivals "cherry picked" the highest earners who could sometimes double their incomes by leaving.[144] In summarizing the problem, the great grandson of one of the founders noted, "You have to have a strategy. I don't think we ever did."[145]

Jenkins and Gilchrest, by contrast, had a clear strategy, but one based on excessive risk and ambition. This pillar of the Dallas legal establishment, and at one point the fastest growing firm in the United States, disbanded in 2007 to avoid prosecution for tax fraud.[146] The firm also paid a $76 million penalty, settled a client class action suit for $81.5 million, and publicly acknowledged that it had "marketed fraudulent tax shelters and failed to exercise effective oversight and control over the firm's tax shelter practice."[147] Underlying the debacle was the desire of a regional firm for a national presence and reputation. Beginning in the late 1990s, Jenkins launched a plan of rapid expansion. To staff eight new offices, leaders looked for lateral acquisitions with premium business. To lure those high earners, the firm needed to boost its profits per partner.[148] Accordingly, in 1998, leaders recruited Paul Dauguerdas, a partner with a highly lucrative tax shelter practice. It was a controversial decision. Some partners questioned the legality of his shelter plans and the potential malpractice exposure that they created. Concerns also surfaced about his "difficult" personality and the compensation structure that he demanded, which gave him an above-average percentage of the revenue that his shelter practice generated, rather than the customary arrangement of a share of the firm's overall profits, with adjustments for revenue generation.[149] The effect was to give him a large stake in growing his practice but not in the firm's overall well-being. Moreover, he would be working from a new branch office in Chicago, which lessened opportunities for informal oversight and integration into the firm culture. On balance, however, firm leaders thought that his practice would be worth the price. No lawyer had ever been sued, much less prosecuted, for giving a shelter opinion and the IRS was not then much concerned with policing abuses.[150] According to William Durbin, the principle champion of Daugerdas and the firm's later chair, his recruitment promised a highly profitable and "not a terribly risky" way to give the firm a presence in another major metropolitan area.[151]

Firm leaders were right about the profits and wrong about the risks, and grossly underestimated both. Daugerdas had initially projected that his practice would generate $6 million in its first year. In fact, by 2000 it was accounting for fifteen times that amount, almost a third of Jenkins's total revenues.[152] In four years, his shelter practice reportedly generated $267 million in revenue for the firm and $95 million for himself.[153] That profit level could not help but raise ethical questions. How could his work be so much more lucrative than that of other top tier firms if it was perfectly legal? Although his practice did dramatically boost profits per partner, he proved difficult in other respects. He failed to disclose side business arrangements, continually complained about compensation, and fought with the Texas partner whom the firm had designated to provide a second opinion on the legality of his shelter opinions. That lawyer, not a shelter expert, was suddenly deluged with an overwhelming volume of fact-sensitive transactions and could scarcely provide close oversight. As Georgetown law professor Milton Regan notes, anyone in that position would face "powerful pressures to sign off on opinions generating such a huge stream of revenue."[154]

In 2001, the problems with Daugerdas had become sufficiently apparent that the firm's governing board agreed in a straw vote to ask him to leave. However, it delayed taking formal action in an effort to close the year in a strong financial position. Then Durbin took over as chair, and was, by his own account, "bottom-line oriented."[155] No ouster occurred. Lawsuits by clients and a competitor, as well as an investigation by the IRS, forced the end of Daugerdas's shelter practice in 2002, but not his departure. As one former Jenkins partner explained, "You don't want to be at war with someone who is a primary witness in defending yourself."[156] To compensate for the lost tax revenue, Durbin proposed de-equitizing some lower earning partners, a highly divisive strategy.

By 2004, internal acrimony and external lawsuits were taking their toll. Durbin was forced to resign, Daugerdas left under pressure, and other lawyers began to depart. Jenkins's new leaders began merger discussions, but found no firm willing to commit until the civil and criminal liability issues were resolved. By the time that happened, it was too late. Departures had escalated and a no-prosecution agreement with the government was conditional on the firm's dissolution. A further posthumous blow to the firm's reputation came with felony convictions of Daugerdas and two other Jenkins tax partners.[157] Looking back on the debacle, Durbin issued a strong statement of regret about his preoccupation with profits and failure to close down the shelter work when problems surfaced. "I wish I could have been more coura-geous. I played a very large part in bringing about the demise of a firm…that I loved."[158]

In 2012, a stunned legal profession watched as one of New York's largest and most distinguished firms, Dewey & LeBoeuf, imploded. No one doubted that leadership failures were partly responsible. Following a merger in 2007, the firm negotiated lavish pay arrangements with key partners and lured laterals with multimillion dollar, multiyear guarantees. The result was gross inequal-ity in compensation; partners' incomes ranged from $300,00 to $7,000,000.[159] To finance expansion, the firm took on massive debt, and when the economic slowdown hit and revenues shrank, the firm kept expanding. Its leader, Steve Davis, was described as a "vision guy, not an execution guy," and the manage-ment committee failed to compensate for his weaknesses.[160] It also failed to demand transparency concerning compensation packages, and partners were not aware that about a third of the partners had guaranteed incomes not tied to performance.[161] Nor did they learn that the firm's obligations in current and deferred compensation exceeded profits by $250 million until the firm was on the edge of bankruptcy.[162] As it became unable to meet its financial obligations, layoffs and an exodus of partners followed. As one expert summed up widely held views, "This absolutely falls into the category: What were they thinking? This was Mismanagement 101 across the board."[163]

The distinctiveness of Dewey's plight has been subject to debate. Certainly some of its problems seem attributable to its own mistakes: the size and dura-tion of compensation guarantees, the amount of long-term debt, and the possible financial irregularities by its chair, which triggered a criminal investi-gation and civil claim for fraud.[164] But some of its problems are widely shared. Representative articles ran under titles such as "Dewey's Fall Underscores Law Firms' New Reality," and "Dewey & LeBoeuf Crisis Mirrors the Legal Industry's Woes."[165] Intense competition for clients and for partners who seem able to deliver them are endemic to the legal market. Many firms have relied on compensation guarantees in order to hire laterally and found that they are "extremely corrosive culturally because they are divorced from individual or firm performance…."[166] As Michael Trotter summarized the situation, "Dewey's problems are [not] just a matter of a management mistake here or there but instead reflect a change in the fundamental competitive environ-ment in the legal services industry." [167] Dewey could not "generate enough legal business at high enough prices to meet the income expectations of its partners."[168] Dewey's woes are widely shared, and in Trotter's views, other firms may well suffer a similar fate.

Lessons for Leaders

"Every unhappy law firm is unhappy in its own way," notes Milton Regan.[169] But some pathologies are more common than others and underscore the leadership lessons noted earlier. One is the importance of a strategic vision that is both inspirational and realistic. As chapter 4 indicated, cognitive biases toward optimism and over-confidence are particularly problematic in leadership settings. To prevent defections, rally the troops, and burnish their own image, leaders are often prone to emphasize the positive. Without a culture and governance structure that encourages transparency, divisive issues and discomfiting trends may get buried. In many of the failed firms, influential partners failed to keep leaders honest, ask tough questions, and demand corrective actions. According to Howrey's consultant Peter Zeughauser, no one on the executive committee "ever put their foot down to ask for more and earlier information."[170] Some Jenkins and Dewey partners similarly "turned a blind eye."[171] Although these tendencies can never be wholly avoided, they can be mitigated by formal checks and balances in oversight, and by informal norms requiring candor and accountability.[172]

A second set of insights fall under the category "be careful what you wish for." A fixation on growth or profits per partner comes at a price. Particularly when leaders see size as a measure of status rather than a rational economic strategy, they are setting themselves up for problems. Steven Kumble helped guide Finley and Kumble to bankruptcy by aspiring to be the biggest law firm in America and to enable lawyers to "make as much money as they could as fast as they could." "Why don't we concentrate on being the best?", asked one irate colleague. "Then we can think about becoming the biggest." "When [we're] the biggest," Kumble responded, "everyone will think we're the best."[173] Everyone didn't. And because money had been the only real glue holding the firm together, partners departed when profits slowed.[174] Firms that expand quickly through mergers, lateral acquisitions, and branch offices have difficulty sustaining a common culture and pursuing core values apart from profits. As in other business contexts, synergies are easier to envision than achieve, and ensuring a good fit requires considerable due diligence at the outset.[175] Gaining consensus can be a daunting task when lawyers are spread across "different economic environments with different risks" and different practice norms.[176] Yet focusing single-mindedly on the one concern that everyone shares—money—raises problems of its own, as several of the preceding examples demonstrate. "Greed is definitely not good" is the lesson that some commentators drew from the demise of Jenkins.[177] But such clichés are beside the point in the world that leaders inhabit. Greed is rampant, and needs to be managed, not simply lamented.

There are no all-purpose prescriptions. One of leaders' greatest challenges lies in balancing concerns of partners whose productivity suffers from factors beyond their control and the reluctance of high earners to subsidize those colleagues. "We are the only industry that carries their wounded," noted one managing partner, and many see this as a luxury their firms cannot afford.[178] "De-equitize the couch potatoes," and "clean out...the weak links [and] deadwood," is their prescription.[179] By contrast, others believe that assisting partners who are victims of market swings or temporary personal problems is part of what distinguishes professional firms from businesses. An excessive focus on rainmaking or billable hours can erode collegiality and cooperation, and devalue other contributions to law firm performance, such as mentoring, recruitment, management, and pro bono service. A central leadership priority should be establishing widely accepted processes for resolving these issues before tensions and departures escalate.

A related priority should be cultivating the sense of group identity and institutional loyalty that tends to reduce self-interested behavior.[180] As law professors Ronald Gilson and Robert Mnookin famously argued, a strong firm culture and firm-specific capital are the best ways to prevent lawyers from "shirking, grabbing, and leaving."[181] To that end, leaders should focus on cultivating the firm's internal and external reputation, treating all lawyers with concern and respect, and modeling institutional commitment.

A related leadership lesson is to beware of quick fixes to long-term difficulties. The financial crises that can precipitate firm failures are often symptomatic of deeper productivity problems and conflicting organizational priorities. Short-term strategies such as additional borrowing or layoffs are no solution to these deeper difficulties. Such strategies may temporarily sustain profits and prevent defections, but they do not increase productivity or efficiency, and they may paper over conflicts that will ultimately prove fatal.[182] Leaders need realistic initiatives to boost performance, such as developing more profitable specialties, and improving staff utilization, client satisfaction, and marketing strategies.[183] For example, one firm helped its real estate practice rebound from a slump in the market by focusing on "premium work for premium clients" and by providing attorneys with personalized development plans and candid feedback.[184] Other firms have begun to develop quality management programs that stress continuous self-assessment through standardization of routine tasks, performance measures, and peer review.[185]

To promote effective governance, firms need to pay more attention to leadership development and succession. One strategy is to institute in-house leadership initiatives. These programs typically offer specially tailored workshops and projects, and provide participants with mentors who design individualized professional development plans and monitor performance.[186] Creating stepping-stone positions designed to build leadership experience can also be useful.[187] Leadership roles should not be used as rewards for successful rainmakers who lack the time and skills to commit to governance.[188] Of equal importance is assisting lawyers manage a smooth transition out of leadership positions. Many of these individuals have their identities tied bound up in their governance role, and may have difficulty envisioning a future with lesser responsibility, power, and prestige.[189] It helps to formalizing a succession plan that provides adequate support for retiring leaders to rebuild their practice or reimagine an alternative. Nurturing new talent and paving the way for their successors is the ultimate test of a successful leader.

Finally, the challenges that leaders encounter in their own firms should encourage involvement in broader debates over practice structures. Other nations and other professions have outpaced American law firms in innovations concerning governance, lay investment, and service delivery.[190] The merits of these initiatives deserve consideration. As Richard Susskind notes, it has been "hard to convince a room full of millionaires that they have their business model wrong."[191] But American firm leaders need to be open to that possibility. In an increasingly globalized practice setting, they need to learn from their competition and to develop professional conduct rules that permit cost-effective innovations. Lawyers with personal leadership experience have much to contribute in wider dialogues about how best to meet the structural challenges facing contemporary law firms.

9

Leadership for Social Change

LEADERS ARE, BY definition, at the forefront of social change and the legal profession is well-represented among them. As government officials and heads of nonprofit organizations and social movements, lawyers play a critical role in cultural transformation. Although their positions vary, they also confront common challenges in defining goals, forging coalitions, mobilizing followers, and attracting support. Yet despite the importance of leaders in social change, their role has only recently received systematic analysis, and little of that analysis has focused directly on lawyers.[1] This chapter aims to help fill that gap.

Drawing from a broader literature on social movements, the discussion below explores ways that lawyer leaders can play a more effective transformative role.[2] Analysis begins with an overview of conditions that are likely to yield such movements and the task of leaders in creating or capitalizing on such conditions. More in-depth analysis then explores two American civil rights campaigns that have brought about major cultural change over the last half century: campaigns challenging discrimination based on race and on sexual orientation.

The Conditions of Social Change

Social change arises from a complex interrelationship of social, economic, and political forces. Leaders both influence and are influenced by those forces. Yet how much leadership matters compared with other factors is difficult to assess. Research on the same social movements often comes to different conclusions. For example, some accounts of Martin Luther King's role in the American civil rights campaign insist that that "the movement made Martin; Martin did not make the movement."[3] According to Clayborn Carson, director of Stanford University's Martin Luther King Papers Project, even without

King "the black struggle would have followed a course of development similar to the one it did."[4] King himself famously suggested as much before a mass meeting during the 1955 Montgomery bus boycott: "If M.L. King had never been born, this movement would have taken place. I just happened to be here. You know there comes a time when time itself is ready for change."[5] Yet others believe that the skills King brought to the movement were critical in shaping its early successes; the "times were ready for King," but so also "King was ready for the times."[6] Cross-cultural research also underscores the importance of leadership capabilities. Similar public policy initiatives in similar circumstances have had different outcomes due to leaders' different skills and strategies.[7]

In any event, whatever the relative importance of leaders, one of their key characteristics is the ability to capitalize on conditions conducive to change. Those conditions often arise from an interplay of social, economic, and political dynamics. For example, the contemporary American women's movement arose at a time when traditional gender roles had fallen increasingly out of step with demographic realities. Increasing longevity and access to birth control meant that women in the 1960s could anticipate spending about two-thirds of their lives without children under eighteen. These changes in family patterns, together with the economy's rising demand for trained workers, propelled growing numbers of women into the workforce. The prejudice they encountered there, as well as in political activities, became a catalyst for change.[8] A related factor was President Kennedy's appointment of a Commission on Women with the official mandate of recommending changes to further the "full realization of women's rights." An unofficial mandate was to discharge political debts to his female campaign workers, none of whom obtained other significant administration posts. Leaders of the Commission took full advantage of their opportunity. Not only did they recommend legislation such as the Equal Pay Act, they also created task forces and a Citizen's Advisory Council that began documenting problems of discrimination and placing them on the political agenda.[9] Other leaders outside the Commission then capitalized on this agenda and created women's legal rights organizations to pursue it.

Another catalyst for social change is some pivotal event, such as a disaster, crisis, or violence that captures widespread attention. For example, media coverage of southern police brutalizing peaceful civil rights protesters in the early 1960s helped build the necessary coalitions for antidiscrimination statutes and enforcement efforts.[10] Coastal oil spills, accidents at the Three Mile Island and Chernobyl nuclear reactors, and mounting evidence of global climate change all raised public consciousness and generated support for environmental organizations.[11] The 1991 televised hearings at which Anita Hill testified before a male-dominated Senate Committee concerning sexual harassment by Supreme Court nominee Clarence Thomas galvanized the women's movement and led to significant advances in women's political representation and policy objectives.[12] That same year, an announcement by the Cracker Barrel restaurant chain that it would terminate employees whose sexual orientation failed to match "normal heterosexual values" raised awareness of homophobia, prompted formation of gay and lesbian workplace task forces, and laid the foundation for other advocacy organizations.[13]

A further impetus for social change comes from widespread recognition of injustice and some general consensus about causes and potentially effective responses.[14] Those perceptions of grievances typically arise less from objective circumstances than from a sense of relative deprivation—peoples' conviction either that their circumstances have fallen short of expectations or that they are disadvantaged relative to another relevant reference group.[15] Occupy Wall Street and its slogan, "we are the 99 percent," is a classic illustration. Another is the gender gap in wages publicized by women's organizations. Social movements often draw on such indignation as well as a sense of collective identity based on shared characteristics, experiences, or ideology.[16] Participants must see their own status and interests connected to those of a broader group, and leaders need ways to build that sense of common purpose.[17]

The Qualities of Leaders

As chapter 1 suggested and studies of social change confirm, what makes for successful leadership depends on context. Campaigns have different needs at different times, stages, and levels. Typically, they benefit from a combination of what sociologists label universal cultural capital, local cultural capital, and symbolic capital.[18] Universal cultural capital, as French theorist Pierre Bourdieu famously described it, refers to individuals' general knowledge, capabilities, and social networks: education, background, analytic abilities, communication skills, and ties to government, media, and funders. Leaders must be able to work effectively in multiple settings with widely different audiences. Local cultural capital refers to individuals' knowledge of the particular groups they are seeking to lead and their shared history or relationships with members. Symbolic capital involves the legitimacy conferred by particular affiliations or positions, such as being a head of an organization, a member of a prominent respected family, a target of repression, or a role model of personal sacrifice.

No single individual may be strong on all these dimensions, but most lawyer leaders stand out on at least one. Louis Brandeis was a leader rich in general social capital. His legendary analytic and organizational abilities helped him orchestrate a broad range of progressive social campaigns. His rebuilding of a moribund American Zionist movement after World War II transformed a federation with a $12,000 budget into a multimillion dollar organization with considerable political power.[19] By communicating a vision of Palestine as a home for displaced and persecuted European Jews, he tapped into Jewish Americans' sense of cultural heritage and religious identity. By contrast, a lawyer who earned a *New York Times Magazine* profile for building local capital is John Rosenberg, the head of the Appalachian Research and Defense Fund. When Rosenberg arrived in Western Kentucky, the local residents saw him as a radical and a communist, and refused to rent him office space.[20] Two decades later, he was inducted into the County Chamber of Commerce Hall of Fame. What makes that honor particularly impressive is that he had spent the intervening years suing the establishment on behalf of the poor. But he had also won broad-based support for his work in local charities and community organizations. Over time, as the executive director of the Kentucky Bar Association put it, "familiarity bred respect."[21]

Symbolic capital comes to lawyers from multiple sources. Some achieve it through family relationships. When naming his 34-year-old brother Attorney General, John Kennedy famously quipped that "I just wanted to give him a little legal practice before he becomes a lawyer."[22] Other leaders earn legitimacy through personal sacrifice. Steve Bright, Director of the Southern Center for Human rights, takes no salary and works the kind of hours that makes others embarrassed ever to refuse his requests by saying "I'm too busy. You'll have to do it yourself."[23] Ralph Nader has gotten similar respect for his Spartan life and sweatshop hours. He also achieved martyr status when his publication of *Unsafe at Any Speed* prompted General Motors's notoriously unsuccessful effort to have private investigators dig up damaging personal information.[24]

Leaders of social change also need the personal qualities identified in chapter 2, particularly those concerning vision and values. Part of what attracts employees, donors, and volunteers is a compelling public purpose. Those at the helm need to communicate an inspiring mission and to exemplify the personal integrity that builds widespread trust and commitment. They also need the inner resolve and resilience that will enable them to stay the course over the sustained period generally necessary for significant progress. Leaders of high-impact organizations tend to share internal leadership and nurture external networks.[25] The less established the organizational structure, the more critical the leader's capabilities, particularly those that involve developing the capabilities of others. Lawyers who are most successful in achieving social impact focus on developing organizational and collaborative capacities.[26] They are willing to sacrifice personal credit and control to achieve effective alliances.[27] Sustained change requires movement-centered leaders, not leader-centered movements.[28] lead - don't overwhelm

Ralph Nader offers a textbook case of a lawyer who lost sight of that difference. In his early consumer organizing work, he was generally successful in avoiding what he described as the "lone ranger effect." "The function of leaders," he often observed, "is to produce more leaders."[29] But his political campaigns in 2000 and 2004 were generally regarded as exercises in self-indulgent narcissism with a significant social cost; he was widely blamed for stealing Florida voters who otherwise would have given Gore a victory over Bush.[30] There are, as one commentator observed, some "colossal egos" in public interest law, and "everyone wants their fiefdom."[31] The most effective leaders are those able to subordinate their own interests to those of a broader movement.

Leadership Challenges

Leaders seeking social change confront many of the same challenges of scale, pace, and complexity described in chapter 2, but also face certain distinctive problems. One involves the diffusion of authority. In *Leadership for the Common Good,* Barbara Crosby and John Bryson note that "anyone who tries to tackle a public problem…sooner or later comes face to face with the dynamics of a shared power world."[32] Leaders of social movements typically lack coercive authority. Even governmental leaders who have such authority discover its limits in advancing social change. Some fail to make the appropriate adjustment. Eliot Spitzer, who was used to the hard power that comes from being New York's attorney general, never fully mastered his more constrained role as governor, in dealing with Albany legislators who didn't play by his rules.[33] American politicians achieve major victories only by persuading key constituencies of the necessity of change and their own stake in achieving it. In confronting important social issues where "no one is in charge," leaders need to rely on soft power and collaborative networks, often involving both governmental and nongovernmental organizations.[34]

Striking the right balance in decision-making processes poses related concerns. Either too much or too little structure can be disabling.[35] Movements can be stifled by what social theorist Robert Michels termed the "iron law of oligarchy," the tendency of leaders to hoard power, and to close off channels for diverse views and grass-roots engagement.[36] But movements can also suffer from the "tyranny of structurelessness" in which the absence of authoritative decision making leads to schisms and prevents coherent coordinated actions.[37] To avoid these pathologies, effective leaders need to create open but authoritative deliberative processes that draw on support from diverse constituencies and ensure accountability for results.[38]

The challenges of establishing such processes are complicated by recent technologies. Online organizing has created new opportunities for participation in social movements by lowering its costs. The potential of social networks to inspire collective action and financial support has been clearly demonstrated in international and domestic political movements. Social media made possible the spread of Arab Spring from Tunisia to Egypt, Yemen, Syria, and surrounding countries.[39] It also facilitated the coordination of Occupy Wall Street protests.[40] Almost 40 percent of American adults have engaged in at least one civic or political activity through social media.[41] On many issues, people can become armchair activists by pushing a few buttons. A case in point is the controversy that erupted when the House of Representative held hearings on birth control insurance coverage by religious institutions and heard testimony only from men. A picture circulated on social media with the caption, "What's wrong with this picture," and Planned Parenthood and NARL began influential online campaigns for petitions and letters to Congress supporting access to birth control. When Rush Limbaugh made offensive comments about a college student who was blocked from testifying in the hearings, online activists circulated petitions asking sponsors to pull advertisements from his radio program. At least 140 companies did so.[42] Activists have also used social networks to solicit pro bono and financial contributions for a broad range of legal rights organizations.[43] A representative example is Spark, a network founded by San Francisco legal activists, whose five thousand members have raised over a million dollars in grants and volunteer services for international grassroots women's organizations.

Yet building sustained support and effective lines of authority online is far more difficult. The Save Darfur Coalition has 1.2 million members, but each has contributed an average of only nine cents.[44] Once the Occupy movement's physical protests declined, its public following and political potential waned. So too, because online organizing networks tend to lack strong centralized leadership, they have difficulty reaching consensus and developing coherent long-term strategies. As Malcolm Gladwell notes, new technologies sometimes "make it easier for activists to express themselves and harder for that expression to have any impact."[45]

Another challenge involves timing. Leaders need to be proactive in developing goals and strategies, but also reactive in light of "windows of opportunity."[46] Effective policy entrepreneurs know when to assume the risks of seeking "big wins" and when to settle for incremental "small wins" that can build confidence, test solutions, and lay foundations for broader change.[47] The issue is frequently complicated by competition within a social movement. For example, lawyers heading public interest organizations have an obvious interest in arriving first at courthouse doors. They benefit from the influence, public attention, and donor support that comes from litigating a landmark case. Politicians gain similar rewards from sponsoring major legislative or policy initiatives. Yet moving too early on an issue can provoke backlash, entrench opposition, and generate unfavorable legal precedents. President Clinton's ill-timed efforts to secure universal health care and end sexual orientation discrimination in the military are textbook cases. Premature escalation of conflict can also demoralize supporters; it deprives them of the small victories that sustain hope and make the ends of activism seem worth its price.[48]

The challenges are compounded by leaders' frequent lack of control over key events, and the need to respond quickly in the face of unforeseen opportunities. Representative examples involve bus boycotts and sit-ins during the early civil rights campaigns. Some of the precipitating incidents arose without advance planning. Rosa Parks's refusal to move to the back of a segregated Montgomery bus was not the product of a coordinated strategy. Nor was a similar decision by two black Tallahassee college students; unlike Parks, they did not even have a history of prior involvement with any civil rights organizations. But once these events occurred, leaders saw the need to seize the momentum and to organize boycotts. Those required volunteers and financial support. Community members were necessary to help supply alternative transportation, and funds were critical to pay the legal fees of activists arrested for organizing and for operating transit vehicles without a license.[49] In some cases, involvement in protests led to an unanticipated broadening of their agendas. In Montgomery, many organizers initially had been wary of being too far out in front of public opinion, and of asking for more than a fairer system of allocating seats on public transit.[50] But resistance stiffened their resolve, and like other activists, they quickly saw the need to challenge segregation head-on. That, in turn, required seeking support beyond the local communities involved and developing coordinated protest strategies against a broad range of public accommodations. In addition to bus boycotts, leaders organized sit-ins at restaurants, sleep-ins at motels, wade-ins at beaches, and knee-ins at churches that excluded blacks.[51]

A third leadership challenge involves the complexity of many social problems and the need to work simultaneously in legislative, administrative, legal, media, business, funding, and grass roots arenas. Leaders of a wide array of public interest organizations have noted the difficulties in dealing with more complicated issues than those facing their predecessors. As the head of the Sierra Club noted, the initial focus of their legal staff was to identify polluters and "just say no. Shut it down. Clean it up."[52] The then-President of the NAACP Legal Defense Fund similarly observed that in the period after the Association was founded, "the evil was clear and visible and easy to organize around. Now evil in this crude form is rare."[53] Pursuit of racial justice requires attention to the structural causes of inequality. The same is true for women's rights organizations. The underpinnings of current gender inequalities are, as the then-President of Legal Momentum pointed out, "more complex and less susceptible to legal solutions" than the overt sexism of earlier eras.[54]

Leaders are also facing these problems in a social and fiscal climate that is less hospitable than the one in which most public interest legal organizations were founded. On some issues, the public has become more complacent; on others, it is more skeptical of the ability of government and advocacy organizations to achieve major social change. Civil rights and women's groups encounter the sense that "we've fixed that."[55] These movements' many visible achievements have eroded the sense of urgency that gave them birth. As a former NAACP Legal Defense Fund president put it, our groups are, "to some degree, victims of our own success."[56] Other organizations, such as those representing poor communities, confront a public "exhausted by their plight" and resistant to initiatives requiring additional resources.[57] So too, the growth in number of social change organizations has increased competition for public attention and donor support. In earlier eras, a small group of organizations did almost all the "heavy lifting."[58] Now, as the president of Public Advocates put it, "there is somebody for every issue."[59]

The growing conservatism of the federal judiciary also has created both substantive and procedural roadblocks to progressive campaigns. Over the last quarter-century, public interest organizations have become particularly wary of focusing too much on litigation; the result is too often "victory in the courts but...not victory in practice."[60] Judges may lack the legitimacy, expertise, and enforcement resources necessary for major reform.[61] Leaders of organizations such as the American Civil Liberties Union, the NAACP Legal Defense Fund, the Natural Resources Defense Council, the Western Center on Law and Poverty, and the National Women's Law Center all have ample experience with legal rights gone wrong.[62] Judicial decisions without a political base to support them are vulnerable to chronic noncompliance, public backlash, and statutory or doctrinal reversal.[63] Litigation is most successful when used in tandem with other strategies to gain public attention, mobilize group support, impose costs, and increase policy leverage. As Ralph Nader once summed it up: "You have to deal with the adversary on all the fronts on which the adversary deals with you."[64]

Leadership Strategies

Although what makes for effective leadership depends heavily on context, experience across a wide range of social movements suggests a few generalizable lessons, and lawyers have much to learn from examples of other successful activists. One key lesson is the importance of multifaceted approaches and strategic planning. Leaders must be ready to take advantage of unforeseen events, but they must do so in light of long-term goals and priorities. Establishing a vision for change requires widespread consultation and continuing reassessment. Leaders need a systematic process for defining objectives, identifying opportunities for leverage, enlisting stakeholders, building coalitions, and evaluating progress. "Issue opportunism" and staying power are both essential; leaders need to spot possibilities for momentum and to maintain a stable, focused presence over a long course of intermittent setbacks and incremental progress.[65]

That process often requires a broad base of support within the affected community as well as potential sympathizers outside it. A textbook example of success is Cesar Chavez's campaign to organize farm workers. The challenges were substantial. Prior organizing efforts by the predominantly white leaders of national labor organizations had been unsuccessful. Intransigence by growers, intimidation by police, and recruitment of immigrant replacements had doomed initial strike efforts.[66] Chavez, who had deep knowledge of the local community as well as ties to other potential support groups, recast the struggle to appeal to both constituencies. He stressed racial injustice, recruited clergy and college students, and organized dramatic protests. One of the most celebrated examples was a pilgrim-like march through farm worker communities timed to arrive on Easter Sunday at the California governor's mansion. The national union affiliate declined to join; its leaders insisted that the struggle was a "labor union dispute, not a civil rights movement or a religious crusade."[67] Chavez and his advisors cast the campaign as all three and exploited the expressive value of social activism. Although they had far fewer financial and organizational resources than the nationally affiliated union, they had more inspiring strategies and more enduring successes.

Most contemporary social change organizations have recognized the need for collaboration at multiple levels. As the president of the National Women's Law Center noted, "Almost never will a single organization have the capacity to achieve major policy change."[68] In a survey of fifty leading public interest organizations, close to 90 percent reported collaboration with grassroots organizations, an even higher percent reported coalitions with other public interest legal organizations, and nearly half were in partnerships with government or private sector organizations.[69] Although such alliances can pose problems of control and credit, they can also reduce costs, increase influence, expand a political base, and prevent duplicative or inconsistent strategies. But to ensure that such collaborations can work effectively, leaders often need to subordinate their own desires for recognition and to accept compromises in pursuit of common ends.

Building sophisticated "collective impact initiatives" among nonprofit, private, and government organizations may require centralized staff and decision-making structures, as well as shared evaluation systems and continuous communication.[70] For example, STRIVE, a nonprofit subsidiary of Knowledge Works, achieved dramatic improvements in Cincinnati students' educational performance through such collaboration. Organizers coordinated efforts by three hundred leaders of local organizations, including heads of influential private and corporate foundations, city government officials, school district representatives, presidents of universities, and executive directors of hundreds of education-related nonprofit groups.[71]

Even when they collaborate, most social change initiatives operate with broad aspirations and limited resources, so leaders need to be particularly adept at scaling modest successes. One strategy involves what psychologists Chip Heath and Dan Heath describe as "looking for bright spots"; other experts call it searching for "positive deviants," i.e., exceptions to general trends that hold potential for progress.[72] An example is Jerry Sternin's campaign to fight child malnutrition in Vietnam during the early 1990s. At the root of the problem was poverty, and the resulting inadequacies in food, sanitation, and clean water. Sternin found such explanations TBU—"true but useless."[73] His organization, Save the Children, lacked the capacity to make significant inroads on poverty. However, in touring rural villages, he noticed that some children fared reasonably well, despite their circumstances, and he began searching for reasons why. He found that the mothers of these children fed them more frequently in smaller amounts than was customary, and also provided a more varied diet. His strategy then was to organize local cooking classes for mothers, which could be replicated throughout the country. The result was to improve the life chances of some 2.2 million children. Similar "bright spot" strategies have yielded significant social change in a wide variety of contexts.[74] Generalizing from these examples, Heath and Heath conclude that leaders facing seemingly intractable social problems may sometimes do best by focusing less on underlying causes and more on scaling small successes.[75] As a *New Yorker* cartoon put it, at times "[w]e need a leader who is not afraid to dream incremental dreams."[76]

It may also be important to appeal to people's sense of identity as well as interests. A case history is Paul Butler's pioneering efforts to save an endangered species of parrot, found only on the Caribbean island of St. Lucia. Hunters, pet seekers, and environmental degradation had put this bird on a path to extinction. The obvious solutions—steep criminal penalties and creation of a parrot sanctuary—would require a groundswell of public support that was notably lacking. Butler, "fresh out of college, working with the forestry department, and armed with a budget in [only] the hundreds of dollars, had to figure out a way to rally the people of St. Lucia behind a parrot that most of them took for granted (and some of them ate)."[77] His answer was an appeal to national pride. He enlisted local businesses in printing bumper stickers and calling cards, and convinced ministers to preach environmental stewardship. One card featured a gorgeous parrot next to a homely American bald eagle, making it obvious whose bird looked better. The message was clear: "This parrot is ours. Nobody else has this but us. We need to cherish it and look after it." The people agreed. They passed tough laws, established a sanctuary, virtually ended illicit trade, and preserved the parrots. The conservation organization Rare has now replicated that strategy in about 120 other campaigns to save endangered species.[78]

That example points up the need for strategic responses to "common action" problems in which no individual has a significant personal stake. The difficulties are compounded in many contexts, such as global warming, where solutions seem technical, consequences are long-term, and actions by any single person or political entity are unlikely to have significant impact. To motivate change in these circumstances, it is helpful to:

- Build a sense of urgency through vivid, dramatic messages that appeal to core values and concerns (show polar bears on melting ice caps, demonstrate personal financial savings from energy conservation);

- Harness peer pressure to create social norms of responsibility (tell people that their neighbors have reduced energy consumption);
- Appeal to consumers' self-image as socially responsible individuals (link product choices to environmental stewardship);
- Advocate specific, readily achievable behavioral changes and reduce their costs (suggest home improvements and provide rebates and lists of contractors).[79]

Once leaders get a "foot in the door" and convince people to take small steps toward social responsibility, their commitment is likely to escalate.[80]

In principle, all these social change strategies seem plausible. In practice, the challenge lies in judging which will be most cost-effective in particular contexts. Lawyers involved in social movements often agree on ends but divide sharply on means. Which small successes are likely to remain small and which realistically can be scaled up? How much compromise to achieve collaboration makes sense? When should leaders wait for greater public, political, or judicial support before pursuing litigation or policy initiatives? How can they prevent ill-conceived actions by other movement supporters from derailing a coherent national strategy? Those issues are the subject of the case studies that follow.

Civil Rights in Social Context
Challenging Segregation

To gain a better sense of the leadership challenges that lawyers face in pursuit of social change, it is useful to explore representative examples in greater depth. One involves the dilemmas facing the NAACP Legal Defense Fund in orchestrating litigation challenges to racial discrimination in the mid-twentieth century. Starting in the 1930s, the NAACP Legal Defense Fund launched a plan to end state-sponsored segregation, which gradually moved from bringing isolated lawsuits to "treat[ing] each case in a context of jurisprudential development."[81] That strategy required assessing any particular challenge in light of multiple factors: were the facts sufficiently favorable, were resources available to develop the case, were the lead lawyers effective advocates, and were courts ready to rule for civil rights plaintiffs? Those questions were in dispute during the run-up to the Supreme Court's landmark school desegregation decision in *Brown v. Board of Education*. How far to push the Court was one of the key considerations. Conventional wisdom is that the Court is never too far ahead of public opinion, particularly on volatile social issues.[82] Surveys at the time indicated that slightly over half of Americans favored segregated public facilities, but 89 percent thought that blacks should have equal opportunities to get a good education.[83] NAACP leaders were convinced that those positions were irreconcilable but unsure whether a majority of Justices would agree. The key issue was whether to continue arguing that schools for blacks were in fact unequal to those for whites in resources and facilities, or whether to push the Court to declare that segregated facilities were inherently unequal.

In *Simple Justice*, Richard Kluger describes an NAACP conference in which participants struggled with this issue.

> "A judge cannot be blamed if he shrinks from precipitating a race riot"[Yale Law School Professor] John Frank told the group…. Unquestionably, the NAACP "should not hesitate in its just demands for fear of reaping the whirlwind" because "judicial victories will not be won without asking for them." But "Vigor is not recklessness," Frank asserted. "The most daring army guards its lines of retreat. So should a litigation strategist." It would be a mistake to push the attack on segregation itself to the exclusion of victories won on lesser grounds (that is, equalization). For if the Court were pushed "inescapably" to a decision on the validity of school segregation where no other element of discrimination is present, "it may decide in behalf of segregation; and the morale and prestige loss to the anti-segregation forces from such a decision would be incalculable."

Howard Law School professor James Nabrit responded with passion. Of those who said blood would run in the streets if the segregation fight was waged in the face of intransigent white-supremacists, Nabrit demanded, "Suppose it does? Shall the Negro child be required to wait for his constitutional rights until the white South is educated, industrialized, and ready to confer these rights on his children's children? No, he thundered".[84]

Although blood did run in the streets, few today doubt that NAACP leaders were right to challenge segregation directly. By the turn of the twenty-first century, close to nine out of ten Americans supported the *Brown* ruling.[85] At the time, however, the issue was by no means clear, and both sides misjudged key considerations that underpinned the decision to claim that separate could never be equal. Some black leaders feared that demands for integration would lead to cuts in already meager financial support for black schools.[86] NAACP advisors such as Harvard law professor Erwin Griswold worried that litigators were moving too fast and that a precipitous adverse decision "might take a generation or more to overcome."[87] Columbia law professor Herbert Wechsler questioned whether a black child attending a segregated school was better off than a black child attending an integrated school, "where he might feel the full brunt of white prejudice."[88] In fact, subsequent research showed that minorities' academic achievement and aspirations were higher in integrated schools, and that these schools had more solid financial support than segregated counterparts.[89]

Leaders behind the *Brown* strategy, for their part, were unprepared for the resistance that it provoked and the consequences of white flight. At the time of his victory in the case, Thurgood Marshall predicted that school segregation would be entirely stamped out within five years.[90] Yet a decade after the decision, 98 percent of black children in the south still attended segregated schools.[91] A half-century after *Brown*, almost three-quarters of black and over three-quarters of Hispanic children attended schools in which minorities dominated, and two out of five attended intensely segregated schools in which 90 percent of students were minorities.[92] Yet ironically enough, the unanticipated degree of southern resistance to *Brown* had further unanticipated consequences. The backlash produced its own backlash. Northern whites reacted with horror to national television coverage of southern police brutalizing peaceful demonstrators and federal troops quelling riots and escorting children to school. This new consciousness of racism created the necessary political support for landmark civil rights legislation, which in turn helped transform the racial landscape.[93]

Yet educational inequalities persisted, and how to respond continued to divide civil rights leaders. The issue attracted widespread attention in the late 1970s when Harvard Law Professor Derrick Bell claimed that the NAACP leadership's single-minded commitment to maximum integration had led the organization to ignore the priorities of black parents, who cared more about educational quality than racial balance. While not questioning the motives of NAACP leaders, Bell challenged their willingness to substitute their own preferences for those of their clients. "Idealism," Bell observed, "though perhaps rarer than greed, is harder to control."[94] A similar dispute surfaced around the same time when Mexican American Legal Defense and Education Fund attorneys reported opposition to NAACP integration efforts that would dilute minority control and undermine barrio solidarity.[95]

Nathanial Jones, NAACP General Counsel, defended the organization's position. The courts, he pointed out, had recognized a right to integration, not to educational quality.[96] Moreover, NAACP leaders' pursuit of integration made sense from a practical as well as doctrinal standpoint. Blacks had learned that "green follows white"; the best way to attract dollars for minority schools was to increase their white enrollment.[97]

Yet over the next two decades, as doctrinal and practical realities shifted, leadership priorities also needed to change. A series of Supreme Court decisions restricting remedies in school desegregation cases, together with growing residential housing patterns, made further integration impossible. Declining inner city financial resources forced the civil rights community to seek new responses to persistent inequalities. Today's debates focus less on racial balance and more on issues such as equitable financing, accountability for student performance, and the role of choice and charter schools. If there are lessons to be learned from prior leadership struggles that could inform these debates, they are the importance of humility and diverse perspectives. Predicting long-term social change is an inherently inexact business. Leaders of wisdom and integrity can be utterly wrong about the consequences of events they set in motion. Recognition of this fact should serve as an invitation not to paralysis but to modesty, and openness to competing views. In the face of uncertainty, leaders' best option may be to fairly consider opposing perspectives and then follow their own moral compass. Or as Thurgood Marshall once summed up his philosophy: "you do what you think is right and let the law catch up."[98]

Public Officials Pursuing Public Interests

What constituted the "right" strategy in the face of southern resistance was the subject of other leadership disputes during the early civil rights era. Among the most significant questions were those confronting Justice Department officials during the Kennedy administration. Neither of the lawyers who led the government's civil rights efforts, Robert Kennedy as Attorney General, and Burke Marshall, as head of the Civil Rights Division, came to their positions with deep knowledge or commitment on racial justice issues. Initially, such issues were not a priority for the Kennedy administration. As Robert Kennedy later acknowledged, "I won't say I lay awake nights worrying about the problems of the Negroes."[99] Neither had these problems been high on the agenda of Burke Marshall, an antitrust litigator with a large Washington law firm. Indeed, as chapter 3 noted, his lack of involvement with civil rights was a main reason for his selection; he was more acceptable to the South than an attorney with a prior record supporting racial justice initiatives, and he was less likely to raise unrealistic hopes among the civil rights community.[100] Yet once events forced the "problems of the Negroes" to become *their* problems, both men grew in their positions and assumed a leadership role in the struggle for social change.

The challenges facing them were substantial. President Kennedy's victory had been a narrow one, dependent on southern electoral votes. He had a thin margin of potential support for his New Frontier domestic priorities and an array of critical international issues that called for his attention. Prudence dictated that his administration should seek only as much progress on civil rights as possible without alienating essential congressional allies or diverting excessive time and political capital from other pressing concerns.[101] Robert Kennedy shared that view. He was furious when Freedom Riders continued to provoke a violent backlash by attempting to desegregate interstate buses just before a crucial international summit. As he told reporters, continuing publicity about "ugly race riots would send the leader of the free world into European palaces with mud on his shoes."[102] In Kennedy's view, civil rights enforcement should focus on litigation protecting voting rights, which promised gradual democratic change with the added dividend of new Democratic voters.[103] Federal sanctions for resistance to segregation were to be avoided, as was any use of troops.[104] The administration wanted nothing that would trigger a blood bath and entrench opposition.

Burke Marshall came to similar views by a somewhat different route. He began with a deep commitment to federalism and a belief that it was neither practical nor desirable for the federal government to assume responsibility for protection of civil rights activities. The Justice Department's tiny staff of federal marshals was grossly inadequate to the task, and a national police force would be a threat to liberty.[105] In the long run, according to Marshall, the most effective solution to racial violence would be to put pressure on local law enforcement officials through the political process. Southern institutions had to be responsible for promoting racial justice because, as Marshall put it, "they are going to be there when we leave."[106]

In the short run, however, Marshall conceded the difficulties in ceding authority to Southern law enforcement officials unwilling to exercise it on behalf of civil rights activists. As local police declined to restrain racist mobs, and white judges and juries declined to convict those responsible for racial violence, the costs of federal inaction escalated. Between 1960 and 1965, there were 26 civil rights related murders, 150 incidents of serious violence, and scores of beatings, bombings, and burnings of black churches.[107] Almost none of the perpetrators were brought to justice. Although Marshall resisted requests for a federal response, he recognized the dilemma that this inaction posed:

> Those who say that civil rights issues cut into the fabric of federalism are correct. They cut most deeply where police power is involved.... There would be vast problems in any attempts at federal control of the administration of justice, even through the moderate method of federal court injunctions. Yet vast problems have been created already by police indifference to Negro rights in the South, and they will grow if the trend is not turned. The loss of faith in law—the usefulness of federal law and the unfairness of local law—is gaining very rapidly among Negro and white civil rights workers. The consequences in the future cannot be foreseen.[108]

The challenges for Justice Department leaders were compounded by their lack of control over key events. Marshall and Robert Kennedy were frequently confronted with unanticipated crises. Neither southern law enforcement agencies nor the Federal Bureau of Information under Herbert Hoover's leadership were willing to supply information that might have alerted the administration to the threat of violent resistance.[109] FBI agents were reluctant to impair cooperative relationships with local police, and Hoover was more interested in spying on civil rights activists than in protecting them.[110]

So too, as the brutality of southern police became more visible, the Justice Department found itself increasingly at odds with the civil rights movement. Victor Navasky summarized the conflict: "the strategy of the movement...was to instigate confrontations while the tactic of the Department was to avoid them."[111] Freedom Riders, a few "nameless...half-suicidal pacifists," could precipitate a national crisis by the simple act of riding an integrated bus into the Deep South.[112] Civil rights leaders recognized the political payoff from exposing scenes of southern police unleashing dogs, fire hoses, and billy clubs on peaceful protesters. These leaders believed that the "national conscience reacted not to injustice but to [southern police chief] Bull Conner's cattle prods."[113] Administration efforts to prevent confrontations also bumped up against the goals of anti-civil rights activists. Burke Marshall's painstaking efforts to craft a peaceful plan for desegregating Birmingham nearly unraveled when white racists bombed the home of Martin Luther King's brother and the motel where King and other civil rights leaders had their headquarters.[114]

The effectiveness of administration leaders' responses to these challenges is a matter of debate. On the positive side of the ledger were Burke Marshall's and Robert Kennedy's leadership styles. Marshall was respected by all sides for "listening endlessly, talking quietly, [and] forever seeking common ground."[115] Kennedy, as chapter 2 noted, had a way of treating Justice Department staff as equal members of a team, which inspired great loyalty and commitment. He listened well and "never lectured."[116] He also was astute and inventive in the use of power to advance racial justice. A famous example occurred during the presidential campaign of 1960. Martin Luther King was arrested for a traffic violation: driving without a valid license. He received a twelve-month suspended sentence on the condition that he not violate any other laws during his year of probation. He was subsequently arrested for a sit-in and sentenced to four months' hard labor for violating the terms of his probation. Republican presidential candidate Richard Nixon did nothing. Democratic candidate John Kennedy called Dr. King's pregnant wife to express his sympathy. Campaign manager Robert Kennedy called the judge and King was released on bail two days later. The case was ultimately closed with a $25 fine and suspended sentence.[117]

In 1961, when activists dragged Freedom Riders from their bus, beat them, and firebombed the bus, Robert Kennedy was shocked and again sprang into action. Although he agreed with the president that the Freedom Riders had deliberately put themselves in harm's way, he felt bound to protect them. When the Greyhound Company couldn't find another driver willing to carry on the dangerous journey, Kennedy called the company office personally. Tapes of the conversation revealed Kennedy grilling a company official. "Do you know how to drive a bus?" ... "Surely someone in the damn bus company can drive a bus, can't they?" In a thinly veiled threat, he added, "I am,—the Government is—going to be very much upset if this group does not get to continue their trip."[118] The trip then did continue to Montgomery, where an angry mob descended on the passengers with lead pipes and baseball bats. Some of the Riders and about fifteen hundred sympathizers subsequently met to hear Martin Luther King preach in Montgomery's First Baptist Church. A howling mob of three thousand surrounded the church. In anticipation of violence, Kennedy had quickly pulled together a motley makeshift army of U.S. marshals, federal prison guards, border patrolmen, and Alcohol, Tobacco, and Firearms agents. When they failed to disperse the crowd with tear gas, Kennedy began to discuss the possibility of federal troops. After eavesdropping on his telephone conversations through the local switchboard, Alabama's governor sent in the state's National Guard.[119]

The crisis was averted, but more followed despite the Kennedys' best efforts to discourage further Freedom Rides. In meetings with civil rights leaders, Kennedy tried to convince them to focus instead on voter registration. Working behind the scenes, he arranged private foundation funding for the effort and a tax exemption for a Voter Education Project that would allow foundations to provide financial support without jeopardizing their tax exempt status.[120] His efforts met with partial success and his stepped-up enforcement of voting rights by Justice Department lawyers further aided the effort.

Backstage maneuvering and informal persuasion was typical of Kennedy's strategies. In the midst of a crisis in Birmingham, he arranged for cabinet members to call on leaders of Alabama businesses to urge them to pressure the Governor for a peaceful resolution.[121] Through adept use of political connections, Kennedy convinced a reluctant Interstate Commerce Commission to issue an unprecedented order desegregating bus terminals. He achieved in months the kind of result that normally took years even if the Commission was willing, which in this case it was clearly not.[122] Kennedy also took over planning for the Martin Luther King's historic 1963 march on Washington, arranging for everything from portable toilets to prerecorded music ready to pipe in over loudspeakers if the rhetoric got out of hand.[123]

When all other efforts failed, Kennedy was also prepared to call in federal troops. That proved necessary in Mississippi in 1962 to enforce a federal decree entitling James Meredith to enroll at the state university. Extended negotiations with Governor Ross Barnett and a federal court order holding him in contempt failed to produce a workable plan for Meredith's enrollment. When Barnett reneged on a deal to allow a secret registration, Kennedy threatened to have the president reveal the duplicity on national television, and claim it as a justification for bringing in outside troops. That convinced Barnett to agree to another surreptitious registration strategy, but he was unable to control the mob of outsiders assembling near the university. After rioters overwhelmed another makeshift army of marshals, border patrolmen, and prison guards, Kennedy ordered the airlift of federal troops. Within several days of the riots at "Ole Miss," twenty-three thousand members of the armed forces assembled in the college town, three times its normal population.[124] James Meredith began attending classes, and ultimately completed a degree, guarded by federal marshals for the duration. It was undoubtedly the most expensive public education in the nation's history.[125] The Ole Miss debacle was also an education for Justice Department leaders, and one from which they learned enough to avoid a similar incident at the University of Alabama.

Once again, the federal courts had ordered the admission of black students, and once again a governor, in this case George Wallace, vowed defiance. The compromise was that he got his opportunity to honor a campaign pledge to "stand at the schoolhouse door" blocking admission, but that the students would be allowed to register peacefully. In preparation for any outbreak of violence, the Alabama National Guard was federalized, and army troops were on standby across the border.[126]

To many civil rights supporters, this forceful defense of the rule of law should have been far more common. Kennedy was particularly faulted for failing to provide federal protection for the voter registration activity that he had personally solicited.[127] At the time, Burke Marshall defended the Department's policy. As he wrote to a civil rights advocate, "we do not have a national police and cannot provide protection in a physical sense...we have no budget for it. There is no substitute under the federal system for the failure of local law enforcement responsibility.[128] But in retrospect, even Marshall wondered whether the administration had leaned "too far over" in its efforts to avoid the use of force.[129] Many others questioned whether the administration also could have done more to pressure local law enforcement to act, or to enlist the FBI in enforcement efforts.

A second leadership failure was the low priority that Kennedy attached to judicial selection. The administration acquiesced in the appointment of segregationist federal judges, and even publicly defended some as upright jurists, even as they became major obstacles to social change.[130] Justice department lawyers ended up spending thousands of hours "trying to counter the obstructionist tactics of its own appointees."[131]

A third failing was Kennedy's refusal to stand up to J. Edgar Hoover. Not only was the FBI head unwilling to charge FBI agents with responsibility to help prevent violence, he also demanded Kennedy's authorization of wiretaps on King and other civil rights activists. Biographer Evan Thomas believes Kennedy's acquiescence reflected concerns about Hoover's extensive files on his brother's sexual affairs while president.[132] There was always the risk that challenging Hoover might result in devastating disclosures. But whatever the reason, Kennedy continued to authorize surveillance of King, including his sexual activities, long after the wiretaps failed to reveal any subversive activity that would justify them.[133]

A final failure was Kennedy's inability to acknowledge his own mistakes or limitations. A representative example occurred when he was asked before a crowd of protestors why the Justice Department employed so few blacks. It was a concern Kennedy himself had shared; only 10 of the Justice Department's

950 lawyers under his leadership were black.[134] Yet instead of admitting the problem and committing the Department to address it, Kennedy responded that "individuals will be hired according to their ability not their color."[135]

This mixed legacy suggests a leader who "commuted between idealism and expediency."[136] Although committed in principle to racial justice, in practice Kennedy steered a prudential course. It was often a thankless task. While civil rights advocates condemned him for doing too little, southerners damned him for doing too much.[137] In trying to strike a balance, Kennedy lurched from crisis to crisis, bringing formidable talents to bear on explosive situations. He was, as his father once put it, "hard as nails" when necessary and he brought that steely determination to seemingly intractable controversies.[138] But most of his civil rights efforts were reactive rather than programmatic, and according to many historians, his failure to anticipate the depth of southern resistance and fully mobilize federal resources slowed the struggle for racial justice.[139] Yet, as other commentators note, the faith that he and Marshall placed in the power of the vote to promote local enforcement of civil rights was not entirely misplaced. Dogged efforts to secure registration of black voters gradually shifted the balance of power and helped to bring new priorities on issues of racial justice. By 1973, the *New York Times* reported the "virtual disappearance" from the South of unpunished random violence against blacks.[140] Kennedy's and Marshall's leadership was doubtless responsible for some of that achievement, but perhaps also for the fact that it took so long.

Competing Views of Common Interests: The Gay Marriage Campaign

A final example of challenges for leaders seeking social change comes from the contemporary campaign for same-sex marriage. At issue are fundamental questions of strategy, priority, and process. As in the debate over *Brown*, a key dispute has involved whether now is the time to bring a matter of fundamental importance before the Supreme Court. Other major concerns are how much priority gay marriage should assume, and how disputes over timing should be decided.

Controversies over the priority to place on gay marriage first came to a head in the late 1980s. Tom Stoddard, executive director of Lambda, squared off against Paula Ettelbrick, the legal director of Lambda, in a debate published by the journal *Out/Look*. Stoddard set forth the political, economic,

and symbolic justifications for treating committed gay and lesbian relationships the same as heterosexual ones, and urged the "gay rights movement [to]
aggressively seek full legal recognition for same-sex marriages."[141] Ettelbrick
disagreed. "Since When Is Marriage a Path to Liberation?," she asked in the
title of her article, and then went on to argue:

> [M]arriage will not liberate us as lesbians and gay men. In fact, it will
> constrain us, make us more invisible, force our assimilation into the
> mainstream, and undermine the goals of gay liberation … : the affirma-
> tion of gay identity and culture; and the validation of many forms of
> relationships.…Justice for gay men and lesbians will be achieved only
> when we are accepted and supported in this society *despite* our differ-
> ences from the dominant culture and the choices we make regarding
> our relationships….As a lesbian, I am fundamentally different from
> non-lesbian women. That's the point. Marriage, as it exists today, is
> antithetical to my liberation as a lesbian and as a woman because it
> mainstreams my life and voice. I do not want [to] be known as "Mrs.
> Attached-To-Somebody-Else." Nor do I want to give the state the
> power to regulate my primary relationship.[142]

As Harvard Law Professor William Rubenstein notes, the Stoddard/
Ettelbrick exchange was "a 'marriage announcement' of sorts, a declaration
that the issue of marriage was moving from the margin to the center of the
lesbian/gay movement."[143] Once there, it continued to evoke controversy.

While Stoddard and Ettelbrick took to the road to argue their positions
before members of the gay community, a parallel debate was occurring among
civil rights leaders. In 1990, some gay Hawaiians asked the local ACLU affiliate
to file a lawsuit challenging the state's marriage law. ACLU lawyers contacted
the organization's National Lesbian and Gay Rights Project in New York for
guidance. Nan Hunter, then Director of the Project, suggested that the lawyers try to gauge support for the case within Hawaii's gay community before
pursuing the issue. Following that advice, the lawyers sent a letter to community leaders asking whether there was "broadly based support for such litigation" in Hawaii. The letter explained that the "ACLU would not want to act
in a manner inconsistent with the opinion of a substantial number of gays
and gay rights activists."[144] The letter drew some sharp protest. One activist
responded, "civil rights should never be construed as a popular opinion issue,
but rather a right of each human being."[145]

The controversy subsided after three lesbian and gay male couples in Hawaii brought their own claim in state court without the support of the ACLU. Once the case was filed, the community's legal organizations provided support. Although the litigation was partially successful, the victory was short-lived. The Hawaii Supreme Court issued the nation's first decision finding that a denial of the right to marriage to same-sex couples constituted sex discrimination. Under the state constitution's equal protection clause, the government therefore needed to show a compelling interest in denying marriage licenses to gay and lesbian couples.[146] The court remanded the case to the trial judge to determine if such an interest existed, but before that occurred, Hawaii voters terminated the case by approving an amendment to the state constitution allowing the legislature to "reserve marriage to opposite-sex couples."

The two decades following the Hawaii litigation witnessed substantial legal and legislative efforts to recognize same-sex marriages, as well as debate within the gay community about the importance of the issue. To some leaders, it was a mistake to view marriage as the preeminent movement goal rather than affirmation of diverse family forms.[147] But the vehemence of conservatives' opposition to same-sex marriage "had the effect of "heightening its importance as the ultimate symbol of LGBT equality."[148] Denial of that right came to be seen as a signal to gays and lesbians that they and their relationships were "less worthy, less legitimate…and less valued."[149] Moreover, in some instances, the community had no choice but to focus on the marriage issue because gay and lesbian couples insisted on litigating it. In 2003, the Massachusetts supreme court became the first to find a state constitutional right to same-sex marriage.[150] The decision produced considerable backlash. Fourteen states subsequently amended their constitutions to prohibit same-sex marriage. However, by 2012, eight states enacted legislation permitting it, and several state supreme courts found state constitutional support for gays' right to marry.

During this period, a coalition of nine lesbian, gay, bisexual, and transgender (LGBT) advocacy organizations came together to develop a coherent strategy. In a statement titled "Make Change, Not Lawsuits," the group warned same-sex couples against filing federal cases, or suing "their home state or their employer to recognize their marriage" until there is a "critical mass of states recognizing same-sex relationships."[151] Losing court cases, the groups argued, would actually delay the struggle to obtain marital rights. Legislation rather than litigation was the preferred course, since losing in legislatures would not set an adverse precedent that would be hard to overturn.

That strategy unraveled in California. Controversy began in 2004 when Mayor Gavin Newsom of San Francisco allowed the issuance of marriage licenses to same-sex couples, on the grounds that the denial of these licenses violated the state constitution's equal protection clause. Newsom's standing shot up in the polls but his decision was short lived. About 4,000 same-sex marriages occurred before the California Supreme Court ordered the city to stop issuing the licenses and voided the marriages. While holding that city officials exceeded their authority by deciding a constitutional question, the court expressed no opinion on that question.[152] Litigation quickly followed "at a time movement leaders did not choose and in a procedural posture they did not desire...."[153] The California Supreme Court subsequently determined that the law limiting marriage to heterosexual couples violated the state constitution, which prompted a ballot initiative to overturn the decision. In the November 2008 elections, California voters narrowly passed Proposition 8 by a 52 percent margin, amending the California state constitution to ban same-sex marriages.

LGBT groups began marshalling their forces for another ballot initiative campaign to reverse Prop 8. In the interim, a Hollywood political strategist, Chad Griffin, approached Ted Olson, the former Solicitor General under George W. Bush, and a partner in Gibson, Dunn, & Crutcher. Griffin wanted Olson to bring a federal lawsuit challenging the constitutionality of Prop 8, and asserting same-sex couples' right to marriage. Olson agreed, and recruited as co-counsel David Boies, who had been his opposing counsel in *Bush v. Gore*. Boies and Olson knew that leaders of gay rights organization were opposed to a federal challenge, and did not consult with them before filing suit. As another lawyer at Gibson Dunn explained, "We did not want to have a big debate about what we felt was the right strategy... We did not want that debate to break out before we launched our suit...."[154]

In justifying that decision, Olson told the *New Yorker,* "There are millions of people in this country who would like to be married—in California, in Arkansas, wherever. Some couple is going to go to some lawyer and that lawyer is going to bring the case. And that case could be the case that goes to the Supreme Court. So, if there's going to be a case, let it be us. Because we will staff it—we've got fifteen, twenty lawyers working on this case and we have the resources to do it, and we have the experience in the Supreme Court."[155]

That Olson and Boies themselves might have something to gain from being lead counsel on a case of this prominence did not escape notice. Many leaders of the gay rights community were furious, and a joint statement by the ACLU and eight prominent gay rights organizations issued a statement condemning the suit. According to that statement, the odds of success were not strong because the "Supreme Court typically does not get too far ahead of either public opinion or the law in the majority of states.... A loss now may make it harder to go to court later...It will take us a lot longer to get a good Supreme Court decision if the Court has to overrule itself. We lost the right to marry in California at the ballot box. That's where we need to win it back."[156]

Many experts on gay rights agreed. Nan Hunter, founder of the ACLU's LGBT project, now a professor at Georgetown law school, denounced the lawsuit as "reckless" because "there is a significant chance of failure if the case reaches the U.S. Supreme Court."[157] However strong a case Olson and Boies might present, "invalidating roughly forty state laws that define marriage as between a man and a woman is an awfully heavy lift for the Supreme Court, and especially for Justices who take a limited view of the scope of the judiciary....I fear that their strategy is: Ted Olson will speak, Anthony Kennedy will listen, and the earth will move. I hope I'm wrong about this—they're excellent lawyers—but I fear, frankly, that there's more ego than analysis in that."[158] Yale Law Professor William Eskridge agreed. "A question that so evenly but intensely divides the country is not one that should be decided by the courts nationwide....It is just not something that this Supreme Court is going to deliver on at this point."[159] The process as well as the substance of the decision to file suit provoked criticism. As Hunter noted, LGBT legal groups had been following a "very careful and deliberate, collaborative" strategy for many years, only to have it "thrown off by an organization with a small number of people who are wealthy enough to pay for a major litigation effort."[160]

The controversy over Boies's and Olson's actions continued once the federal trial judge in the case issued an order specifying issues for the parties to consider. He identified a wide range of matters on which gay rights groups had expertise, including the history of discrimination against gays and lesbians, and their ability to provide an optimal child rearing environment. Three gay advocacy organizations then attempted to join the lawsuit as interveners. Kate Kendall, head of the National Center of Lesbian Rights pointed out that "[b]etween our organizations, we've litigated in a trial setting almost every single one of those issues. That's invaluable experience...."[161] Olson and Boies opposed the groups' intervention. "We very much wanted their help and support," Olson later explained. "But we represent clients, and we have to retain control of the case—not only the strategic decisions but also the pace of litigation. As soon as you have five captains of the ship, it's very hard to control the ship."[162] The trial court denied the motion to intervene, and the groups ended up supporting the litigation informally, by supplying briefs and experts.

How the decision to file suit will play out is too soon to tell. The plaintiffs were successful at the trial level, and prevailed again in the court of appeals, although on narrower grounds than Olson and Boies had argued. Rather than finding that gay and lesbian couples had a right to marriage under the federal constitution, the court reasoned that couples already granted that right under the state constitution could not have the right taken away without a legitimate non-discriminatory reason, which was absent in the ratification of Prop 8. This narrow holding, along with some technical standing issues, gave the Supreme Court alternatives to reaching the constitutional issue after it granted review. But that was clearly not the result that Olson and Boies were seeking. For present purposes, the interesting question is less what the Court will do than what leaders should do when considering whether to bring high-risk cases. What factors should they consider and how should they make the decision?

Leaders of gay rights groups had strong reasons for believing that federal litigation on same-sex marriage should wait for a more receptive climate. Time was clearly on their side. Polling data showed a dramatic increase in support for gay marriage over the last two decades, particularly among younger voters. A 2013 survey in found that Americans favored recognition of same-sex marriage by a 58 to 36 margin, the exact flip of a similar survey just seven years earlier, when the margin was 36 to 58.[163] President Obama's endorsement of the right reflected and reinforced that trend. When individuals changed their views, they did so in the direction of marriage equality.[164] One factor that most strongly predicts support for equal rights for gays and lesbians is knowing someone in those categories. In one study, 65 percent of those who knew someone gay supported gay marriage or civil unions, compared with only 35 percent of those who did not know someone gay.[165] As more gays and lesbians have come out of the closet, their social environment has improved, and as that has happened, more have felt able to come out of the closet. This trend is likely to continue, and to increase support for same-sex marriage. That, in turn, will increase the comfort level for the Court in declaring a right that is widely accepted. Justices are always wary about pushing too far too fast, and triggering a backlash that will derail a decision. Giving same-sex marriage a chance to gain support through state legal and political processes has much to recommend it.

Of course, Olson had a point when he responded that some gay couples do not want to wait for a more receptive climate, and may file a suit without the resources and experience that he and Boies can bring to the case. But Olson and Boies can scarcely be disinterested in assessing the risks of such a suit against the risks of an adverse precedent in the case they contemplated filing. Why not defer to the leaders of the gay rights organizations about whether it made sense to sue now? These leaders are likely to be less self-interested and better informed about the concerns of those who will be most affected by the decision.

This is, of course, not a responsibility we impose on most lawyers. And it is one Olson resisted. As he put it, "If people are being hurt by discrimination...then who are we as lawyers to say 'Wait ten years'?"[166] Under accepted ethical rules, once attorneys accept a case, their obligation is to represent the lawful objectives of the client as the client conceives them.[167] But attorneys also have ethical discretion in deciding whether to accept a case, and those who aspire to be leaders of social change need to consider the interests of a broader constituency than the individuals willing to bring or bankroll litigation. In declining even to consult with gay leaders before filing suit, Olson and Boies hardly set an example of responsible leadership. And even if their decision turns out to pay off, the preemptory method by which it was reached is not one that will generally serve a social movement.

WHAT QUALITIES STAND out among the leaders most effective in pursuit of social change? One is the capacity to see around corners: to recognize and capitalize on the conditions conducive to reform and to anticipate and address the sources of resistance. Equally important is the ability to work in multiple settings with multiple constituencies. Leaders must be able to build a sense of shared urgency and identity among their followers, and to develop collaborative relationships with potential allies. That, in turn, requires deep knowledge of the communities affected and a willingness to consult widely on goals and strategies. Above all, leaders need resilience, resolve, and a commitment to interests broader than their own.

The Leader's Legacy

"WE HAVE ALL occasionally encountered top persons who couldn't lead a squad of seven-year-olds to the ice cream counter," noted John Gardiner.[1] This book has aimed to keep lawyers from becoming any of those persons. To that end, this chapter concludes with a review of key insights about effective leaders and thoughts on the legacy that leadership makes possible.

Qualities of Leadership

Leadership is a process, not a position, a relationship, not a status. A title may give someone subordinates but not necessarily followers. To recall Joseph Nye's metaphor, having a fishing license does not mean you will catch fish.[2] Leadership is earned.

The qualities and styles necessary to the task vary somewhat by context. Yet although research reveals no uniform profile of the ideal leader, certain characteristics appear effective for most leadership situations: vision, ethics, technical competence, interpersonal skills, and personal skills such as self-awareness and self-control.[3] The need for such qualities has never been greater. Contemporary leaders confront a landscape of increasing competition, complexity, scale, pace, and diversity. Many decisions play out on a wider stage, with less time for informed deliberation. What further complicates these challenges is the "leadership paradox": the frequent disconnect between the qualities that enable individuals to attain positions of power and the qualities that are necessary to perform effectively once they get there. Successful leadership requires subordinating interests in personal achievement in order to create the conditions for achievement by others.

In developing the necessary strategies and skills, experience is critical, as is reflection about experience. Aspiring leaders need to seek opportunities for exercising influence, obtaining candid advice, and learning from their own mistakes, as well as from research and case studies. Those who have obtained positions of power can assist the process by creating "learning organizations" that will effectively generate, transfer, and incorporate knowledge that can develop new leaders.[4]

One of the key skills that leaders need to learn is decision making. Leaders who are most successful have developed habits of conscious deliberation before and after they act. Rather than simply reacting to events, successful leaders consider what they most want to achieve and anticipate what might stand in the way. After they act, these leaders reflect on what worked and what did not, and what they might do differently in the future.[5] Skilled decision makers also recognize that even the most thoughtful processes are subject to biases in perception, memory, and problem solving. Sound judgment depends on recognizing bounded rationality and building in appropriate correctives. Information that is vivid or consistent with stereotypes and self-interest will be disproportionately "available" to skew decision making unless leaders make conscious adjustments. In cost-benefit calculations, psychic numbing and the salience of individual victims can lead to overinvestment in short term remedies and underinvestment in long-term preventative strategies. Groupthink and related dynamics can also sabotage effective policymaking and risk management. Creating processes that will ensure independent and diverse points of view is an essential leadership skill.

Mastering strategies of influence is equally critical. Power comes in multiple currencies, and often the most obvious rewards and sanctions are less available or effective than other persuasive approaches, such as reciprocity and peer pressure. These techniques are essential in building relationships in a world in which boundaries separating leaders and followers are increasingly blurred. Most lawyers "lead from the middle." They are leaders in some contexts, and followers in others. In either case, they require interpersonal skills such as empathy and active listening that foster trust and mutual respect. Leaders also need strategies for innovation and conflict management. They need to overcome inertia, chart a path for change, and create environments that reward and sustain it. In dealing with conflict, avoidance is generally to be avoided. The preferable approach is generally collaborative problem solving, in which parties build on shared concerns in search of mutual gain. Leaders can facilitate the process, not only by assisting individual dispute resolution, but also by creating "conflict competent" organizations. Channels for candid dialogue and bottom-up evaluations can help identify problems before they escalate.

Finally, leaders need communication skills. That requires knowing their objectives, their audience, their occasion, and their substance. To create messages "made to stick," speakers should look for material that is succinct, unexpected, credible, and emotionally appealing. They should avoid the curse of knowledge; less is often more, stories are more memorable than statistics, and visual images are often the most powerful persuasive strategy.

Values in Leadership

Effective leadership depends not only on skills but also on values. Challenges often arise because values are in conflict and ethical commitments are in tension with situational pressures. Dilemmas of dirty hands, which require immoral means to achieve moral ends, are particularly common in political life. Although many of these dilemmas lack clear answers, leaders should be accountable for their responses, and their choices should serve public, not just personal interests. To reinforce moral behavior, leaders need to address the peer pressures, cognitive biases, and diffusion of responsibility that compromise moral judgment. Ethical conduct is highly situational, and research on the banality of evil makes clear how readily minor missteps or mindless conformity can entrap individuals in major misconduct. To maintain their moral compass, leaders as well as followers should consult widely, enlist allies, observe bright line rules, and cultivate self-doubt. Those in leadership positions can also foster ethical conduct by setting the tone at the top, and establishing appropriate reward and oversight structures.

Leaders also need private lives that are consistent with public and organizational responsibilities. Power both imposes special obligations and creates special temptations. Leaders not only have more than the customary opportunities for abuse, they are surrounded by subordinates reluctant to challenge it. Self-serving biases can further reinforce leaders' sense of entitlement and invulnerability. The result is a steady stream of scandal, fed by media eager to fill a continuous news cycle, and technologies that make misconduct more visible. In this climate, crisis management has become a critical part of the leadership toolkit, and the art of apology is an essential skill. So too, is the capacity to use scandal as a catalyst for corrective action. Market meltdowns and environmental disasters can supply the urgency for organizational and regulatory reform. Where personal conduct is at issue, leaders need to be attentive to even the appearance of impropriety. In an era of increasing transparency and instant notoriety, those in positions of power need to consider how private conduct would look in public settings before it is too late to change.

Leadership in Context

Contemporary leaders face a host of challenges, and diversity is high among them. Despite considerable progress over the last half-century, women and minorities are significantly underrepresented in positions of influence. Unconscious stereotypes, in-group biases, and inflexible workplace structures remain substantial obstacles. There are strong reasons to address them. Women and minorities constitute an increasing share of today's talent, and effective performance in an increasingly multicultural environment demands an equal playing field. When well-managed, diversity also can enhance the quality and legitimacy of decision making. To that end, women and minorities need to be proactive in seeking opportunities, mentors, and feedback that will enhance their qualifications, and leaders of organizations need to promote initiatives that address unconscious bias and structural barriers, and that monitor and reward progress on diversity-related issues.

Leaders of law firms face further, distinctive challenges. Competition from within and outside the profession has intensified, and technological innovations have reduced demand for services while increasing their pace. Clients want to pay less, lawyers want to earn more, and firms' growth in size and lateral hiring have eroded a sense of collegiality and shared mission. Leaders also face trade-offs between short-term profits and long-term investments in collective concerns such as mentoring, quality of life and pro bono service. In mediating these competing demands, leaders need to consult broadly and develop a strategic plan that is not only responsive to market realities, but also that cultivates a sense of institutional identity and loyalty.

Those who head movements for social change face comparable challenges. Leaders play a pivotal role in creating or capitalizing on conditions for progress. Their ability to inspire followers, enlist allies, attract public support, and reinforce shared identities can provide the foundations for social transformation. However, conflicts often arise about timing or strategies, such as when to litigate, which cases to bring, and who should decide. One distinguishing feature of great leaders is the ability to mediate such disputes, and to build coherent unifying strategies in pursuit of common ends.

The Legacy of Leadership

Leadership not only poses special challenges and special obligations, it can also bring exceptional rewards. Those that are most fulfilling are generally not, however, the extrinsic perks that accompany positions of power. A wide array of psychological research suggests that satisfaction with work depends on feeling effective, exercising strengths and virtues, and contributing to socially valued ends that bring meaning and purpose.[6] As one British military leader put it, "You make a living by what you get; you make a life by what you give."[7] Individuals who are motivated by "intrinsic aspirations" such as personal growth and assisting others tend to be more satisfied than those motivated primarily by extrinsic aspirations, such as wealth or fame.[8] Part of the reason is that extrinsic desires, expectations, and standards of comparison increase as rapidly as they are satisfied. Leaders can become trapped on a "hedonic treadmill": the more they have, the more they need to have.[9] So too, money and status are positional goods; individuals' satisfaction depends on how they compare relative to others, and increases in wealth or position are readily offset by changes in reference groups.[10] The arms race in law firm partner compensation reflects this dynamic. Leaders who look hard enough can always find someone getting more.

How then can individuals with high needs for achievement and recognition find greatest fulfillment? Laura Nash and Howard Stevenson of the Harvard Business School studied leaders who by conventional standards had achieved "success that lasts."

> Our research uncovered four irreducible components of enduring success: happiness (feelings of pleasure and contentment); achievement (accomplishments that compare favorably against similar goals others have strived for); significance (the sense that you've made a positive impact on people you care about); and legacy (a way to establish your values or accomplishments so as to help others find future success).[11]

The challenge for leaders is how to set priorities that strike a balance among all four domains.

"Legacy" is often the hardest form of success to measure. The philosopher William James insisted that the greatest use of life is to spend it on something that outlasts it but what that something is depends on personal values. Contemporary leadership experts agree. They underscore the need for a larger purpose but warn against confusing fame with legacy.[12] A focus on ensuring recognition of a legacy can get in the way of achieving it; leaders can be tempted to hoard power, status, and credit, or to strike out in bold but ill-considered directions. Too much emphasis on others' perception can also deflect attention from leaders' own goals.[13] As English essayist Charles Montague noted, "There is no limit to what a man can do so long as he does not care a straw who gets the credit for it."[14]

An important distinction for leaders is between "making a difference" and "making 'my' difference and making sure everyone knows it."[15] No one can ever control how others will ultimately interpret their contributions; pigeons may nest on their monuments.[16] Many leaders recognize as much. When asked about what would be his legacy during the close of his presidential term, Bill Clinton resisted the question. He wanted to focus his attention on substantive issues; "the legacy would take care of itself..."[17] Earl Warren also tried to avoid fixating on public perceptions, which helped him withstand the vicious attacks that accompanied his opinions on civil rights: billboards asking to "impeach Earl Warren" and commentators claiming " I would not impeach Earl Warren. I would lynch him."[18]

Thinking about legacy is helpful only if it directs attention to ultimate goals and values, not if it diverts energy into futile quests for lasting glory. That concern with values should begin sooner rather than later. Priorities and relationships formed early in a career create the foundations for later achievements. It is never too soon for leaders to think about what they would like said at their eulogy.

Leaders cannot fully determine their legacies, but they can be conscious of how their daily interactions and priorities affect other individuals and institutions. For a lasting contribution, leaders' priorities should include supporting the careers of subordinates as well as their own. As one expert notes, "the ultimate test of a leader is not whether he or she makes smart decisions...but whether he or she teaches others to be leaders and builds an organization that can sustain its success even when he or she is not around."[19]

When asked how he wished to be remembered, Supreme Court Justice Thurgood Marshall responded: "He did what he could with what he had."[20] Leaders have many ways to leave a legacy. For most, it is less through grand triumphs than through smaller cumulative acts that improve the lives around them.

Notes

CHAPTER I

1. Neil W. Hamilton, Ethical Leadership in Professional Life, 6 U. St. Thomas L. Rev. 358, 361 (2009).
2. For lawyers' representation in the population, see James Podgers, State of the Union: The Nation's Lawyer Population Continues to Grow, But Barely, ABA J. l, July 1, 2011, http://www.abajournal.com/magazine/article/state_of_the_union_the_nations_lawyer_population_continues_to_grow_but_bare/.

   Approximately 10 percent of the CEOs of Fortune 50 companies are lawyers. See Mark Curriden, CEO, Esq., ABA J., May 1, 2010, http://www.abajournal.com/magazine/article/ceo_esq/.
3. For corporate expenditures, see Doris Gomez, The Leader as Learner, 2 Int'l J. Leadership Stud. 280, 281 (2007). For inadequate curricula in academic institutions that claim to be developing leaders, see Nitin Nohria & Rakesh Khurana, Advancing Leadership Theory and Practice, in Handbook of Leadership Theory and Practice 3–5 (Nitin Nohria & Rakesh Khurana, eds., 2010). See also Hamilton, Ethical Leadership, at 370. For discussion of the few law school programs, see Leary Davis, Competence as Situationally Appropriate Conduct: An Overarching Concept for Lawyering, Leadership and Professionalism, 52 Santa Clara L. Rev. 725, 748–749 (2012); Susan Swain Daicoff, Expanding the Lawyer's Toolkit of Skills and Competencies, 52 Santa Clara L. Rev. 795, 838–839 (2012). See generally Law and Leadership: Integrating Leadership Studies into the Law School Curriculum (Paula Monopoli & Susan McCarty, eds. 2013).
4. Pew Research Center, A Paradox in Public Attitudes: Men or Women, Who's the Better Leader? 15 (2008).
5. Gallup, Honesty/Ethics in Professions (2010), htpp://www.gallup.com/poll/1654/honesty-ethics-professions.aspx.
6. Marc Galanter, The Faces of Mistrust: The Image of Lawyers in Jokes, Public Opinion, and Political Discourse, 65 U. Cin. L. Rev 805, 7809 (1998).

7. Harris Poll, March 5, 2009; The Harris Poll Annual Confidence Index Rises 10 Points (March 5, 2009), available at http://www.harrisinteractive.com/harris_poll/pubs/Harris_Poll_2009_03_05.pdf.

8. Mark C. Miller, The High Priests of American Politics: The Role of Lawyers in American Political Institutions 60 (1995).

9. ABA Section of Litigation, Public Perceptions of Lawyers: Consumer Research Findings 19 (2002), http://www.americanbar.org/content/dam/aba/migrated/marketresearch/PublicDocuments/public_perception_of_lawyers_2002.authcheckdam.pdf.

10. Robert Post, On the Popular Image of the Lawyer: Reflections in a Dark Glass, 75 Ca. L. Rev. 379, 380 (1987).

11. ABA Section of Litigation, Public Perceptions of Lawyers, at 7.

12. Miller, The High Priests, at 65; Francis K. Zemans & Victor G. Rosenblum, The Making of a Public Profession xv (1981); Willard Hurst, The Growth of American Law 359 (1950).

13. Alexis de Tocqueville, Democracy in America Volume 1 283 (H. Reeve translation 1835).

14. Joseph A Schlesinger, Lawyers and American Politics: A Clarified View, 1 Midwest Journal of Political Science 26, 276 (1957).

15. John Milton Cooper Jr., Woodrow Wilson: A Biography 32 (2009) (quoting Wilson).

16. Heinz Eulau & John D. Sprague, Lawyers in Politics 144 (1964).

17. Barbara Kellerman, The End of Leadership 157 (2011).

18. For values, see Robert W. Cullen, The Leading Lawyer: A Guide to Practicing Law and Leadership 34–41 (2010) (discussing integrity); Larry Richard, Leadership: Competencies in Law, in Law and Leadership, at 42 (citing integrity); Warren Bennis, On Becoming a Leader 40–41 (2d ed. 1994) (citing integrity and trust); Montgomery Van Wart, Dynamics of Leadership in Public Service: Theory and Practice 16, 92–119 (2005) (citing integrity and an ethic of public service); James M. Kouzes & Barry Z. Posner, The Leadership Challenge 21 (1995) (citing honesty). For personal skills, see Daniel Goleman, Richard Boyatzis, & Annie McKee, Primal Leadership: Realizing the Power of Emotional Intelligence 253–256 (2002) (citing self- awareness, and self- management); Van Wart, supra, at 16 (citing self-direction). For interpersonal skills, see Goleman, Boyatzis, & McKee, Primal Leadership, at 253–256 (citing social awareness, empathy, persuasion, and conflict management). For vision and inspirational ability see Bennis, On Becoming a Leader, at 33; Kouzes and Posner, supra, at 21; Cullin, The Leading Lawyer, at 33, 42. For competence, see id.; Lorsch, A Contingency Theory, at 417; Noel M. Tichy & Warren G. Bennis, Judgment: How Winning Leaders Make Great Calls (2007) (describing importance of judgment); Cullin, The Leading Lawyer, at 41 (discussing technical competence).

19. These included ability to influence and build coalitions (42 percent); inspiration and passion (34 percent); vision (29 percent); listening (24 percent); good communication (25 percent); ability to attract followers (21 percent); empathy (21 percent); integrity (17 percent); courage (16 percent); humility (16 percent); respect for others (12 percent). Only one quality, business understanding (21 percent) involved technical and analytical skill. Maureen Broderick, The Art of Managing Professional Services (2010), excerpted in Maureen Broderick, Leading Gently, The American Lawyer, December, 2010, 63–64.

20. Broderick, Leading Gently, at 63–64.

21. For the listed qualities see Thomas DeLong, John Gabarro, & Robert J. Lees, When Professionals Have to Lead, excerpted in The American Lawyer, December 2007, 125–129. For views of managing partners, see Kenneth Van Winkle Jr., The Managing Partner's Role in Today's World, in Managing a Law Firm 25, 46–47 (2010); Abraham C. Reich & Mark L. Silow, Democracy, Transparency and Rotation: Keys to Running a Successful Law Firm, in Managing a Law Firm, supra, 73, 81; Cullin, The Leading Lawyer, at 120–123.

22. Napoleon Bonaparte, Napoleon in His Own Words 4 (Comp. Jules Beartaut, 1916).

23. Richard, Leadership Competencies in Law, at 46; Larry Richard, Herding Cats: The Lawyer Personality Revealed, 29 Report to Legal Management 1, 4 (Altman Weil Aug. 2002); Susan Daicoff, Lawyer, Know Thyself: A Review of Empirical Research on Attorney Attributes Bearing on Professionalism, 46 Am. U. L. Rev. 1337, 1349, 1390–1391 (1997).

24. Mark Milner, Defining The Gift of a Far-Sighted Few; Mark Milner Looks at One Man's Quest to Pin Down What Might Be Thought Too Intangible—That Elusive Ability to See Further Than the Rest, The Guardian, June 9, 2000 (quoting Bush).

25. Richard, Herding Cats, at 4.

26. Id., at 9; Daicoff, Lawyer, Know Thyself, at 1422–1424 (noting also the costs to professionalism of such attributes).

27. Richard, Leadership Competencies in Law, at 46; Richard, Herding Cats at 4, 9; Larry Richard & Lisa Rohrer, A Breed Apart?, American Lawyer, July/Aug. 20011, at 43, 44; Daicoff, Lawyer, Know Thyself at 1392–1394 (noting lawyers' orientation toward logical analysis rather than interpersonal concerns).

28. Richard, Herding Cats at 9; Susan Daicoff, Asking Leopards to Change Their Spots: Should Lawyers Change? A Critique of Solutions to Problems with Professionalism by Reference to Empirically-Derived Attorney Personality Attributes, 11 Geo. J. Legal Ethics 547, 588–589 (1998).

29. Douglas B. Richardson & Douglas P. Coopersmith, Learning to Lead, The American Lawyer, July, 2008, at 57.

30. Jennifer A. Chatman & Jessica A. Kennedy, Psychological Perspectives on Leadership, in Handbook of Leadership Theory and Practice, at 169, 174.

31. The Wisdom of Laotse 114 (trans. & ed. Lin Yutang, 1948).

32. Robert Hogan & Robert B. Kaiser, What We Know about Leadership, 9 Rev. of Gen. Psychol. 169, 176 (2005). Jeffrey Pfeffer, Power: Why Some Have It—and Others Don't 199–200 (2010).

33. Pfeffer, Power, at 221–222. In the nonprofit sector, the problem is sufficiently common with founders of organizations that experts have coined the label "founder's syndrome." Leslie R. Crutchfeld and Heather McLeod Grant, Forces for Good: The Six Practices of High Impact Nonprofits 124, 140 (2008).

34. Manfred Kets de Vries & Elisabet Engellau, A Clinical Approach to the Dynamics of Leadership and Executive Transformation, in Handbook of Leadership Theory and Practice, 183, 195 (Nohria & Khurana, eds., 2010); Terry L. Price, Explaining Ethical Failures of Leadership, in Ethics, The Heart of Leadership 130–31 (Joanne B. Ciulla, ed., 2d. ed. 2004); George R. Goethals, David W. Messick and Scott T. Allison, The Uniqueness Bias: Studies of Constructive Social Comparison, in Social Comparison: Contemporary Theory and Research, 149, 153–155 (Jerry Suls and Thomas Ashby Wills, eds., 1991). See also Roderick M. Kramer, The Harder They Fall, Harv. Bus. Rev., October 2003, at 61.

35. Peter Drucker, What Makes an Effective Executive?, Harv. Bus. Rev. June, 2004, at 63.

CHAPTER 2

1. Bernard Bass, Bass and Stogdill's Handbook of Leadership: Theory, Research, and Managerial Applications 11 (3d ed. 1990) (noting that "[t]here are almost as many definitions of leadership as there are persons who have attempted to define the topic"); Gareth Edwards, In Search of the Holy Grail: Leadership in Management (Working Paper LT-GE-00-15 Ross-on-Wye, United Kingdom, Leadership Trust Foundation 2000).

2. Roger Gill, Theory and Practice of Leadership 9 (2006); Joseph C. Rost, Leadership for the Twenty-First Century 38 (1991).

3. John W. Gardner, On Leadership 3 (1990).

4. Joseph S. Nye Jr., The Powers To Lead 19 (2008).

5. Paul Hoffman, Lions in the Streets 40 (1973).

6. Gardner, On Leadership, at 34.

7. Gill, Theory and Practice of Leadership, 253: Ronald E. Riggio, The Charisma Quotient (1987).

8. See R. J. House, Path-Goal Theory of Leadership: Lessons, Legacy and Reformulated Theory, 7 Leadership Quarterly, 323(1996); Michael E. Brown & Linda K. Trevino, Is Values-Based Leadership Ethical Leadership?, in Emerging Perspectives on Values in Organizations 151, 168 (Steven W. Gilliland, Dirk D. Steiner, & Daniel Skarlicki, eds., 2003).

9. Nye, The Powers to Lead, at 15.

10. Nye, The Powers to Lead, at 121–122.

11. For popular support, see George C. Edwards, On Deaf Ears: The Limits of the Bully Pulpit 87, 105 (2003). For organizations, see Jim Collins, Level 5 Leadership: The Triumph of Humility and Fierce Resolve, Harv. Bus. Rev., Jan. 2001, at 73; Gill, Theory and Practice of Leadership, at 253.

12. Collins, Level 5 Leadership, at 73; Gill, Theory and Practice of Leadership, at 253.

13. For Marshall, see Nicholas deB. Katzenbach; Burke Marshall, in The Yale Biographical Dictionary of American Law 359 (Roger K. Newman, ed., 2009). For Christopher, see Warren Christopher, L.A. Times, March 20, 2011, at A1; Bill Clinton, Warren Christopher, Time, April 4, 2011, at 26. For Cox, see Ken Gormley, Archibald Cox Conscience of a Nation 153 (1999). For Griswold, see Roger K. Newman, Erwin Griswold, in The Yale Biographical Dictionary, supra at 239–240. For Doar, see Roger K. Newman, John Doar, in The Yale Biographical Dictionary, at 167–168.

14. Hoffman, Lions in the Streets, at 9 (quoting Cravath).

15. Frank Rich, It's a Bird, It's a Plane, It's Obama, N. Y. Times, April 4, 2010, at WK9; David Remnick, The Bridge: The Life and Rise of Barak Obama 361 (2011).

16. James Wolcott, One Cool Cat, Vanity Fair, September 2010, 2–6 ("aloof," "professorial"); George Packer, Obama's Last Year, The New Yorker, March 15, 2010, at 46, 49 ("tone deaf," "technocratic") (quoting aides and Barney Frank); George Lakoff, The Policy Speak Disaster for Health Care, Truthout, August 20, 2009 ("policy speak").

17. Wolcott, One Cool Cat at 211 (quoting Richard Cohen on "cannot emote").

18. Wolcott, One Cool Cat at 211 (no drama); Hillel Italie, Critics Assess Obama's Speeches, Capital Culture, January 26, 2010.

19. Ezra Klein, Obama's Gift, The American Prospect, January 3, 2008.

20. James McGregor Burns, Leadership 244 (1978). See also Robert C. Solomon, Ethical Leadership, Emotion and Trust: Beyond "Charisma," in Ethics: The Heart of Leadership 83, 93 (Joanne B. Ciulla, ed., 2d. ed. 2004); Gardner, On Leadership, at 35.

21. Barbara Kellerman, Bad Leadership (2004); D. L. Dolitch & P. Cairo, Why CEOS Fail: The 11 Behaviors that Can Derail Your Climb to the Top and How to Manage them (2003); Robert M. Fulmer & Jay Alden Conger, Growing Your Company's Leaders (2004); Ronald J. Burke, Why Leaders Fail: Exploring the Darkside, 27 International J. of Manpower 91 (2006).

22. Jack Zenger and Joseph Foleman, Ten Fatal Flaws That Derail Leaders, Harv. Bus. Rev., June 2009, at 18–19.

23. In a sample of one hundred leaders of large firms, the trait that stood out was ambition. Larry Richard, Leadership Competencies in Law, in Law and Leadership: Integrating Leadership Studies into the Law School Curriculum 47 (Paula Monopoli & Susan McCarty, eds., 2013).

24. For early development of the contextual approach, see Fred E. Fiedler, A Theory of Leadership Effectiveness (1967); Fred E. Fiedler, Leadership: A New Model,

in Leadership 230–241 (Cecil Austin Gibb, ed., 1969). For discussion of its contemporary applications, see Robert Goffee and Gareth Jones, Why Should Anyone Be Led by You?, Harv. Bus. Rev., September, 2000, at 63–64; Jay Lorsch, A Contingency Theory of Leadership, in Handbook of Leadership Theory and Practice, 411–424 (2010).

25. See Cheryl Lavin, Nader the Dragonslayer Still Breathing Fire, Chicago Tribune, July 13, 1986, at C1; Tamara Straus, From Hero to Pariah in One Documentary, S. F. Chronicle, Mar. 11, 2007, at PK-28 (reviewing the documentary, An Unreasonable Man).

26. Marcia Coyle, A Supreme Court Memoir, Nat'l l L. J.l, October 3, 2011, at 27 (quoting Stevens); Scott Bob Woodward & Scott Armstrong, The Brethren: Inside the Supreme Court 66, 174, 256 (1979); Jeffrey Toobin, The Nine 29 (quoting Rehnquist).

27. Gardner, On Leadership, at 5–6, 47.

28. Center for Creative Leadership, When It Comes to Leadership Talent (2009).

29. See Richard Susskind, Tomorrow's Lawyers 61 (2013); Nancy Levit & Douglas O. Linder, The Happy Lawyer: Making a Good Life in the Law 53–73 (2010); Deborah L. Rhode, In the Interests of Justice 24–38 (2000). For an overview of such trends in the workplace generally see Jeffrey Pfeffer & John F. Veiga, Putting People First for Organizational Success, 13 Acad. Management Executive 37, 45 (1999).

30. For the role of poor leadership and internal rivalries in accounting for law firm difficulties and failures see William G. Johnson, The Anatomy Law Firm Failures, Mar. 2004, http://www.Hildebrandtblog.com/Hildebrandt-Institute. For examples, see Rhode & Packel, Leadership, at 65–69; and chapter 8.

31. David Maister, The Trouble with Lawyers, American Lawyer, April, 2006, at 13, 20. See also Larry Richard, Herding Cats: The Lawyer Personality Revealed, The Personality and Practice, LAWPRO Magazine, Winter 2008, at 1, 3.

32. See Deborah L. Rhode, Public Interest Law: The Movement at Midlife, 60 Stan. L. Rev. 2027 (2008).

33. Montgomery Van Wart, Dynamics of Leadership in Public Service 186 (2011) (quoting David Sarnoff).

34. For the growth in large firms see Scott L. Cummings, The Politics of Pro Bono, 52 UCLA Law Review 1, 3, 34–36 (2004). For public interest organizations, see Rhode, Public Interest Law, at 2031. For a general review of the growth of large multi-office firms, see George P. Baker & Rachel Parkin, The Changing Structure of the Legal Services Industry and the Careers of Lawyers, 84 N. C. L. Rev. 1635, 1643, 1648–1650 (2006).

35. For the rise of in-house counsel, see Colin P. Marks, The Anticipation Misconception, 99 Ky. L. J. 9, 57 (2011) Baker & Parkin, The Changing Structure at 1654. For statistics indicating a 40 percent increase in businesses with over 500 employees in the last two decades, see United States Bureau of the Census,

1988–2006 SUSB Totals for United States, http://www2.census.gov/econ/susb/data/us_state_total_1988-2006.xls. The growth may have leveled off in the wake of the recession.

36. Bob Johansen, Leaders Make the Future 11 (2009).

37. Michael Fullan, Leading in a Culture of Change 2 (2001).

38. Elizabeth Vrato, The Counselors 51 (2002) (quoting Jamie Gorelick).

39. See Nancy Levit & Douglas O. Linder, The Happy Lawyer 6–7 (2010); Daicoff, Lawyer, Know Thyself, at 1407–1409; Deborah L. Rhode, Forward: Personal Satisfaction in Professional Practice, 58 Syr. L. Rev. 217 (2008).

40. Nye, The Powers to Lead, at 2.

41. For discussion of shared and distributed leadership, see Richard Bolden, Beverley Hawkins, Jonathan Gosling & Scott Taylor, Exploring Leadership: Individual, Organizational, and Societal Perspectives 35–39 (2011); Bruce J. Avolio, Fred O. Walumbwa, & Todd J. Weber, Leadership: Current theories, Research, and Future Directions, 60 Annual Rev. Psych. 421, 442–443 (2009).

42. Maister, The Trouble with Lawyers, at 13. For discussion of lawyers' need for autonomy and the difficulties that poses for leadership, see Larry Richard & Susan Raridon Lambreth, What Does It Take to Develop Effective Law Firm Leaders?, Law Practice Today, Mar. 2006, http://www.abanet.org/lpm/lpt/articles/pmqa03061.shtml; Leadership Partners or Managing Partners, Law Office Management and Administration Report, Oct., 2010, at 5. For resistance to innovation, see Susskind, Tomorrow's Lawyers, at 61, 165.

43. Van Wart, Dynamics of Leadership at 55–56.

44. Barbara C. Crosby & John M. Bryson, Leadership for the Common Good 161–162 (2005).

45. Bradley P. Owens & David R. Hekman, Modeling How to Grow: An Inductive Examination of Humble Leader Behaviors, Contingencies, and Outcomes, 55 Academy Management J. 787 (2012); Collins, Level 5 Leadership, at 6.

46. Roderick Kramer, The Harder They Fall, Harv. Bus. Rev., October, 2003, at 58–66, and Terry L. Price, Explaining Ethical Failures of Leadership, in Ethics, The Heart of Leadership 130–31 (Joanne B. Ciulla, ed., 2d. ed. 2004); discussion in chapters 1 and 7.

47. Daniel Goleman, Leadership That Gets Results, Harv. Bus. Rev. March–April, 2000, at 78.

48. Goleman, Leadership That Gets Results, at 78. The sample of 3,871 executives was compiled by the Hay McBer consulting firm from a database of approximately 20,000 executives.

49. Goleman, Leadership That Gets Results, at 78–80.

50. Goleman, Leadership That Gets Results, at 80.

51. The discussion in this section draws on my article for a leadership symposium, Developing Leadership, 52 Santa Clara L. Rev. 689 (2012). For research on Goleman's six styles in law firms, see Susan Snyder & Sara Littauer, Leadership

Flexibility: How Outstanding Partners Get Results, 7 Strategies: Journal of Legal Marketing, 4 (2005).

52. Goleman, Leadership That Gets Results, at 82.

53. Goleman, Leadership That Gets Results, at 82.

54. Snyder & Littauer, Leadership Flexibility, at 7. Snyder and Littauer use the term "directive" to describe this style.

55. Goleman, Leadership That Gets Results, at 83.

56. Roderick M. Kramer, The Great Intimidators, Harv. Bus. Rev. Feb. 2006, at 88, 96.

57. Kramer, The Great Intimidators, at 90.

58. Kramer, The Great Intimidators, at 90.

59. Kramer, The Great Intimidators, at 92 (quoting Thomas).

60. Kramer, The Great Intimidators, at 92.

61. See generally Fred J. Cook, The Army-McCarthy Hearings (1971); Robert Shogan, No Sense of Decency (2009). For McCarthy's fall and censure, see generally Arthur V. Watkins, Enough Rope (1954).

62. Amy Singer, A Passion for Organization, American Lawyer, December 1999, at 24–25.

63. Evan Thomas, The Man to See 206 (1991).

64. Peter Elkind and Jennifer Reingold with Doris Burke, Inside Pfizer's Palace Coup, Fortune, Aug. 15, 2011, at 76.

65. John Maggs, Boss Nader, 36 National Journal 1796, 1798 (2004); Charles McGarry, Citizen Nader 208 (1972).

66. Maggs, Boss Nader, at 1798 (quoting employee).

67. Thomas Ferraro, Nader at 50: The "White Knight" is Still a Driven Man, Hot on the Trail of the Bad Guys, Chicago Tribune, January 4, 1985, at C1.

68. Ferraro, Nader at 50, at C1 (quoting Nader). For a first-time offense, however, the likely sanction would not be severe. Among the options Nader contemplated was a prescribed regimen of apple juice. Id.

69. Isaac Eisler, Shark Tank: Greed, Politics and the Fall of Finley Kumble, One of America's Largest law Firms 153–154 (1990).

70. See Deborah L. Rhode & Barbara Kellerman, Women and Leadership: the State of Play, in Women and Leadership: The State of Play and Strategies for Change 1, 7 (Barbara Kellerman and Deborah L. Rhode, eds., 2007); Sheryl Sandberg, Lean In: Women, Work, and the Will to Lead 39–41 (2013); Cecilia Ridgeway, Framed By Gender: How Gender Inequality Persists in the Modern World 115 (2011); Alice H. Eagly and Linda L. Carli, Through the Labyrinth: The Truth About How Women Become Leaders, 106 (2007); Joan Williams, Reshaping the Work-Family Debate 98 (2010).

71. See Rhode & Kellerman, Women and Leadership at 7; Laurie A. Rudman & Peter Glick, Prescriptive Gender Stereotypes and Backlash Toward Agentic Women, 57 J. Social Issues 743 (2001). For the persistence of such sex stereotypes, see

research summarized in Deborah L. Rhode & Joan Williams, Legal Perspectives on Employment Discrimination, in Sex Discrimination in the Workplace (Faye J. Crosby, Margaret S. Stockdale, & S. Ann Ropp, eds., 2007).

72. Alice H. Eagly and Steven J. Karau, Role Congruity Theory of Prejudice Toward Female Leaders, 109 Psych, Rev. 573, 576 (2002); Dawn L. Brooks and Lynn M. Brooks, Seven Secrets of Successful Women 195 (New York: McGraw Hill, 1997); Linda Babcock & Sara Laschever, Women Don't Ask, 87–88 (2003).

73. Neela Banerjee, The Media Business: Some "Bullies" Seek Ways to Soften Up: Toughness Has Risks for Women Executives, N. Y. Times, Aug. 10, 2001, at C1.

74. Suzanne Braun Levine & Mary Thom, Bella Abzug 201 (2007) (quoting Brownie Ledbetter on Rosalynn Carter's assessment as "rude"); id. at XIII ("cantankerous"); id. At 19 (quoting Amy Swerdlow "abusive and "not kind"); id., at 150 (quoting Eileen Shanahan about being harsh to staff and having high levels of turnover).

75. In his presidential news conference announcing Abzug's departure as Chair, Carter noted that "there has not been good cooperation between the committee and the cabinet members, or my advisors or me, and I felt it was necessary to change the chairperson." Levine & Thom, at 221 (quoting Carter).

76. For the importance of likeability, see Steve Arneson, How Much Does Likeability Influence How We View Leaders?, Leadership Examiner, (Mar. 1, 2009), http://www.examiner.com/leadership-in-national/how-much-does-lieability-influence-how-we-view-leaders; Tim Sanders, The Likeability Factor: How to Boost Your L-Factor and Achieve Your Life's Dreams (2005). For the particular importance of likeability for women see Sandberg, Lean In, at 39–41. For the destructive effects of bullying on physical and mental health and job performance, see the research summarized in Pamela Lutgen-Sandvik et al., Workplace Bullying: Causes, Consequences, and Corrections, in Destructive Organizational Communication 41, 46–47 (Pamela Lutgen-Sandvik, & Beverly Davenport Sypher, eds., 2009).

77. Nye, The Powers to Lead, at 82.

78. Kramer, The Harder They Fall, at 94.

79. Kramer, The Harder They Fall, at 94.

80. See Scott W. Sprier, Mary H. Fontaine, and Ruth L. Malloy, Leadership Run Amok: The Destructive Potential of Overachievers, Harv. Bus. Rev., June 2006, at 72, 74–79.

81. Liz Wiseman with Greg McKeown, Multipliers: How the Best Leaders Make Everyone Smarter 102 (2010).

82. Goleman, Leadership, at 83.

83. Goleman, Leadership, at 83–84.

84. Goleman, Leadership, at 84.

85. For the "low trust" environment of many firms, see Maister, The Trouble With Lawyers, at 13.

86. D. Anthony Butterfield & James P. Grinnell, "Re-viewing" Gender Leadership, and Managerial Behavior: Do Three Decades of Research Tell Us Anything?, in Handbook of Gender and Work 223, 235 (Gary N. Powell ed., 1999); Alice H. Eagly, Mona G. Makhijani, & Bruce G. Klonsky, Gender and The Evaluation of Leaders, 111 Psych. Bull. 17 (1992); Jeanette N. Cleveland, Margaret Stockdale, & Kevin R. Murphy, Women and Men in Organizations: Sex and Gender Issues at Work 106–107 (2000); Rochelle Sharpe, As Leaders, Women Rule: New Studies Find that Female Managers Outshine Their Male Counterparts in Almost Every Measure, Businessweek Online, Nov. 20, 2000, http/www.businessweek.com/2000/00_47/b3708145.htm.

87. See Eagly & Carli, Through the Labyrinth, at 187.

88. Amy Wilentz, Yellow Pantsuit, in Thirty Ways of Looking at Hillary Clinton 1, 6 (Susan Morrison, ed., 2008).

89. The phrase originally comes from Mary Mary Sue Coleman, President of the University of Michigan, and is explored in Linda Babcock & Sara Laschever, Ask For It 252–255 (2008), and Sandberg, Lean In, at 48.

90. Babcock & Laschever, Ask for It. at 253–266.

91. Goleman, Leadership at 84; Snyder & Littauer, Leadership Flexibility, at 6.

92. Victor Navasky, Kennedy Justice 359 (Rev. Ed. 2000).

93. Navasky, Kennedy Justice at 348, 355.

94. Navasky, Kennedy Justice at 444.

95. Jonathan Alter, Woman of the World, Vanity Fair, June, 2011, http://www.vanityfair.com/politics/features/2011/06/hillary-clinton-201106

96. Alter, Woman of the World.

97. Michael Kelly, Lives of Lawyers Revisited 100 (2007).

98. Joel Rosenblatt, The Great Sonsini, Cal. Lawyer, Oct. 2004, at 22, 28.

99. Philippa Strum, Brandeis: Beyond Progressivism 56 (1993) (letter to William Dunbar).

100. Goleman, Leadership, at 85.

101. See Rhode & Packel, Leadership, at 166–168. Studies by the Leadership Development Institute and the Center for Creative Leadership estimate between 20 to 40 percent of leaders' time is spent on conflicts. Craig E. Runde & Tim A. Flanagan, Becoming a Conflict Competent Leader 12 (2007) (explaining the need to directly address conflict and an overview of strategies). See generally Barbara A. Nagle Lechman, Conflict and Resolution (2008); Ho-Wan Joeng, Understanding Conflict and Conflict Analysis (2008).

102. Goleman, Leadership, at 85.

103. Rhode, Public Interest Law, at 2050 (all but 5 percent of leading organizations report extensive staff involvement).

104. Goleman, Leadership, at 85.

105. Goleman, Leadership, at 85.

106. Goleman, Leadership, at 85.

107. John Heilemann & Mark Halperin, Game Change 188 (2010).

108. Heilemann & Halperin, Game Change, at 194.

109. Heilemann & Halperin, Game Change, at 196.

110. Goleman, Leadership, at 85.

111. The quote has variously been attributed to Oscar Wilde, George Orwell, and George Bernard Shaw. See The Problem with Google Is Similar: Too Many Results, Ask Metafilter (Jan. 28, 2007) http://ask.metafilter.com/55890/The-problem-with-Google-is-similar-too-many-results

112. Goleman, Leadership, at 86.

113. William Kuntsler with Sheila Isenberg, My Life as a Radical Lawyer (1994).

114. Kuntsler with Isenberg, My Life, at 395.

115. Kuntsler with Isenberg, My Life, at 396.

116. Kuntsler with Isenberg, My Life, at 396.

117. Charles McCarry, Citizen Nader 183 (1972).

118. McCarry, Citizen Nader, at 183.

119. Thomas Whiteside, Profiles: A Countervailing Force II, New Yorker, October 15, 1973, at 52, 56.

120. Whiteside, Profiles, at 56.

121. Goleman, Leadership, at 86.

122. Goleman, Leadership, at 86.

123. Goleman, Leadership, at 86.

124. Whiteside, Profiles at 52 (quoting Robert Fellmeth).

125. Whiteside, Profiles, at 60 (describing responsibilities given to staff); Juan Williams, Return from the Nadir, Washington Post, May 23, 1982, at 6 (describing Nadir's ability to enlist a million supporters in campus Public Interest Research Groups and to launch careers of major public figures). For overviews of his legacy, see Patricia Cronin Marcello, Ralph Nader: A Biography 1 (2004).

126. Whiteside, Profiles, at 55 (quoting Reuben Robinson).

127. Goleman, Leadership, at 87.

128. Juan Williams, Thurgood Marshall: American Revolutionary 53–57, 94 (1998); Genna Rae McNeil, Charles Hamilton Houston: 1895–1950, 32 Howard L. Rev. 469, 472–473 (1989). For Marshall's mentoring, see Constance Baker Motley, My Personal Debt to Thurgood Marshall, 101 Yale L. J. 19, 22 (1991).

129. See Raymond C. Fisher, Warren M. Christopher '49, Stanford Lawyer, Spring 2011, at 13, 81–85.

130. Babcock served as Assistant Attorney General for the Civil Division under the Carter administration, and Kaye served as dean of the Boalt Hall School of Law at Berkeley and as president of the Association of American Law Schools. I personally am a major beneficiary of mentoring by them both.

131. Goleman, Leadership, at 87.

132. Rhode and Packel, Leadership at 56, 166; Deborah L. Rhode, From Platitudes to Priorities: Diversity and Gender Equity in Law Firms, 24 Geo. J. Legal Ethics 1041, 1067 (2011).

133. Rhode, Platitudes, at 1054, American Bar Association Commission on Women in the Profession, Visible Invisibility: Women of Color in Law Firms 15–16 (2006).

134. For the inadequacy of mentoring, see Rhode, Platitudes at 1071. For the inadequacy of leadership succession programs, see Ida Abbott, Taking the Lead, 21 Management Solutions (Winter 2008) http://www.IdaAbbott.com/sites/default/files/news-archive/news21.html.

135. For the absence of skills, see Goleman, Leadership at 78; for the problems experienced by women and minorities see American Bar Association Commission on Women in the Profession, Visible Invisibility, at 15–21; Leigh Jones, Mentoring Plans Failing Associates, National L. J., Sept. 18, 2006, at 1; Rhode & Kellerman, Women and Leadership, at 10–11, 22; Rhode, Platitudes at 1072. Senior men often report discomfort or inadequacy discussing "women's issues," and minorities express reluctance to raise diversity-related concerns with those who lack experience or empathy. Ida Abott & Rita Boags, Minority Corporate Counsel Association, Mentoring Across Differences: A Guide to Cross-Gender and Cross-Race Mentoring (2004).

136. Rhode, Platitudes, at 1972; Jones, Mentoring at 1; Minnesota State Bar Association, Best Practices Guide, Diversity and Gender Equity in the Legal Profession 70–71, 77–79 (2008).

137. Abbott & Boags, Mentoring Across Differences.

138. For an example, see David Wilkins, On Being Good and Black, 112 Harv. L. Rev. 1924, 1927 (1999) (reviewing Paul M. Barrett The Good Black: A True Story of Race in American (1999) (discussing Katten Mungen's failure to effectively support and mentor a black associate who later sued the firm for race discrimination and noting one commentator's characterization of the problem as "business as usual mismanagement").

139. See generally National Association of Law Placement (NALP), Update on Associate Attrition (2010); NALP, Keeping the Keepers II: Mobility and Management of Associates (2004).

140. Jill Schachner Chanen, Early Exits, ABA. J., (2006), at 33, 36, http://abanet.org/women/woc/EarlyExits.pdf.

141. Jack Zenger & Joseph Folkman, Ten Fatal Flaws That Derail Leaders, Harv. Bus. Rev., June 2009, at 18.

142. Goleman, Leadership, at 87.

143. Goleman, Leadership, at 87. See also Snyder & Littauer, Leadership Flexibility, at 7–8.

144. Adrian Gostick & Scott Christopher, Levity Effect 139 (2008); Bell Leadership Institute, Humor Gives Leaders the Edge (2012), http//www.bellleadership.com/pressresleases/press_template.php?id=15; Bruce J. Avolio et al., A Funny Thing Happened on the Way to the Bottom Line: Humor as a Moderator of Leadership Style Effects, 42 Academy of Management Journal 2190 (1999); William Decker & Denise Rotondo, Relationships Among Gender, Type of Humor, and Perceived Leader Effectiveness 13 J. Managerial Issues 450 (2001).

145. C.B. Crawford, Strategic Humor in Leadership: Practical Suggestions for Appropriate Use, 4 Speech/Conf. Papers 17 (1994); Eric J. Romero and Anthony Pescosolido, Humor and Group Effectiveness, 61 Human Relations 395 (2008); Eric J. Romero & Kevin W. Cruthirds, The Use of Humor in the Workplace, 59 Academy Management J. 69 (2006).

146. Kevin T. Baine, Wit, Wisdom and Compassion In Memoriam: Justice Thurgood Marshall, 20 Hastings Constitutional L. Q. 497, 499 (1993). See also Susan Low Block et al., Remembering Justice Thurgood Marshall: Thoughts From His Clerks, 1 Geo. J. Pov. L. and Pol'y 9 (1993) (comments of Susan Low Block).

147. Williams, Thurgood Marshall at 207.

148. Williams, Thurgood Marshall, at 286.

149. Williams, Thurgood Marshall, at 171–172.

150. Williams, Thurgood Marshall, at 172 (quoting Marshall).

151. See Deborah L. Rhode, Letting the Law Catch Up, 44 Stan. L. Rev. 1259, 1267 (1992) (quoting Marshall).

CHAPTER 3

1. For firms, see Douglas B. Richardson & Douglas P. Coopersmith, Learning to Lead, American Lawyer, July, 2008, at 57, and Susan G. Manch with Michelle C. Nash, Learning From Law Firm Leaders xii (2012). For law schools, see Neil W. Hamilton, Ethical Leadership in Professional Life, 6 U. St. Thomas L. J. 358, 370 (2009).

2. For studies on twins finding that 70 percent of leadership traits were learned, see Richard D. Arvey et al., The Determinants of Leadership Role Occupancy: Genetic and Personality Factors, 17 Leadership Quarterly 1 (2006); Bruce Avolio, Pursuing Authentic Leadership Development, in Handbook of Leadership Theory and Practice 739, 752 (Nitan Nohria & Rakesh Khurana, eds., 2010). See also Warren G. Bennis & Bert Nanus, Leadership: Strategies for Taking Charge 207 (1997); Sharon Daloz Parks, Leadership *Can* Be Taught (2005).

3. James M. Kouzes & Barry Z. Posner, The Truth About Leadership 119 (2010). See also Caroll Dweck, Mindset: The New Psychology of Success 7 (2006) (noting that people who believe talent can be developed are best at confronting their mistakes and learning from them).

4. Douglas A. Ready, Jay A. Conger, and Linda A. Hill, Are You a High Potential?, Harv. Bus. Rev. June, 2010, at 78, 82.

5. Thomas Harry Williams, Huey Long 34 (1969).

6. Jacob Heilbruner, Interim Report, N. Y. Times Book Rev, May 30, 2010, at 12.

7. Roger Gill, Theory and Practice of Leadership 275 (2006); Peter E. Drucker, Managing Oneself, Harv. Bus. Rev., March–April 1999, at 68–69; Doug Lennick & Fred Kiehl, Moral Intelligence: Enhancing Business Performance and Leadership Success 239 (2008).

8. Noel H. Tichy & Warren Bennis, Judgment 10 (2002).

9. For the survey of managing partners, see Leadership Partners or Managing Partners, Law Office Management & Administration Report 1, 6 (2010). For the role of leadership in law firm dissolution, see chapter 8, Deborah L. Rhode & Amanda Packel, Leadership: Law, Policy, and Management 63–69 (2011); and Hildebrandt, The Anatomy of Law Firm Failures, November 19, 2008, available at http://www.Hildebrandt.com/The-Anatonomy-of-Law-Firm-Failures,

10. Warren Bennis & Burt Nanus, Leaders: The Strategies for Taking Charge 76 (1985), quoted in Carol Tavris & Eliot Aronson, Mistakes Were Made (but not by me) 225, n. 9 (2007).

11. Lennick & Kiehl, Moral Intelligence, at 245–248.

12. Id. For discussion of research showing performance improvement when people receive praise and recognition, see Thomas J. Peters & Robert H. Waterman, In Search of Excellence: Lessons from America's Best Run Corporations 58–59 (2004); David DeSteno & Piercarlo Valdesolo, Out of Character 114–115 (2011).

13. Drucker, Managing Oneself, at 65.

14. James M. Kouzes & Barry Z. Posner, A Leader's Legacy 28 (2006). See also Larry Richards, Herding Cats: The Lawyer Personality Revealed, 29 Report of Legal Management 1, 3 (Altman Weil, 2002) (noting that lawyers score low on resiliency, which means that they tend to be defensive and resistant to negative feedback).

15. Kouzes & Posner, A Leader's Legacy, at 28.

16. National Association for Law Placement Foundation (NALPF), How Associate Evaluations Measure Up: A National Study of Associate Performance Assessments 74 (2006).

17. Robert Hargrove, Masterful Coaching 302 (2008) (quoting Galbraith).

18. For the classic description, see Lee Ross, The Intuitive Psychologist and His Shortcomings; Distortions in the Attribution Process, in 10 Advances in Experimental Social Psychology 173–220 (Leonard Berkowitz, ed., 1977).

19. For discussion of such biases, see Thomas Peters and Robert Waterman, In Search of Excellence 58 (2004); Leary Davis, Competence as Situationally Appropriate Conduct: An Overarching Concept for Lawyering, Leadership and Professionalism, 52 Santa Clara L. Rev. 725, 764 (2012).

20. David G. Myers, The Inflated Self: How Do I Love Me? Let Me Count the Ways, Psychology Today, May, 1980, at 16.

21. Robert Hargrove, Masterful Coaching, 124 (2008). See also Chris Argyris, Teaching Smart People How to Learn, Harv. Bus. Rev, May–June, 1991, at 99–109.

22. Hargrove, Masterful Coaching, at 124.

23. Hargrove, Masterful Coaching, at 124; Argyris, Teaching Smart People, at 100.

24. Morgan W. McCall Jr., The Experience Conundrum, in Handbook of Leadership Theory and Practice 679, 692–693; Ben W. Heineman Jr., & David B. Wilkins, The Lost Generation?, American Lawyer, March 1, 2008, 85.

25. McCall, The Experience Conundrum, at 699.

26. Richardson & Coopersmith, Learning to Lead, at 57.

27. Larry Richard, Herding Cats: The Lawyer Personality Revealed, 29 Report to Legal Management 1, 4, 9 (Altman Weil Aug. 2002); Susan Daicoff, Lawyer, Know Thyself: A Review of Empirical Research on Attorney Attributes Bearing on Professionalism, 46 Am. U. L. Rev. 1337, 1349, 1390–1391 (1997).

28. For an overview, see Daniel Goleman, Richard Boyatzis & Annie McKee, Primal Leadership: Learning to Lead with Emotional Intelligence (2002); Susan Swain Daicoff, Expanding the Lawyer's Toolkit of Skills and Competencies, 52 Santa Clara L. Rev. 795, 840–842 (2012).

29. Richard J. Leider, The Ultimate Leadership Task: Self-Leadership, in The Leader of the Future: New Visions, Strategies, and Practices for the Next Era 189 (Frances Hesselbein, Marshall Goldsmith, & Richard Beckhard, eds., 1997).

30. Jim Collins, Level 5 Leadership: The Triumph of Humility and Fierce Resolve, Harv. Bus. Rev., January 2001, at 2 (quoting Smith).

31. Marshal Ganz & Emily Shin, Learning to Lead, in Handbook of Leadership Theory and Practice, at 353, 365.

32. Joseph Nye, The Powers to Lead 24 (2008); Jay A. Conger, Leadership Development Initiatives, in Handbook of Leadership Theory and Practice, at 712,714; James M. Kouzes & Barry Z. Posner, The Truth About Leadership 121 (2010).

33. See Mentkowski & Associates, Learning That Lasts: Integrating Learning, Development and Performance in College and Beyond 120–121 (2000); Muriel Bebeau, Promoting Ethical Development and Professionalism: Insights from Educational Research in the Professions, 5 U. St. Thomas L. J. 366, 384–385 (2008) (summarizing research); Deborah L. Rhode, Ethics by the Pervasive Method, 42 J. Legal Ed. 31, 46 (1992); William M. Sullivan et al., Educating Lawyers: Preparation for the Profession of Law 135 (2007); M. Neil Browne, Carrie L. Williamson & Linda L. Barkacs, The Purported Rigidity of an Attorney's Personality: Can Legal Ethics be Acquired?, 30 J. Legal Prof. 55 (2006).

34. Steven Hartwell, Promoting Moral Development Through Experiential Teaching, 1 Clinical L. Rev. 505 (1995); Neil Hamilton & Lisa M. Brabbit, Fostering Professionalism Through Mentoring, 37 J. Legal Educ. 102 (2007); National Research Council, Learning and Transfer, in How People Learn 51–78 (John D. Bransford et al., eds., 2000). For the pressures that need to be addressed, see Deborah L Rhode, If Integrity Is the Answer, What Is the Question?, 72 Fordham L. Rev. 333 (2003).

35. For examples of teaching materials, see Rhode & Packel, Leadership; Law and Leadership (Paula Monopoli & Susan McCarty, eds., 2013).

36. Lisa A. Boyce, Stephen J. Zaccaro, & Michelle Zaanis Wisecarver, Propensity for Self-Development of Leadership Attributes: Understanding, Predicting, and Supporting Performance of Leader Self-Development, 21 Leadership Q. 159 (2010).

37. Warren Bennis, On Becoming a Leader 108–109 (2002).
38. Michele Coleman Mayes & Kara Sophia Baysinger, Courageous Counsel 122 (2011) (quoting Richard St. John).
39. Boyce, Zaccaro, & Wisecarver, Propensity for Self-Development of Leadership Attributes: Understanding, Predicting, and Supporting Performance of Leader Self-Development, 21 The Leadership Quarterly 161 (2010).
40. Douglas A. Ready, Jay A. Conger, & Linda A. Hill, Are You a High Potential, Harv. Bus. Rev., June 2010, at 82; Linda A. Hill, Developing the Star Performer, in Leader to Leader 296 (Frances Hesselbein & Paul M. Cohen, eds., 1999); David V. Day, Leadership Development: A Review in Context, 11 The Leadership Quarterly 581 (2001).
41. See William A. Cohen, Drucker on Leadership 139–140, 193 (2010); John P. Kotter, What Leaders Really Do, Harv. Bus. Rev. 68, May–June 1990, 103; Sheri-Lynne Leskiw and Parbudyal Singh, Leadership Development: Learning from Best Practices, 28 Leadership and Organizational Development Journal 444, 450–454 (2007).
42. McCall, The Experience Conundrum, at 679, 683–685.
43. Peter Senge, The Fifth Discipline: The Art and Practice of the Learning Organization 3 (1990).
44. D. A. Gavin, Building a Learning Organization, Harv. Bus. Rev., July-August, 1993, 78, 79.
45. Robin J. Ely, Herminia Ibarra, & Deborah M. Kolb, Taking Gender into Account: Theory and Design for Women's Leadership Programs 474, 480 (2011).
46. Argyris, Teaching Smart People, at 99.
47. Argyris, Teaching Smart People, at 107.
48. Argryris, Teaching Smart People, at 100.
49. This discussion of lawyers' career paths draws on Deborah L. Rhode, What Lawyers Lack: Leadership, 9 University of St. Thomas L. J. 471 (2011).
50. John Gardner, On Leadership 117 (1990).
51. Doug Lennick and Fred Kiel, Moral Intelligence, 240 (2007).
52. Richard Leider, The Ultimate Leadership Task, in The Leader of the Future 189–198 (Frances Hesselbein, Marshall Goldsmith, & Richard Beckhard, eds., 1997).
53. Elizabeth Vrato, Counselors 85 (2002) (quoting Marshall).
54. Marian Wright Edelman, Lanterns: A Memoir of Mentors 61 (1999).
55. Constance Baker Motley, Equal Justice Under Law: An Autobiography 97 (1998).
56. Cheryl Lavin, Nader: the Dragon Slayer Still Breathing Fire, Chicago Tribune, July 13, 1986, at A1, A5 (quoting Nader).
57. Lavin, Nader, at A5 (quoting Nader). See also Thomas Ferraro, Nader at 50: The White Knight Is Still a Driven Man, Hot on the Trail of the Bad Guys, Chicago Tribune, January 4, 1985, at 1 (quoting Nader's statement: "I enjoy achieving justice in society. That's my greatest satisfaction").

58. Paul Farhi, Miles to Go: In Ralph Nader's Race for Reform, This Is No Time to Slow Down, Washington Post, June 25, 2008, at C1 (quoting Paul Krugman).

59. Lavin, Nader, at A5 (quoting Nader)

60. Lavin, Nader, at A5.

61. Lavin, Nader, at A5 (quoting Nader).

62. Thomas Whiteside, A Countervailing Force II, New Yorker, October 15, 1973, at 62.

63. Hillary Rodham Clinton, in Encyclopedia of Arkansas History and Culture, http://www.encyclopediaofarkansas.net/encyclopediea/entry-detail.aspx?entryID-2744.

64. Jeff Gerth & Don Van Natta, Her Way 31 (2007).

65. Tribute to Sandra Day O'Connor, comments of Justice Stephen G. Breyer, 119 Harv. L. Rev. 1242 (2006); Sandra Day O'Conner & Alan Day, Lazy B: Growing Up on a Cattle Ranch in the American Southwest (2002); Joan Biskupic, Sandra Day O'Connor 7–21 (2005).

66. Williams, Thurgood Marshall, at 62–63, 73, 76–77, 84–85.

67. Williams, Thurgood Marshall, at 193, 272–274.

68. Williams, Thurgood Marshall, at 274–276.

69. Drew Days, Confessions of an Improbable Professor, Yale Law Report, Summer 2011, at 50, 51.

70. Barbara Babcock, Woman Lawyer: The Trials of Clara Foltz 7–8 (2011).

71. Babcock, Woman Lawyer, at 8.

72. Babcock, Woman Lawyer, at 33. Foltz originated the concept of the public defender.

73. Hillary Rodham Clinton, Living History 69 (2003).

74. Clinton, in Encyclopedia of Arkansas History and Culture.

75. Biskupic, O'Connor, at 28.

76. Biksupic, O'Connor, at 31 (quoting O'Connor).

77. Biskupic, O'Connor, at 31.

78. Biskupic, O'Connor, at 72–78.

79. Sandra Day O'Connor, Preface, in Women and Leadership: The State of Play and Strategies for Change xiv (Barbara Kellerman & Deborah L. Rhode, eds., 2007).

80. The suit was Murray v. Pearson. See Richard Kluger, Simple Justice: The History of Brown v. Board of Education and Black America's Struggle for Equality 187–194 (1975); Michael D. Davis & Hunter R. Clark, Thurgood Marshall: Warrior at the Bar, Rebel on the Bench 11, 78–79 (1992).

81. Babcock, Woman Lawyer, at 44–57. The victory didn't help Foltz, because by the time the case was decided she could no longer afford to be a student. Id., at 57.

82. Barbara Allen Babcock, Feminist Lawyers, 50 Stan. L. Rev. 1689, 1694 (1998) (quoting Foltz).

83. Babcock, Feminist Lawyers, at 1694.

84. For the costs of formal complaints, which still persist, see Deborah L. Rhode, From Platitudes to Priorities: Diversity and Gender Equity in Law Firms, 24 Geo. J. Legal Ethics 1041, 1059 (2011).

85. Suzanne Braun Levine & Mary Thom, Bella Abzug 27, 29 (2007).

86. Williams, Thurgood Marshall, at 178 (quoting Marshall).

87. William Safire & Leonard Safir, Leadership 220 (1990) (quoting Rockefeller).

88. Victor Navasky, Kennedy Justice 162 (2000) (quoting Byron White).

89. Arthur L. Liman with Peter Israel, Lawyer: A Life of Counsel and Controversy 35 (1998).

90. Liman with Israel, Lawyer, at 35.

91. Warren Christopher, Chance of a Lifetime 35 (2001).

92. Christopher, Chance of a Lifetime., at 123.

93. Christopher, Chance of a Lifetime, at 105, 123.

94. Ken Gormley, Archibald Cox: Conscience of a Nation, 141 (1999).

95. Biskupic, Sandra Day O'Connor, at 80 (quoting O'Connor).

96. Biskupic, O'Connor, at 83. Other commentators were harsher. According to the Nation, "Judge O'Connor's record is not even close to Supreme Court quality. She was not an exceptional lawyer or legal scholar; nor is she an outstanding judge." Id., (quoting Nation).

97. Biskupic, Sandra Day O'Connor, at 71–72, 76–77.

98. Biskupic, O'Connor, at 75.

99. Vrato, Counselor, at 128.

100. Richard Nixon, In the Arena 195 (1990).

101. Developing Law Firm Leaders, Law Practice Management, October, 2003, at 27, 30 (quoting Nancy Geenan).

102. Developing Law Firm Leaders, at 30 (quoting Ronald Ruma).

103. Developing Law Firm Leaders, at 30 (quoting Wendy Tice-Wallner).

104. Mayes & Baysinger, Courageous Counsel 96 (quoting Daley).

105. Id., at 28, 30.

106. Eliott Richardson declared his willingness to run for president if there was an "organized, well-financed, massive draft movement on my behalf." Harry Whitten, Richardson Still Has Foot in the Political Door, Honolulu Star-Bulletin, Dec. 12, 1978 (quoting Richardson). After a distinguished career in public service, Richardson spent his final years in a private practice that never lived up to expectations. See James Abourezk, Oh Congress, My Congress, Washington Post, June 16, 1980 (describing Richardson as "bored with private life to the point that he cares about little else but public service").

107. Biskupic, Sandra Day O'Connor, at 75 (quoting Henry Habitch).

108. Elinor Smith, in Aviation Pioneers: An Anthology (2006), available at http://www.ctie.monash.edu.au/hargrave/smith_e.html.

109. Doug Lennick & Fred Kiehl, Moral Intelligence: Enhancing Business Performance and Leadership Success 97 (2005).

110. Gill, Theory and Practice, at 273–277; Day, Leadership Development, at 594.

111. Constance Baker Motley, Equal Justice Under Law: An Autobiography 41, 56 (1998).

112. Barbara Allen Babcock, Feminist Lawyers, 50 Stan. L. Rev. 1689, 1705 (1998). Motley herself received funds for her college and law school education from a male philanthropist. Motley, Equal Justice, 45.

113. Gormley, Archibald Cox at 86 (quoting Richardson).

114. Gormley, Archibald Cox, at 86 (quoting Richardson quoting Cox).

115. Evan Thomas, The Man to See, 330, 331–332 (1992).

116. Thomas, The Man to See, at 330.

117. Thomas, The Man to See, at 330.

118. Liman with Lazarus, Lawyer, at.3.

119. Liman with Lazarus, Lawyer, at 3.

120. John Heilemann & Mark Halperin, Game Change: Obama and the Clintons, McCain and Palin, and the Race of a Lifetime 28 (2010) (quoting Obama's 2005 statement to his Senate chief of staff, Pete Rouse).

121. Id. See also NPR, All Things Considered, November 19, 2007 (describing Obama's consultations with former federal judge and congressman Abner Mikva, campaign manager Dan Shomon, and strategist David Axelrod).

122. Heilemann & Halperin, Game Change, at 34, 36–37.

123. David Remnick, The Joshua Generation: Race and the Campaign of Barack Obama, The New Yorker, November 17, 2008, at 68 (quoting Axelrod).

124. NPR, All Things Considered, (comments of Michelle Obama). See also Heilemann & Halperin, Game Change, at 87–88.

125. Daniel J. Boorstein, A Case of Hypochondria, in The Spirit of '70; Six Historians Reflect on What Ails the American Spirit, Newsweek, July 6, 1970, at 19 (discussing education generally).

126. Michael Burlingame, The Inner World of Abraham Lincoln 194 (1994); Vrato, Counselors, at 129.

CHAPTER 4

1. Jonah Lehrer, How We Decide 159 (2009) (quoting Simon and citing research).

2. Jon Hanson & David Yosifon, The Situational Character: A Critical Realist Perspective on the Human Animal, 93 Geo. L. J. 1, 37 (2004).

3. David Eagleman, Incognito: The Secret Lives of the Brain 4 (2011); Daniel Kahneman, Thinking, Fast and Slow 20–21 (2011); Jonathan Haidt, The Emotional Dog and its Rational Tail: A Social Intuitionist Approach to Moral Judgment, 108 Psychological Review 814, 822, 828 (2001).

4. Gerd Gigerenzer, Heuristics, in Heuristics and the Law 17 (Gerd Gigerenzer & Christoph Engel, eds., 2006).

5. Montgomery Van Wart, Dynamics of Leadership in Public Service: Theory and Practice 329–330 (2005).

6. Dolly Chugh & Max Bazerman, Bounded Awareness: What You Fail to See Can Hurt You, 6 Mind and Society 1 (2007).

7. Christopher Chabris & Daniel Simons, The Invisible Gorilla: And Other Ways Our Intuitions Deceive Us (2010).

8. Kahneman, Thinking Fast and Slow, at 24.

9. Max H. Bazerman & Ann E. Tenbrunsel, Blind Spots: Why We Fail to Do What's Right and What to Do About It 7, 33 (2011).

10. Fritz Heider, The Psychology of Interpersonal Relations (1958); Paul Brest & Linda Hamilton Krieger, Problem Solving, Decision Making, and Professional Judgment: A Guide for Lawyers and Policymakers 332 (2010).

11. Bazerman and Tenbrunsel, Blind Spots, at 83.

12. Lee Ros & Donna Shestowsky, Contemporary Psychology's Challenge to Legal Theory and Practice, 97 Northwestern L. Rev. 108 (2003).

13. Bazerman & Tenbrunsel, Blind Spots, at 57.

14. Philip Tetlock, Expert Political Judgment: How Good is It? How Can We Know? (2005).

15. Richard Nisbett & Lee Ross, Human Inference Strategies and Shortcomings in Social Judgment 45 (1980) (vivid information); Bazerman & Tenbrunsel, Blind Spots, at 92 (incremental change); Kahneman, Thinking Fast and Slow at 80 (selective recall of information that confirms prior views).

16. Paul Brest, Quis Custodiet Ipsos Custodes? Debiasing the Policy Makers Themselves, in The Behavioral Foundations of Policy (Eldar Shafir, ed., 2011).

17. Karen E. Jenni and George Loewenstein, Explaining the "Identifiable Victim Effect," 14 Journal of Risk and Uncertainty 235 (1997).

18. James Friedrich et al., Psychophysical Numbing: When Lives Are Valued Less as the Lives at Risk Increase, 8 Journal of Consumer Psychology 277, 285 (1999).

19. Nisbett & Ross, Human Inference, at 43 (quoting Stalin).

20. Don Van Natta Jr. & Abby Goodnough, 2 Cambridge Worlds Collide in Unlikely Meeting, N. Y. Times, July 26, 2009, at A13.

21. Abby Goodnough, Harvard Professor Jailed; Officer Is Accused of Bias, N. Y. Times, July 21, 2009, at A13.

22. Gates Police Report (2009), http://www.scribd.com/doc/17512830/Gates-Police-Report.

23. Good Morning America, Henry Louis Gates Jr.: I'm Outraged, http://www.youtube.com/watch?v=AeRK_olc3yQ&feature=fvsr.

24. John Hechinger & Simmi Aujla, Police Drop Charges Against Black Scholar, Wall Street Journal, July 22, 2009, at A6.

25. Katharine Q. Seelye, Obama Wades Into a Volatile Racial Issue, N. Y. Times, July 23, 2009, http://www.nytimes.com/2009/07/23/us/23race.html.

26. Anahad O'Connor, Beer Summit Goes for a Second Round, N. Y. Times, October 30, 2009, http://thecaucus.blogs.nytimes.com/2009/10/30/beer-summit-goes-for-a-second-round/.

27. Ben W. Heineman Jr., A Due Process Teaching Moment—WASTED, The Atlantic, July 25, 2009, http://www.theatlantic.com/politics/archive/2009/07/a-due-process-teaching-moment-wasted/22124/.

28. Heineman, A Due Process Teaching Moment.

29. Jeff Zeleny, Obama Expresses His Regrets on Gates Incident, The Caucus, The Politics and Government Blog of The Times, July 24, 2009, http://thecaucus.blogs.nytimes.com/2009/07/24/obama-expresses-his-regrets-on-gates-incident/? ge=4.

30. Seelye, Obama Wades into a Volatile Racial Issue.

31. The Borowitz Report, Funny Times, September 2009, at 5.

32. The Daily Show with Jon Stewart, July 30, 2009.

33. Abby Goodnough, Gates Reflects on Beers at the White House, The Caucus, The Politics and Government Blog of The Times, July 31, 2009, http://thecaucus.blogs.nytimes.com/2009/07/31/gates-reflects-on-beers-at-the-white-house/.

34. Slavisa Tasic, Are Regulators Rational? 17 Journal des Economistes et des Etudes Humaines (2011); Matt Ridley, Studying the Biases of Bureaucrats, Wall Street Journal, October 23, 2010, at C4.

35. Ken Auletta, Non-Stop News, New Yorker, June 25, 2010, 38.

36. Heineman, A Due Process Teaching Moment.

37. Harold J. Leavitt, Suppose We Took Groups Seriously, in Man and Work in Society 67–77 (Eugene L. Cass & Frederick G. Zimmer, eds., 1975).

38. Irving L Janis, Groupthink: Psychological Studies of Policy Decisions and Fiascoes (1982).

39. Brest & Krieger, Problem Solving, at 597.

40. Irving Janis, Groupthink, 4–5; Susan Cain, The Rise of the New Groupthink, New York Times, January 13, 2012, at Wk1, 6.

41. Steven G. Rogelberg, Janet L. Barnes-Farrell, & Charles A Lowe, The Stepladder Technique: An Alternative Group Structure Facilitating Effective Group Decisionmaking, 77 Journal of Applied Technology 730 (1992).

42. Gene Rowe & George Wright, Expert Opinions in Forecasting: The Role of the Delphi Technique, in Principles of Forecasting 125 (J. Scott Armstrong, ed., 2001).

43. Report of the Select Committee on Intelligence on the U.S. Intelligence Community's Prewar Intelligence Assessments on Iraq, 108th Congress 2d. Session, Senate Report 106–301, 18 (July 9, 2004).

44. Paul Brest, Quis Custodiet Ipsos Custodes? Debiasing the Policy Makers Themselves.

45. Doris Kearns Goodwin, Team of Rivals: The Political Genius of Abraham Lincoln (2005).

46. Michael Kranish & Scott Helman, The Real Romney 238 (2012) (quoting Eric Kriss).

47. Hillary Rodham Clinton, Living History 289 (2003).

48. Liz Wiseman with George McKeown, Multipliers: How the Best Leaders Make Everyone Smarter 137–138 (2010).

49. Wiseman with McKeown, Multipliers, at 138 (quoting David Brooks).

50. Peter Wallsten and Jonathan Weisman, Pressure Builds on Obama to Shake Up Inner Circle, Wall Street J., November 2, 2010, A 4; David Rothkopf, Managing the Oval Office, N. Y. Times, January 20, 2013, at 6.

51. David Leonhardt, If Fed Missed That Bubble, Will It See a New One?, N. Y. Times, January 5, 2010, A1.

52. Carol A. Needham, Listening to Cassandra: The Difficulty of Recognizing Risks and Taking Action, 78 Fordham L. Rev. 2329 (2010).

53. See Roland Benabou, Groupthink: Collective Delusions in Organizations and Markets, National Bureau of Economic Research Working Paper 14764 (March, 2009).

54. The following discussion is drawn from Deborah L. Rhode, David Luban, & Scott L. Cummings, Legal Ethics 419–23 (6th ed. 2013); James B. Stewart, The Kona Files: How an Obsession With Leaks Brought Scandal to Hewlett-Packard, The New Yorker, Feb. 19, 2007, at 152; Sue Reisinger, Saw No Evil, Corporate Counsel, Jan. 1 2007, at 68; Peter Waldman & Don Clark, Probing the Pretexters, Wall St J., Sept. 29, 2006, at B1; and Lawrence Hurley, Congress Asks HP: Where Were the Lawyers?, San Francisco Daily J., Sept. 29, 2006, at 1, 9.

55. Waldman & Clark, Probing the Pretexters,

56. Reisinger, Saw No Evil, at 72–73.

57. Reisinger, Saw No Evil, at 73–75.

58. Reisinger, Saw No Evil, at 74–75.

59. Marianne Moody Jennings, Business Ethics: Case Studies and Selected Readings 186 (2008).

60. David Streitfeld, California and the West; HP Said to Have Spied on Lawyer; Phone records of Larry Sonsini were Accessed in the Boardroom Leak Probe, a Source Says, Los Angeles Times, September 19, 2006 at C2.

61. Hewlett-Packard Pretexting Scandal: Hearing Before the Subcommittee on Oversight and Investigations of the House Committee on Energy and Commerce, 109th Congress, September 28, 2006 Washington, D.C., at 75.

62. Seth Hettena, Ready for the Next Scandal, The American Lawyer, October 1, 2010, at 17.

63. Damon Darlin, Adviser Urges H.P. to Focus on Ethics Over Legalities, N. Y. Times, October 4, 2006, at C3 (quoting Schwartz).

64. Brest & Krieger, Problem Solving, at 556–562.

65. Hearing before the Subcommittee on Oversight and Investigations of the House Committee on Energy and Commerce, Hewlett-Packard's Pretexting Scandal, 109th Congress, 2006, at 13.

66. Peter J. Burke et al., eds., Advances in Identity Theory and Research (2003); Sheldon Stryker & Peter J. Burke, The Past, Present, and Future of an Identity

Theory, 63 Social Psychology Quarterly 28 (2000); Cassandra Burke Robertson, Judgment, Identity and Independence, 42 Conn. t L. Rev. 1, 14–20 (2009).

67. Hugh Gunz & Sally Gunz, Hired Professional to Hired Gun: An Identity Theory Approach to Understanding the Ethical Behavior of Professionals in Non-Professional Organizations, 60 Human Relations 851, 882–886 (2007).

68. Stanley Milgram, Obedience to Authority: An Experimental View (1974).

69. Martin Mayer, The Lawyers 363 (1967).

70. Robert B. Cialdini, Influence: The Psychology of Persuasion (2007); Lionel Tiger and Robin Fox, The Imperial Animal (1971); Alvin W. Gouldner, The Norm of Reciprocity: A Preliminary Statement, 25 American Sociological Rev. 161 (1960).

71. Lincoln Caplan, Skadden: Power, Money, and the Rise of a Legal Empire 11 (1994) (quoting Flom).

72. Kranish & Helman, The Real Romney, at 241 (quoting Democratic legislator).

73. Kranish & Helman, The Real Romney, at 266.

74. Jane Mayer, Schmooze or Lose, New Yorker, August 27, 2012, 24–31.

75. Cialdini, Influence, at 26 (quoting Keating).

76. Ron Suskind, Confidence Men: Wall Street, Washington, and the Education of a President 12 (2011).

77. Susskind, Confidence Men, at 51.

78. Solomon E. Asch, Effects of Group Pressure upon the Modification and Distortion of Judgment, in Groups, Leadership, and Men (Harold S. Guetzkow ed., 1951).

79. Tina Rosenberg, Join the Club: How Peer Pressure Can Transform the World (2011).

80. Robert Cialdini, Harnessing the Science of Persuasion, Harv. Bus. Rev., October 2001, at 76. For early adopters, see Kerry Patterson, Joseph Grenny, David Maxfield, Ron McMillan, and Al Switzler, Influencer: The Power to Change Anything 148–150 (2008).

81. Hal G. Rainey, Understanding and Managing Public Organizations 233 (2003).

82. Montgomery Van Wart, Dynamics of Leadership in Public Service: Theory and Practice 209–213 (2005).

83. Frederick Herzberg, One More Time: How Do You Motivate Employees?, Harv. Bus. Rev., September–October 1987, at 6–12.

84. Daniel H. Pink, Drive: The Surprising Truth About What Motivates Us 45–46, 59 (2009). See generally Alfie Kahn, Punished by Rewards: The Trouble with Gold Stars, Incentive Plans, A's, Praise, and Other Bribes (1999).

85. Herzberg, One More Time, 6, 8–9. However, extrinsic factors contribute to job dissatisfaction, and retention and recruitment will suffer if concerns involving salary, job security, and workplace relationships go unaddressed.

86. Warren Bennis, Introduction, in The Art of Followership: How Great Followers Create Great Leaders and Organizations xxiv, xxvi (Ronald E. Riggio, Ira Chaleff, & Jean Lipman-Blumen, eds., 2008).

87. Barbara Kellerman, Followership: How Followers are Creating Change and Changing Leaders 8 (2008). See also Barbara Kellerman. The End of Leadership 37–55 (2012).

88. Robert Nye, Power and Leadership, in Handbook of Leadership Theory and Practice 312 (Nitin Nohria & Rakesh Khurana, eds., 2010).

89. Nannerl O. Keohane, Thinking About Leadership 30 (2010).

90. Kellerman, Followership, at 10.

91. Kellerman, Followership, at 55–59.

92. Bennis, Introduction, at xxvi. See Kellerman, Followership, at 55–59.

93. Lynn R. Offerman, When Followers Become Toxic, Harv. Bus. Rev., January, 2004, at 55, 57, 59; Jon P. Howell & Maria J. Mendez, Three Perspectives on Followership, in Riggio, Chaleff, & Lipman-Bluman, eds., The Art of Followership, 25, 35.

94. James W. Robinson, Jack Welch and Leadership: Executive Lessons From the Master CEO 154 (2001).

95. Roger Gill, Theory and Practice of Leadership 140 (2006).

96. William A. Cohen, Drucker on Leadership: New Lessons From the Father of Modern Management 219 (2009); Gill, Theory and Practice of Leadership, at 216; Bruce J. Avolio & Rebecca J. Reichard, The Rise of Authentic Followership, in The Art of Followership, at 325, 329–335.

97. Ronald A. Heifetz, Leadership Without Easy Answers 92 (1994) (quoting Ruckelshaus).

98. Heifetz, Leadership, at 92 (quoting Ruckelshaus).

99. Heifetz, Leadership, at 94.

100. Heifetz, Leadership, at 97.

101. Deputy Secretary Paul Wolfowitz Interview with Peter Boyer of the New Yorker, June 18, 2002, http:www.defenselink.mil/transcripts.aspx?transcriptid=3527 (quoting Eric K. Shinseki).

102. John P. Kotter & Leonard A. Schlesinger, Choosing Strategies for Change, Harv. Bus. Rev., March-April 1979, at 106. Since that account, the pace of change has undoubtedly accelerated.

103. Hal G. Rainey, Understanding and Managing Public Organizations 16–18 (2003) (discussing public opinion).

104. Ilana RItov & Jonathan Baron, Status-Quo and Omission Biases, 5 Journal of Risk and Uncertainty 49 (1992)

105. Law Firm Leadership 2010 Research on Current Practices and Responsibilities, 10 Law Office Management and Administration 20 (October 2010).

106. Van Wart, Dynamics of Leadership in Public Service, at 40; Sandford Borins, Loose Cannons and Rule Breakers, or Enterprising Leaders: Some Evidence about Innovative Public Managers, 60 Public Admin. Rev. 498, 499 (2000).

107. Mark Gerzon, Leading Through Conflict: How Successful Leaders Transform Differences Into Opportunities 208 (2006).

108. Richard Susskind, The End of Lawyers? Rethinking the Nature of Legal Services (2010): Richard Susskind, Tomorrow's Lawyers (2013); J. Stephen Poor, Re-Engineering the Business of Law, N. Y. Times DealBook, May 7, 2012, http://dealbook.nytimes.com/2012/05/07/re-engineering-the-busines-of-law/.

109. Cohen, Drucker on Leadership, at 1; Noel M. Tichy &d Warren G. Bennis, Judgment: How Winning Leaders Make Great Calls 58 (2007) (quoting Drucker).

110. Van Wart, Dynamics of Leadership, at 40; Borins, Loose Cannons, at 503.

111. Stephen P. Robbins & Timothy A. Judge, Organizational Behavior 625–626 (13th ed. 2009); John P. Kotter, in Making Change Happen, in Leader to Leader: Enduring Insights on Leadership from the Drucker Foundation's Award-Winning Journal 69, 70–71(Frances Hesselbein & Paul M. Cohen, eds., 1999).

112. Peter M. Senge, The Practice of Innovation, in Hesselbein & Cohen, eds., Leader to Leader, at 55, 60.

113. Peter Firestein, Crisis of Character: Building Corporate Reputation in the Age of Skepticism 128, 133 (2009).

114. Susskind, Tomorrow's Lawyers, at 56; Richard Susskind, Storm Warning, Amer. Lawyer, February 2013, at 38.

115. Ronald A. Heifitz & Donald L. Laurie, The Work of Leadership, Harv. Bus. Rev. Dec. 2001, at 132.

116. Kerry Patterson et al., Influencer: The Power to Change Anything 68–69, 102 (2008).

117. John P. Kotter & Dan S. Cohen, The Heart of Change 18, 30–31 (2002).

118. David Maister, Strategy and the Fat Smoker; Doing What's Obvious But Not Easy 171–176 (2008).

119. Robbins and Judge, Organizational Behavior, 623–624; Kotter and Schlesinger, Choosing Strategies for Change, at 109; Gerzon, Leading Through Conflict, at 209.

120. Kotter, Making Change Happen, 70.

121. Van Wart, Dynamics of Leadership, at 54; Maureen Broderick, The Art of Managing Professional Services: Insights From Leaders at the World's Top Firms 105–107 (2011).

122. Cain, The Rise of the New Groupthink, at 6.

123. Robbins and Judge, Organizational Behavior, 623; Kotter & Schlesinger, Choosing Strategies for Change, at 107; Larina Kase, The Confident Leader: How the Most Successful People Go From Effective to Exceptional 11 (2008).

124. Barbara C. Crosby & John M. Bryson, Implementing New Policies, Programs and Plans, in Leadership for the Common Good: Tackling Public Problems in a Shared-Power World 335 (Barbara C. Crosby & John M. Bryson, eds., 2005).

125. Kelly Patterson, Joseph Grenny, Ron McMillan, and Al Switzler, Crucial Confrontations 27 (2004).

126. See Douglas Stone, Bruce Patton, & Sheila Heen, Difficult Conversations: How to Discuss What Matters Most (1999): Cynthia M. Phoel, Feedback that Works,

11 Harv. Management Update 3 (2006); Robert E. Quinn et al., Becoming a Master Manager 62 (5th ed. 2011); A.J. Schuler, Overcoming Resistance to Change: Top Ten Reasons for Change Resistance, http://www.schulersolutions. com/resistance_to_change.html.

127. See Tina Rosenberg, Join the Club: How Peer Pressure Can Transform the World 48 (2011).

128. Senge, The Practice of Innovation, at 65 (quoting O'Brien).

129. Kotter, Making Change Happen, at 71.

130. Melanie Wakefield et al., Effect of Televised, Tobacco Company-Funded Smoking Prevention Advertising on Youth Smoking-Related Beliefs, Intentions, and Behavior, 96 American J. Public Health 2154–2460 (2006).

131. Rosenberg, Join the Club, at 82.

132. See Deborah L. Rhode & Alice Woolley, Comparative Perspectives on Professional Regulation, 80 Fordham L. Rev., 2761, 2764–2769 ((2012).

133. Rhode & Woolley, Comparative Perspectives, 2783–2784.

134. James Moliterno, A Profession in Crisis, Chapter 10 (forthcoming, 2013).

135. Id., http://www.forbes.com/sites/avidan/2012/01/23/kodak-failed-by-asking-the-wrong-marketing-question/

136. Steven Johnson, Where Good Ideas Come From: The Natural History of Innovation 41, 58, 166, 246 (2010).

137. Chip Heath & Dan Heath, Switch: How to Change Things When Change is Hard 16–20 (2010).

138. Studies by the Leadership Development Institute and the Center for Creative Leadership estimate between 20 to 40 percent. Craig E. Runde & Tim A. Flanagan, Becoming a Conflict Competent Leader: How You and Your Organization Can Manage Conflict Effectively 12 (2006). Other research estimates that the average executive spends the equivalent of seven weeks a year (roughly 15 percent of his or her time) dealing with workplace disputes. Gerzon, Leading Through Conflict, at 34.

139. Quinn et al., Becoming a Master Manager, at 89 (quoting William Wrigley).

140. Barbara A. Nagle Lechman, Conflict and Resolution 4 (2008); Runde & Flanagan, Becoming a Conflict Competent Leader, at 115.

141. Runde & Flanagan, Becoming a Conflict Competent Leader, at 21.

142. Ho-Wan Joeng, Understanding Conflict and Conflict Analysis 5 (2008).

143. Quinn et al., Becoming a Master Manager, at 89.

144. See Kenneth R. Melchin & Cheryl A Picard, Transforming Conflict Through Insight 36–38 (2008);Joeng, Understanding Conflict and Conflict Analysis at, 8–13; Lechman, Conflict and Resolution, at 8; Runde & Flanagan, Becoming a Conflict Competent Leader, at 28–35.

145. See Jeong, Understanding Conflict, at 74; Runde & Flanagan, Becoming a Conflict Competent Leader, at 49.

146. Robert Mnookin, Why Negotiations Fail: An Exploration of Barriers to the Resolution of Conflict, 8 Ohio State J. Dispute Resolution 236, 245 (1993).

147. Carol Tavris & Eliot Aronson, Mistakes Were Made (but not by me) 42 (2007).

148. Connie Green, Leader Member Exchange and the Use of Moderating Conflict Management Styles, 19 Internat'l J. Conflict Management 92 (2008).

149. Jeong, Understanding Conflict, at 30; Lechman, Conflict and Resolution, at 21–22.

150. David L. Bradford & Allan R. Cohen, Power Talk: A Hands-on Guide to Supportive Confrontation, in Power Up: Transforming Organizations Through Shared Leadership 321, 323, 345 (Allan R. Cohen & David L. Bradford, eds., 1998).

151. John Heilemann & Mark Halperin, Game Change 188 (2010).

152. Juan Williams, Thurgood Marshall 228 (2000) (quoting Marshall).

153. Runde & Flanagan, Becoming a Conflict Competent Leader, at 117, 161.

154. Patterson et al., Crucial Conversations, at 122.

155. Runde & Flanagan, Becoming a Conflict Competent Leader, at 45; Jeswald W. Salacuse, Ten Ways That Culture Affects Negotiating Style: Some Survey Results, 14 Negotiation J. 221 (1998); Deborah A. Prentice and Dale T. Miller, eds., Cultural Divides: Understanding and Overcoming Group Conflict (2001). See also discussion in chapter 2.

156. Manfred Kets de Vries & Elizabet Engellau, A Clinical Approach to the Dynamics of Leadership and Executive Transformation, in Nohria & Khurana, Handbook of Leadership Theory and Practice, 183, 199.

157. Gary Goodpaster, A Primer on Competitive Bargaining, 2 J. Dispute Resolution 325 (1996).

158. Green, Leader Member Exchange, at 96; Jeong, Understanding Conflict, at 40; Runde & Flanagan, Becoming a Conflict Competent Leader, at 44.

159. William Ury & Roger Fisher, Getting to Yes: Negotiating Agreement Without Giving In (2d. ed. 1991).

160. Robert S. Adler, Benson Rosen, & Elliot M. Silverstein, Emotions in Negotiation: How to Manage Fear and Anger, 14 Negotiation J. 161 (1998).

161. Melchin & Picard, Transforming Conflict Through Insight, at 79; Lechman, Conflict and Resolution, at 28 (noting that experts estimate that less than 10 percent of communication comes from substantive content; the rest comes from facial gesture, tone, and so forth).

162. Bradford & Cohen, Power Talk: A Hands-on Guide to Supportive Confrontation, at 331.

163. Ben Heineman Jr., How to Say No to Your CEO, 25 ACC Docket 38, 39 (2007).

164. Fisher & Ury, Getting to Yes, at ix.

165. James White, The Pros and Cons of Getting to Yes, 34 J. Legal Education 115, 123 (1984) (comments of Roger Fisher).

166. Melchin & Piccard, Transforming Conflict, at 79–80; Van Wart, Dynamics of Leadership in Public Service, at 222; Bradford & Cohen, Power Talk, at 340 (discussing toothless promises); Kathleen M Eisenhardt, Jean L. Kahwajy, & L. J. Bourgeois III, How Management Teams Can Have a Good Fight, Harv. Bus.

Rev., July-August, 1997, at 2; Robert Hargrove, Masterful Coaching 235–245 (3d ed. 2008).

167. Susan Letterman White, Power and Influence for Lawyers: How to Use It to Develop Business and Advance Your Career 134 (2011).

168. Robert Gordon, Book Review: Louis D. Brandeis: A Life, 60 Journal Legal Education 549, 555 (2011).

169. Runde & Flanagan, Becoming a Conflict Competent Leader, 171; Van Wart, Dynamics of Leadership, 221–224.

170. Tom R. Tyler, Why People Obey the Law (2006); Readings in Procedural Justice (Tom R. Tyler, ed., 2005).

171. Mark Gerzon, Leading Through Conflict 69 (2006).

172. Ken Gormley, Archibald Cox: Conscience Of A Nation 70 (1999).

173. Gormley, Archibald Cox, at 72 (quoting Cox).

174. Gormley, Archibald Cox, at 76.

175. Susan G. Manch with Michelle C. Nash, Learning From Law Firm Leaders 91 (2012).

176. For Americans generally, public speaking is the most feared or second most feared event. Fear of Public Speaking Statistics, http://www.speech-topics-help.com/fear-of-public-speaking-statistics.html; Daniel J. DeNoon, Fear of Public Speaking Hardwired: Speech Anxiety Worse for Some, but Most Can Overcome it, Webmdhealthnews, www.wemd.com/ansiety-panic/guide/20061101/fear-public-speaking.

177. Chip Heath & Dan Heath, Made to Stick: Why Some Ideas Survive and Others Die 242–43 (2007).

178. Heath & Heath, Made to Stick, at 244.

179. Robert B. Reich, Locked in the Cabinet, excerpted in the New Yorker, April 21, 1997, at 43.

180. Warren Christopher, Chances of Lifetime: A Memoir 187 (2001).

181. Fred J. Cook, The Army McCarthy Hearings: A Senator Creates a Sensation Hunting Communists 27–28 (1971).

182. Cook, The Army McCarthy Hearings, at 260.

183. Richard Nixon, In the Arena: A Memoir of Victory, Defeat, and Renewal 212 (1990) (quoting Wilson).

184. P. G. Wodehouse, The Girl in Blue 100–101(1971).

185. Jay A. Conger, The Necessary Art of Persuasion, Harv. Bus. Rev., May/June, 1998, at 85, 88; Belle Linda Halperin & Richard Richards, Mastering the Art of Leadership, in The Handbook for Teaching Leadership 135, 138 (Scott Snook, Nitin Nohira, & Rakesh Khurana, eds., 2012).

186. Nixon, In the Arena, at 212.

187. Will Rogers, Sanity Is Where You find It: An Affectionate History of the United States in the 20s and 30s 167 (Donald Day, ed., 1935).

188. Joy Elizabeth Hayes, Did Herbert Hoover Broadcast the First Fireside Chat: Rethinking the Origins of Roosevelt's Radio Genius, 7 J. Radio Studies 77, 79 (2000).

189. Lawrence W. Levine & Cornelia R. Levine, The Fireside Conversations: America Responds to FDR During the Great Depression 10 (2002).

190. Mathew A. Baum & Samuel Kernell, Economic Class and Popular Support for Franklin Roosevelt in War and Peace, 65 Public Opinion Q 198, 218, 223–224 (2001); B. R. Smith, FDR's Use of Radio During the War Years, 4 Radio Studies 76 (1997). For the limited effect of presidential communication on approval ratings, see George C. Edwards III, On Deaf Ears, The Limits of the Bully Pulpit 29, 79 (2003). For the effect of FDR's address on public confidence and support for policies, see id., at 79, 99.

191. Charlene Li, Open Leadership: How Social technology Can Transform the Way You Lead 11–12 (2010); Doris A Graber, Mass Media and American Politics 194 (8th ed., 2008).

192. Ian Urbina, Obama's Social Media Outposts Join the Campaign, N. Y. Times, June 18, 2011.

193. Kellerman, The End of Leadership 56 (noting that a third of CEO's are using social media to connect to stakeholders); Richard Perez-Pena, Talking Tough and Drawing Viewers, Christie Is a YouTube Star, N. Y. Times, November 30, 2010 (discussing merger of entertainment and substance).

194. Heath & Heath, Made to Stick, at 114–115.

195. Heath & Heath, Made to Stick, at 16–18.

196. Roger Gill, Theory and Practice of Leadership 260–262 (2006); David M. Armstrong, Managing by Storying Around: A New Method of Leadership (1992).

197. Patterson et al., Influencer, at 60 (describing experiment in which students were asked to recall information several weeks later).

198. Heath & Heath, Made to Stick, at 75.

199. Gettysburg Address, reprinted in Rizer, Lincoln's Counsel, at 200.

200. Leon A. Harris, The Fine Art of Political Wit, at 148–149 (1964).

201. Roger Morris, Richard Milhous Nixon: The Rise of An American Politician 779–781 (1990).

202. The speech is available at the History Place, Great Speeches Collection, http://www.historyplace.com/speeches/nixon-checkers.htm.

203. Morris, Nixon, at 844–845.

204. Eric J. Sundquist, "We Dreamed a Dream": Ralph Ellison, Martin Luther King Jr., and Barack Obama, Daedalus (Winter 2011), at 114.

205. Barack Obama, Candidate for U.S. Senate in Illinois, Keynote Address at the Democratic National Convention, (July 27, 2004) (transcript available at http://www.washingtonpost.com/ac2/wp-dyn/A19751-2004Jul27?language=printer.

206. Barack Obama, Inaugural Address, January 20, 2009, available at http://www. presidency.ucsb.edu/ws/index.php?pid=44&st=&st1=.

207. Frank Rich, It's a Bird, It's a Plane, It's Obama, N. Y. Times, April 3, 2010, at WK9.

208. Joe Klein, The Natural: The Misunderstood Presidency of Bill Clinton 40, 79 (2002).

209. Randall Kennedy, The Persistence of the Color Line: Racial Politics and the Obama Presidency 78–80 (2011); Carol McNamera, Barak Obama's Postracial Presidency, in The Obama Presidency in the Constitutional Order 165 (Carol McNamera & Melanie M. Marlowe, eds. 2011); David Remnick, The Bridge: The Life and Rise of Barak Obama 3–4, 14–15 (2010).

210. Kennedy, The Persistence of the Color Line, at 120.

211. Richard Ford, The Race Card: How Bluffing About Bias Makes Race Relations Worse 365 (2008).

212. Frederick C. Harris, The Price of a Black President, N. Y. Times, Oct. 28, 2012, at WK9.

213. Jodi Kantor, For President, a Complex Calculus of Race and Politics, N. Y. Times, October 21, 2012, A1 (quoting Tavis Smiley). See also Gary Dorrien, The Obama Question: A Progressive Perspective 11 (2012) (discussing critiques of Obama by left African Americans).

214. George Lakoff, The Policy-Speak Disaster for Health Care, Truthout, Aug. 20, 2009.

215. Lakoff, The Policy-Speak Disaster.

216. One representative poll during the health care reform debates found that 41 percent of Americans believed that Obama's healthcare reform bill would in fact institute "death panels."CNN Opinion Research, September 11–13, 2009, http://i2cdn.turner.com/cnn/2009/images/09/14/rel14b2.pdf.

217. Jacob S. Hacker, The Road to Nowhere 143 (1997).

218. George C. Edwards III, On Deaf Ears: The Limits of the Bully Pulpit 170 (2003) (quoting Clinton).

219. Matt Bai, Still Waiting for the Narrator in Chief, N. Y. Times Magazine, November 4, 2012, at 16.

220. Amitai Etzioni, Needed: A Progressive Story, The Nation, May 5, 2010, at 22–23.

221. George Packer, Obama's Lost Year, New Yorker, March 15, 2010, at 46 (quoting aide).

222. Packer, Obama's Lost Year, at 49 (quoting Frank).

223. Bill Keller, Scoring Obama's Debate, N. Y. Times, October 4, 2012.

224. Gail Collins, The Season of Debates, N. Y. Times, October 4, 2012.

225. George Lakoff, Why Obama Lost the First Debate, October 4, 2012, http://www.huffingtonpost.com/george-lakoff/obama-first-debate.

226. Edwards, On Deaf Ears, at 184 (quoting Clinton).

227. James W. Ceaser, Glen E. Thurow, Jeffrey Tulis, & Joseph M. Bessette, The Rise of the Rhetorical Presidency, Presidential Studies Quarterly 163 (1981).

228. For the importance of first impressions, see Jeffrey Pfeffer, Power: Why Some People Have It and Others Don't 148–149 (2010).

229. Jon Meacham, Thomas Jefferson, The Art of Power 354, 363 (2012).

230. Deborah L. Rhode, The Beauty Bias 30–31(2010).

231. Rhode, Beauty Bias,, at 9, 60.

232. Jonathan Alter, Woman of the World, Vanity Fair, June 2011, available at http://www.vanityfair.com/politics/features/2011/06/hillary-clinton-201106.

233. Sylvia Ann Hewlett et al., The Sponsor Effect: Breaking Through the Last Glass Ceiling, Harv. Bus. Rev., January, 2011, at 31, 33.

234. Mark J. Green, The Other Government: The Unseen Power of Washington Lawyers 57 (1975).

235. Caryl Rivers, Mockery of Katherine Harris, WomenEnews.org, November 29, 2000 (quoting Boston Herald columnist) http://womensenews.org/story/commentary/001129/mockery-katherine-harris-shows-double-standard.

236. Hewlett, The Sponsor Effect, at 32.

237. Heath & Heath, Made to Stick, at 6–7 (quoting Abe Silverman).

238. Heath & Heath, Made to Stick, at 6–7.

239. Howard Gardner, Changing Minds: The Art and Science of Changing Our Own and Other People's Minds 86(2004).

240. Gardner, Changing Minds, at 76.

241. Sarah A. Soule, *Contention and Corporate Social Responsibility* (2009).

242. See Cliff Atkinson, Beyond Bullet Points: Using Microsoft PowerPoint to Create Presentations That Inform, Motivate, and Inspire (2007).

243. Samuel Johnson, The Lives of the Most Eminent English Poets: With Critical Observations on Their Works vol. 1 158 (1819).

244. Gloria Steinem, Address at Stanford University, January 27, 2012 (quoting Kennedy).

245. Leon A. Harris, The Fine Art of Political Wit 94 (1964) (quoting Lincoln).

246. Doris Kearns Goodwin, Team of Rivals: The Political Genius of Abraham Lincoln 54 (2005): Harris, Political Wit, at 100.

247. Harris, Political Wit, at 103.

248. Charles McGrath, Streep Dons Thatcher's Armor, N. Y. Times, Dec. 23, 2011, at Arts & Leisure 1.

249. Harris, Political Wit, at 243 (quoting John Billings).

250. Ryan A. Malphurs, "People Did Sometimes Stick Things in my Underwear": The Function of Laughter at the U.S. Supreme Court, 10 Communication L. Rev. 48 (2012) (quoting Floyd).

251. Hillary Rodham Clinton, Living History 183 (2003).

252. Joann M. McCabe, The Fear of Public Speaking; 20 Ways to Get Over It, The Toastmaster 18 (2006).

253. Arthur Rizer, Lincoln's Counsel: Lessons from America's Most Persuasive Speaker 188 (2010): Harold Holzer, Lincoln the Orator, 58 American Heritage 40 (Winter 2009).
254. Smith, FDR's Use of Radio, at 84.
255. Nixon, In the Arena, at 213 (quoting Randolph Churchill).
256. John W. Gardner, On Leadership 51 (1990) (quoting Churchill).
257. William Safire, Prolegemon, in William Safire and Leonard Safire, Leadership 19 (1990) (quoting Eisenhower).

CHAPTER 5

1. See sources cited in Deborah L. Rhode, Where is the Leadership in Moral Leadership?, in Moral Leadership: The Theory and Practice of Power, Judgment, and Policy 8 (Deborah L. Rhode, ed., 2006).
2. Rhode, Where is the Leadership in Moral Leadership, at 8.
3. Tom Morris, If Aristotle Ran General Motors: The New Soul of Business 157 (1999).
4. Gallup Organization, Honesty/Ethics in Professions, (Nov. 28, Dec. 1, 2011), http://www.gallup.copm/poll/1654/honesty-ethics-professions.aspx.
5. Seven percent of Americans have high or very high confidence in congressional representatives. For law firm leaders, confidence runs at 11 percent. See Chapter 1.
6. Louis Brandeis, The Opportunity in the Law, in Louis Brandeis, Business: A Profession 313, 321 (1914).
7. Harlan F. Stone, The Public Influence of the Bar, 48 Harv. L. Rev. 1 (1934)
8. Anthony Kronman, The Lost Lawyer (1993); Sol M. Linowitz with Martin Mayer, The Betrayed Profession, sources cited in Deborah L. Rhode, The Professionalism Problem, 39 William & Mary L. Rev. 283, 284 (1998).
9. James McGregor Burns, Leadership 19 (1978).
10. John Gardner, The Moral Aspect of Leadership 9, 10, 13 (1987).
11. Barbara Kellerman, Bad Leadership: What It Is, How It Happens, Why It Matters 12 (2004).
12. For a summary, see Rhode, Moral Leadership, at 17.
13. Tom R. Tyler & Steven L. Blader, Social Identity and Fairness and Judgment: Emerging Perspectives on Values in Organizations 63, 67–79 (Dirk D. Steiner & Daniel P. Starlicki, eds., 2003); Lynn Sharp Paine, Value Shift: Why Companies Must Merge Social and Financial Imperatives to Achieve Superior Performance 46 (2002).
14. Paine, Value Shift, at 45–46; Kim S. Cameron, David Bright, & Arran Caza, Exploring the Relationships Between Organizational Virtuousness and Performance, 47 American Behavioral Scientist 766, 773(2004).
15. See Linda Klebe Trevino & Gary R. Weber, Managing Ethics in Business Organizations: Social Scientific Perspective 233 (2003); Paine, Value Shift, at 42–44.

16. Trevino & Weaver, Managing Ethics, at 233; Paine, Value Shift, at 45; Robert B. Cialdini, Social Influence and the Triple Tumor Structure of Organizational Dishonesty, in Codes of Conduct: Behavioral Research into Business Ethics 53–56 (David Messick & Anne E. Tenbrunsel, eds., 1996).

17. James M. Kouzes & Barry Z. Posner, The Truth About Leadership 46 (2010).

18. Thomas H. Peters and Robert P. Waterman, In Search of Excellence: Lessons from America's Best-Run Companies 279 (1982). See also Robert C. Solomon, Ethics and Excellence: Cooperation and Integrity in Business 44, 47 (1993).

19. Rosabeth Moss Kanter, How Great Companies Think Differently, Harv. Bus. Rev., November, 2011, at 66, 73.

20. Moral Development: Advances in Research and Theory 36–49 (James Rest, ed., 1994).

21. William Damon, The Moral Advantage: How to Succeed in Business by Doing the Right Thing 3 (2004).

22. Richard Reeves, The Trouble With Lawyers: The Case of James St. Clair, New York, July 29, 1974, at 27.

23. Elizabeth Chambliss, New Sources of Managerial Authority in Large Law Firms, 22 Geo. J. Legal Ethics 63, 89 (2009); Robert L. Nelson, Partners with Power 255 (1988).

24. Thomas M. Jones, Ethical Decision Making by Individuals in Organizations: An Issue-Contingent Model, 16 Acad. Management Rev. 366, 376 (1991).

25. For the effects of empathy and solidarity, see Nancy Eisenberg, Altruistic Emotion, Cognition, and Behavior 30–56 (1986); Martin L. Hoffman, Empathy and Prosocial Activism, in Social and Moral Values: Individual and Societal Perspectives 65–85 (Nancy Eisbenberg, Janusz Reykowski, & Ervin Staub, eds., 1989). For devaluation, see Albert Bandura, Moral Disengagement in the Perpetration of Inhumanities, 3 Personality and Soc. Psych. Rev. 193 (1999).

26. Lincoln Caplan, Skadden: Power, Money, and the Rise of a Legal Empire 122 (1993) (quoting Joe Flom).

27. Caplan, Skadden, at 147 (quoting Susan Getzendanner).

28. Kimberly Kirkland, Ethics in Large Firms: The Principle of Pragmatism, 35 Memphis L. Rev. 631, 722(2005); Mark C. Suchman, Working Without a Net; The Sociology of Legal Ethics in Corporate Litigation, 67 Fordham L. Rev. 837, 853 (1998)

29. Paul Hoffman, Lions in the Street 38 (1973).

30. Ann E. Tenbrunsel & David Messick, Ethical Fading: The Role of Self-Deception in Unethical Behavior, 17 Social Justice Research 223, 224 (2004); see also Francesca Gino & Max H. Bazerman, When Misconduct Goes Unnoticed: The Acceptability of Gradual Erosion in Others' Unethical Behavior, 45 J. Experimental Soc. Psychol. 708 (2009).

31. Philip Zimbardo, The Lucifer Effect : Understanding How Good People Turn Evil (2007); Neil Hamilton & Verna Monson, the Positive Empirical Relationship

of Professionalism to Effectiveness in the Practice of Law, 24 Geo. J. Legal Ethics 137, 141, 182 (2011);

32. Ronald R. Sims & Johannes Brinkmann, Enron Ethics (Or: Culture Matters More than Codes), 45 J. Business Ethics 243, 247 (2003). See also Bethany McLean & Peter Elkind, Smartest Guys in the Room: The Amazing Rise and Scandalous Fall of Enron (2003).

33. Donald C. Langevoort, The Organizational Psychology of Hyper-Competition: Corporate Irresponsibility and the Lessons of Enron, 70 George Wash. L. Rev. 968, 970 (2002).

34. Rebecca Roiphe, The Ethics of Willful Ignorance, 24 Geo. J. Legal Ethics 187 (2011).

35. John M. Doris, Lack of Character: Personal and Moral Behavior 141 (2002); Gino & Bazerman, When Misconduct Goes Unnoticed.

36. David Eagelman, Incognito: The Secret Lives of the Brain 4 (2011); Jonathan Haidt, The Emotional Dog and its Rational Tail: A Social Intuitionist Approach to Moral Judgment, 108 Psych. Rev. 814, 822–888 (2001).

37. David DeSteo & Piercarlo Valdesolo, Out of Character 33–35 (2011).

38. Steven Brill, Fatal Arrogance, American Lawyer, October 1988, at 35, 34.

39. Milton C. Regan, Eat What You Kill, 54, 60–62 (2004).

40. Claudiea MacLachlan & Harver Berkman, Littl Rock's Bar Shaken to its Core: Local Lawyers are Reeling as Washington Woes Come Home to Roost, Nat'l L. J., April 11, 1994, at 18.

41. Susan Koniak, When Did Overbilling Become a Habit, N. Y. Times, May 2, 1998, at 15 (quoting Hubbell).

42. Lisa Lerman, Blue Chip Bilking: Regulation of Billing and Expense Fraud by Lawyers, 12 Geo. J. Legal Ethics 205, 259–262 (1999).

43. Lerman, Blue Chip Bilking, at 276; Benjamin Wittes, It Could Happen to You: Hubbell's Plea Spotlights Firm Billing Problems, Legal Times, December 12, 1994, at 7.

44. Wittes, It Could Happen to You, at 7.

45. Lerman, Blue Chip Bilking, at 275; Wittes, It Could Happen to You (quoting the president of a fraud auditing company).

46. Susan Saab Fortnoy, Ethics Counsel's Role in Combating the "Ostrich Tendency," Professional Lawyer 131, 134–135 (2002).

47. Lerman, Blue Chip Bilking, at 281 (quoting Roy Simon). See also Lisa G. Lerman, A Double Standard for Lawyer Dishonesty: Billing Fraud Versus Misappropriation, 34 Hofstra L. Rev. 847, 864–865, 872 (2006).

48. Ann Colby & William Damon, Some Do Care 307 (1994); Deborah L. Rhode, Pro Bono in Principle and in Practice 61–62, 65 (2005).

49. For robber barons, see Nancy Liseger & Frank Lisius, A Law Unto Itself: The Story of the Law Firm of Sullivan and Cromwell 31 (1988). For asbestos companies, see Paul Brodeur, Outrageous Misconduct: The Asbestos Industry on Trial (1985).

For tobacco companies, see David Margolick, Tobacco: Its Middle Name, Law Firm Thrives, for Now, N. Y. Times, Nov. 20, 1992. For savings and loan companies, see Lincoln Savings and Loan Association v. Wall, 743 F. Supp. 901 (D.D.C. 1990). For nine financial scandals involving companies such as Enron, Worldcom, and HealthSouth, see Association of the Bar of the City of New York, Report of the Lawyer's Role in Corporate Governance 22–30 (2006). For lawyers' role in conduct leading to the recent financial crisis, see Katherine Franke, Occupy Wall Street's Message for Lawyers, Nat'l Law J., November 21, 2001; Doreen McBarnet, Financial Engineering or Legal Engineering? Legal Work, Legal Integrity, and the Banking Crisis, in The Future of Financial Regulation (Iain G. MacNeil & Justin O'Brien, eds., 2010).

50. John Thompson, The Prosecution Rests, but I Can't, N. Y. Times, April 9, 2011. For more details, see Vivian Berger, No Recompense for John Thompson's Stolen Years, Nat'l L. J., June 20, 2011.

51. Peter Irons, Justice at War 204–206 (1993).

52. Irons, Justice at War, at 290–291.

53. Irons, Justice at War, at 350–351.

54. Bernard Williams, Politics and Moral Character, in Public and Private Morality 58 (Stuart Hampshire, ed., 1978).

55. Irons, Justice at War, at, 350–351.

56. C.S. Lewis, The Inner Ring, in C.S. Lewis, They Asked for a Paper: Papers and Addresses 146–147 (1962)

57. Trevino & Weaver, Managing Ethics in Organizations, at 181; James R. Rest & Darcia Narvaez, Moral Development in the Professions (1994).

58. Augusto Blasi, Bridging Moral Cognition and Moral Action: A Critical Review of the Literature, 88 Psych. Bull. 1, 37–41 (1980): Lynn L. Dallas, A Preliminary Inquiry into the Responsibility of Corporations and their Officers and Directors for Corporate Climate: The Psychology of Enron's Demise, 35 Rutgers L. J. 1, 18 (2003).

59. John Braithwaite, Crime, Shame, and Reintegration 147 (1989).

60. J. Scott Armstrong, Social Irresponsibility in Management, 5 J. Business Research 185 (1977).

61. Michael Useem, Leadership Moment 178 (1998) (quoting Deryck Maughan).

62. Linda Grant, Taming the Bond Buccaneers. at Salomon Brothers, Los Angeles Times Magazine, February 16, 1992, at 22. For the Salomon culture generally, see Michael Lewis, Liar's Poker 63–67, 69–70, 73, 75–76, 81–83 (1989).

63. Carol J. Loomis, Warren Buffet's Wild Ride at Salomon, Fortune, October 27, 1997, at 118.

64. In re Gutfreund, Securities Exchange Release No. 34-31554 (December 3, 1992).

65. Grant, Taming the Bond Buccaneers, at 22.

66. Useem, Leadership Moment, at 197.

67. Hannah Arendt, On Violence 38–39(1970).

68. Rhode, Where is the Leadership in Moral Leadership, at 30; David Luban, Making Sense of Moral Meltdowns, in Moral Leadership, 57–58; David M. Messick & John Darley, How Organizations Socialize Individuals into Evildoing, in Codes of Conduct, at 13–65.

69. Sims & Brinkmann, Enron Ethics, at 252–253.

70. Keith A. Findley & Michael S. Scott, The Multiple Dimensions of Tunnel Vision in Criminal Cases, 2006 Wisconsin L. Rev. 291, 292 (2006). Myrna Raeder, What Does Innocence Have to Do With It?: A Commentary on Wrongful Convictions and Rationality, 2003 Mich. St. L. Rev. 1315, 1327.

71. Robert Pack, The Lawyers of Watergate, Washington Lawyer, July/August, 1999, at 25; John Dean, Watergate: Lessons for Today, Nearly 40 Years Later, Ohio Lawyer, July/August, 2011, at 11. Half of those indicted or named as coconspirators were lawyers. Richard Harris, The Watergate Prosecutions, New Yorker, at 51. Of the key participants in the cover up, only H. R. Haldeman was not a lawyer.

72. For a list of lawyers and offenses see Kathleen Clark. The Legacy of Watergate for Legal Ethics Instruction, 51 Hastings L. J. 673, 678–682 (1999).

73. Watergate and Related Activities. Phase I: Watergate Investigation, Senate Select Committee on Presidential Campaign Activities, Presidential Campaign Activities of 1972, Book 3, 1013, 1054 (June 25, and 26, 1973).

74. John W. Dean III, Blind Ambition 34 (1976).

75. Dean, Blind Ambition, at 35.

76. Stanley I. Kutler, The Wars of Watergate: The Last Crisis of Richard Nixon 355 (1990).

77. Kutler, Wars of Watergate, at 249.

78. The White House Transcripts 142 (Gerald Gold, ed., 1974).

79. Dean, Watergate, at 14 (describing his ignorance of the law as well as facts).

80. Michael A Genovese & Iwan W. Morgan, Introduction, Remembering Watergate, in Watergate Remembered: The Legacy for American Politics 7 (Michael A. Genovese & Iwan W. Morgan, eds., 2012).

81. Genovese & Morgan, Introduction, at 7.

82. Richard Nixon, In the Arena 34 (1990).

83. Genovese & Morgan, Introduction, at 7.

84. Genovese & Morgan, Introduction, at 11.

85. Dean, Blind Ambition, at 34 (quoting Chotiner).

86. Herbert S. Parmet, Richard M. Nixon 173(2008).

87. Earl Krogh, Statement, N. Y. Times, January 25, 1974, at 16. See also Mark Curridan, The Lawyers of Watergate, ABA J. June 212, at 38 (quoting Krogh's claim that "national security was at stake").

88. William H. Simon, Wrongs of Ignorance and Ambiguity: Lawyer Responsibility for Collective Misconduct, 22 Yale J. Reg. 1, 14–15 (2005).

89. David Frost's Interview with Richard Nixon (May, 1977), in Great Interviews of the 20th Century, The Guardian, at http://www.guardian.co.uk/theguardian/2007.

90. Dean, Blind Ambition, at 34 (quoting Chotiner).

91. Dean, Blind Ambition, at 47 (quoting Krogh).

92. Dean, Blind Ambition, at 34.

93. The Watergate Hearings 227 (1973).

94. Genovese & Morgan, Introduction, at 20; Parmet, Richard Nixon, at 146. For a review of the Saturday Night Massacre see Ken Gormley, Archibald Cox: Conscience of a Nation, 323–371(1997).

95. Nixon, In the Arena, at 41.

96. Genovese & Morgan, Introduction, at 13 (quoting Colson).

97. Dean, Blind Ambition, at 31.

98. ABA Standards for the Approval of Law Schools, Standard 302(a)(iii) (1974).

99. Harry W. Jones, Lawyers and Justice: The Uneasy Ethics of Partisanship, 23 Villanova Law Review 957, 959 (1978).

100. John Dean stated, "I knew that the things I was doing was wrong…. A course in legal ethics wouldn't have changed anything." Thomas Likona, What Does Moral Psychology Have to Say to the Teacher of Ethics, in Ethics Teaching in Higher Education 129 (Daniel Callahan & Sissela Bok, eds., 1980) (quoting Dean).

101. Curridan, The Lawyers of Watergate, at 41.

102. Rhode, If Integrity Is the Answer, What Is the Question? 72 Fordham L. Rev. 333 (2003); William Sullivan et al., Educating Lawyers: Preparation for the Profession of Law 135(2007; M. Neil Browne, Carrie L. Williamson, & Linda L. Barkacs, The Purported Rigidity of an Attorney's Personality: Can Legal Ethics Be Acquired?, 30 J. Legal Prof. 55 (2006); Steven Hartwell, Promoting Moral Development Through Experiential Teaching, 1 Clinical L. Rev. 505 (1995); Neil Hamilton & Lisa M. Babbit, Fostering Professionalism Through Mentoring, 37 J. Legal Educ. 102 (2007); National Research Council, Learning and Transfer, in How People Learn 51–78 (2000)

103. William Sullivan et al., Educating Lawyers, at 134–135.

104. Michael Walzer, Political Action: The Problem of Dirty Hands, 2 Philosophy and Public Affairs 160 (1973)

105. Walzer, Political Action, at 161.

106. Walzer, Political Action, at 168.

107. Stuart Hampshire, Public and Private Morality, in Stuart Hampshire et al. eds., Public and Private Morality 50 (1978).

108. Richard M. Nixon, Leaders 324 (1982).

109. T. Harry Williams, Huey Long 748 (1969) (quoting Long).

110. Williams, Huey Long, at 34 (quoting Long).

111. Williams, Huey Long, at 160 (quoting supporter).

112. Williams, Huey Long, at 748 (quoting Long).

113. Bernard Shaw, quoted in John Rohr, Ethics for Bureaucrats 8, 9 (1978), and Stephen K. Bailey, Ethics and the Politician 6 (1960).

114. Jonathan Alter, The Defining Moment 102 (2006).

115. Alter, Defining Moment, at 306 (quoting Roosevelt).

116. Joan Biskupic, Sandra Day O'Connor 52–53 (2005).

117. Bksupic, Sandra Day O'Connor, at 61.

118. Biskupic, Sandra Day O'Connor, at 84.

119. The statement released by campaign manager Jim Messina appears at http://www.barackobama.com/news/entry/we-will-not-play-by-two-sets-of-rules.

120. The press briefing is available at http://www.whitehouse.gov/the-press-office/2012/02/07/press-briefing-press-secretary-jay-carnay-272012.

121. Kristoff, Waiting for Mitt the Moderate, N. Y. Times, January 4, 2012, at A25.

122. Michael D. Shear, Erik Eckholm, & Ashley Parker, Once Again, Social Issues Test Romney, N. Y. York Times, Oct. 9, 2011 at A1; Romney's Path on Abortion, N. Y. Times, Feb 2, 2012, at A1, A19.

123. Shear, Eckholm, & Parkeer, Once Again Social Issues Test Romney, at A1.

124. Michael Kranish & Scott Helman, The Real Romney 258 (2012).

125. Kristoff, Waiting for Mitt, at A 25.

126. Steve Toles, Washington Post, November 30, 2011.

127. Bernard Williams, Politics and Moral Character, in Public and Private Morality, 69.

128. Lynnne L. Dallas, A Preliminary Inquiry into the Responsibility of Corporations and Their Officers and Directors for Corporate Climate: The Psychology of Enron's Demise, 35 Rutgers L. J. 1, 40 (2003); Chris Moon & Clive Bonny, Attitudes and Approaches, In Business Ethics: Facing Up to the Issues 34 (Chris Moon & Clive Bonny, eds., 2001); W. Michael Hoffman, Integrating Ethics into Business Cultures, in Business Ethics, at 43–44.

129. John Gibeaut, Telling Secrets: When In- House Lawyers Sue Their Employers, They Find Themselves in the Middle of the Debate on Client Confidentiality, ABA J., Nov. 2004 at 39, 73; Roberta Ann Johnson, When It Works—and Why 93 (2003); Fred Alford, Whistleblowers, Broken Lives and Organizational Power 1, 19–20 (2001); Terence Miethe, Whistleblowing at Work: Tough Choices in Exposing Fraud, Waste, and Abuse on the Job 149–208 (1999).

130. See the cases cited in Deborah L. Rhode, David Luban, & Scott L. Cummings, Legal Ethics 394–398, 933–935 (6th ed. 2013): Gibeaut, Telling Secrets, at 39.

131. Myron Glazer & Penina M. Glazer, Whistleblowers: Exposing Corruption in Government and Industry 207 (1989) (quoting Hugh Kaufman).

132. Johnson, Whistleblowing, at 50; Alford, Whistleblowers, at 31–32.

133. Alford, Whistleblowers, at 21.

134. John Dalla Costa, The Ethical Imperative: Why Moral Leadership is Good for Business 87 (1998).

135. APR Panelists Examine Why Prosecutors Are Largely Ignored by Disciplinary Offices, 22 ABA /BNA Lawyers' Manual on Professional Conduct 90 (2006) See also Deborah Jane Cooper et al., The Myth of Prosecutorial Accountability After Connick v. Thompson, 121 Yale L. J. Online 203 (2011).

136. Fred Zacharias, The Professional Discipline of Prosecutors, 79 N. Car. L. Rev. 721 (2001).

137. See Cooper et al., The Myth of Prosecutorial Accountability.

138. Mike Scarcella & Zoe Tillman, A Lack of Leadership Dooms Case, Nat'l L. J., March 19, 2012, at A1, A4.

139. Investigation into the Office of Legal Counsel's Memoranda Concerning Issues Relating to the Central Intelligence Agency's Use of Enhanced Interrogation Techniques on Suspected Terrorists (July 29, 2009) (OPR Report).

140. OPR Report, at 228.

141. OPR Report, at 226–237.

142. David Margolis, Memorandum for the Attorney General of Decision Regarding the Objections to the Findings of Professional Misconduct in the Office of Professional Responsibility's Report of Investigation, January 5, 2010.

143. The Torture Lawyers, N. Y. Times, Feb. 25, 2010, at A26.

144. Stephen Gillers, Letter to the Editor, N. Y. Times, March 4, 2010, at A26; David Cole, Torture Lawyers on Trial, The Nation, March 1, 2010, at 7.

145. NBC News Special, Decision Points, interview of George W. Bush by Matt Lauer, November 8, 2010, available at http://www.msnbc.msn.com/id/40076644/ns/politicsw-decision_points.

146. Phillipa Strum, Brandeis: Beyond Progressivism 50 (1993).

147. Melvin L. Urofsky, Louis D. Brandeis: A Life 354 (2009).

148. American Bar Association, Canons of Professional Ethics, Canon 4 and Canon 12 (1908).

149. Jerold Aurbach, Unequal Justice; Lawyers and Social Change in Modern America 282 (1976).

150. Philip P. Lochner, The No Fee and Low Fee Legal Practice of Private Attorneys, 9 Law and Soc'y Rev. 431, 442, 446 (1975).

151. ABA Model Rules of Professional Conduct, Rule 6.1ABA Standing Committee on Pro Bono and Public Service, Supporting Justice II; A Report on the Pro Bono Work of American Lawyers 21 (2009).

152. Chris Johnson, Choppy Waters, American Lawyer, July/August, 2011. Some of the most profitable of the 200 also had among the poorest pro bono records. Id

153. See research summarized in Corporation for National Community Service, The Health Benefits of Volunteering: A Review of Recent Research (2007); Deborah L. Rhode, Pro Bono in Principle and Practice 58–59 (2005); Alan Luks with Peggy Payne, The Healing Power of Doing Good xii, 17–18, 45–54, 60 (2d ed. 2001); John Wilson & Marc Musick, The Effects of Volunteering on the Volunteers, 62 Law and Contemp. Problems 141, 150–159 (1999); Marc A. Musick, A. Regula Herzog & James S. House, Volunteering and Mortality Among Older Adults: Findings From a National Sample, 548 J. Gerontology S173, S178 (1999).

154. Rhode, Pro Bono, at 30–31.

155. Scott L. Cummings & Deborah L. Rhode, Managing Pro Bono: Doing Well by Doing Better, 78 Fordham L. Rev. 2357, 2401, 2405 (2010).

156. Cummings & Rhode, Managing Pro Bono, at 2402–2403.

157. Deborah L. Rhode, Public Interest Law: The Movement at Midlife, 60 Stan. L. Rev. 2027, 2071 (2008).

158. ABA Standards for Programs Providing Civil Legal Services to Persons of Limited Means (Standard 2.12)

159. Kurt Baier, The Moral Point of View 1 (1965).

CHAPTER 6

1. Laura Kipnis, How to Become a Scandal 8, 21(2010).

2. Ari Adut, On Scandal: Moral Disturbances in Society, Politics, and Art 80 (2008).

3. Peter Firestein, Crisis of Character: Building Corporate Reputation in the Age of Skepticism 41 (2009).

4. Judith Sklar, Ordinary Vices 48 (1984).

5. G.R. Goethals, David W. Messick and S. T. Allison, The Uniqueness Bias: Studies of Constructive Social Comparison, in Jerry M. Suls & Thomas Ashby Wills, Social Comparison: Contemporary Theory and Research 149, 161–162 (1991).

6. John Schwartz, Resumes Made for Fibbing, N.Y. Times, May 23, 2010, at WK5.

7. Piercarlo Valdesolo & David DeSteno, The Duality of Virtue: Deconstructing the Moral Hypocrite, 44 J. Experimental Social Psychology 1334 (2008).

8. Joris Lammers, Diederick A. Stapel and Adam D. Galinsky, Power Increases Hypocrisy: Moralizing in Reasoning, Immorality in Behavior, 21 Psychological Science 737 (2010).

9. See surveys cited in Lammers, Stapel and Galinsky, Power Increases Hypocrisy, 738; Adam D. Galinsky, Joe C. Magee, Deborah H. Gruenfeld, Jennifer A. Whitson, & Katie A. Lijenquist, Social Power Reduces the Strength of the Situation: Implications for Creativity, Conformity and Dissonance, 95 J Personality and Social Psychology 1450 (2008).

10. Dennis F. Thompson, Restoring Responsibility: Ethics in Government, Business, and Healthcare 216–217 (1995).

11. Ruth Grant, Hypocrisy and Integrity 26 (1997). See also Shklar, Ordinary Vices, at 54 (arguing that to fail in aspirations is not hypocritical).

12. Sklar, Ordinary Vices, at. 78.

13. Grant, Hypocrisy and Integrity, 181.

14. Shklar, Ordinary Vices, at 70.

15. Alan Ehrenhalt, Hypocrisy Has Its Virtues, N. Y. Times, February 6, 2001, at A19.

16. Marvin Kitman, Supersource for Scandal: Reporters are Wasting Time and Money on Politicians' Dirty Secrets. Let's Get it All Organized in a "Sin Bin," Los Angeles Times, April 6, 2008, at 9.

17. Peter Furia, Democratic Citizenship and the Hypocrisy of Leaders, 41 Polity 114, 123 (2009).

18. Suzanne Dovia, Making the World Safe for Hypocrisy, 34 Polity 3 (2001).

19. Andrew Young, The Politician 206–207 (2010).

20. Maureen Dowd, Running with Scissors, N. Y. Times, April 21, 2007, at A25.

21. Maureen Dowd, Feliz Cumpleaños, and Adiós, N. Y. Times, August 8, 2010, at WK9.

22. Jay Leno, Laugh Lines, N. Y. Times, August 15, 2010, at WK2.

23. Dowd, Feliz, at WK9 (quoting Axelrod).

24. Mitt Romney Struggles to Talk Wealth Ahead of South Carolina Primary, Huffington Post, http:/www.huffingtonpost.com/2012/01/20/mitt-romney-tax-returns-wealth-south-carolina-primary-2012_n_1219563.html.

25. Gerard Baker, Sex Americana, Wall Street J., June 27–28, 2009, at W1 (quoting Bennett).

26. David Rosenham, Moral Character, 27 Stan. L. Rev. 925, 926 (1975). See also Walter Mischel, Personality and Assessment 21–26 (1968).

27. Hugh Hartshorne and Mark A. May, Studies in the Nature of Character: Studies in Deceit, Book I, 377–390, 407–412; Book II, 211–221 (Book II) (1928); Hugh Hartshorne & Mark A. May, Studies in the Nature of Character, Book 2, 211–212. See Mischel, Personality and Assessment, at 250–226; Daryl J. Bem & Andrea Allen, On Predicting Some of the People Some of the Time: The Search for Cross Situational Consistencies in Behavior, 81 Psych. Rev. 506 (1974), Walter Mischel & Yuichi Shoda, A Cognitive Affective System Theory of Personality: Reconceptualizing Situations, Dispositions, Dynamics and Invariance in Personality Structure, 102 Psych. Rev. 246 (1995).

28. Hartshorne & May, Studies in Deceit, Book II, at 211–221.

29. Samuel D. Warren and Louis Brandeis, The Right to Privacy, 4 Harv. L. Rev. 196 (1890).

30. Gary Hart's Judgment, N. Y. Times, May 5, 1987, at A34.

31. Liptak, Taking it Personally, Yale Alumni Magazine, March 1988, at 29 (quoting Calabresi).

32. Jonah Lehrer, The Power Trip, Wall Street J., August 14–15, 2010, at W1.

33. Sharon Jayson, What Makes the Powerful Cheat?, USA Today, November 13, 2012, at 2D (quoting psychologist Frank Farley).

34. Roy F. Baumeister & John Tierney, Willpower: Rediscovering the Greatest Human Strength (2011); Stephanie Rosenbloom, Ambition + Desire=Trouble, N. Y. Times, June 19, 2011, at ST2.

35. Paul K. Piff et al., Higher Social Class Predicts Increased Unethical Behavior, 109 Proceedings of the National Academy of Sciences of the United States of America 4083 (2012).

36. Peter J. Boyer, The Bribe, New Yorker, May 19, 2008, at http://www.newyorker.com/reporting/2008/05/19/080519fa_fact_boyer

37. Boyer, The Bribe, (quoting Scrubbs).

38. Boyer, The Bribe, (quoting Scrubbs ally).

39. Laura Kalman, Abe Fortas 324–326, 352, 377 (1990). See also Bruce Allen Murphy, Fortas: The Rise and Ruin of a Supreme Court Justice (1988).

40. Kalman, Abe Fortas, at 322, 377 (quoting Fortas and describing his lifestyle).

41. Kalman, Abe Fortas, at 573.

42. D. Kevin McNeir, Kwame Kilpatrick: The Rise and fall of Detroit's "Hip Hop" Mayor, Miami Times, July 12, 2012.

43. Kwame Kilpatrick, 2008 Detroit State of the City Address, http://www.detroit-news.com/article/20080311/METRO/803110464.

44. Steve Fainaru, University to Manage Home Costs of President, N. Y. Times, August 27, 2010, at A17.

45. Yale Provost Resigns After Dispute Over Cost of Renovating Home, N. Y. Times, May 2, 1979, at B5; Allison T. Stark, Yale Provost Quits Over Home Expenses Conflict, Washington Post, May 2, 1979, at A14.

46. In the Matter of Representative Charles B. Rangel, Adjudicatory Subcommittee from the Committee on Standards of Official Conduct, U.S. House of Representatives, November 16, 2010.

47. Senate Panel to Senator Craig: You Discredited the Chamber, at http://www.cnn.com/2008/POLITICS/02/12/larry.craig/index.html; at http://www.cnn.com/2008/Politics/02/13/larry.craig/index.html.

48. David M. Halbfinger, Paterson Fined $62,125 Over World Series Tickets, N. Y. Times, December 20, 2010, at A1.

49. Roderick Kramer, The Harder They Fall, Harv. Bus. Rev. October, 2003, at 58.

50. Bryan Burrough, Marc Dreier's Crime of Destiny, Vanity Fair, November, 2009, at http://www.vanityfair.com/business/features/2009/11/marc-dreier200911.

51. Burrough, Marc Dreier's Crime of Destiny.

52. Kramer, The Harder They Fall, at 1.

53. Kramer, The Harder They Fall, at 1.

54. Baumeister & Tierney, Willpower, at 126–127.

55. Carl Hulse, Ensign Apologizes in Farewell Speech, N. Y. Times, May 2, 2011, at http://thecaucus.blogs.nytimes.com/2011/05/02/ensign-apologizes-in-farewell-speech/.

56. Nathan Koppel, Former Florida Lawyer Pleads Guilty to Ponzi Scheme, Wall Street J., January 27, 2010, at http://online.wsj.com/article/SB10001424052748704094304575029013194919020.html.

57. Jon Burstein et al., Lawyer returns as Uproar Grows, Sun-Sentinel (Fort Lauderdale, Florida), November 4, 2009 at A1 (quoting Rothstein).

58. Brittany Wallman et al., Life in the Fast and Secret Lane, Sun Sentinel (Fort Lauderdale, Florida), November 6, 2009.

59. In re Rothstein, Rosenfeldt, Aldler, P.A., Case No. 09-34791, U.S. Bankruptcy Ct. S. Dist. Fl. At 5.

60. Jonah Lehrer, The Power Trip, Wall Street J., August 14–15, 2010, at W1, W2 (noting that abuses are prevented when people know they're being monitored).

61. George Orwell, The Art of Donald McGill, in Essays, 373, 383 (John Carey, ed., 2002).

62. For men's sense of entitlement, see Ronald F. Levant & Gary R. Brooks, Men and Sex: New Psychological Perspectives 87 (1997).

63. Nicholas Confessore, Ungoverned, N. Y. Times Book Review, July 4, 2010, at 15 (quoting Spitzer). See Peter Elkind, Rough Justice: The Rise and Fall of Eliot Spitzer (2010).

64. Andrew Young, The Politician 289 (2010) (quoting Edwards' interview with Bob Woodruff).

65. For accounts of the scandal, see Allan Nevins, Grover Cleveland: A Study in Courage 162–169 (1932); Henry F. Graff, Grover Cleveland 60–65 (2002); Richard E. Welch, The Presidencies of Grover Cleveland 36–39 (1988); see generally Charles Lachman, A Secret Life: The Lies and Scandals of President Grover Cleveland (2011).

66. Audit, On Scandal, at 179, 218; See also Ken Gormley, The Death of American Virtue: Clinton vs. Starr 413 (2010).

67. Mike McGreevey, Confession (2006).

68. Paul Kane & Carol D. Leaning, Senate Ethics Committee: Ensign Violated Federal Laws, Washington Post, May 12, 2011 at http://www.washingtonpost. com/politics/ethics-committee-to-unveil-ensign-probe-findings-in-senate-speeches/2011/05/12/AFhRvAoG_story.html.

69. Marion Clark & Rudy Masa, Rep. Wayne Hays' $14,000-a-Year-Clerk Says She's His Mistress, Washington Post, May 23, 1976, http://www.washingtonpost.com/ wp-srv-longterm/tours/scandal/elizray.htm (Quoting Ray, "I can't type, I can't file, I can't even answer the phone").

70. See Sheryl Gay Stolberg, Naked Hubris: When It Comes to Scandal, Girls Won't Be Boys, N. Y. Times, June 12, 2011, at WK1 (quoting democratic strategist Celinda Lake about public's tendency to be more judgmental about women than men); Julia Baird Newsweek, Girls Will be Girls. Or Not., Newsweek, March 31, 2008, http://www.newseek.com/id/128621 (quoting Northwestern Professor Gunnbjorg Lavoll's explanation of the harsher social consequences for women); Levant & Brooks, Men and Sex, at 84, 87 (noting higher frequency of infidelity in men and noting that it is often socially accepted).

71. Rebecca Dana, Why Women Don't Have Sex Scandals, The Daily Beast, December 11, 2009.

72. Stolberg, Naked Hubris, at WK1.

73. Backpage, Newsweek, June 7, 2010, at 56; Piercarlo Vandesolo & David Desteno, The Duality of Virtue: Deconstructing the Moral Hypocrite, 44 J. Exper. l Social Psych. 1334, 1337 (2008) (quoting Foley).

74. E. J. Dionne Jr., Give Him a Break: Sen. Vitter Has Sinned, But It's Time to Stop Nosing into our Politicians' Private Lives, Pittsburgh Post Gazette, July 13, 2007, at B7.

75. Paul Farhi, Bad News Travels Fast, and Furiously, Washington Post, March 14, 2008 (quoting Frank).

76. Peter Elkind, Rough Justice: The Rise and Fall of Eliot Spitzer (2010); Lloyd Constantine, Journal of the Plague Year: An Insider's Chronicle of Eliot Spitzer's Short and Tragic Reign (2010); Kristi Keck, Surviving a Political Sex Scandal, CNN.com, July 14, 2009, 1, available at http://www.cnn.com/2009/POLITICS/07/14/political.sex.scandal.survival/index.html.

77. Jenny Sanford, Staying True (2010); Elizabeth Edwards, Resilience: Reflections on the Burdens and Gifts of Facing Life's Adversities (2009).

78. Paul Farhi, Bad News Travels Fast, and Furiously, Washington Post, March 14, 2008, at C1.

79. Kipnis, How to Become a Scandal, at 5.

80. Peter H. Kim, Removing the Shadow of Suspicion: The Effects of Apology Versus Denial for Repairing Competence Versus Integrity-Based Trust Violations, 89 J. Applied Psychology 107 (2004).

81. Donald L. Ferrin, Peter H. Kim, Cecily D. Cooper, & Kurt T. Dirks, Silence Speaks Volumes: The Effectiveness of Reticence in Comparison to Apology and Denial for Responding to Integrity- and Competence-Based Trust Violations, 92 J. Applied Psych. 893, 894 (2007).

82. Bill Clinton, Response to Lewinsky Allegations, Jan. 26, 1998, http://miller-center.org/scripps/archive/speeches/detail/3930: Larry Craig, Press Conference August 28, 2007 http://www.foxnews.com/story/0,2933,294961,00.html.

83. Christopher Dehane, Mark Fabiani, & Bill Guttentag, Masters of Disaster: The Ten Commandments of Damage Control 31 (2012).

84. Hearit, Crisis Management by Apology, at 208; Ferrin, Kim, Cooper, & Dirks, Silence Speaks Volumes, at 893.

85. Ferrin, Kim, Cooper, and Dirks, Silence Speaks Volumes, at 906.

86. Noam Cohen, Word for Word/Mixed Messages: Swimming With Stock Analysts, or Sell Low and Buy High…Enthusiastically, N. Y. Times, May 5, 2002, at 4, 7; Patrick McGeehan, $100 Million Fine for Merrill Lynch, N. Y. Times, May 22, 2002, at A1.

87. Steven J. Scher and John M. Darley, How Effective Are the Things People Say to Apologize? Effects of the Realization of the Apology Speech Act, 26 Psycholinguistic Res. 127, 130 (1997).

88. Deborah Tannen, The Power of Talk: Who Gets Heard and Why, Harv. Bus. Rev., Sept.–Oct. 1995, at 143.

89. Douglas A. Cooper, CEO Must Weigh Legal and Public Relations Approaches, 48 Public Relations J. l 40 (1992).

90. Jennifer K. Robbennolt, Apologies and Legal Settlement: An Empirical Examination, 102 Mich. L. Rev. 460, 469, 491–499 (2003).

91. Eric Dash, So Many Ways to Almost Say I'm Sorry, N. Y. Times, April 18, 2010, Wk4 (quoting Charles Prince).

92. Jennifer Robbennolt, Attorneys, Apologies, and Settlement Negotiations, 13 Harvard Negotiation Review 1349, 362 (2008); Kenichi Ohbuchi, Masuyo Kameda, & Nariyuki Agarie, Apology as Aggression Control: Its Role in Mediating Appraisal of and Response to Harm, 56 J. Personality and Social Psych. 219, 224–226 (1989); Dehane, Fabiani, & Guttentag, at 74.

93. Graham Dobbs, Political Apologies: Chronological List, http://reserve.mg2.org/apologies.htm.

94. Lisa Belkin, Unforgivable, N. Y. Times Magazine, July 4, 2010, at 10 (noting that hospitals have found that a disclose and apologize policy has reduced litigation costs); Jennifer Robbennolt, Apologies and Settlement Levers, 3 J. of Empirical Legal Studies 333 (2006); Robbennolt, Attorneys, Apologies, and Settlement Negotiation, 354–355.

95. Robbennolt, Attorneys, Apologies, and Settlement Negotiation, at 356; Robbennolt, Apologies and Settlement Levers, at 336–337.

96. Robbennolt, Apologies and Settlement Levers.

97. Scher and Darley, How Effective Are the Things People Say, 132; Hearit, Crisis Management by Apology, at 69; Paul Vitello, I Apologize. No, Really, I'm Serious, I…, N. Y. Times, Feb. 21, 2010, at WK2; Nick Smith, I was Wrong 140–42 (2008).

98. Dodds, Political Apologies.

99. Mark D. West, Secrets, Sex, and Spectacle: the Rules of Scandal in Japan and the United States 285, 294 (2006) (quoting Shozo Shibuya, Techniques of Apology 152 (2003)).

100. The President's Address Announcing His Intention to Resign, 10 Weekly Comp. Pres. Doc. 1014, 1015 (Aug. 8, 1974).

101. Trip Gabriel, The Trials of Bob Packwood, N. Y. Times Magazine, August 29, 1993, at http://www.nytimes.com/1993/08/29/magazine/the-trials-of-bob-packwood.html?pagewanted=all&src=pm. (quoting Packwood and citing number of complaints).

102. Rhonda Schwartz, Brian Ross, and Chris Francescani, Edwards Admits Sexual Affair, Lied as Presidential Candidate, ABC News, The Blotter, Aug. 8, 2008, http://abcnews.go.com/Blotter/story?id=5441195#.ULgak2f4Kio.

103. Last Night's Address: In his Own Words, N. Y. Times, August 18, 1998, at A12.

104. John M. Broder, Testing of a President: In Moscow, Clinton Defends his TV Admission on Lewinsky Case, N. Y. Times, September 3, 1998, at A1.

105. Bill Clinton, My Life 803 (2004).

106. New York Times, President Clinton's Address at the National Prayer Breakfast, N. Y. Times, September 12, 1998, at A12. For an analysis of Clinton's apologies,

see Images, Scandal, and Communication Strategies of the Clinton Presidency (Robert E Denton Jr. & Rachel L. Holloway, eds., 2003).

107. Susan Dominus, Doing Something Sketchy? It's Harder to Cover Up Now, N. Y. Times, March 21, 2008, at B6; Farhi, Bad News Travels Fast, at http://www.washingtonpost.com/wp-dyn/content/article/2008/03/13/AR2008031304354.html.

108. Jon Decker, Crisis Management and Penn State, Nat'l l Law J., November 21, 2011, at 43.

109. Hastert, Top Aides Knew of Foley Allegation, Roll Call Magazine, September 30, 2006. The House Ethics committee investigated claims that the Republican leadership knew of allegations of sexual advances. See Jonathan Weisman, Hastert Aides Interest Ethics Panel: Staff Members' Knowledge of Foley's Actions With Former Pages in Question, Washington Post, October 11, 2006 (noting that one of the aides allegedly knowledgeable was an attorney).

CHAPTER 7

1. National Association for Legal Career Professionals (NALP), Women and Minorities in Law Firms by Race and Ethnicity, NALP Bulletin, January, 2012; Minority Corporate Counsel Association, Diversity and the Bar, Sept. Oct. 2012, at 30.

2. ABA Commission on Women in the Profession, A Current Glance at Women in Law, 2011, http://www.americanbar.org/content/dam/aba/uncategorized/2011/cwp_current_glance_statistics_2011. Institute for Inclusion in the Legal Profession, The State of Diversity and Inclusion in the Legal Profession (2011); Minority Corporate Counsel Association, MCCA Survey: Women General Counsel at Fortune 500 Companies Reaches New High, Aug. 8, 2012, at 1.

3. Deborah L. Rhode, Perspectives on Professional Women, 40 Stan. L. Rev. 1163, 1173–1174 (1988).

4. United States Census Bureau, Statistical Abstract of the United States: 1970, at 227, table 337 (1970).

5. Deborah L. Rhode, David Luban, & Scott L. Cummings, Legal Ethics 1008 (6th ed. 2012); Donna Fossum, Women in the Legal Profession: A Progress Report, 67 Women L. J. 1 (1981).

6. Bradwell v. Illinois, 83 U.S. 130, 141 (1872) (Bradley, J., concurring).

7. Rhode, Perspectives on Professional Women, at 1170–1171.

8. Virginia G. Drachman, Sisters in Law: Women Lawyers in Modern American History 244 (1998).

9. Lucy R. Tunis, I Gave Up My Law Books for a Cookbook, American Magazine, July, 1927, at 34; Drachman, Sisters in Law, at 247.

10. Drachman, Sisters in Law, at 179–180.

11. For Harvard, see Rhode, Perspectives on Professional Women, at 1171; for Hastings, see Barbara Babcock, Woman Lawyer: The Trials of Clara Foltz, 7–8

(2011); for Columbia, see Jerold S. Auerbach, Unequal Justice: Lawyers and Social Change in Modern America 295 (1976).

12. Cynthia Fuchs Epstein, Women in Law 51 (1981) (quoting Frances Marlatt, quoting Stone).

13. J. R. Pole, The Pursuit of Equality in American History 311 (1978); Drachman, Sisters in Law, at 229, 240.

14. Karen Berger Morello, The Invisible Bar: The Woman Lawyer in America 1638 to the Present 203, 205 (1986); Fred Strebeigh, Equal: Women Reshape American Law 153, 149 (2009); Erwin O. Smigel, The Wall Street Lawyer: Professional Organization Man? 46–47 (1964) (finding only eighteen women lawyers in large firms out of 1,755 practicing in New York in 1957).

15. Drachman, Sisters in Law, at 215, 217.

16. Morello, Invisible Bar, at 147; Maria Chávez, The Rise of the Latino Lawyer: New Study Reveals Inspiring Successes, Lingering Obstacles, ABA J., Oct., 2011, at 39.

17. These characteristics were even presumed sufficient to disqualify some applicants to the bar in jurisdictions with rigorous moral character inquiry. See Douglas, The Pennsylvania System Governing Admission to the Bar, 54 Rep. A.B.A.701, 703–705 (1929); Auerbach, Unequal Justice, at 123, 127 (quoting Harlan Stone regarding undesirable applicants).

18. Auerbach, Unequal Justice 123 (quoting Henry Taft). Report of the Committee on Professional Ethics, 29 Rep. A.B.A. 600, 601 (1906).

19. Auerbach, Unequal Justice, at 66.

20. Darwin Payne, Quest for Justice: Louis A. Bedford Jr. and the Struggle for Equal Rights in Texas 112 (2009); Morello, The Invisible Bar, at 153.

21. Geraldine Segal Blacks in the Law: Philadelphia and the Nation, 102–103 (1983); Payne, Quest for Justice, at 28.

22. Payne, Quest for Justice, at 14, 103.

23. Morello, Invisible Bar, at 148.

24. Morello, Invisible Bar, at 145–146.

25. Morello Invisible Bar, at 146–147.

26. See Jane M. Friedman, America's First Woman Lawyer: The Biography of Myra Bradwell 38 (1993).

27. Babcock, Woman Lawyer, at 8.

28. Elizabeth Vrato, The Counselors 165, 169 (2002).

29. Maria Chávez, Everyday Injustice: The Latino Profession and Racism 1 (2011).

30. Genna Rae McNeil, Charles Hamilton Houston, 3 Black L. J. 123, 124 (1973).

31. Cruz Reynoso, The Lawyer as a Public Citizen, 55 Maine L. Rev. 336, 347–349 (2003).

32. Carol Sanger, Curriculum Vitae (Feminae): Biography and Early American Women Lawyers, 46 Stan. L. Rev. 1245, 1254 (1994).

33. Constance Baker Motley, Equal Justice: An Autobiography 45 (1998).

34. David A. Canton, Raymond Pace Alexander: A New Negro Lawyer Fights for Civil Rights in Philadelphia 13 (2010).

35. P.J. Pierce, "Let Me Tell You What I've Learned": Texas Wisewomen Speak 230 (2002).

36. Juan Williams, Thurgood Marshall: American Revolutionary 53–57, 94 (1998); Genna Rae McNeil, Charles Hamilton Houston: 1895–1950, 32 Howard L. Journal 469, 472–473 (1989). For Marshall's mentoring, see Constance Baker Motley, My Personal Debt to Thurgood Marshall, 101 Yale L. J. 19, 22 (1991).

37. Belva A. Lockwood, My Efforts to Become a Lawyer, Lippincott's Monthly Magazine, February, 1888; Morello, Invisible Bar 38 (quoting Lockwood).

38. Morello, Invisible Bar, at 149.

39. Morello, Invisible Bar, at 70, 74; Drachman, Sisters in Law, at 152–167.

40. Morello, Invisible Bar, at 156.

41. Jon Meacham, Thomas Jefferson, The Art of Power 366 (2012) (quoting Robert Troup); Doris Kearns Goodwin, Team of Rivals: The Political Genius of Abraham Lincoln 265 (quoting Chicago press account); Evan Thomas, The Man to See 429, 535 (1992).

42. Kim Isaac Eisler, Shark Tank: Greed, Politics and the Collapse of Finley Kumble, One of America's Largest Law Firms 64 (1990).

43. Jill Norgren, Rebels at the Bar: The Fascinating Forgotten Stories of America's First Women Lawyers 5 (2012).

44. Tribute to Mrs. Constance B. Motley, House of Representatives, October 18, 2005 (Comments of Rep. Bennie G. Thompson).

45. Marian Wright Edelman, Lanterns: A Memoir of Mentors 79 (1995).

46. Suzanne Braun Levine & Mary Thom, Bella Abzug 39 (2007).

47. Tribute: The Legacy of Ruth Bader Ginsburg and WRP Staff, American Civil Liberties Union, March 7, 2006, http://www.aclu.org/womens-rights/tribute-legacy-ruth-bader-ginsburg-and-wro-staff; Fred Strebeigh, Equal 36 (2009).

48. Jeanine Becker, Myra Colby Bradwell: Sisterhood, Strategy and Family, http://www.womenslegalhistory.stanford.edu (quoting Bradwell); Sanger, Curriculum Vitae, at 1265; Norgren, Rebels at the Bar (quoting claims).

49. Drachman, Sisters in Law, at 64.

50. Catherine B. Cleary, Lavinia Goodell, First Woman Lawyer in Wisconsin, Wis. Mag. Hist. 243, 249 (1991).

51. Joan Biskupic, Sandra, Day O' Connor 39 (2005) (quoting journalists and Senate colleague).

52. Biskupic, O' Connor, at 72–78. In supporting her appointment, Barry Goldwater described her as "epitomizing the 'American ideal of a mother and wife…'" Id., at 85 (quoting Goldwater).

53. Strebeigh, Equal, at 166.

54. Strebeigh, Equal, at 207.

55. Nancy Gertner, In Defense of Women: Memoirs of an Unrepentant Advocate 238 (2011).

56. See Vrato, Counselors, at 157 (noting that Patricia Wald's receipt of a position as Assistant Attorney General owed much to President Carter's pledge to appoint women); Ruth Bader Ginsburg, Women on the Bench, 12 Colum. J. Gender & L., 370 (2003) (describing speculation that her appointment at Columbia in 1972 was the result of affirmative action precipitated by pressure from the federal Office of Civil Right).

57. Deborah L. Rhode, Speaking of Sex: The Denial of Gender Inequality 169 (1997) (quoting Barbara Babcock).

58. White House Project Report, Benchmarking Women's Leadership 8 (2010) (citing Roper public opinion polls).

59. Steven J. Harper, The Lawyer Bubble 91–93 (2013); National Association of Women Lawyers [NAWL]and the NAWL Foundation, Report of the Seventh Annual National Survey on Retention and Promotion of Women in Law Firms 12 (October, 2012).

60. Thomas Thaelkeld, Measuring the Progress of the Nation's Legal Leaders 21 (MCCA 2012).

61. Nancy Levit & Douglas O. Linder, The Happy Lawyer: Making a Good Life in the Law 11(2010).

62. A study of young lawyers by the American Bar Foundation (ABF) found that women attained equity partner status at about half the rate of men. Ronit Dinovitzer et al., After the JD II: Results from a National Study of Legal Careers 63 (2009). A study by the federal Equal Employment Opportunities Commission found that male lawyers were five times as likely to become partners as their female counterparts. EEOC, Diversity in Law Firms 9 (2003), http://www.eeoc.gov/stats/reports/diversitylaw/indesx.html. For studies controlling for factors see Theresa M. Beiner, Not All Lawyers Are Equal: Difficulties That Plague Women and Women of Color, 58 Syr. L. Rev. 317, 328 (2008); Mary C. Noonan, Mary E. Corcoran, & Paul N. Courant, Is the Partnership Gap Closing for Women? Cohort Differences in the Sex Gap in Partnership Chances, 37 Soc. Sci. Res. 156, 174–175 (2008).

63. see NAWL, Seventh Annual National Survey, at 14–15; Amy Kolz, The Law of Small Numbers, American Lawyer, January 2013, at 86; Maria Pabon Lopez, The Future of Women in the Legal Profession: Recognizing the Challenges Ahead By Reviewing Current Trends, 19 Hastings Women's L. J. 53, 71 (2008); and Joan C. Williams & Veta T. Richardson, New Millennium, Same Glass Ceiling?: The Impact of Law Firm Compensation Systems on Women 14 (Project for Attorney Retention & Minority Corporate Counsel Association, 2010).

64. Ronit Dinovitzer et al., After the JD: First Results of a National Study of Legal Careers 58 (2004); Lopez, The Future of Women, at 69; Nancy J. Reichman & Joyce S. Sterling, Sticky Floors, Broken Steps, and Concrete Ceilings in Legal Careers, 14 Tex. J. Women & L. 27, 47 (2004).

65. Thaelkeld, Measuring the Progress, at 30.

66. See Deborah L. Rhode, From Platitudes to Priorities: Diversity and Gender
Equity in Law Firms, 24 Georgetown Journal of Legal Ethics 1041, 1046 (2011);
Marc Galanter & William Henderson, The Elastic Tournament: A Second
Transformation of the Big Law Firm, 60 Stanford Law Review 1917 (2008).
67. Vivia Chen, Prisoner's Dilemma, The American Lawyer, June 2011, at 16.
68. Maria Chávez, Everyday Injustice Latino Professionals and Racism 73 (2011).
69. MCCA, Sustaining Pathways to Diversity: The Next Steps in Understanding and
Increasing Diversity and Inclusion in Large Firms 30 (2010).
70. John M. Conley, Tales of Diversity: Lawyers' Narratives of Racial Equity in
Private Firms, 31 Law & Social Inquiry 831, 841–842, 851–852 (2006).
71. Nicholas Vandersky, March 5, 2012, response to Leslie Bennetts, Women and
the Leadership Gap, The Daily Beast, http://www.thedailybeast.com/news-
week/2012/03/04/the-stubborn-gender-gap.print.html.
72. Robert Drell, Personal Interview, Stanford, CA, February 7, 2012.
73. Kolz, The Law of Small Numbers, at 86.
74. Linda Bray Chanow & Lauren Stiller Rikleen, Power in Law: Lesson from the
2011 Women's Power Summit on Law and Leadership 8–10(2012); Anna Fels,
Necessary Dreams: Ambition in Women's Changing Lives 48–50 (2004).
75. Sheryl Sandberg, Lean In: Women, Work, and the Will to Lead 12–26 (2013).
76. MCCA, Sustaining Pathways to Diversity, at 25.
77. Id., at 15.
78. ABA Commission on Women in the Profession, Visible Invisibility19 (2006).
79. Deepali Bagati, Women of Color in U.S. Law Firms 13 (2009).
80. Bagati, Women of Color, at 13.
81. Anna Scott, Diversity Has Been a Casualty of Law Firm Cutbacks, San Francisco
Daily J., March 17, 2010, at 4. For other employers, see Bennetts, The Leadership
Gap.
82. Maria Chávez, Everyday Injustice 72 (2011); Jill L. Cruz & Melinda S. Molina,
Hispanic National Bar Association National Study on the Status of Latinas in the
Legal Profession, Few and Far Between: The Reality of Latina Lawyers, 37 Pepp.
L. Rev. 971, 1010 (2010); Garner K. Weng, Racial Bias in Law Practice, California
Magazine, January 2003, 37–38; Lu-in Wang, Race as Proxy: Situational Racism
and Self-Fulfilling Stereotypes, 53 DePaul L. Rev. 1013, 1014 (2004). Some leaders
report this concern as well. Susan B. Manch with Nichelle Nash, Learning From
Law Firm Leaders 153 (2012).
83. Institute for Inclusion in the Legal Profession, The State of Diversity, at 76; LeeAnn
O'Neill, Hitting the Legal Diversity Market Home: Minority Women Strike
Out, The Modern American, Spring, 2007, at 7, 9; Bagati Women of Color, at 37;
ABA Commission, Visible Invisibility, at 25; Sonia M. Ospina & Erica G. Foldy,
A Critical Review of Race and Ethnicity in the Leadership Literature: Surfacing
Context, Power, and the Collective Dimensions of Leadership, 20 Leadership Q.
876, 880 (2009).

84. David A. Thomas, The Truth About Mentoring Minorities: Race Matters, Harv. Bus. Rev. April, 2001, at 99, 104.

85. Lynette Clemetson, "The Racial Politics of Speaking Well," N.Y. Times, Feb. 4, 2007, Sec. 4, at 1.

86. Ella L. J. Edmondson Bell & Stella M. Nkomo, Our Separate Ways: Black and White Women and the Struggle for Professional Identity 145 (2001).

87. Eli Wald, Glass Ceilings and Dead Ends: Professional Ideologies, Gender Stereotypes and the Future of Women Lawyers at Large Law Firms, 78 Fordham L. Rev. 2245, 2256 (2010); Crystal L. Hoyt, Women, Men, and Leadership: Exploring the Gender Gap at the Top, 47 Social & Personality Psychology Compass 484, 491 (2010); Cecilia L. Ridgeway & Paula England, Sociological Approaches to Sex Discrimination, in Sex Discrimination in the Workplace 189, 195 (Faye J. Crosby, Margaret S. Stockdale, & S. Ann Rupp, eds., 2007). Even in experimental situations where male and female performance is objectively equal, women are held to higher standards, and their competence is rated lower. Martha Foschi, Double Standards in the Evaluation of Men and Women, 59 Social Psychology 237 (1996). For the special pressures faced by women of color, see Gladys Garcia Lopez, Nunca Te Toman En Cuenta [They Never Take You Into Account]; The Challenges of Inclusion and Strategies for Success of Chicana Attorneys, 22 Gender & Society 590, 598, 603–604 (2008).

88. Deborah L. Rhode & Joan Williams, Legal Perspectives on Employment Discrimination, in Sex Discrimination in the Workplace, at 235, 245; MCCA, Sustaining Pathways to Diversity, 32.

89. Monica Beirnat, M. J. Tocci, and Joan C. Williams, the Language of Performance Evaluations: Gender-Based Shifts in Content and Consistency of Judgment, 3 Soc. Psych. & Personality Science 186 (2011).

90. ABA Commission, Visible Invisibility, at 83. For other research, see Reichman & Sterling, Sticky Floors, at 63–64.

91. Manch with Nash, Learning From Law Firm Leaders, 153.

92. Hewlett et al., Sponsorship Effect, at 24; Michele Mayes and Kora Sophia Baysinger, Courageous Counsel 129 (2011 (quoting Dana Mayer).

93. Deborah L. Rhode & Barbara Kellerman, Women and Leadership: The State of Play, in Women and Leadership: The State of Play and Strategies for Change 7 (Barbara Kellerman & Deborah L. Rhode, eds., 2007); Catalyst, Women Take Care, Men Take Charge: Stereotyping of Business Leaders (2005); Linda L. Carli & Alice H. Eagly, Overcoming Resistance to Women Leaders: The Importance of Leadership Styles, in Women and Leadership, at 127–129; Wald, Glass Ceilings, at 2256.

94. Alice Eagley, Female Leadership Advantage and Disadvantage: Resolving the Contradictions, 31 Psychology of Women Quarterly 1, 5, 9 (2007); Carli & Eagly Overcoming Resistance, at 128–129; Laurie A. Rudman and Stephen E. Kilianski, Implicit and Explicit Attitudes Toward Female Authority, 26 Personality and Social Psych. Bull. 1315 (2000).

95. D. Anthony Butterfield and James P. Grinnell, Reviewing Gender, Leadership, and Managerial Behavior: Do The Decades of Research Tell Us Anything?, in Handbook of Gender and Work 223, 235 (Gary N. Powell, ed., 1998); Jeanette N. Cleveland, Margaret Stockdale, & Kevin R. Murphy, Women and Men in Organizations: Sex and Gender Issues at Work 106–107 (2000).

96. Sandberg, Lean In, at 41; Alice Eagly & Steven Karau, Role Congruity Theory of Prejudice Toward Female Leaders, 109 Psych. Rev. 574 (2002); Alice H. Eagly, Achieving Relational Authenticity in Leadership, 16 Leadership Quarterly 470 (2005); Catalyst, The Double Bind Dilemma for Women in Leadership: Damned if You Do, Damned if You Don't (2007); Linda Babcock and Sara Laschever, Women Don't Ask: The High Cost of Avoiding Negotiation—and Positive Strategies for Change 87–89 (2007); Michele Mayes & Kara Sophie Baysinger, Courageous Counsel 131 (2011).

97. Eagly & Carli, Overcoming Resistance, at 130; Hoyt, Women, Men, and Leadership, at 486; Joan C. Williams & Veta T. Richardson, The Project for Attorney Retention and Minority Corporate Counsel Association, New Millennium, Same Glass Ceiling?: The Impact of Law Firm Compensation Systems on Women 48 (2110), Laurie A. Rudman, To Be or Not To Be (Self-Promoting), The Consequences of Counterstereotypical Impression Management, in Power and Influence in Organizations 290 (Roderick M. Kramer & Margaret A. Neale, eds., 1998).

98. Francis Flynn, Cameron Anderson, and Sebastien Brion, Too Tough Too Soon, Familiarity and the Backlash Effect 2011 (Stanford Business School, unpublished paper).

99. Rick Schmidt, Prophet and Loss, Stanford Magazine, March/April, 2009 (quoting Arthur Levitt), http://www.stanfordalumni.ofg/news/...born/html; Michael Hirsh, Capitol Offense: How Washington's Wise Men Turned America's Future Over to Wall Street 12, 1 (2010) (quoting Robert Rubin and unnamed staffer).

100. Schmidt, Prophet and Loss (quoting Michael Greenberger).

101. Katha Pollitt, Hillary Rotten, in Thirty Ways of Looking at Hillary: Reflections by Women Writers 16–18 (Susan Morrison, ed., 2008).

102. Marie Cocco, Misogyny I Won't Miss, Washington Post, May 15, 2008, at A14; Kathleen Deveny, Just Leave Your Mother out of It, Newsweek, March 17, 2008, at 32.

103. David L. Hamilton & Jim W. Sherman, Stereotypes, in Handbook of Social Cognition 1–68 (Robert S. Wyler & Thomas K. Scrull, eds., 1994); For confirmation bias generally, see Paul Brest & Linda Krieger, Problem Solving, Decision Making and Professional Judgment 277–289 (2010).

104. Lopez, The Future of Women, at 65.

105. Robin Ely, Herminia Ibarra, & Deborah M. Kolb, Taking Gender into Account: Theory and Design for Women's Leadership Development Programs, 10 Academy of Management Learning & Education 474, 477 (2010); Martha

Foschi, Double Standards in the Evaluation of Men and Women, 59 Soc. Psych. Q. 237 (1996); ABA Commission, Visible Invisibility, at 27.

106. Williams & Richardson, New Millennium, at 49–50; Ridgeway & England, Sociological Approaches, at 197; Marilyn B. Brewer & Rupert J. Brown, Intergroup Relations in The Handbook of Social Psychology 554–594; (Daniel T. Gilbert, Susan T. Fiske, & Gardner Lindzey, eds., 1998); Susan T. Fiske, Stereotyping, Prejudice and Discrimination, in Handbook of Social Psychology, at 357–414.

107. The term comes from Pierre Bourdieu, The Forms of Capital, in Handbook of Theory and Research for the Sociology of Education 241, 248 (John G. Richardson, ed., 1986). For discussion in the legal context, see Cindy A. Schipani, Terry M. Dworkin, Angel Kwolek-Folland, & Virgina G. Maurer, Pathways for Women to Obtain Positions of Organizational Leadership: The Significance of Mentoring and Networking, 16 Duke J. Gender L. & Pol'y 89 (2009); Fiona Kay & Jean E. Wallace, Mentors as Social Capital: Gender, Mentors, and Career Rewards in Legal Practice, 79 Sociological Inquiry 418 (2009).

108. For minorities, see ABA Commission, Visible Invisibility, at 18; David Wilkins & G. Mitu Gulati, Why Are There So Few Black Lawyers in Corporate Law Firms: An Institutional Analysis, 84 Cal. L. Rev. 493 (1996). For women, see Reichman & Sterling, at 65; Timothy O'Brien, Up the Down Staircase, N. Y. Times, March 19, 2006, at A4; Williams & Richardson, New Millennium, at 16–17.

109. ABA Commission on Women in the Profession, Visible Invisibility, at 35; Jill Schachner Chanen, Early Exits, ABA J. August, 2006, at 36.

110. Sarah Dinolfo, Christine Silva, & Nancy M. Carter, High Potentials in the Pipeline: Leaders Pay it Forward 7 (Catalyst 2012). For one of the few surveys finding widespread evidence of the dynamic, see Peggy Drexler, The Tyranny of the Queen Bee, Wall Street J., March 2-3, at C2.

111. Dinolfo, Silva, & Carter, High Potentials, at 7.

112. See studies cited in Rhode, Platitudes, at 1071–1172.

113. Sylvia Ann Hewlett, with Kerrie Peraino, Laura Sherbin, & Karen Sumberg, The Sponsor Effect: Breaking Through the Last Glass Ceiling, Harv. Bus. Rev. Research Report 5 (2010): Herminia Ibarra, Nancy M. Carter, & Christine Silvia, Why Men Still Get More Promotions, 88 Harv. Bus. Rev. 80 (2010); Robin J. Ely, Herminia Ibarra, & Deborah M. Kolb, Taking Gender Into Account: Theory and Design for Women's Leadership Development programs, 10 Academy of Management Learning & Education 474, 478 (2011).

114. ABA Commission on Women in the Profession, Visible Invisibility, at 14.

115. For the role of sexual concerns see Hewlett et al., Sponsor Effect, at 35. For race-related barriers in mentoring, see Monique R. Payne-Pikus, John Hagan, Robert L. Nelson, Experiencing Discrimination: Race and Retention in America's Largest Law Firms, 44 Law & Society Rev. 553, 561 (2010).

116. ABA Commission on Women in the Profession, Visible Invisibility, at 27. See also Thomas, Truth About Mentoring Minorities, at 105.

117. ABA Commission on Women in the Profession, Visible Invisibility, at 15–16: Marc Galanter and William Henderson, The Elastic Tournament, 60 Stan. L. Rev. 1868, 1914–1916 (2008); Payne-Pikus, Hagan, Nelson, Experiencing Discrimination, at 576.

118. Institute for Inclusion in the Legal Profession, The State of Diversity, 46.

119. Bagati, Women of Color, at 16; ABA Center on Racial and Ethnic Diversity, Diversity in the Legal Profession: The Next Steps 43 (2010).

120. ABA Commission on Women in the Profession, Visible Invisibility, at 21; Galanter and Henderson, The Elastic Tournament, at 1916; David B. Wilkins & G. Mitu Gulati, Why are There So Few Black Lawyers in Corporate Law Firms, 84 Cal. L.Rev. 493, 565–571 (1996).

121. ABA Commission, Visible Invisibility, at 21.

122. Williams & Richardson, New Millennium, at 42.

123. ABA Commission, Visible Invisibility, at 21; LeeAnn O'Neill, Hitting the Legal Diversity Market Home; Minority Women Strike Out, Modern American, Spring, 2007, at 10.

124. Linda A. Mabry, The Token, California Lawyer, July, 2006, at 76.

125. For sleep, see Law is Second Most Sleep-Deprived Profession, Federal Survey Finds, ABA J. Newsletter, March 2, 2012, abajournalreppt@aconnectionbar. org. For long hours, see Anahad O'Connor, Long Work Hours Can Cause Depression, New York Times, Feb. 7, 2012, at D5. For lawyers' disproportionate depression and substance abuse, see Nancy Levit & Douglas O. Linder, The Happy Lawyer: Making a Good Life in the Law 6(2010); Martin P. Seligman, Paul R. Verkuil, & Terry H. Kang, Why Lawyers are Unhappy, 23 Cardozo L. Rev. 33 (2001).

126. National Association for Law Placement, Most Lawyers Working Part-Time Are Women—Overall Number of Lawyers Working Part-Time Remains Small (December 17, 2009 news release).

127. Paula A. Patton, Women Lawyers: Their Status, Influence, and Retention in the Legal Profession, William & Mary J. of Women & L. 173, 180 (2005). For lower partnership rates, see Theresa Beiner, Not All Lawyers Are Equal: Difficulties That Plague Women and Women of Color, 58 Syracuse L. Rev. 317, 326 (2008); Kenneth G. Dau-Schmidt, Marc S. Galanter, Kaushik Mukhopadhaya, & Kathleen E. Hull, Men and Women of the Bar, 16 Mich. J. Gender & Law 49 (2009); Mona Harrington & Helen His, Women Lawyers and Obstacles to Leadership, MIT Workplace Center 28-29 (2007).

128. See Deborah L. Rhode, Balanced Lives for Lawyers, 70 Fordham L. Rev. 2207, 2213 (2002); For stigma see Holly English, Gender on Trial 212 (2003) (reporting perceptions about slackers); Lopez, Future of Women, at 95; Cynthia Thomas Calvert, Linda Bray Chanow, & Linda Marks, Reduced Hours, Full Success: Part-Time

Partners in U.S. Law Firms (The Project for Attorney Retention, 2009) (reporting that even among lawyers who had achieved partnership, about 40 percent feel stigma from taking part-time schedules).

129. Bureau of Labor Statistics, American Time Use Survey 2010 (2011).

130. Harrington & His, Women Lawyers and Obstacles to Leadership, at 17.

131. Nancy Gertner, In Defense of Women: Memoirs of an Unrepentant Advocate 246 (2011).

132. Ronit Dinovitzer et al., After the JD II, at 62.

133. NALP, Most Lawyers Working Part-Time Are Women; Joan C. Williams, Reshaping the Work-Family Debate 89 (2010) (quoting Derek Bok).

134. Dau-Schmidt, Galanter, Mukhopadhaya, & Hull, Men and Women, at 112–113; Levit & Linder, Happy Lawyer, at 12–13.

135. Vivan Chen, At Law Firms the Kids Are All Right, American Lawyer, Oct. 17, 2011, at 4.

136. Marci Krufka, The Young & the Restless, Law Practice, July/Aug. 2004, at 48; Galanter and Henderson, Elastic Tournament, at 1922–1923.

137. Earl Warren, The Memoirs of Chief Justice Earl Warren 173 (1977).

138. Sheryl Gay Stolberg, He Breaks for Band Recitals, New York Times, February 14, 2010, at S1, S10.

139. Fareed Zakaria, Interview, Time, January 30, 2012, at 31 (quoting Obama).

140. Stolberg, He Breaks for Band Recitals, at S11.

141. Ann-Marie Slaughter, Why Women Still Can't Have it All, Atlantic, July/August 2012, at 85.

142. Galanter and Henderson, Elastic Tournament, at 1921.

143. Cynthia Calvert, Linda Chanow, & Linda Marks, Project for Attorney Retention, Reduced Hours, Full Success: Part-Time Partners in U.S. Law Firms 13, 22 (2009).

144. Calvert, Chanow & Marks, Reduced Hours, at 9, 13, 21.

145. Deloitte and Touche has been a leader. See Susan Sturm, Second Generation Employment Discrimination: A Structural Approach, 101 Colum. L. Rev. 458, 493 (2001).

146. Levit & Linder, Happy Lawyer, at 170; Wal-Mart Legal News, Nov. 2009, at 1; Calvert, Chanow, & Marks, Reduced Hours, at 10–12.

147. See Eyana J. Smith, Employment Discrimination in the Firm: Does the Legal System Provide Remedies for Women and Minority Members of the Bar?, 6 U. Pa. J. Labor & Emp. L.789 (2004).

148. Title VII of the federal Civil Rights Act prohibits employment discrimination based on race, color, religion, sex or national origin. 42 US. Code Section 2000 (e)(2). For an overview, see Katherine T. Bartlett, Deborah L. Rhode, & Joanna Grossman, Gender and Law: Theory, Doctrine, Commentary 89 (6th ed. 2013).

149. Rhode & Williams, Legal Perspectives on Employment Discrimination, at 243; Riordan v. Kaminers, 831 F. 2d 690, 697 (7th Cir. 1987).

150. The problem is true of employment discrimination litigation generally. See Laura Beth Nielson & Robert L. Nelson, Rights Realize? An Empirical Analysis of Employment Discrimination Litigation as a Claiming System, 2005 Wisconsin Law Review 663; Linda Hamilton Krieger, The Watched Variable Improves: On Eliminating Sex Discrimination in Employment, in Sex Discrimination in the Workplace, at 296, 309–310.

151. ABA Commission on Women in the Profession, Visible Invisibility, at 20 (aggressive, bitch); Williams & Richardson, New Millennium, at 38 (confrontational); Reichman & Sterling, Sticky Floors, at 65 (bitch); Marcia Coyle, Black Lawyer's Life, Suit Told by a White Author, National L. J., Jan. 11, 1999, at A14 (quoting Mungen) (angry black).

152. For the advice, see Robert Kolker, The Gay Flannel Suit, N.Y. Magazine, Feb. 26, 2007, http://nymag.com/news/features/28515/; ABA Commission on Women in the Profession, Visible Invisibility at 21. For negative consequences following complaints about compensation, see Williams & Richardson, New Millennium, at 38.

153. ABA Commission on Women in the Profession, Visible Invisibility, at 27.

154. Kolker, Gay Flannel Suit.

155. Deborah L. Rhode, What's Sex Got to Do With It: Diversity in the Legal Profession, in Legal Ethics: Law Stories 233, 246 (Deborah L. Rhode & David Luban eds., 2005) (quoting Charles Kopp).

156. Rhode, What's Sex Got to Do with It, at 235.

157. Ezold v. Wolf, Block, Schorr & Solis-Cohen, 751 F. Supp. 1175, 1184–1186 (E.D. Pa.1990), reversed, 983 F.2d 509 (3d Cir. 1992), *cert. denied*, 510 U.S. 826 (1993).

158. Ezold v. Wolf, Block, Schorr & Solis-Cohen, 751 F. Supp. 1175.

159. 983 F.2d 509 528 (3d Cir. 1992). See Rhode, What's Sex Got to Do With It, at 243.

160. Rhode, What's Sex Got To Do With It, at 245 (quoting Robert Segal).

161. Equal Opportunity Commission v. Bloomberg, 778 F. Supp. 458, 485 (S.D.N.Y 2011).

162. Amelia J. Uelman, The Evils of Elasticity: Reflections on the Rhetoric of Professionalism and the Part-Time Paradox in Large Firm Practice, 33 Fordham Urban L. J. 81, 83 (2005).

163. Sturm, Second Generation, at 468, 470–71, 475–476.

164. Scott Mitchell, MCAA Presents its Recent Findings: Law Firm Diversity, Diversity & B., Dec. 2001, quoted in David B. Wilkins, From "Separate is Inherently Unequal," to "Diversity is Good for Business"; The Rise of Market-Based Diversity Arguments and the Fate of the Black Corporate Bar, 117 Harvard L. Rev. 1548, 1570 (2004).

165. Austin Manifesto on Women in Law, Adopted at the Women's Power Summit on Law and Leadership, sponsored by the Center for Women in Law at the University of Texas School of Law, May 1, 2009.

166. See Anita Williams Woolley et al., Evidence for a Collective Intelligence factor in the Performance of Human Groups, 330 Science 686 (2010); Cynthia Estlund, Putting Grutter to Work: Diversity, Integration and Affirmative Action in the Workplace, 26 Berkeley Journal of Employment and Labor Law Review 1, 22 (2005); Steven A. Ramirez, Diversity and the Boardroom, 6. Stan. J. L. Bus. & Fin. 85 (2000); Rhode & Kellerman, Women and Leadership, at 16; Douglas E. Brayley & Eric S. Nguyen, Good Business: A Market-Based Argument for Law Firm Diversity, 34 J. Legal Profession 1, 13 (2009).

167. Narda Zacchino & Robert Scheer, They Shot the Messenger, Ms., Fall, 2009, at 34.

168. Pew Research Center, A Paradox in Public Attitudes: Men or Women, Who's the Better Leader? 15 (2008).

169. Brayley & Nguyen, Good Business, at 13–14; Cedric Herring, Does Diversity Pay?: Race, Gender, and the Business Case for Diversity, 74 American Sociological Rev. 208 (2009); David A. Carter et al., Corporate Governance, Board Diversity, and Firm Value, 38 Financial Review 33, 51 (2003).

170. Brayley & Nyugen, Good Business, at 34; Deborah L. Rhode & Amanda Packel, Diversity on Corporate Boards: How Much Difference Does Difference Make (Rock Center for Corporate Governance, Working Paper 89, 2010).

171. See studies discussed in Brayley & Nguyen, Good Business, at 13, Wilkins, From "Separate is Inherently Unequal," at 1588–1590; Frank Dobbin, Jiwook Jung, & Alexandra Kalev, Corporate Board Diversity and Stock Performance: The Competence Gap or Institutional Investor Bias (2010); Jonathan S. Leonard, David L. Levine & Aparna Joshi, Do Birds of a Feather Shop Together? The Effects on Performance of Employees Similarity With One Another and With Customers, 25 J. Organizational Behavior 731 (2004).

172. A Call to Action: Diversity in the Legal Profession Commitment Statement, http://www.tools.mcca.com/CTA/commitment_statement.html.

173. Neta Ziv & Christopher Whelan, Privatizing the Profession: Clients' Control of Lawyers' Ethics, 80 Fordham L. Rev. 2577 (2012).

174. Ziv & Whelan, Privatizing the Profession, at 2597–2600; Claire Tower Putnam, Comment: When Can a Law Firm Discriminate Among Its Own Employees to Meet a Client's Request? Reflections on the ACC's Call to Action, 9 U. Pa. J. Lab. & Emp. L. 657, 660 (2007): Karen Donovan, Pushed by Clients, Law Firms Step Up to Diversity Efforts, N. Y. Times, July 211, 2006, C6.

175. California Minority Counsel Program, Diversity Business Matters: Corporate Programs Supporting Business for Diverse Outside Counsel 18 (2011).

176. Melanie Lasoff Levs, Carrot Money to Diversity, Diversity & the Bar, Sept. Oct. 2008, 59.

177. Mary Swanton, 18th Annual Survey of General Counsel: Survey Snapshots, Inside Counsel, July 2007, at 55.

178. Catalyst, Women in Corporate Leadership, 15, 21; Eleanor Clift and Tom Brazaitis, Madame President, 321, 324 (2003).

179. Linda Babcock and Sara Laschever, Ask For It 252 (2008).

180. Babcock and Laschever, Ask For It, at 252–262.

181. Joan Biskupic, Sandra Day O'Connor 56 (2009) (quoting B. Wynn).

182. Ely, Ibarra, & Kolb, Taking Gender Into Account; Erin White, Female Training Classes Flourish, Wall St. J., September 25, 2006, B3. The Leadership Council on Legal Diversity also offers a fellowship program for minorities on the leadership track.

183. Mayes & Baysinger, Courageous Counsel, at 82.

184. Mayes and Baysinger, Courageous Counsel, at 69.

185. Mayes and Baysinger, Courageous Counsel, at 75

186. Susan A Berson, The Rules (For Women), ABA J., January 2012, at 28; Chanow & Rikleen, Power in Law, at 15.

187. Frank Dobbin, Alexandra Kalev, Erin Kelly, Diversity Management in Corporate America, Context Fall 2007, at 21; Catalyst, Advancing Women in Business, at 6, 12–13; Catalyst, Women of Color in Corporate Management, at 69.

188. Frank Dobbin & Alexandra Kalev, The Architecture of Inclusion: Evidence from Corporate Diversity Programs, 30 Harv. J. L. & Gender 279, 283 (2007); Jeanine Prime, Marissa Agin, Heather Foust-Cummings, Strategy Matters: Evaluating Company Approaches for Creating Inclusive Workplaces 6 (Catalyst, 2010); Beiner, Not All Lawyers, at 333.

189. ABA Presidential Initiative Commission on Diversity, Diversity in the Legal Profession: The Next Steps 23 (2010).

190. Emilio J. Castilla, Gender, Race and Meritocracy in Organizational Careers, 113 Am. J. Sociology 1479, 1485 (2008); Stephen Benard, in Paik, & Shelley J. Correll, Cognitive Bias and the Motherhood Penalty, 59 Hastings L. Rev., 1359, 1381 (2008).

191. Bagati, Women of Color, 49; Rhode & Kellerman, Women and Leadership, at 27; Ridgeway & England, Sociological Approaches, at 202; Ely, Ibarra, & Kolb, Taking Gender into Account, at 481; Joanna Barsh & Lareina Lee, Unlocking the Full Potential of Women at Work 11 (McKinsey & Company, 20012).

192. Dobbin & Kalev, The Architecture of Inclusion, at 293–294; Dobbin, Kalev & Kelly, Diversity Management, at 23–24.

193. Tiffany N. Darden, The Law Firm Caste System: Constructing a Bridge Between Workplace Equity Theory and the Institutional Analyses of Bias in Corporate Law Firms, 30 Berkeley Journal of Employment and Labor Law 85, 100 (2009). For the limited research and mixed or negative findings on effectiveness, see Deborah L. Rhode, Social Research and Social Change: Meeting the Challenge of Gender inequality and Sexual Abuse, 30 Harv. J. Law and Gender 11, 13–14 (2007); Elizabeth Levy Paluck, Diversity Training and Intergroup Contact: A Call to Action Research, 62 J. l Social Issues 577, 583, 591 (2006).

194. Dobbin & Kalev, The Architecture of Inclusion, at 293–295; Dobbin, Kalev, & Kelly, Diversity Management, at 23–25.

195. Darden, The Law Firm Caste System, at 117; Diane Vaughan, Rational Choice, Situated Action, and the Social Control of Organizations, 32 Law & Society Rev. 23, 34 (1998).

196. NALP National Survey on Retention and Promotion of Women in Law Firms, November 2007, 15.

197. Schipiani et al., Pathways, at 131; Alexandra Kalev, Frank Dobbin, Dobbin, & Erin Kelley, Best Practices or Best Guesses: Assessing the Efficacy of Corporate Affirmative Action and Diversity Policies, 71 American Sociological Rev. 589, 594 (2006); Rhode & Kellerman, Women and Leadership, at 30.

198. Bob Yates, Law Firms Address Retention of Women and Minorities, Chicago Lawyer (March 2007).

199. Dobbin, Kalev & Kelly, Diversity Management, at 25.

200. Kalev Dobbon, & Kelly, at 594; Rhode & Kellerman, Women and Leadership at 30; Cindy A. Schipani et al., Pathways for Women to Obtain Positions of Organizational Leadership: The Significance of Mentoring and Networking, 16 Duke Journal of Gender, Law and Policy, 89, 100–101 (2009); Abbott, The Lawyer's Guide to Mentoring, at 25, 32–33.

201. Minnesota State Bar Association, Diversity and Gender Equity in the Legal Profession, Best Practices Guide, http:///www.mnbar.org/committes/DiversityImplementation/DiversityBestPracticesGuideFinal.pdf; Manch with Nash, Learning From Law Firm Leaders, at 111.

202. Minnesota State Bar Association, Diversity and Gender Equity.

203. Minority Corporate Counsel Association, Mentoring Across Differences, http://www.mcca.com/_data/n_001/rsources/live/GoldBookExecutiveSummary.pdf.; Leigh Jones, Mentoring Plans Failing Associates, National L. J. September 15, 2006, http://www.law.com/jsp/nlj/PubArticleNLJ.jsp?id=900005462642.

204. Catalyst, The Pipeline's Broken Promise 5 (2010); Manch with Nash, Learning From Law Firm Leaders, at 163.

205. Sara Eckel, Seed Money, American Lawyer, September 2008, at 20.

206. Eckel, Seed Money, at 20 (quoting Ruth Ashby).

207. Frederick A. Miller and Judith H. Katz, The Inclusion Breakthrough: Unleashing the Real Power of Diversity 37–38 (2002).

CHAPTER 8

1. The American Bar Association's dated figures show 74 percent of lawyers in private practice; of those, slightly under half (48 percent) are in solo practice and slightly over half (52 percent) are in firms. ABA Lawyer Statistical Report 6 (2004).

2. ABA Lawyer Statistical Report, at 8.

3. Laurie Bassi and Daniel McMurrer, Leadership and Large Firm Success: A Statistical Analysis,http://www.mcbassi.com/resources/documents/WhitePaper-leadershipAndLawFirmSuccess.pdf.

4. Paul M. Barrett, White Shoe Blues, Business Week, April 23–29, 2012, at 6; Bradford W. Hildebrandt and James W. Jones, *The Anatomy of Large Firm Failures* (Somerset, NJ: Hildebrandt, Nov. 19, 2008), 3, http://www.hildebrandt.com/Hubbard. FileSystem/files/Publication/a018bee0-b710-493c-8f07-006057d169b8/Presentation/PublicationAttachment/7d0507dd-0ed4-4b0e-901f-0.

5. Marc Galanter & William Henderson, The Elastic Tournament: A Second Transformation of the Big Law Firm, 60 Stan. L. Rev. 1867, 1869 (2008).

6. Thomas J. DeLong, John J. Gabarro, & Robert J. Lees, Firm Leaders Survey, American Lawyer, Dec. 2007, at 125, 128.

7. See Elizabeth Chambliss, Measuring Law Firm Culture, in Law Firms, Legal Culture, and Legal Practice: Studies in Law, Politics and Society 1, 3, 5–8 (Austin Sarat, ed., 2010).

8. Chambliss, Measuring Culture, at 9, 19.

9. For discussion, see Marc Galanter & William Henderson, The Elastic Tournament, at 1874; Marc Galanter & Palay, Tournament of Lawyers: The Transformation of the Big Law Firm 37–76 (1991).

10. Paul Hoffman Lions in the Street, 5 (1973), quoting Robert T. Swaine, The Cravath Firm and its Predecessors (1946–1948).

11. Robert T. Swaine, The Cravath Firm and its Predecessors 5, 9 (1946–1948).

12. Milton C. Regan Jr., Eat What You Kill 20 n. 4 (2004).

13. Galanter & Henderson, The Elastic Tournament, at 1873; see Erwin O. Smigel, The Wall Street Lawyer 209 (1964).

14. Swaine, The Cravath Firm, 143.

15. Hoffman, Lions in the Street, at 55, Galanter & Henderson, Elastic Tournament, at 1873.

16. Smigel, Wall Street Lawyer, at 211.

17. Smigel, Wall Street Lawyer, at 199, 211 (quoting anonymous Cravath alumnus quoting de Gersdorff).

18. For examples, see chapter 1 and Thomas, The Man to See, at 433 (describing "total control" demanded by Edward Bennett Williams) and Swaine, The Cravath Firm 1–12 (describing Cravath system); Hoffman, Lions in the Street, at 5 (describing Cravath as a tyrant).

19. Nancy Lisager & Frank Kpsius, A Law Unto Itself: The Untold Story of the Law Firm of Sullivan & Cromwell 28, 32 (1988).

20. Robert Gordon, A Firm of Their Own, 2 Jurist- Books on Line (1999), http://jurist.law.pitt.edu/lawbooks/revmar99.htm; Harold M. Hyman, Craftsmanship and Character: A History of the Vinson & Elkins Law Firm of Houston, 1917–1997, 301–308 (1998).

21. Hyman, Craftsmanship and Character, at 283 (quoting Elkins).

22. Hyman, Craftsmanship and Character, at 283.

23. Hayman, Craftsmanship and Character, at 283.

24. Smigel, Wall Street Lawyer, at 238.

25. Hoffman, Lions in the Street, at 76.

26. Hoffman, Lions in the Street at 30 (quoting anonymous lawyer's description of Phillips, Nizer, Benjamin, Drim & Ballon).

27. Smigel, Wall Street Lawyer, at 37. See also Spencer Kaw, Wall Street Lawyers, Fortune, February, 1958, at 192, and Eli Wald, The Rise and Fall of the Wasp and Jewish Law Firms, 60 Stan. L. Rev. 1803 (2008).

28. Louise Bernikow, Ginsburg Rose to Court from Gender Battles, Women's enews, July 31, 2006 (quoting Ginsburg) http://womensenews.org/story/the-courts/060731/ginsburg-rose-court-gender-battles.

29. Mark J. Green, The Other Government: The Unseen Power of Washington Lawyers 34 (1978).

30. Smigel, Wall Street Lawyer, at 47.

31. Gordon, A Firm of Their Own; Hyman, Craftsmanship and Character, at 15; Hoffman, Lions in the Street, at 126.

32. See Deborah l. Rhode, From Platitudes to Priorities: Diversity and Gender Equity in Law Firms, 24 Geo. J. Legal Ethics 1041 (2011).

33. Thomas J. De Long, John Garro, & Robert J. Lees, When Professionals Have to Lead 9–10 (2007).

34. Mark Chandler, Address at the Northwestern School of Law Securities Regulation Institute, State of Technology in Law (Jan. 25, 2007), http://blogs.cisco.com/news/cisco_general_counsel_on_state_of_technolgy_in_the_law.

35. Richard E. Susskind, The End of Lawyers?: Rethinking the Nature of Legal Services (2010); Richard E. Susskind, Tomorrow's Lawyers (2013).

36. Kim Isaac Eisler, Shark Tank: Greed, Politics, and the Collapse of Finely Kumble, One of America's Largest Law Firms 84 (1990).

37. Deborah L. Rhode, In the Interests of Justice: Reforming the Legal Profession 35 (2000); Ashby Jones, Law-Firm Life Doesn't Suit Some Associates, Wall Street J., May 23, 2006, at B6.

38. Marie Beaudette, Associates Leave Firm in Droves, Nat'l L. J. October 6, 2003, at A1 (quoting Mark Plotkin)

39. See Jennifer Smith, Firms Keep Squeezing Associates, Wall Street J., January 30, 2012, at B1, B4; Chapter 7; Deborah L. Rhode, Balanced Lives: Changing the Culture of Workplace Practices 20 (ABA Commission on Women in the Profession, 2002). For general discussion of the costs of excessive workloads, see Sylvia Ann Hewlett & Carolyn Buck Luce, Extreme Jobs: The Dangerous Allure of the 70 Hour Workweek, Harv. Bus. Rev. Dec., 2006; Jill Andresky Fraser, White-Collar Sweatshop 36–37 (2001).

40. Stephen P. Younger, Shaping Our Profession: A Blueprint for the Future, 82 N.Y. State Bar J. 5, 5 (July/Aug. 2010); National Association for Law Placement Foundation, Update on Associate Attrition 4 (2010).

41. Younger, Shaping Our Profession, at 5; Patti Giglio, Rethinking the Hours, Legal Times, Nov. 8, 2004, at 33.

42. Dinovitzer and Garth, (noting that graduates of elite law schools are least satisfied).

43. Georgetown Law Center for the Study of the Legal Profession, Report on the State of the Legal Market (2013); Eli Wald, Forward: The Great Recession and the Legal Profession, 78 Fordham Law Review 2052 (2010); Larry E. Ribstein, The Death of Big Law, 2010 Wisc. L. Rev. 749, 751; Altman Weil, Law Firms in Transition (2011).

44. Altman Weil, Law Firms in Transition (98 percent viewed focus on efficiency as permanent change and 90 percent expected more price completion). See also Georgetown Law Center for the Study of the Legal Profession, Report on the State of the Legal Market, at 17.

45. Altman Weil, Law Firms In Transition.

46. Peter Lattman, Dewey & LeBoeuf Crisis Mirrors the Legal Industry's Woes, New York Times, April 26, 2012, at B7 (quoting Michael Trotter). See Michael Trotter, Declining Prospects 89 (2012) ("there are more good lawyers and law firms than there are clients").

47. Barrett, White Shoe Blues, at 7 (45,000 graduates for 25,000 job openings).

48. Susan G. Manch with Michelle C. Nash, Learning From Law Firm Leaders 139 (2012); Developing Law Firm Leaders, 29 Law Practice Management 27–28 (2003).

49. Altman Weil, Law Firms in Transition.

50. David Maister, The Trouble With Lawyers, The American Lawyer April 2006, 100; Larry Richard, Herding Cats: The Lawyer Personality Revealed, LAWPRO Magazine, Personality and Practice, Winter, 2008, at 1, 3; Jeff Foster, Larry Richard, Lisa Rohrer, and Mark Sirkin, Understanding Lawyers: The Personality Traits of Successful Practitioners (Hildebrandt White Paper, 2010).

51. Leadership Partners or Managing Partners, 10 Law Office Management & Administration Rep. 1, 5 (2010): Elizabeth Chambliss, New Sources of Managerial Authority in Large Law Firms, 63 Geo. J. Legal Ethics, 77 (2009).

52. Maister, The Trouble With Lawyers, 100; Michael Kelly, The Lives of Lawyers Revisited 180–181 (2007); Steven J. Harper, The Lawyer Bubble: A Profession in Crisis xiv (2013).

53. Dan M. Kahan, The Logic of Reciprocity: Trust, Collective Action, and the Law, 102 Mich. L. Rev. 71, 74 (2002).

54. Leadership Partners or Management Partners; Eisler, Shark Tank, at 84. See chapter 1.

55. Michael Rosen, Managing Partners Wear Two Hats Well, California Lawyer, May, 2012 at 16 (quoting Dale Goldsmith).

56. Rosen, Managing Partners, at 16.

57. See chapter 1; Manch with Nash, Learning From Law Firm Leaders, at X.

58. +Peter D. Zeughauser and Ron Beard, Rewarding Leadership, The American Lawyer, January 2008, 60.

59. Leadership Partners or Management Partners, 7.

60. Ida Abbott, Taking the Lead, www.IdaAbbott.com; Developing Law Firm Leaders, Law Practice Management, Oct. 2003, at 27, 31–32.

61. Cartoon by Robert Weber, The New Yorker, June 6, 1998, at 5.

62. Steven Harper, Fed to Death, American Lawyer, December, 2011, at 61, 62. See Harper, The Lawyer Bubble, at 72.

63. Steven Brill, "Ruining the Profession," American Lawyer, July/August, 1996, 5.

64. Nathan Koppel & Vanessa O'Connell, Pay Gap Widens at Big Law Firms as Partners Chase Star Attorneys, Wall Street J., Feb.8, 2011, at A1, A12.

65. Peter Lattman, A Once-Ambitious Law Firm, Reduced to Grim Dispatches, N. Y. Times, May 2, 2012, at A1, B7.

66. Maister, The Trouble with Lawyers, at 100.

67. Amy Kolz, A Waste of Money?, American Lawyer, Sept. 2011, at 72 (quoting Ralph Baxter).

68. Kolz, A Waste of Money, at 72.

69. Kolz, A Waste of Money, at 74.

70. See sources cited in Deborah L. Rhode, Foreword: Personal Satisfaction and Professional Practice, 58 Syr. L. Rev. 217, 229 (2008).

71. Daniel Kahneman et al., Would You Be Happier if You Were Richer? A Focusing Illusion, 312 Sci. 1908, 1910 (2006). See also David G. Meyers, The Pursuit of Happiness: Who is Happy—and Why 39 (1992); Robert H. Frank, How Not to Buy Happiness, 133 Daedalus 69, 69–71 (2004); William C. Compton, Introduction to Positive Psychology 62 (2004).

72. Jonathan Lindsey, After the Pie Has Been Sliced: Reducing Friction Over Distribution, reprinted in PLI, Law Firm Leadership & Management Institute 2010, (Course Handbook Series B-1787); Mike Papantonio, Legal Egos on the Loose, ABA J., Sept. 1999, at 108. For general discussion, see Robert H. Frank and Philip J. Cook, The Winner Take All Society 41, 66 (1995); John R. O'Neill, The Paradox of Success: When Winning at Work Means Losing at Life 29–30 (1994).

73. Jonathan Lindsey, Lateral Partner Satisfaction: A Decade of Perspective 7 (2007).

74. Rhode, Foreword: Personal Satisfaction and Professional Practice, at 231–233.

75. Exclusive LOMAR Survey Data, Law Firm Leaders Share Views on Their Challenges and Triumphs in 2008 for 2008 and Beyond, Law Office Management &Administration Report, Feb., 2008; Conley, How Bad is It, 2009–2012.

76. Marc Galanter, "Old and in the Way": The Coming Demographic Transformation of the Legal Profession and Its Implications for the Provision of Legal Services, 1999 Wis. L. Rev. 1081, 1085. For a general discussion, see Deborah L. Rhode, Senior Lawyers Serving Public Interests: Pro Bono and Second Stage Careers, 21 Professional Lawyer 1 (2011) Kenneth G. Dau-Schmidt, Esther F. Lardent, Reena N. Glazer, & Kellen Ressmeyer, "Old and Making Hay": The Results of the

Pro Bono Institute Firm Survey on the Viability of a "Second Acts" Program to Transition Attorneys to Retirement Through Pro Bono Work, 7 Cardozo Public L. Pol'y, and Ethics J. 321, 324 (2009).

77. Almost nine out of ten Americans between the ages of 65 and 74 are able to work. Laura L. Carstensen, A Long Bright Future: An Action Plan for a Lifetime of Happiness, Health, and Financial Security 31 (2009).

78. In an Altman Weil survey, half of firms with at least 50 lawyers had mandatory retirement policies Altman Weil, Flash Survey on Lawyer Retirement (2007), http://www.altmanweil.com/LawyerRetirement. Of firms with 50–99 attorneys, 39 percent had such policies. A *New York Times* survey of firms with over 100 lawyers found that 60 percent had mandatory policies. Julie Creswell & Karen Donovan, Happy Birthday, Vacate Your Office, New York Times, December 8, 2006, at C1. A Pro Bono Institute survey of firms averaging 391 lawyers reported that 42 percent had such policies and 37 percent had an express target retirement age. Dau-Schmidt, Lardent, Glazer & Ressmeyer, Old and Making Hay, at 333. The average age under mandatory policies was 67 and the target age was 66.

79. Elizabeth Goldberg, Grey Matters, American Lawyer, December 2007, at 119. See also Nelson D. Schwartz, Easing Out the Gray-Haired. Or Not, N. Y. Times, May 28, 2011, at B1 (describing difficulties of terminating partners whose billings decline). In the Altman Weil survey of lawyers in management positions, 38 percent favored mandatory policies. Altman Weil, Flash Survey.

80. ABA Report to the House of Delegates, No. 10A (August 2007), http://adwww2. americanbar.org/sdl/Pages/ABAPolicyADS.aspx.

81. Amy Cavalier, Legal Industry Tackles Ageism, Daily Record (Rochester), Sept. 24, 2010.

82. EEOC v. Sidley Austin Brown & Wood, 406 F. Supp. 991 (N.D. Ill. 2005); Nate Raymond, Faced With Suit, Kelley Drye Drops Retirement Policy, N. Y. L. J., April 12, 2010, at 1.

83. Goldberg, Grey Matters, at 119.

84. Michael D. Shear & John Schwartz, Law Firm Won't Defend Marriage Act, N. Y. Times, April 25, 2011 (quoting firm Chair Robert D. Hayes Jr.). See Deborah L. Rhode, King and Spaulding Was Right to Withdraw, Nat'l L. J., May 9, 2011, at 42.

85. Jennifer Rubin, Why Did King & Spaulding Dump Its Client?, Washington Post blog, April 26, 2011, at http:www.washingtonpost.com/blogs/right-turn/post/why-did-king-and-spaulding-dump-its-client/2011/03/29/AFCgWmqEblog.html.

86. Shear & Schwartz, Law Firm Won't Defend (quoting Stephen Gillers).

87. David Dat, King & Spaulding: More DOMA Drama, Above the Law, May 13, 2011, http://wbovethelaw.com/2011/05/king-spalding-more-doma-drama-plus-salary-amd-bonus-news/.

88. William H. Herndon and Jesse W. Weik, *Herndon's Lincoln* 215 (Douglas L. Wilson and Rodney O. Davis, eds., 2006) (1888).

89. Blaine Harden & Saundra Torry, N.Y. Law Firm to Advise Swiss Bank Accused of Laundering Nazi Loot, Washington Post, Feb. 28, 1997, at A3; Edward A. Adams & Daniel Wise, Controversy Ruffles Cravath Over Representing Swiss Bank, N.Y. L.J. March 3, 19997, at A1.

90. Blaine Harden When Client, Justice are "Incompatible"; Lawyers Protest Firms Representation of Bank That Laundered Nazi Loot, Washington Post, March 13, 1997, at A15.

91. Id. (quoting Liman).

92. See William Glaberson, New York Loses a Top Legal Ally in Suit Over Guns, N. Y. Times, April 17, 2004, at A1, A7.

93. A Less Gilded Future, The Economist, May 7, 2011, at 73.

94. For lawyer skepticism, see chapter 1. For experts, see Maureen Broderick, The Art of Managing Professional Services 121–146 (2011); De Long, Gabarro, & Lees, When Professionals Have to Lead, Mark Shapiro, Why Must Law Firms Be Strategic, in PLI, Law Firm Leadership & Management Institute 2010 (Course Handbook Series B-1787).

95. Broderick, The Art of Managing Professional Services, at 222.

96. Broderick, The Art of Managing professional Services, at 37.

97. For examples of firms that gave quite different priorities to profits, see Michael Kelly, The Lives of Lawyers Revisited: Transformation and Resilience in the Organizations of Practice (2007).

98. Broderick, the Art of Managing Professional Services, at 183.

99. Barry Schwartz & Kenneth Sharpe, Practical Wisdom 248–250 (2010); Kelly, Lives of Lawyers Revisited, at 130–143.

100. James C. Collins and Jerry Porras, Built to Last: Successful Habits of Visionary Companies, 46–68, Chapter 3: More Than Profits (1994); Rosabeth Moss Kanter, How Great Companies Think Differently, Harv. Bus. Rev., November, 2011 http://hbr.org/2011/11/how-great-companies-think-differently/ar/1.

101. Kelly, Lives of Lawyers Revisited, at 222.

102. Leadership Partner or Managing Partner, Law Office Management and Administration Report, October 2010, at 1, 5; Broderick, The Art of Managing Professional Services, at 267.

103. Kelly, Lives of Lawyers, at 151. See also John M. Conley, How Bad Is It Out There?; Teaching and Learning About the State of The Legal Profession in North Carolina, 82 N. Carolina L. Rev. 1943, 1970, 2007 (2004).

104. Joel Rosenblatt, The Great Sonsini, California Lawyer, October 2004, at 23–29.

105. Lincoln Caplan, Skadden: Power, Money, and the Rise of a Legal Empire 317 (1993); Kelly, Lives of Lawyers Revisited, at 150–151; Broderick, Leadership: Characteristics Grooming Selection, in PLI Law Firm Leadership and Management Institute, 467, 480; Broderick, The Art of Managing Professional Services, at 269–271.

106. Developing Law Firm Leaders, at 31 (comments of Rachel Shaming).

107. Kelly, Lives of Lawyers Revisited, at 153.
108. For the diversity in workable structures, see Conley, How Bad is it Out There, at 2003–2004. For the widely accepted "autocracy" at Jones Day, see Susan Letterman White, Power and Influence for Lawyers: How to Use It to Develop business and Advance Your Career 54 (2011). For the direct democracy at Paul Weiss, see Arthur Liman with Peter Israel, Lawyer 61–62 (1998). For changes at Skadden, see Lincoln Caplan, Skadden: Power, Money, and the Rise of a Legal Empire 314–316 (1993). For changes at Gibson Dunn, see Toni Massaro, F. Daniel Frost and the Rise of the Modern American Law Firm, 76, 81 (2011).
109. Broderick, The Art of Managing Professional Services, at 240, 247; Kelly, Lives of Lawyers, at 187.
110. Chambliss, Measuring Law Firm Culture, 23; Tom R. Tyler & Steven L. Blader, The Group Engagement Model: Procedural Justice, Social Identity and Cooperative Behavior, 7 Personality and Soc. Psych. Rev. 349 (2003).
111. Broderick, The Art of Managing Professional Services, at 269. See also Kelly, Lives of Lawyers Revisited, 165, 204.
112. Julie Triedman, The Fall of Howrey, The American Lawyer, June 1, 2011 (quoting John Briggs).
113. Steven Brill, Leadership, American Lawyer, September 1983, at 18.
114. Martin Mayer, The Lawyers 335 (1966).
115. For survey data, see Rhode, Senior Lawyers Serving Public Interests; Altman Weil Flash Survey.
116. See Rhode, Senior Lawyers Serving Public Interests. The Senior Attorneys Initiative for Legal Services has developed sample policies that call on firms to integrate pro bono planning into their structured retirement process and to have their pro bono committee or coordinator meet with seniors on a regular basis to discuss their interest in public interest projects. Senior Attorneys Initiative for Legal Services, Sample Law Firm Pro Bono Policies for Senior Lawyers (May 6, 2011).
117. Ida Abbott, Taking the Lead, www.IdaAbbott.com; Douglas B. Richardson and Douglas B. Coopersmith, How a Law Firm Learned to Train its Leaders, American Lawyer, July, 2008, at 2.
118. Broderick, Managing Professional Services, at 474.
119. Id., Chapter 2. For examples, see Kelly, Lives of Lawyers, 171, and Manch with Nash, at 165–85. For the value of such self-conscious management, see Chambliss, Measuring Law Firm Culture, at 25.
120. Jim Collins, Level 5 Leadership: The Triumph of Humility and Fierce Resolve, Harv. Bus. Rev., January 2001, at 1, 7.
121. For fistfights, see Eisler, Shark Tank, 131; for vases, see Karen Dullon, Last Days at Lord Day, American Lawyer, May 2004, at 40.
122. Bradford W. Hildebrandt and James W. Jones, The Anatomy of Large Firm Failures (2008), 3, http://www.hildebrandt.com/Hubbard.FileSystem/files/

Publication/a018bee0-b710-493c-8f07-006057d169b8/Presentation/ PublicationAttachment/7d0507dd-0ed4-4b0e-901f-01.

123. Hildebrandt, The Anatomy of Law Firm Failures.

124. For an earlier discussion of some of these failures see Deborah L. Rhode & Amanda Packel. Leadership: Law, Policy, and Management 65-69 (2011).

125. Susan Kostal, SanFrancisco online, The Brobeck Mutiny (2003), http://www.sanfranmag.com/story/brobeck-mutiny.

126. Jonathan Glater, West Coast Law Firm Closing After Dot-Com Collapse, N. Y. Times, Jan. 31, 2003, at C1; Todd Wallack and Harriet Chang, Top S.F. Dot-com Law Firm to Close: Brobeck, Phleger, & Harrison Grew with Tech Boom, San Francisco Chronicle, Jan. 31, 2003, at A1.

127. Kostal, The Brobeck Mutiny.

128. Kostal, The Brobeck Mutiny (quoting Snow).

129. Kostal, The Brobeck Mutiny.

130. Kostal, The Brobeck Mutiny.

131. Glater, West Coast Law Firm Closing After Dot-Com Collapse.

132. Jason Fagone, Wrongful Death, Philadelphia Magazine, June 2009, 2, 4, 6, http://www.phillymag.com/articles/wrongful_death/.

133. Fagone, Wrongful Death. See also Gina Passarella, No Easy Answers in Wolf Block's Demise, Legal Intelligencer, March 25, 2009.

134. A Less Gilded Future, at 74; Steven Pearlstein, Why Howrey Law Firm Could Not Hold It Together, Washington Post, March 19, 2011.

135. Julie Triedman, The Fall of Howrey, American Lawyer, June, 2011, at 49–55.

136. Id., at 51; Pearlstein, Why Howrey Firm Could Not Hold It Together; Marisa M. Kashino, A Tale of Two Law Firms, Washingtonian, Dec. 2011, at 76.

137. Kashino, A Tale of Two Firms, at 75 (quoting John Briggs).

138. Triedman, Fall of Howrey, at 51, 52.

139. Kashino, A Tale of Two Firms, at 74 (quoting John Briggs).

140. Triedman, Fall of Howrey, at 54 55 (quoting Peter Zeughauser).; Kashino, A Tale of Two Firms, at 74–78.

141. Kashino, A Tale of Two Firms, at 123 (quoting Ruyak).

142. Carlyn Kolker, An Unquiet Death, American Lawyer, November, 2006; Ellen Rosen, The Complicated End of an Ex-Law Firm, N. Y. Times, February 9, 2007, at C7.

143. Jonathan D. Glater, Law Firm That Opened Borders is Closing Up Shop, N. Y. Times, Aug. 30, 2005, at C1.

144. Nathan Koppel, Coudert Brothers Votes to Disband Storied Law Firm, Wall Street J. l, Aug 19, 2005, at B 2 (quoting Peter Zeughauser). For income, see Glater, Law Firm That Opened Borders, at C1.

145. Glater, Law Firm That Opened Borders, at C1 (quoting Frederic Coudert).

146. Milton C. Regan Jr., Taxes and Death: The Rise and Demise of an American Law Firm, in Studies in Law, Politics, and Society: Law Firms, Legal Culture, and Legal Practice (Austin Sarat, ed., 2010).

147. Jenkens & Gilchrist, Statement, March 29, 2007, http://www.justice.gov/tax/ usaopress/2007/txdv07jenkins&gilchristnppr.pdf.

148. Regan, Taxes and Death; Firm Dissolutions, Law Firm Management, June 2007, at 1.

149. Regan, Taxes and Death., at 137. See also Nathan Koppel, How a Bid to Boost Profits Led to a Law Firm's Demise, Wall Street J., May 17, 2007, at A1.

150. Regan, Taxes and Death, at 140–141.

151. Nathan Koppel, Bid to Boost Profits, at A1 (quoting William Durbin Jr.).

152. Regan, Taxes and Death, at 139.

153. Regan, Taxes and Death, at 139; Katie Fairbank & Terry Maxon, How Jenkins Lost Its Way: As Law Firm Dissolves, Leaders Have No Doubt Tax Scheme to Blame, Dallas Morning News, April 1, 2007, at A1.

154. Regan, Taxes and Death, at 140.

155. Koppel, Bid to Boost Profits, at A1 (quoting William Durbin).

156. Koppel, Bid to Boost Profits, at A16 (quoting Marshall Simmons).

157. Bob Van Voris, Lawyer Daugerdas Seeks New Trial Based on Juror Misconduct, Bloomberg News, Aug. 15, 2011. The lawyers sought a new trial based on lies by a juror. A third lawyer plead guilty and testified for the government.

158. Nathan Koppel, Bid to Boost Profits, at A16 (quoting William Durbin)

159. Peter Latmann, Assigning Blame in Dewey's Collapse, N. Y. Times, May 14, 2012, at B1; Jennifer Smith, Ashby Jones, & Steve Eder, Woes at Law Firm Deepen, Wall Street J. l, April 28, 29, at A1, A4.

160. Smith, Jones & Eder, Woes at Law Firm Deepen, at A4 (quoting partner).

161. Casey Sullivan, Dewey Downfall is Cautionary Tale for Firms, San Francisco Daily Journal, May 24, 2012, at 1, 5.

162. Julie Triedman, Sara Randazzo, & Brian Baxter, House of Cards, American Lawyer, July/August 2012, at 53.

163. James B. Stewart, Dewey's Fall Underscores Law Firms' New Reality, N. Y. Times, May 5, 2012, at B1, B6 (quoting Bruce MacEwen). For other experts, see Peter Lattman, Lean times for a Law Firm, N. Y. Times, March 16,2012, at B1.

164. The civil claim by an ex-partner claims that the former chairman and other law firm leaders misrepresented Dewey's financial circumstances to induce him and other successful partners to join the firm, and then used the capital they invested to pay themselves. Jennifer Smith, Dewey's Former Leaders Sued, Wall Street J.l, June 14, 2012.

165. Stewart, Dewey's Fall, at A1; Peter Lattman, Dewey & LeBoeuf Crisis Mirrors the Legal Industry's Woes, N. Y. Times, April 26, 2012, at B7.

166. Stewart, Dewey's Fall, at B6 (quoting Bruce MacEwen).

167. Lattman, Dewey & LeBoeuf Crisis, at B7 (quoting Trotter).

168. Trotter, Declining Prospects, at 223.

169. Regan, Taxes and Death, at 142.

170. Triedman, The Fall of Howrey, at 51 (quoting Zeughauser).

171. Firm Dissolution, Partner's Report for Law Firm Owners, June, 2007, at 5 (quoting Jenkins lawyer).

172. Assigning a specific partner an independent oversight role may sometimes be a useful strategy. Aric Press, A Partner Protection Plan, American Lawyer, June 2012.

173. Eisler, Shark Tank, at 13, 65.

174. Harper, Lawyer Bubble, at 108.

175. For illusions of synergy, see Paul B. Carroll & Chunka Mui, Billion Dollar Losses 15–16 (2009).

176. Rosen, The Complicated End, at C7 (quoting Ward Bower).

177. Firm Dissolutions, Partner's Report for Law Firm Owners, June, 2007, at 5–6.

178. What Law Firm Leaders Are Saying, 28 Of Counsel 5, 7 (June, 2009).

179. Kimberly Kirkland, Ethics in Large Firms: The Principles of Pragmatism, 35 U. Memphis L. Rev. 631, 678 (2004) (quoting partner); Kelly, Lives of Lawyers, at 220 (quoting partners).

180. George A. Akerlof & Rachel E. Kranton, Identity and the Economics of Organizations, 19 J. Econ. Persp. 9, 9–16, 27–29 (2005). For Vinson & Elkins' "company culture," see Hyman, Craftsmanship and Character, at 17.

181. Ronald J. Gilson & Robert H. Mnookin, Sharing Among the Human Capitalists: An Economic Inquiry into the Corporate Law Firm and How Partners Split Profits," 37 Stan. L. Rev. 313, 375–381 (1985).

182. Ronald A. Heifetz and Marty Linsky, Leadership on the Line: Staying Alive Through the Dangers of Leading 59 (2002); Koppel, Recession Batters Law Firms, at A11.

183. Peter D. Zeughauser, Stuck on You, American Lawyer, October, 2011, at 63, 64.

184. DeLong, Gabarro, and Lees, When Professionals Have to Lead, American Lawyer, at 125–129.

185. William H. Simon, Where is the Quality Management in the Legal Profession, 2012 Wisc. L. Rev. 87.

186. Sarah Kellogg, Queasy Street, Washington Lawyer, June, 2009, at 28, 30; Richardson and Coopersmith, Learning to Lead, at 57, 58; For a model leadership development program, see Manch with Nash, Learning From Law Firm Leaders, at 187–212.

187. Manch with Nash, Learning From Law Firm Leaders, at 181.

188. Manch with Nash, Learning From Law Firm Leaders, at 27.

189. Manch with Nash, Learning From Law Firm Leaders, 169–71.

190. Simon, Quality Management; Christine Parker, Tahlia Godon, and Steve Mark, Regulating Law Firm Ethics Management: An Empirical Assessment of an Innovation in Regulation of the Legal Profession in New South Wales, 37 J. Law & Soc'y 466, 467 (2010); John Britton & Scott McLean, Incorporated Legal Practices: Dragging the Regulation of the Legal Profession into the Modern Era, 11 Legal Ethics 241 (2olo).

191. Trotter, Declining Prospects, at 64 (quoting Richard Susskind). See also Susskind, Storm Warning, at 38.

CHAPTER 9

1. For inattention, see Sharon Erickson Nepstad and Clifford Bob, When do Leaders Matter? Hypotheses on Leadership Dynamics in Social Movements, 11 Mobilization: An International Journal 1 (2006); Aldon D. Morris & Suzanne Staggenborg, Leadership in Social Movements, in The Blackwell Companion to Social Movements 171 (David A Snow, Sarah A. Soule, & Hanspieter Kriesi, eds., 2004), Colin Barker, Alan Johnson, and Michael Lavalette, Leadership Matters: An Introduction, in Leadership and Social Movements 1 (Colin Barker, Alan Johnson, & Michael Lavalette, eds., 2001).

2. For social movements generally, see Thomas R. Rochon, Culture Moves: Ideas, Activism, and Changing Values (1998); Gary T. Marx & Doug McAdam, Collective Behavior in Oppositional Settings: The Emerging Social Movement, in Collective Behavior and Social Movements (Gary T. Marx & Doug McAdam, eds., 1993); Doug McAdam, Political Opportunities: Conceptual Origins, Current Problems, and Future Directions, in Comparative Perspectives on Social Movements: Political Opportunities, Mobilizing Structures, and Cultural Framings (Doug McAdam, John D. McCarthy, & Mayer N. Zald, eds.,1996); John D. McCarthy and Mayer N. Zald, Resource Mobilization and Social Movements: A Partial Theory, in Collective Behavior and Social Movements, 40, 43(Russell L. Curtis & Benigno A. Aguirre, eds., 1993).

3. Alan Johnson, Self Emancipation and Leadership, in Leadership and Social Movements 96, 99 (Colin Barker, Alan Johnson, & Michael Lavalette, eds., 2001) (quoting civil rights activist Ella Baker).

4. Clayborne Carson, Reconstructing the King Legacy: Scholars and National Myths, in We Shall Overcome: Martin Luther King and the Black Freedom Struggle 243, 246 (Peter J. Albert and Robert Hoffman, eds., 1993).

5. David J. Garrow, Bearing the Cross: Martin Luther King Jr. and the Southern Christian Leadership Conference, 56 (1st Perennial Classics ed., 2004) (quoting King).

6. Aldon Morris, A Man Prepared for the Times: A Sociological Analysis of the Leadership of Martin Luther King Jr., in We Shall Overcome, at 36.

7. Joe Wallis and Brian Dollery, Market Failure, Government Failure, Leadership and Public Policy 119 (1999).

8. Deborah L. Rhode, Justice and Gender 54–55 (1989).

9. Rhode, Justice and Gender, at 56; Thomas R. Rochon, Culture Moves: Ideas, Activism and Changing Values 207 (1998).

10. McAdam, Culture and Social Movements, at 40.

11. Rochon, Culture Moves, at 8; McAdam, Culture and Social Movements, at 40.

12. Rochon, Culture Moves, at 190–198; Deborah L. Rhode, Sexual Harassment, 65 S. Cal. L. Rev. 1459 (1992).

13. Nicole C. Raeburn, Working it Out: The Emergence and Definition of the Workplace Movement for Lesbian, Gay, and Bisexual Rights, in Research in *Social*

Movements: Conflicts and Change 187 (Daniel J. Myers & Daniel M. Cress, eds., 2004).

14. Bert Klandermans, The Demand and Supply of Participation: Social-Psychological Correlates of Participation in Social Movements, in The Blackwell Companion, at 360, 362 Marshall Ganz, Leading Change: Leadership Organization and Social Movements, in, Handbook of Leadership Theory and Practice 527, 533 (Nitin Nohria & Rakesh Khurana, eds., 2010); McCarthy & Zald, Resource Mobilization and Social Movements, at 40.

15. Joan Neff Gurney and Kathleen J. Tierney, Relative Deprivation and Social Movements: A Critical Look at Twenty Years of Theory and Research, in Collective Behavior and Social Movements, at 141. See also Herbert Buner, Social Problems as Collective Behavior, in Collective Behavior and Social Movements, 54 (noting that harmful conditions are not sufficient to mobilize a movement; they need to be legitimated as a problem that can be addressed by social action).

16. Scott A. Hunt and Robert D. Benford, Collective Identity, Solidarity, and Commitment, in Blackwell Companion, 433, 439; Rochon, Culture Moves, at 124–161.

17. Rochon, Culture Moves, at 104.

18. Morris and Staggenborg, Leadership in Social Movements, at 174–175; Sharon Erickson Nepstad & Clifford Bob, When Do Leaders Matter? Hypotheses on Leadership Dynamics in Social Movements, in 11 Mobilization: An Internat'l J. 1 (2006).

19. Melvin L. Urofsky, Louis D. Brandeis: A Life 399–419 (2009).

20. Michael Winerip, What's a Nice Jewish Lawyer Like John Rosenberg Doing in Appalachia, N. Y. Times Magazine, June 29, 1997, at 26.

21. Winerip, What's a Nice Jewish Lawyer, at 27 (quoting Bruce Davis).

22. Evan Thomas, Robert Kennedy: His Life 110–111 (2000).

23. Cynthia Cotts, Trumpeting the Cause of Civil, Human Rights, National L. J., Aug. 24, 1998, at C15.

24. See the discussion of Nader's personal life in chapter 2 and the General Motors suit in Charles McCarry, Citizen Nader 25–27 (1972).

25. Leslie R. Crutchfield & Heather McLeod-Grant, Local Forces for Good, Stan. Social Innovation Rev., Summer 2012, at 36.

26. Sonia Ospina and Erica Foldy, Toward a Framwork of Social Change Leadership (2005), available at http://ssrn.com/abstract=1532332.

27. For discussion of the structures conducive to social impact, see John Kania and Mark Kramer, Collective Impact, Stan. Social Innovation Rev., Winter, 2011.

28. The distinction was used to criticize Martin Luther King. See Alan John, Self-Emancipation and Leadership: The Case of Martin Luther King, in Leadership Matters. at 106.

29. McCarry, Citizen Nader, at 183.

30. Todd Gitlin, Ralph Nader and the Will to Marginality, Dissent, Spring, 2004 at 5; Gabriel Sherman, Nader's Traitors: Public Enemy No. 1, New Republic, May 7, 2008, at 7–8.

31. Ann Southworth, Lawyers of the Right: Professionalizing the Conservative Coalition 31 (2008).

32. Barbara C. Crosby & John M. Bryson, Leadership for the Common Good: Tackling Public Problems in a Shared-Power World 3 (2005).

33. Peter Elkind, Rough Justice: The Rise and Fall of Eliot Spitzer (2010); Nicholas Confessore, Ungoverned, N. Y. Times Book Rev., July 2, 2010, at 15.

34. Ricardo S. Morse, Integrative Public Leadership: Catalyzing Collaboration to Create Public Value, 21 Leadership Quarterly 231, 243 (2010).

35. Morris and Staggenborg, Leadership and Social Movements, at 189–190.

36. Colin Barker, Robert Michels, and the "Cruel Game," in Leadership and Social Movements, at 24.

37. Barker, Johnson, and Lavalette, Leadership Matters, at 12–14.

38. Marshall Ganz, Resources and Resourcefulness: Strategic Capacity in the Unionization of California Agriculture, 105 Am. J. Soc. 1003, 1014–1016 (2000).

39. Raymond Schillinger, Social Media and the Arab Spring: What Have We Learned, The Huffington Post September 20, 2011, http://www.huffingtonpost.com/raymond-schillinger/arab-spring-social-media_b_970165.html; The People Formerly Known As the Audience, The Economist, July 7, 2011, http://www.economist.com/node/18904124.

40. See Andrew Grossman & Jack Nicas, Wall Street Protest Digs In, Spreads, Wall Street J., October 3, 2011, at A6.

41. Julianna Goldman, Obama Winning Social Media, If #hashtagwars Really Matter, Bloomberg, October 21, 2012, http://www.bloomberg.com/news/2012-10-22/obama-winning-social-media-if-hashtagwars-really-matter.html.

42. Judd Legum, Think Progress, March 12, 2012 http://thinkprogress.org/media/2012/03/12/442673/141-companies-advertising-rush-limbaugh/?mobile=nc.

43. See Monitor Institute, Catalyzing Networks for Social Change (2011), http://www.monitorinstitute.com/downloads/Catalyzing_Networks_for_Social_Change.pdf.

44. Malcolm Gladwell, Small Change: Why the Revolution Will Not be Tweeted, New Yorker, October 4, 2010, at 42. See Andy Smith and Jennifer Aaker, The Dragonfly Effect: Quick, Effective, and Powerful Ways to Use Social Media to Drive Social Change (2010).

45. Gladwell, Small Change, at 42.

46. Joe Wallis & Brian Dollery, Market Failure, Government Failure, Leadership and Public Policy 145 (1999).

47. Crosby & Bryson, Leadership for the Common Good, at 275–278.

48. Crosby & Bryson, Leadership for the Common Good, at 122.
49. Lewis M. Killian, Organization, Rationality and Spontaneity in the Civil Rights Movement, in Collective Behavior and Social Movements, 209, 214–216.
50. Gail Collins, When Everything Changed 110 (2009).
51. Rochon, Culture Moves, at 7.
52. Deborah L. Rhode, Public Interest Law: The Movement at Midlife, 60 Stan. L. Rev. 2027, 2035 (2008) (quoting Carl Pope).
53. Rhode, Public Interest Law, at 2035 (quoting Ted Shaw).
54. Rhode, Public Interest Law, at 2035 (quoting Kathy Rogers).
55. Rhode, Public Interest Law, at 2045 (quoting Irma Herrera).
56. Rhode, Public Interest Law, at 2040 (quoting Ted Shaw).
57. Rhode, Public Interest Law, at 2045 (quoting Brian Stevenson).
58. Rhode, Public Interest Law, at 2033 (quoting Jon Davison, Lambda Legal).
59. Rhode, Public Interest Law, at 2033 (quoting Jamienne Studley).
60. Rhode, Public Interest Law, at 2043 (2008) (quoting Barbara Olshansky).
61. Gerald N. Rosenberg, The Hollow Hope: Can Courts Bring About Social Change? (1991); Ross Sandler & David Schoenbrod, Democracy By Decree: What Happens When Courts Run Government (2003); Kenneth Lee, Where Legal Activists Come From, American Enterprise, June 2001, at 50.
62. Rhode, Public Interest Law, at 2043.
63. Stuart A. Scheingold,The Politics of Rights, xxiv (2004), Kevin R. Den Dulk, In Legal Culture, but Not of It: The Role of Cause Lawyers in Evangelical Legal Mobilization, in Cause Lawyers and Social Movements 199, 200 (Austin Sarat and Stuart Scheingold eds., 2006); Ann Southworth, Lawyers and the "Myth of Rights" in Civil Rights and Poverty Practice, 8 Boston U. Public Interest L. J. 1469(1999).
64. Nan Aron, Liberty and Justice for All: Public Interest Law in the 1980s and Beyond 90 (1989) (quoting Nader).
65. Steven Telles, The Rise of the Conservative Legal Movement 232 (2010); Jeffrey M. Berry, Effective Advocacy for Nonprofits, in Nonprofit Advocacy and the Policy Process, Volume 2, Exploring Organizations and Advocacy 1–8 (Elizabeth J. Reid and Maria D. Montilla, eds., 2001).
66. J. Craig Jenkins & Charles Perrow, Insurgency of the Powerless: Farm Workers Movements (1946–1972), in Collective Behavior and Social Movements, 341: 351–352; Marshall Ganz, Resources and Resourcefulness: Strategic Capacity in the Unionization of California Agriculture, 1959–1966, 105 Am. J. Soc. 1003, 1033–1044 (2000).
67. Ganz, Resources and Resourcefulness, 1039.
68. Rhode, Public Interest Law, at 2064 (quoting Marcia Greenberger).
69. Rhode, Public Interest Law, at 2064, 2067.
70. John Kania and Mark Kramer, Collective Impact, Stan. Social Innovation Rev., Winter, 2011, at 36, 38.

71. Kania & Kramer, Collective Impact, at 36.
72. Chip Heath and Dan Heath, Switch: How to Change Things When Change is Hard 28 (2010).
73. Heath and Heath, Switch, at 28 (quoting Sternim).
74. See the work summarized by the Positive Deviance Initiative at Tufts, http://www.positivedeviance.org/materials/bib_subj.html.
75. Heath & Heath, Switch, at 29–39, 40.
76. New Yorker, Dec. 22, 29 2003.
77. Heath & Heath, Switch, at 150.
78. Heath & Heath, Switch, at 151. For a history, see http://rareconservation.org/about/page.php?subsection=history.
79. Deborah L. Rhode & Lee D. Ross, Environmental Values and Behaviors: Strategies to Encourage Public Support for Initiatives to Combat Global Warming, 26 Virg. Environ. L. J. 161, 167–68, 187 (2008).
80. For examples, see Heath and Heath, Switch, 159–161, Rhode and Ross, Environmental Values, at 181.
81. Derrick A. Bell Jr., Serving Two Masters: Integration Ideals and Clients' Interests in School Desegregation Litigation, 85 Yale L. J. 470, 473 (1976).
82. See generally Barry Friedman, The Will of the People (2009).
83. Michael Murakami, Desegregation, in, *Public Opinion and Constitutional Controversy* 18, 19–20 (Nathaniel Persily, Jack Citrin, & Patrick J. Egan, eds., 2008).
84. Richard Kluger, Simple Justice: The History of Brown v. Board of Education and Black America's Struggle for Equality 535–536 (1977).
85. Gary Orfield & Erica Frankenberg, Reviving Brown v. Board of Education: How Courts and Enforcement Agencies Can Produce More Integrated Schools, in Brown at 50: The Unfinished Legacy 195 (Deborah L. Rhode & Charles J. Ogletree, Jr., eds. 2004).
86. Juan Williams, Thurgood Marshall 181 (1998).
87. Mark Tushnet, Making Civil Rights Law 138 (1990).
88. Kluger, Simple Justice, at 530.
89. Orfield & Frankenberg, Reviving Brown v. Board of Education, at 192; Nathanial R. Jones, Correspondence: School Desegregation, 86 Yale L. J. 378, 380 (1976).
90. Cass R. Sunstein, Did Brown Matter?, in Brown at 50, at 119.
91. Sunstein, Did Brown Matter, at 119; Orfield & Frankenberg, Reviving Brown v. Board of Education, at 189.
92. Steven G. Breyer, Turning Brown's Hope into Reality, in Brown at Fifty, 145.
93. Michael Klarman, From Jim Crow to Civil Rights: The Supreme Court and the Struggle for Racial Equality 364 (2004); Ronald A. Heifitz, Leadership without Easy Answers 129-149 (1994).
94. Bell, Serving Two Masters, at 504.
95. Gary Orfield, Must We Bus? 212 (1978).

96. Jones, Correspondence, at 379.

97. Jones, Correspondence, at 380.

98. Deborah L. Rhode, Letting the Law Catch Up, in Brown at 50, at 151 (quoting Marshall).

99. Victor S. Navasky, Kennedy Justice 97 (1970).

100. Michael Belknap, The Vindication of Burke Marshall: The Southern Legal System and the Anti-Civil-Rights Violence of the 1960s, 33 Emory L. J. 93, 94 (1984); Nicholas deB Katzenbach, Some of it Was Fun: Working with RFK and LBJ 15 (2008).

101. Harold C. Fleming, The Federal Executive and Civil Rights: 1961–1963, 94 Daedalus 921, 922 (1965).

102. Thomas, Robert Kennedy 131; Taylor Branch, Parting the Waters 473 (1988).

103. Thomas, Robert Kennedy, at 127; Branch, Parting the Waters, at 382.

104. Fleming, The Federal Executive, at 922; Thomas, Robert Kennedy, at 127; Katzenbach, Some of it Was Fun, at 42; Branch, Parting the Waters, at 434.

105. Belknap, The Vindication of Burke Marshall, at 96.

106. Belknap, The Vindication of Burke Marshall, at 96 (quoting Marshall).

107. Belknap, The Vindication of Burke Marshall, at 102.

108. Fleming, The Federal Executive, at 937 (quoting Marshall).

109. Kenneth O'Reilly, The FBI and the Civil Rights Movement During the Kennedy Years—From the Freedom Rides to Albany,54 J. Southern Hist. 201 (1988).

110. Belknap, The Vindication of Burke Marshall at 204, O'Reilly, The FBI, at 203, Thomas, Robert Kennedy at 262–262.

111. Navasky, Kennedy Justice, at 205.

112. Branch, Parting the Waters, at 433.

113. Navasky, Kennedy Justice, at 205.

114. Thomas, Robert Kennedy, at 243; Schlesinger, Robert Kennedy, at 329–330; Branch, Parting the Waters, 793–802.

115. Schlesinger, Robert Kennedy, at 329.

116. Katzenbach, Some of it Was Fun, 29.

117. Histories of the period recount the facts somewhat differently. Compare Walter Lord. The Past That Would not Wait, 114 (1965) with Navasky, Kennedy Justice, xx. The facts in the text were taken from contemporaneous news accounts. Georgia Refuses to Free Dr. King, N. Y. Times, Oct. 27, 1960 at 22; Dr. King and the Law, N.Y. Times, October 30, 1960; Martin Luther King Traffic Case Closed, Boston Globe, April 8, 1961; Auto Case Penalty Eased for Dr. King, N. Y. Times, April 8, 1961, at 43; Dr. King is Jailed for Georgia Protest, N. Y. Times, July 11, 1962, at A1.

118. Thomas, Robert Kennedy, at 129. See Arthur Schlesinger, Robert Kennedy and His Times 296 (1978)

119. Thomas, Robert Kennedy, at 131: Schlesinger, Robert Kennedy, at 297.

120. Thomas, Robert Kennedy, at 132; Navasky, Kennedy Justice, at 21; Branch, Parting the Waters, at 479.

121. Navasky, Kennedy Justice, at 183.

122. Navasky, Kennedy Justice, at 21; Branch, Parting the Waters, at 432.

123. Thomas, Robert Kennedy, at 250–251.

124. Thomas, Robert Kennedy, at 203. For other accounts, see Schlesinger, at 316–317; Branch, Parting the Waters, at 658–659.

125. Katzenbach, Some of it Was Fun, at 79.

126. Schlesinger, Robert Kennedy, at 341.

127. Belknap, The Vindication of Burke Marshall, at 103; Schlesinger, Robert Kennedy, at 303.

128. Schlesinger, Robert Kennedy, at 304 (quoting Marshall).

129. Burke Marshall Oral History Interview—JFK#1, May 29, 1964, Interview 1 John F. Kennedy Library).

130. Branch, Parting the Waters, at 311.

131. Navasky, Kennedy Justice, at 245, 254, 260. See also Schlesinger, Robert Kennedy, at 307.

132. Thomas, Robert Kennedy, at 263–264.

133. Thomas, Robert Kennedy, at 263; Schlesinger, at 360; Branch, Parting the Waters, at 908.

134. Thomas, Robert Kennedy, at 127.

135. Thomas, Robert Kennedy, at 249; Jack Newfield, Robert Kennedy: A Memoir 22–23 (1969).

136. Navasky, Kennedy Justice, at xiii.

137. Michael R. Belknap, Civil Rights During the Kennedy Administration, 23 Law & Soc. Rev. 921, 922 (1989).

138. Schlesinger, Robert Kennedy, at 97 (quoting Joseph Kennedy).

139. Belknap, Civil Rights, at 922–923; Navasky, Kennedy Justice, at 97; Katzenbach, Some of it Was Fun, at 83.

140. Belknap, The Vindication of Burke Marshall, at 110.

141. Tom Stoddard, Why Gay People Should Seek the Right to Marry, 2 Out/Look, Nat's Gay & Lesbian Q 9 (Fall, 1989).

142. Paula L. Ettelbrick, Since When Is Marriage a Path to Liberation, 2 Out/Look, Nat'l Gay & Lesbian Q. 9, 14 (Fall 1989).

143. William B. Rubenstein, Divided We Litigate: Addressing Disputes Among Group Members and Lawyers in Civil Rights Campaigns, 106 Yale L. J. 1623, 1635 (1997).

144. Rubenstein, Divided We Litigate, at 1637 (quoting letter).

145. Rubenstein, Divided We Litigate, at 1637 (quoting letter).

146. Baehr v. Lewin, 852 P.2d 44, 59–68 (Haw. 1993)

147. Katherine M. Franke, Stop Sanctifying Marriage, in NYT Room for Debate on Family Ties Without Tying the Knot, February 16, 2012, http://blogs.law.

columbia.edu/genderandsexualitylawblog/2012/02/16/nyt-room-for-debate-
on-family-ties-without-tying-the-knot-katherine-franke-stop-sanctifying-mar-
riage/; Elizabeth Cooper, Who Needs Marriage?: Equality and the Role of the
State, 8 Journal Law and Family Studies 325 (2005); Michael Warner, The Trouble
with Normal (1999). For an overview, see Suzanne A. Kim, Skeptical Marriage
Equality, 34 Harvard J. L. & Gender 37 (2011).

148. Scott Cummings and Douglas Nejaime, Lawyering for Marriage Equality, 57
UCLA L. Rev. 1306 (2010).

149. Theodore Olson, The Conservative Case for Gay Marriage, Newsweek, January
9, 2010, at 48. See also Evan Wolfson, Why Marriage Matters: America, Equality,
and Gay People's Right to Marry (2004).

150. Goodridge v. Department of Health, 798 N.E. 2d 941 (Mass. 2003).

151. Chuleenan Svetvilas, Anatomy of a Complaint: How Hollywood Activists Seized
Control of the Fight for Gay Marriage, California Lawyer, January 20, 2010, at 24.

152. Lockyer v. City and County of San Francisco, 95 P.3d 459 (Cal. 2004).

153. Cummings and Nejaime, Lawyering for Marriage Equality, at 1309.

154. Svetvilas, Anatomy of a Complaint at 22.

155. Margaret Talbot, A Risky Proposal: Is it Too Soon To Petition the Supreme Court
on Gay Marriage, The New Yorker, January 18, 2010 at 44 (quoting Olson).

156. Talbot, A Risky Proposal, at 41. See Michael J. Klarman, From the Closet to the
Alter: Courts, Backlash, and the Struggle for Same- Sex Marriage (2012).

157. Svetvilas, Anatomy of a Complaint, 22 (quoting Hunter).

158. Talbot, A Risky Proposal, at 48 (quoting Hunter).

159. Talbot, A Risky Proposal, at 42 (quoting Eskridge).

160. Svetvilas, Anatomy of a Complaint, at 22 (quoting Hunter).

161. Svetvilas, Anatomy of a Complaint, at 27 (quoting Kendall).

162. Svetvilas, Anatomy of a Complaint, at 27 (quoting Olson).

163. Frank Bruni, Marriage and the Supremes, N. Y. Times, March 24, 2013, at sr 3.

164. Patrick Egan and Nathaniel Persily, Public Opinion and Constitutional
Controversy 235 (2008).

165. Michael Klarman, Why Gay Marriage is Inevitable, Los Angeles Times, February
12, 2012, at A27.

166. Talbot, A Risky Proposal, at 42 (quoting Olson).

167. American Bar Association, Rule 1.2, Model Rules of Professional Conduct
(2012).

CHAPTER 10

1. John Gardiner, On Leadership 2 (1990).

2. Joseph S. Nye Jr., The Powers to Lead 19 (2008).

3. For values, see Warren Bennis, On Becoming a Leader 32-33 (2d ed. 1994) (citing integrity, trust); Montgomery Van Wart, Dynamics of Leadership in

Public Service: Theory and Practice 16, 92–119 (2005) (citing integrity and an ethic of public service); James M. Kouzes and Barry Z. Posner, The Leadership Challenge 21 (1995) (citing honesty). For personal skills, see Daniel Goleman, Richard Boyatzis, and Annie McKee, Primal Leadership: Realizing the Power of Emotional Intelligence 253–56 (2002) (citing self-awareness, self-management); Van Wart, Dynamics, 16 (citing self-direction). For interpersonal skills, see Goleman, Boyatzis, and McKee, Primal Leadership, 253–256 (citing social awareness, empathy, persuasion, conflict management). For vision, see Bennis, On Becoming a Leader, at 33 (citing vision); Kouzes and Posner, Leadership Challenge, at 21 (citing forward-looking, inspiring). For competence, see id.; Jay Lorsch, A Contingency Theory of Leadership, in *Handbook of Leadership Theory and Practice* 417 (Nitin Nohria and Rakesh Khurana, eds., 2010). For judgment, see Noel M. Tichy & Warren G. Bennis, Judgment: How Winning Leaders Make Great Calls (2007). See chapter 1.

4. David. A. Garvin, Building a Learning Organization, Harv. Bus. Rev. July–August, 1993, at 78, 79.

5. Linda A. Hill and Kent Linebeck, Being the Boss: The Three Imperatives for Becoming a Great Leader 215 (2011).

6. David G. Myers, The Pursuit of Happiness: Who is Happy—and Why 32–38 (1992); David G. Myers & Ed Diener, Who is Happy, Psych. Social Science 6, 10, 17 (1995); Christopher Peterson and Martin E.P. Seligman, Character Strengths and Virtues: A Handbook and Classification (2004). William C. Compton, Introduction to Positive Psychology 48-49, 53–54 (2004); Ed Diener et al., Subjective Well-Being: Three Decades of Progress, 125 Psych. Bull. 276 (1999).

7. Air Vice-Marshal Sir Norman Duckworth Kerr MacEwen, http://www.quotatio.com/m/macewen-norman-quotes.html.

8. Christopher P. Niemiec, Richard M. Ryan, and Edward L. Dei, The Path Taken: Consequences of Attaining Intrinsic and Extrinsic Aspirations, 43 J. Res. In Personality 291 (2009).

9. Martin E. P. Seligman, Authentic Happiness: Using the New Positive Psychology to Realize Your Potential for Lasting Fulfillment 49 (2002); Ed Diener, Richard E. Lucas, and Christie Napa Scollon, Beyond the Hedonic Treadmill: Revising the Adaptation Theory of Well –Being, 61 Am. Psychologist 305 (2006).

10. Robert H. Frank, How Not to Buy Happiness 133 Daedalus 69, 69–71 (2004); Myers, The Pursuit of Happiness, 39; Sonja Lyubomirsky, The How of Happiness 48 (2008).

11. Laura Nash and Howard Stevenson, Success that Lasts, Harv. Bus. Rev., February 2004, at 102, 104. For an extended version of their argument, see Laura Nash & Howard Stevenson, Just Enough: Tools for Creating Success in Your Work and Life (2004).

12. For the need for a higher purpose see Thomas J. DeLong, Flying Without a Net 48 (2011). For fame and legacy, see J. Patrick Dobel, Managerial Leadership and the Ethical Importance of Legacy, in *Public Ethics and Governance: Standards and Practices in Comparative Perspective* (Denis Saint-Martin and Fred Thompson, eds., 2004): 195, 200–203.

13. Robin J. Ely, Herminia Ibarra, & Deborah M. Kolb, Taking Gender into Account: Theory and Design for Women's Leadership Programs 10 Acad. Management Learning & Edu. 474, 487 (2011).

14. Fred Shapiro, Yale Book of Quotations 532 (2006) (quoting Montague).

15. Dobel, Managerial Leadership, 201.

16. Dobel, Managerial Leadership, at 201.

17. Bill Clinton, My Life 875 (2004).

18. Earl Warren, The Memoirs of Chief Justice Earl Warren 305, 325 (1977).

19. Ray Blunt, Leaders Growing Leaders for Public Service, reprinted in The Jossey-Bass Reader in Non-Profit Public Leadership 41 (2010) (quoting Noel Tichy).

20. Ruth Marcus, Plain-Spoken Marshall Spars with Reporters, Washington Post, June 29, 1991, at A1, A10.

Index